Population, Environment and Development

A Global Challenge for the 21st Century

Population, Environment and Development

A Global Challenge for the 21st Century

Edited by

B.R.K. Sinha
Professor of Geography, Faculty of Science
Banaras Hindu University,
Varanasi, India.

NEW NC CENTURY

New Century Publications
New Delhi, India

NEW CENTURY PUBLICATIONS
4800/24, Bharat Ram Road,
Ansari Road, Daryaganj,
New Delhi – 110 002 (India)

Tel.: 011-2324 7798, 4358 7398, 6539 6605
Fax: 011-4101 7798
E-mail: indiatax@vsnl.com • info@newcenturypublications.com
www.newcenturypublications.com

Editorial office:
LG–7, Aakarshan Bhawan
4754-57/23, Ansari Road, Daryaganj,
New Delhi – 110 002

Tel.: 011-4356 0919

First Published: **September 2009**

ISBN: **978-81-7708-217-3**

Published by New Century Publications and printed at Salasar Imaging Systems, New Delhi.

Designs: Patch Creative Unit, New Delhi

PRINTED IN INDIA

CONTENTS

Part II: Environmental Aspects

Part III: Developmental Profile

Part IV: Population-Environment-Development: Inter-linkages

Foreword

The population, environment and development interact among them and are a concern for the scientist, scholars and global developmental planners. Development affects environment and growing population needs exploitation of the physical resources. Everywhere in the world particularly the developing countries strive for higher pace of economic development. This means negative effects on environment. Therefore a policy that encourages a compromise between the two is in the best interest of the people. Least environmental damage ought to a part of a universal development policy. There is already a greater awareness now to limit the population growth. This awareness needs to be converted into an active policy of zero population growth. All these issues have been discussed in the book in which contributors from different parts of the world have made significant inroads in understanding the relationship among population, environment and development with a view to maintain a sustainable growth strategy. This book is highly recommended for libraries and classroom adoption for graduate and post - graduate studies.

Ashok K. Dutt
Professor Emeritus
Geography and Planning
Professor Emeritus of Urban Studies
The University of Akron
Akron, OH 44325-5005
USA

Appreciation of the Book

This book is an elegant volume of geographical essays edited by Professor Sinha. It opens with a clear, firm and concise statement of purpose and conceptual setting. The concepts employed are deeply rooted in the traditions of geography, for example those of space, connectivity, population, development and environment. The spatial perspective in the essays leads the authors to identify general patterns. The book will be widely read, and will have a greater impact among social scientists including geographers. This book has a great value, both for scholarly contributions to research on population, environment and development issues as well as excellent readings for the general public interested in human resource development.

P. P. Karan

P.P. Karan,
Department of Geography/
Japanese Studies,
University of Kentucky,
Lexington,
KY 40506-0027, USA

Acknowledgements

I place on record my deep sense of gratitude to each of the contributors to this volume for his/her significant contribution, patience and cooperation. I also wish to record my deep appreciation to the internationally known geographer Dr. Ashok K. Dutt, Professor Emeritus, Geography and Planning, Professor Emeritus, Urban Studies, University of Akron, USA for his affection, good wishes, generosity and academic encouragement. I am grateful to Professor Dutt and his wife Dr. Hiran H. Dutta, Professor Emeritus, Department of Biological Sciences, Kent State University, Kent for helping and assisting my USA visit which, in turn, helped me in making personal contacts with several contributors. I am also thankful to Professor P.P. Karan, Department of Geography/Japanese Studies, University of Kentucky, Lexington, USA for his helpful suggestions. I remain ever grateful to my wife Mrs. Meera Rani Sinha and my lovely daughters Ekta Sinha and Chaitanya Sinha for their love, constant inspiration, assistance, sacrifice and endurance in achieving the goal of this publication. Thanks are also due to Mr. Sandeep Sury, Chief Executive, New Century Publications, New Delhi for accepting the manuscript, meticulously handling it and finally publishing this book.

B.R.K. Sinha

About the Book

Human and natural resources are the basis of all economic activities. Economic activities in turn affect the quantity and quality of natural and environmental resources. Economic activities change the stock of natural resources. The change of stock calls for appropriate trade-off between the needs of present and future generations. Economic growth without environmental considerations can cause serious damage to the quality of life of the present and future generations.

The concept of sustainable development advocates economic progress in an environmentally responsible manner. Sustainable development attempts to strike a balance between the demands of the economic development and the need for protection of the environment. It seeks to combine the elements of economic efficiency, intergenerational equity, social concerns and environmental protection.

This book is a collection of essays penned by an international group of distinguished scholars from the United States, Canada, United Kingdom, Hungary, Romania, South Korea, Japan and India. Contributions included in this book focus on interaction between population, environment and development in various areas of the world.

The book provides fresh thoughts and broad understanding of the current issues and challenges to be faced in the present century pertaining to complex inter-relationships between population, environment and development. It makes a significant departure from the existing pattern of literature available on the subject.

This book brings together the ideas of scholars in the field of population, environment and development. Their respective contributions are socially relevant for the contemporary society. The book is useful for a cross-section of readers including geographers, demographers, environmentalists, development economists, legislators and others interested in the dynamics of modern growth process.

Editor's Profile

Professor B.R.K. Sinha (b. 1956) is currently Professor of Geography, Faculty of Science, Banaras Hindu University (BHU), Varanasi, India. He obtained B.A. Honours (1977) and M.A. (1979) degrees from Patna University, and Ph.D. (1988) from the Maharaja Sayajirao (M.S.) University of Baroda. During 1982-1988 he worked as a UGC Research Fellow and Teaching Assistant at the M.S. University of Baroda. Dr. Sinha joined Visva-Bharati (a Central University), Santiniketan, West Bengal in 1988, where he served as a Lecturer and Reader, and since March 2004 as Professor. Dr. Sinha joined Banaras Hindu University as Professor of Geography in June 2007. The areas of his teaching and research interest are population geography, cartography and human resource development. He is internationally recognized for his research on geography of human resource development. He has published nearly 50 research papers/articles in national and international journals. He has participated in 31 National and 23 International seminars/conferences. On invitation from professional geographical organizations, he has visited Czech Republic, South Korea, Romania, UK and USA.

Contributors and Their Affiliations

Name	Affiliation	E-mail
Ann Novogradec	BAS, MES, Ph.D. Candidate (ABD), Faculty of Environmental Studies, York University, Toronto, ON, Canada.	ann.novogradec@rogers.com
Aurel Gheorghilas	Lecturer, Department of Human Geography, University of Bucharest, Bucharest, Romania	aghgeo@yahoo.com
Bhagwati Joshi	Department of Geography, Kumaon University, Nainital, India.	...
Bindu M. Bhatt	Senior Lecturer, Department of Geography, M.S. University, Baroda, India.	bindoobhatt@rediffmail.com
B.R.K. Sinha	Professor, Department of Geography, Faculty of Science, Banaras Hindu University, Varanasi, India.	sinha_brk@yahoo.co.in
Christopher Cusack	Professor, Department of Geography, Keene State College, Keene, NH 03435-2001, USA.	ccusack@keene.edu
Eva Edit Kiss	Associate Professor, Geographical Research Institute, Hungarian Academy of Sciences, 1112.Budapest Budaörsi út 45. Hungary.	kisse@helka.iif.hu
George M. Pomeroy	Professor, Geography-Earth Science Department, Shippensburg University, Shippensburg, USA.	gmpome@ship.edu
Liliana Dumitrache	Professor and Head, Department of Human Geography, University of	dosaredumitrache@yahoo.com

	Bucharest, Romania.	
Mariana Mirela Nae	Department of Human Geography, University of Bucharest, Romania.	mirellanae@yahoo.com
Michael O'Neal. Campbell	Department of Geography and Sociology, University of Strathclyde, Graham Hills Building, 50, Richmond Street, Glasgow, G1 1XN, Scotland, UK.	ecol55@hotmail.com
M. K. Khandelwal	Associate Professor, Department of Geography, University of Rajasthan, Jaipur, India.	...
Nak- Hun Song	Professor, Urban Studies, Kangwon Development Research Institute, Kangwon-DO, 200-041, South Korea.	snh@kdri.re.kr
Nanda R. Shrestha	Florida A&M University, USA.	nanda.shrestha@famu.edu
Norman Johnson	Florida A&M University, USA.	...
Parbati Nandi	Professor, Department of Geography, Visva-Bharat, Santiniketan, West Bengal, India.	nandiparbati@yahoo.com
P.C. Tiwari	Department of Geography, Kumaon University, Nainital, India.	pctiwari@yahoo.com
Raghuvanshi Jogender Singh	Department of Geography, M.S. University, Baroda, India.	r_jogender@rediffmail.com
Ram Bilas	Professor, Department of Geography, Faculty of Science, Banaras Hindu University, Varanasi, India.	rambilas@bhu.ac.in

Rama Prasad	Associate Professor, Department of Geography, Rajasthan University, Jaipur, India.	ramaprasad10@gmail.com
Rameshwari Pandya	Reader, Department of Home Science, Extension and Communications, Faculty of Home Science, M.S. University, Baroda, India.	amurt40@hotmail.com
Rani Singh	Research Scholar, Department of Geography, Rajasthan University, Jaipur, India.	...
Richard McQown	Professor, Geography-Earth Science Department, Shippensburg University, Shippensburg, USA.	...
Samuel Thompson	Professor, Department of Geography, Western Illinois University, Tillman, Macomb, IL, USA.	s-thompson@wiu.edu
S.C. Mukhopadhyay	Department of Geography, Calcutta University, Kolkata, India.	deepa_2005kolkata@rediffmail.com
Shio Muni Yadav	Professor, Department of Geography, B.N. Mandal University, Madhepura, Bihar, India.	...
Shii Okuno	Professor in Local Economic Development and Economic Geography, Faculty of Information Science, University of Marketing and Distribution Sciences, Kobe Japan.	shii_okuno@red.umds.ac.jp
Shivaji Prasad	Department of Geography, Frostburg State University, Maryland, USA.	sprasad@ frostburg.edu
Wilbur I. Smith	Florida A&M University, USA.	...

Editor's Note on the Book

Population, environment and development are challenging global issues in the 21st century. Population being a human branch, environment a physical or natural branch and development an outcome of the interaction of the two are very vital from the viewpoint of peace, prosperity and posterity. In this sense, the study of interaction of population, environment and development becomes important for creating a world of peace, comfort and security.

This book contains 23 research contributions grouped into four parts.

Part I of the book, consisting of 8 chapters, deals with various dimensions of surging population of the world. Problems, particularly health concerns, posed by growing population in different geographical regions of the world have been addressed and examined.

The work of **Nanda R. Shrestha, Norman Johnson, and Wilbur I. Smith** (USA) concentrates on the four traditions (Malthusian, Marxist, Neo-Malthusian, and Neo-liberal) of population-poverty analysis. They have reviewed the underlying concepts of these four traditions. Population according to them is a defining barometer of any society as it shapes—and is, in turn, shaped by—the process of social and economic development. One result of this interactive process is that where there is population, there is poverty. Population and poverty are thus intrinsically intertwined, permeating virtually every facet of life and of society. Yet, the questions about what causes poverty and how to tackle it remains, often imbued with political slants and ideological biases.

Their work reveals the nature of the ongoing population-poverty debate, showing that it remains mired in an ideological cul-de-sac. They lay out in the concluding section of their work a way out of the cul-de-sac. Specifically, they treat poverty as an ecosystem with three basic causes—population growth (Malthusian and Neo-Malthusian stance), social class structure (Marxist position), and the lack of economic or market freedom (Neo-liberal contention). What is proposed, therefore, is a policy framework focused on transforming these three causes of poverty into a nexus of complementary weapons to achieve the shared goal of defeating poverty.

Samuel Thompson (USA) addresses the problems of aging population (a result of the greying of the baby boomers) in America. He points out that America is undergoing a dramatic demographic change in the coming years. With a slow population growth and the aging of the baby boomers, the country is turning into an aging society. As a result, there will be more people aged 65 or above by the year 2010 and beyond. Since there has not been a precedent of such a large-scale aging population in the history of America, the pending increase in the old population poses several challenges in terms of meeting the needs of the elderly population in the country. The country will have to provide the aged population with appropriate housing, easier mode of transportation and adequate healthcare facility. How the country absorbs and provides for all the elderly will determine the quality of life of the senior population in the 21st century.

The work of **Christopher Cusack** (USA) is to some extent similar to that of Samuel Thompson. He looks at the problems of rapid population aging and deals with the associated socio-economic problems in common with the physician geographic mal-distribution. His work indicates that the increasing numbers of geographically dispersed elderly persons has made the provision of adequate health care difficult. Shortages of physicians and health care facilities, particularly in rural areas, have resulted in the phenomenon of physician geographic mal-distribution. He concludes that the areas of greatest concern are rural counties ranging from the Texas-Mexico border to the heart of Appalachia. Awareness of this disparity has resulted in only marginally successful remedial solutions. Other countries can learn from the US experience. Governments alone are likely to be unable to accommodate the needs of their growing elderly populations.

Assessment and evaluation of impact of undocumented aliens in the Organ Pipe Cactus National Monument in Arizona, USA, as carried out by **George M. Pomeroy and Richard McQown** (USA) is of great academic interest. Their assessment and evaluation shows that the heavy volume of undocumented aliens crossing public lands in Arizona has disastrous environmental impacts. They employed two matrices for assessing micro-level and macro-level assessment and evaluation of the impacts of undocumented aliens. The two matrices became an important tool in assessing, evaluating, and prioritizing efforts to minimize impacts due to undocumented alien traffic.

Liliana Dumitrache (Romania) in her paper 'Changing Geography of Health and Health Care in Romania in the Last Decade of the 20th Century' has tried to present the picture of health status and health care of Romanian population. The First part of her study concentrates on general mortality, structure of deaths by main causes, infant mortality, life expectancy and the incidence of certain diseases as factors of health state of the Romanian population. She calculated and employed health index to show health disparities within Romania. The second part of her study analyses health care as one of the most important determinants of health status. She has recommended improvement in the population sanitary behaviour and socio-economic status to raise the status of health of the Romanian people.

The work of **Eva Edit Kiss** (Hungary) is on the 'State of Health of the Hungarian Population in the Period of Transition'. She reveals that despite an indisputable social and economic progress, Hungary has inherited a heavily polluted environment in settlements and a population with deteriorating state of health from the socialist period. After 1989, however, radical social and economic reforms took place which considerably affected the population's state of health. She concludes that in the period of transition the state of health of the Hungarian population has deteriorated and spatial and social variations in the state of health have increased. This is based on the statistical data relating to some indicators of state of health

Education being a process of teaching and learning plays crucial role in all aspects of life of a person as it opens the windows of several life supporting opportunities by enhancing knowledge, skills and awareness. **Rameshwari Pandya** (India) has pin-pointed the significance of population education and has considered it as very important means for solving the problem of population growth. She suggests that imparting education helps in developing awareness among citizens in understanding the major problems of over-population and aims at developing an informed individual. Population education is the only desirable solution for it. Population education in a broad way can be defined as 'an educational programme which provides for a study of the population situation in the family, community, nation and the world, with the purpose of developing in the students a rational and responsible attitude and behaviour towards this situation.

Health care is an important aspect of geographical study as it is one of the essentials of health promotion. **Aurel Gheorghilas** (Romania) has considered health care as a very important preoccupation of population and the analysis of it is necessary. The quality of medical assistance becomes an important element of individual security or insecurity. The quality of medical services is differently perceived from one lifestyle to another and from one community to another. She has highlighted that in rural environment of the Catchment Area of Raul Targului River in Romania the medical need is less than that in urban one. On the other hand, the territorial village surgeries often provide only the role of local health status and of transferring centres for the sick to the urban medical units.

Part II of the book contains 7 chapters relating to description and analysis of environmental issues.

Cancer is a dangerous disease. It is very much linked with the environment. The work of **Ann Novogradec** (Canada) on 'Cancer and the Environment' is a significant contribution to this book. She has examined the relationship between cancer and the environment. She has very intensively reviewed the cancer and environment related concepts. She has made a multi-level analysis and has applied an assessment tool with a view to prevent, minimize or eliminate cancer and other ill health effects. In an attempt to decrease cancer risk, an assessment tool, which is commonly used in the field of business, is suggested as a supplementary measure to assist in the identification of strengths, weaknesses, opportunities and threats pertaining to contributing factors associated with cancer causation and prevention.

Shivaji Prasad (USA) in his paper 'Health of Coastal Waters and Estuaries of the United States of America' deals with the consequences of anthropogenic pollutions along the coasts of the USA. This study focuses mainly on the status of coastal waters and estuaries of the USA. The American coastlines, in general, and its Eastern coasts in particular, are under intense stress due to coastal developments and anthropogenic pollutions. Numerous coastal restoration programmes at local-to-regional level are needed to tackle various ecological impacts on coastal benthic environments.

Kumaon Himalaya is an important part of the Himalayas and during the recent past it has become a focal zone from the point of view of water resource and overall development. The study of **P.C. Tiwari and Bhagwati Joshi** (India) throws light on the environmental status of water resources in Kumaon Himalaya as water is one of the most fundamental and critical natural resources on the earth. This study deals with the glaciers, the rivers and streams, springs and natural lakes, water resource potential, status of water resource utilization, environmental changes and their impact on the geo-hydrology, retreat of glaciers, drying of springs and diminishing lake ecosystems.

Environmental degradation is one of the challenging issues of the 21st century and remains a great problem for the entire community of the world. The contribution of urban centres in degrading environmental quality is at the maximum. The study of **Ram Bilas** (India) is based exclusively on the pollution statistics of Ghaziabad City. He informs that air pollution is a serious problem for the inhabitants of this city. With a progress in living standard and growing need for faster communications, the number of vehicles has been increasing. In the city, heavy vehicles such as city buses, trucks, cars and other vehicles run day and night and emit huge amounts of gaseous pollutants in the air.

Kosi Plain is of great concern because the Kosi is a very furious river and inundates vast areas almost every year. It is called as the sorrow of Bihar. Hence, the physical and cultural landscape of Kosi Plain becomes important. **Shio Muni Yadav** (India) has tried to discuss the salient physical and cultural characteristics of this area which in turn will be important from the point of view of development. Kosi has handicapped the physical and cultural landscape of the study area by its floods and shifting courses.

Parbati Nandi (India) in her paper "Mitigation and Management of Technological Hazards" gives a description of natural and technological hazards and focuses on the Gujarat earthquake, Indian Ocean Tsunami and hurricane Katrina as well as avian influenza.

Bindu, M. Bhatt and Raghuvanshi Jogender Singh (India) have highlighted the concept and brief history of water harvesting. They have also described the water harvesting scenario of India and have focused on the solution of rural and urban problems with regard to water resource.

Part III of the book incorporates 4 papers which present different aspects of the development process.

Urban policy is one of the important aspects of development. The paper by **Nak-Hun Song** (South Korea) is a good contribution to this book. His work is mainly concerned with the urban policies in South Korea and focuses on how to restrain Seoul's growth and to induce balanced national urban development across the country.

Human resource development is considered as the core concept in the field of geography of development and human welfare as it helps the people in maintaining the social mobility and in achieving the growth of wealth, prosperity. 'Spatio-temporal Analysis of Urban Human Resources Development in India', written by the editor, **B.R.K. Sinha** (India) aims at mapping the stock of urban human resources and investigating spatial and temporal variation by gender in the pattern of urban human resource development.

The evaluation of the quality of life must take into consideration the urban policy and the urban development planning. The paper 'Patterns of Urban Living and Quality of Life in Bucharest during the Post-communist Period', by **Mariana Mirela Nae** (Romania) examines the urban changes affecting the citizens' quality of life, urban regeneration initiative (which generally focuses on urban residential neighbourhoods and also on the former communist industrial units) and the uncontrolled urban sprawl, due on an inefficient legislation.

The study of **M.K. Khandelwal** (India) on 'Women Participation in Dairying: A Case Study of Rajasthan, India' is an interesting and useful contribution to this volume. Dairying plays a vital role in the subsistence economy of rural and semi-urban areas. A large section of arid area's population depends on the livestock. The study of the participation of women in dairy development becomes an essential and important exercise. Dairying is the major source of income for many families in Rajasthan.

Part IV of the book, consisting of 4 papers, deals with inter-linkages between population, environment and development.

The study of **Shii Okuno** (Japan) on 'Status of Population, Development and Quality of Life in Japan' is concerned with population and development, environment, and quality of life in Japan. Population growth in the last century and socio-economic development of Japan are the focus of the study. Vital statistics, causes of death, and daily calorie intake in Japan are indicative of development and quality of life.

The study on 'Environment, Population and Land Use Conflicts in the Coastal Savannah of Ghana' carried out by **Michael O'Neal Campbell** (UK) examines environmental access and social change in a case study of the Tuba-Aplaku Plains of the Coastal Savanna of Ghana. His narrative broadens the concept of environmental change to include multi-directional change, where rural populations and livelihood decision-making may contribute to both degradation and enrichment.

"People, Environment and Development of the Upper Ganga Basin Area, Uttarakhand, India" is an applied geo-morphological study conducted by **S.C. Mukhopadhyay** (India). He has explored and evaluated the complexities concerning the recent changes (since 1980) both in the physical and cultural parameters of the tribal people (especially Bhotias, Rajis) of the Upper Ganga Basin.

Environment and demography are the two important aspects of geography. Demographic traits of population and environment are intimately related. **Rama Prasad and Rani Singh** (India) in their paper have made an attempt to explain the relation between environment and demography in Dholpur district of Rajasthan, India. The study evaluates the effect of population on environment and suggests ways to reduce the hostile relationship between the two.

The editing of the book was facilitated by cooperation of the contributors, but I am responsible for any editorial error.

B.R.K. Sinha

Introduction by the Editor

In the 21st Century interaction between population, environment and development is one of the challenging global issues. Geography is concerned with the study of interaction between population, environment and development in space and time. Population (human population) is very vital factor and crucial agent of change or production, environment (a situation around the human population) is full of opportunities for human population and development (a creation of socially and culturally useful values) becomes a source of human welfare. In fact, the core concept of human welfare lies in the complex interconnections and interactions of population, environment and development. Positive or right interaction between population and environment becomes the means of good achievement, the source of human well-being and negative or improper interaction creates a serious threat to human civilization. Therefore, an intensive study of the above three geographical elements in a globalized regime of the 21st century is very vital from the point of view of our aspiration of peace, prosperity and posterity. In this sense, population, environment and development must be viewed in detail and interlinked together for creating a world of peace, comfort and security.

Different scholars from different disciplines and regions have studied the themes 'population, environment and development' differently and from different angles. Traditionally, man and environment and environment and development have been the fields of special study. Some scholars such as Nag, P. (2001, p. 5) and Amanda Banks (1994, p. 7) have given emphasis on man and environment whereas Kayastha, S.L. (1989), Ion, M.A.C. (1994, p. 93), Robin, F.W. (1994, p. 163), World Commission (1988) have laid emphasis on environment and development. Doroa, R.S. (1990) has throws light on man, development and environment. Similarly, Richard, Peet (2003) in the contents of his book 'Radical Geography' has used the terms environment, resources and people. Clive, Potter (1994, p. 120) studied Environmental Change, Population and Society in Poland and showed relations among them. Nag, P.; Kumar, C.K. and Sengupta, S. (2001) published their edited book on 'Environment, Population and Development'. Here they have considered 'environment' in the beginning, 'population' in the middle and 'development' in the end. But author's thinking and approach is certainly different.

In geography, particularly in population geography, population is placed in the centre of all geographical phenomena. Meaning to say that on the earth human being is central and considered as primary element around which all other geographical phenomena are arranged and derive their meaning and significance. Unless human being marks any human imprint (either by acting or using its intellectual and physical energies) on the earth or in the environment, the importance of environment remains inconclusive. Human being lives in surroundings or in surrounding situation (environment) in which different kinds of resources for human survivals are available either in actual or potential form. Since, environment is just the next immediate element to human being from its use point of view; author places the word 'environment' after population. When, human being interacts with his nature or environment for creating and obtaining resources of their benefits, human activities start interfering the structure of environment and the landscape of cultural values comes under the process of formation. The creation of cultural landscape endowed with cultural values (the result of the interaction of population and environment) is known as development. In fact, development is the end result of the interaction between human beings and environment. Since this is the end value and serves the purpose of population of an area at a given point of time, author considers it as tertiary element. However, no one has any meaning in isolation of others. Therefore, the three must be put together to give a comprehensive meaning.

Part I: Population Dimensions

Population is a dynamic phenomenon and a complicated notion in Geography. Population (humans) is the most important and dominant species on this planet. Population being the central or vital living element of the planet earth has been given first place in the structure of this book. The importance of population is clearly seen in the statement of Trewartha, G.T. (1969, p. 2). According to him population servers as the point of reference from which all other geographic elements are observed, and from which they all, singly or collectively, derive significance and meaning. According to him human population provides the essential backgrounds for all geography. Population being a geographic element plays a crucial rolė in the process of spatial organisation as it is the most dynamic and the central element in such process. Rubenstein, J. M. and Bacon, R. S. (1990, p. 37) population and its study is the basis for understanding a wide variety of issues in human geography as well as in other disciplines. Others consider human population as the creature on the earth. It is the origin, the subject and the purpose of all social institutions. Thyagarajan, M.T. and Khan, B.A. (2002, p. 60) considered population as a valuable resource for the growth of economy which in turn achieve a high quality of life. Al-Suwaidi, J.S. (2003) viewed human being as the producer of knowledge, a resource that companies and countries alike can leverage as an asset.

Recently, population studies have been greatly emphasised because they provide a central theme around which revolve other geographic thoughts and ideas, hence population studies should be placed in the fore front of geographical research. With the increase in population across space and time it is necessary to know not only the dynamic ideas about the place of population in geographic literature but also the quality and quantity of population in different parts of the world. This is because in some areas the pressure of population on cultivated land is so high that it nullifies the pace of economic development of a region as well as jeopardises the measures of planning on both social and economic fronts (Mondal, Vyanga and Prasad 1989, p. 4). The human being is the only culture building architect on the earth surface, and accordingly he adopts and creates an environment. Population as the creative element and surveyor of resources occupies a dominant position in geographical studies. Hence, the number of persons at a place is the focal point of geographical investigation. Without population the universe is resource less because only those elements of nature are considered resources which are needed and utilised by man. Thus, it is population who creates and uses all types of resources and builds social, cultural, economic, religious, political, etc. landscape on the earth.

Population is very important element in geography upon which all aspects of life of the people depend. Without knowing the population situation of an area no one can proceed far for any sort of developmental plans and policies. Population plays a duel role in producing and consuming the resources. Population is the creator as well as the destroyer of resources on the earth. Population alters even the very rigid limit of nature by the use of his mind and body. In this sense population is considered as an active factor of production that extracts, exploits, harnesses natural endowments from the earth and converts them into usable cultural goods for satisfying the wants of people of an area. Population being a vital resource builds social, economic, cultural, and political organisations for the development of a nation.

Definition is an important part of a subject that explains the nature of it. Population is an aggregate of people of an area. According to Webster's encyclopaedic unabridged dictionary of English language, population is the total number of persons inhabiting a country, city or in a district or area. It also includes the number or body of inhabitants of a particular race, or class in a place. Oxford advanced learner's dictionary of current English defines population as the number of people living in a place, country, etc. or a special section of them. According to Valentei, D; Kvasha, A and Ivanov, S. (1986 pp. 5-7) "the word population variably brings to one's mind varied images, problems and solutions."

Further they stated that population is a sum of people reproducing itself, a social phenomenon, a result of society's development and a condition required for its development. Therefore, population is the sum of social relations between people since man is essentially the sum of social relations. In the words of Valentey, D.I. (1978, p. 11) population is the aggregate of the people carrying on their life activity within a certain society. Population is always a complex and multiform aggregate of the people living in a given area and performing the natural basis of a given social community. Clarke, John I. (1965, p.5) stated that the term 'population' is commonly used with reference to all other members of plants and animal's kingdoms, it may also be noted that in a statistics population has an even wider meaning. He distinguished human population from animal population in several ways such as, in terms of number, fertility, mortality, importance, etc. Odum Eugene P. (1971, p. 162) defines population as a collective group of organisms of the same species or other groups within which individuals may exchange genetic information occupying a particular space. Each and every organism is an integral part of the ecosystem and has its impact over it. In context of population geography, population means human population. Human population not only uses the environment as habitat but through its multifarious activities changes certain natural processes in space and the ecosystem.

From such definitions of population it can be said that human population is the sum total of persons inhabiting an area at particular point of time. Sum total of persons makes a particular size of population. Population is a dynamic geographic element as the size of population changes from place to place and from time to time due to interplay of fertility, mortality and mobility.

Classification of population is another aspect upon which the analysis of all elements of quantitative and qualitative nature of population is made. Since population possesses several quantitative and qualitative characteristics, population can be divided into different groups. First of all population is divided into male and female depending upon gender. Further, population is also divided into five groups depending upon actual and potential working age. These are infants belonging to 0-4 years, school going age group children between 5 and 14 years, younger working or more active or more mobile and more energetic population of 15-34 yeas age group, older working or less active or less mobile or less energetic population of 35-59 year age group and senile or aged or less utilisable or superannuated population of 60&+ year.

Gender, age and actual and potential working capacity are the important biological characteristics of population and serve as the basis for above classification. Depending upon social and cultural composition of a region, particularly in context of India, population is divided into higher caste, other backward caste, scheduled caste and scheduled tribes. Similarly, on the basis of religion population is also classified as Hindu, Muslim, Christen, Sikh, Buddhist, etc. These groups of population become very important for analysing the spatial coverage and their contribution to the social development. Marital status also plays an important role in the society and population is grouped into unmarried, married, divorced/separated, widow/widowers, etc. The study of such population characteristics pin points the situation of marital status. Literacy and education are very vital cultural characteristics of population and play a very crucial role in all sided development of an area. Depending upon variation in education population is classified as illiterate and literate and educated people.

Further, literate and educated people may also be classified as primary, junior secondary, secondary, higher secondary, graduate and post-graduate people. This approach of population classification is vital in analysing the quality of population. Similarly, population is also classified as healthy and unhealthy population on the basis of health status, the result of diseases, food, nutrition, environment, etc. Likewise, population of an area (in terms of human resource) is also classified as undeveloped, under developed and developed or unskilled, semi-skilled and skilled. This is on the basis of human resource development levels and skills of individuals respectively. Another important approach of population classification is economic criteria. Considering characteristic of population in economic terms population is classified as active population and inactive population. Those participating in economically productive processes known as active population and those found not participating in economic process known as economically inactive population. Similarly, active population is also called as working population and inactive as non-working population. Further, on the basis of occupation in which persons work are known as agricultural and non-agricultural population.

Agricultural populations are also classified as primary workers, (involved in cultivation, animal husbandry, mining and quarrying, etc.), and non-agricultural population as secondary workers (involved in construction and industrial activities) and tertiary workers (involved in trade and commerce, transport and communication and other services). Similarly, non-working population is further classified as child population, household working population, student population, idle population. Depending upon variation in the use of labour input measured in terms of man-days or working hours, working population is classified as under-utilized, adequately-utilized (or fully utilized), and over-utilized. Distribution and concentration of population in space serve as a basis for classifying population as dense population, agglomerated population, and sparse population or dispersed population. Depending upon mobility population is classified as resident or permanent and floating population. Political boundary is also taken into consideration while classifying population.

Depending upon political boundaries of the continent or country, population is called as Asian, African, American, Australian, as well as for example Indian, Chinese and Japanese, etc. However, there is role of language too in such classification. This approach becomes important while dealing with the population of a particular country. On the basis of size of population and resources available to support this, population is divided into optimum, under, and over population. Optimum population means the population of a region which permits the maximum income per head. According to Chandna, R.C. (1999, p. 306) optimum population is that state of equilibrium between the population and the resources, which satisfies the well defined needs of all the members of a community and which varies both in time and space. If the increase in population is followed by an increase of per capita income, the country is known as having under population. But if the increase in population leads to a decrease in per capita income, the country is known as having over-population. This situation asks for decline in population till per capita income is maximised. Such classification of population becomes very important while analysing variation in the carrying capacity of resources of a country. Finally, depending upon the nature of area or land population is also classified as rural and urban population. This classification is of paramount importance in having detailed analysis of population of rural and urban areas. Thus, all the above classification is very much useful in analysing the quantitative and qualitative dimensions of population of an area.

Dimension of population occupies the central position in geographical study of a region because it becomes the foundation upon which other aspects of geography depend. Dimension stands for size, extent, component or aspect of population. Zelinsky, W. (1966, pp. 55-57) has used the word dimension for different population characteristics. According to him dimension means the components or attributes or characteristics of human population. Similarly, Newman J.L. and Matzke, G. E. (1984, pp. 2-5) have shown twenty two dimensions of quantitative and qualitative nature of population and its problems. He has also used the word aspects in place of dimension in which different population characteristics are included. Singh, S.N. and Yadav, K.N.S. (1982, pp. 393-410) have given emphasis on different quantitative and qualitative characteristics of population under the study of dimension of rural urban migration in India. Aperyan, V. (1976, p.11); Premi, M.K.; Ramanamma, A. and Bambawale, V. (1983, pp.10-11); Henk, R.; Ton Dietz and Leo, D.H. (1992, pp. 50-53); Ghosh B. N. (1985, pp. 145-150); Coates, B.E.; Johnston R.J.; Knox, P.

L. (1977, pp. 5 & 66) have included different population characteristics of quantitative nature in the dimension of population. Some of them have explained dimensions as aspects of population also. Human Development Report (1998, p. 20) took into consideration health, knowledge, participation and human security as the dimensions of population and stressed that the assessment of all these is essential in the progress of human development. From the above it is clear that dimension stands for different quantitative and qualitative aspects or components or characteristics of population.

Quantitative and qualitative are the two terms qualifying for different meanings. The former stands for size, magnitude, dimension, amount, sum etc. that can be measured directly in number and weight and lend to statistical treatment. The term qualitative on the other hand stands for nature, capacity, ability, knowledge, skill, mental or physical attributes, trait, aptitude, value, motivation and other characteristics of man that can not be measured in terms of number or weight and do not, therefore, lend themselves as easily to statistical treatment as quantitative characteristics. In this way quantity is measured directly in terms of number or weight and quality in terms of grade or level of the characteristics and these two becomes the basic aspects of population. However, both the quantity and quality of a person are inalienably related to each other and the exclusion of any quality from the quantity or from the mind and body of a person is not justifiable and possible. Gosal, G. S. (1996, p. 2) rightly observed and explained that the quality of population is interrelated with its numbers. The word quality here does not have meaning at all if it is excluded from quantities. Therefore, each population element or trait of quantitative and qualitative groups is of paramount importance and plays a very crucial role in all sided development of a region. All developmental plans and policies depend primarily on the quantitative and qualitative situation of population. Particularly qualitative aspect of population accelerates the speed of desired level of development.

Part II: Environmental Aspects

The study of environment is one of the challenging global issues. This is not confined to geography only but also to other allied subjects. The environment is an important, integral, complex, dynamic and continuously developing system. It has always been considered as a vital factor for the survival of life on the earth. Hartshorne Richard (1968, pp. 42-47) considered the earth as physical (natural) body which is the home of man. According to him it provides the means and nurtures our life. Here, he viewed physical body (the earth) as physical environment which is a source of life supporting means. Ryabchikov, A. (1975, p. Preface) has rightly emphasized the importance of natural environment.

According to him the natural environment is essential for the existence of man and is the primary source of his life and social production. The study of environmental aspect in the world of human society becomes important because environment or each environmental region is endowed with varying quality of life support layer on the living earth. Environment is the source of resources that support the life of human beings, animals, plants and other organisms of this planet earth. It directs and determines the existence, growth and development of humans and other life forms and their activities.

Environment provides various types of conditions in terms of terrain, soil, water, air, weather etc. for the plants and animals and affects their life style and activities. The successful survival of all lives on the earth (the foundation of all life) in general and human being in particular highly depends on the prevailing environment of the places in time. In fact, every aspect of life (social, cultural, economic and political) of the people of a place is completely related to the environment of their places in space and time. Purohit, Shammi and Agrawal (2004, pp. 1-4) highlighted the importance of environment and stated that the environment particularly physical environment provides both habitation and raw materials for the synthesis of organic food. All life processes are dependent on this environment. Environment (the circumstances or conditions) affects an individual or community located at a particular place on a particular point of time. Populations (humans) inhabit the natural world as well as the built or technological, social and cultural world and are influenced by the environment related to such aspects. In this way, environment is the key factor and plays a great deal in the growth and development of all forms of life. In context of human population it becomes very vital and influences all kinds of activities. The role and effect of environment is apparently seen in agriculture, industry, commerce, construction, transport and communications, in all types of institutions of learning and production and of health as well as in all other kinds of human activities relating to social, cultural, economic and political aspects.

Meaning of environment is an integral part of this study and reveals the nature and subject matters of this. Environment with all forms of life or life bearing layer (a shallow layer) lies at or close to vital interfaces between the basic earth realms: the atmosphere (gaseous realm), the hydrosphere (water realm), and the lithosphere (solid mineral realm). According to Strahler, A.N. and Strahler, A.H. (1977, pp. 2-3) environment can broadly be defined as that which surrounds all life forms between the realm of atmosphere, hydrosphere and lithosphere. Hartshorne Richard (1968, pp. 42-47) considered the physical body or physical world as natural environment which environs human being. Generally natural environment is treated as environment (in solid, liquid and gaseous form so called lithospheric, hydrospheric and atmospheric environment).

Therefore, environment should be considered as all those phenomena on this living earth which surround both the human and living world. According to Park, J.E. and Park, K. (1983, p. 27) environment includes climate, water, air, soil, social and economic conditions under which we live. It can be defined as the aggregate of all external conditions and influences affecting the life and development of an organism, human behaviour or society. Turk, Jonathan (1985, p. 1) stated that the earth on which we live is environment. It includes all the physical parts of the earth such as air, soil, minerals, rocks, water, and all living organism, such as animals and plants. All these are important and surround human beings. Daubenmire, R. F. (1974, p. 2) considered environment as the set of surroundings which influences an organism. In fact, any internal force, substance or condition that affects in any way becomes a factor of their environment and the sum total of such factors constitutes an environment.

Bhattacharya (1991, p. 9) defined environment as a living space in which human and other living species are likely to change due to the activities of the species. De and Bose (1991, p. 135) regarded environment as the sum total of conditions of the surroundings within which an organism or group of organisms or an object exists. Mitra (1991, p. 199) explain the environment as the aggregate of all external conditions and influences affecting the life and development of an organism, human behaviour or society. Swarup, Mishra, and Jauhari (1992, pp. 4-7) define environment as pervasive which pervades from one's own home to work place and throughout the socio-economic system involving the various fields of industry, agriculture, urbanization, transportation and so on. Michael, A. (2000, p. 94) considered environment as conditions of work or the type of work an individual carries out, the culture, climate and management style in the organization, the social group within which individuals work. Jeanne and Roger (2001, p. 309) defined environment in terms of services, products and resources. They stated that environment is a product of several interactive processes of different components of a system. The interactive processes between living and non-living things such as soil, water, vegetation and animals generate products and services, which act both as inputs for the continuity and performance of the system and as its output. Hence, for practical purposes, it is often difficult to separate, 'environment as services and products' from, 'environment as manifested by the status of the resources'.

Saxena, H.M. (1999, p. 1) stated that the term 'environment' is etymologically meant for surroundings. It is a complex of many variables which surrounds human beings as well as all living organisms. It is the sum total of all conditions, agencies and influences which affect the development, growth, life and death of an organism, species or race. Park, C.C. (1980) considered environment as the sum total of conditions which surround man at a given point of time in space. According to Singh, Savindra (2004, pp. 9-15) environment is a comprehensive word which in general refers to surroundings but in geographical perspective it includes abiotic (physical-land, air and water) and biotic (plants and animals including man and his several functions, organizations and institutions) components of the life supporting layer-the biosphere. The dictionary meaning of the word 'environment' is a surrounding, external conditions influencing development or growth of people, animals or plants; living or working conditions etc. This stands with three questions-what is surrounded? by what surrounded?, and where surrounded?. The answer of these questions is living object in general and human being in particular is surrounded, living objects are surrounded by physical attributes (natural environment), and living objects are surrounded in space or habitat respectively. In fact, the environment is equated with nature wherein physical components of the planet earth viz. land, water, air etc. support and affect life in the biosphere. The opinion of Dikshit, K.R. (1984, pp. 68-83) is to some extent different. He took into consider the views of others and stated that environment can be defined as a holistic view of the world as its functions at any point of time, with a multitude of spatial elemental or socio-economic systems distinguished by quality and attributes of space and mode of behaviour of biotic and abiotic forms. He further commented that environment should be taken into consideration in context of our concern and priorities. Our immediate concern is the quality of space we live in, the air we breathe, the food we eat, the water we drink and the resources we draw from the environment to support our economy.

Some others describe the word 'environment' as 'natural environment' and include all the biotic and abiotic elements, factors, and conditions that have some impact on growth and development of certain organism. Environment often changes after some time and therefore many organisms have ability to adapt to these changes. However, tolerance range is not the same with all species.

Author defines environment as everything or conditions around and about a geographic space at certain time in which human beings and other living organisms live and function. Environment may broadly be considered in different context. In natural or physical context environment includes lithospheric, hydrospheric and atmospheric conditions; in relational context it is the surroundings in which an organization operates, including air, water, land, natural resources, flora, fauna, humans and their interrelations. In organizational context environment may be considered as a working condition or working climate or working atmosphere and relation in which both man and machine work in producing a use value. In social context environment refers to the social surroundings or conditions or circumstances in which both the living and non-living systems of a society do exist. In cultural context environment relates housing, diet, culture, tourism, politics, legislation, technology, science, religion, language, the mass media and communications, organizations, educational and health institutions or infrastructure, etc. which influence the individuals in the society at a particular point of time in space. In economic context it stands for the economic condition or state of an area that affects both the human and natural phenomena on a given point of time. It also includes investment climate (a condition in which someone has to invest money, talents, energies etc. in an economic activity), land, labour, capital and other resource conditions. In psychological context environment may be considered as physical or interpersonal conditions or surroundings that affect mood, attitude, aptitude, interest, feelings and behaviour of a person or persons at any location in space and time. Environment may be stable or unstable, balanced or imbalanced which has its bearings on health and prosperity of the living organisms of that space. When the balance of environment is disturbed either due to natural calamity or by the action of human beings, it affects the health, mind and life of human and other population.

An approach of classifying environment provides broader understanding of different types of environment. Park, J.E. and Park, K. (1983, pp. 14-28) have classified environment as internal and external. The former pertains to each and every component part, every tissue, organ and organ-system and their harmonious functioning within the body system and the latter consists of those things to which human beings are exposed after conception. The external is further divided into physical, biological and psycho-social. Physical environment relates non-living things such as water, air, housing, soil, climate, heat, light, radiation, noise etc. with which human being is in constant interaction. Biological environment includes living things which surrounds human population. The living things in biological sense are the viruses and other microbial agents, insects, rodents, animals and plants. The psycho-social environment is a creation of humans and includes cultural values, customs, habits, beliefs, attitudes, moral, religion, education, occupation, standard of living, community life, health services, social and political organization. Human being is exposed to the social environment through literature, arts, press, radio, television, mass media and communication. Environment is also classified as macro and micro. The macro environment is the general environment to which a person is exposed. It includes water, air, food, etc. The micro environment stands for personal environment that includes the individual's life style and way of living.

Swarup, Mishra, and Jauhari (1992, pp. 4-7) made an attempt to classify environment as natural, built, technological, social, economic, political, moral, cultural, historical and aesthetic. Sonnenfeld, J. (1972, pp. 244-251) proposed fourfold classification of environment. These are geographical, operational, perceptual and behavioural. Chapman, Keith (1979, pp. 46 and 80) considered environment as physical or human. According to him physical environment can be treated as constraints (barriers) and as an opportunity of resources. Human environment constitutes roads, factories, fields or other cultural landscape or resources as human environment. According to Pacione, Michael (1988, p. 221) environment may be represented at three analytical levels: Physical space - tangible elements on the ground such as the layout of cities and the spatial ordering of family compounds; social space - relating to social and economic organization, including divisions of labour between the sexes and generations; and metaphysical space - the ordering of the visible and invisible universe to form a cosmology or the world system. Thus, environment may be physical, social and spiritual.

The approach of classification of environment of Singh, Savindra and Dubey, A. (1983) is to some extent different. They took into consideration the structure as the basis of classification. On the basis of structure environment may be – physical or abiotic (non-living) and biological or biotic (living). On the basis of physical characteristics or state physical or abiotic may be solid, liquid and gas which represent the lithosphere, hydrosphere and atmosphere. Thus, the three basic divisions of environment may be termed as lithospheric environment, hydrospheric environment and atmospheric environment. Biotic environment may be floral (plant) and faunal (animals) including human population. Grigg, D.B. (1984) classified environment in contents of his book as physical, economic, social, political and cultural.

Similarly, Ramakrishna, V. (2002, p. 45) classified environment as biological, physical, chemical and social. Richard, Peet (2003, pp. 117-118) made an attempt to classify environment as physical, social, economic, family and local environment. Author classifies environment as physical or natural and built or human. Natural environment can be sub-divided into land, water and air. Human environment can be sub-divided into social, cultural, religious, economic and political. Human environment can also be sub-divided into agricultural, industrial, mining, commercial, organizational, technological, etc.

Part III: Developmental Profile

Development is another challenging issue of the study in the era of globalization. Development of any kind in any form in space and time is prerequisite and a basis of survival of human beings, animals and plants on the earth. Without development every aspect of life and activity of people will halt. Development is of immense practical utility and significance. It is equally important for all the regions in both the developed and the developing countries. It helps solve the problems of population and abridges the disparities among different regions of the world. In the words of Johnston, R.J. (1994, pp. 128-130) development is historical, diverse, complex and contradictory and a central feature of human condition. It enables people in societies to make their own histories and geographies under conditions of their own choosing. This is the means by which such conditions of human existence might be achieved. Development would necessarily involve people in productive, crisis-free and non-exploitative set of relation with nature in the production of their material lives and in the struggle to remove operation and exploitation from the relations between themselves. Goel, R.L. (1998, p. 1) highlighted the importance of development. He mentioned that development (economic development) is the basic need of human societies. It makes them prosperous and ensures better quality of life for their people. Economic development provides the ultimate solution of wide spread poverty among nations. Nations are poor because they lack development or they have inadequate development or the fruits of development are inequitably distributed. It is through development that nations can be put on the path of prosperity so that their citizens could live longer and enjoy higher and better standard of living. For better standard of living, economic development should not be rapid but it should also be of better quality. Weeks, J.R. (1998, p. 438) noted that development is concerned with improving the welfare of human beings.

Different scholars have defined development differently and in their own ways. According to Johnston, R.J. (1994, pp. 128-129) development is a process of becoming and a potential state of being. It means it is a process and state of change in the quantitative and qualitative value. In broader sense, it is an historical and essentially geographical process not only because of its own variable and particular characteristics, but also because it is a product of conscious human labour operating in specific sets of social, material and natural conditions. Hirenmath, G.K. (2005, p. 98) development is the multidimensional process involving changes in the structures, attitudes and institutions as well as the acceleration of economic growth, the reduction of inequalities and eradication of poverty. Development is both a physical reality and a state of mind in which the society has through some combinations of social, economic and institutional processes secured the means of obtaining a better life.

According to Al-Ebraheen, Yousef, H. (2003, p. 85) development concepts have undergone a significant change in recent times, with growing concern regarding the knowledge based economy. Traditional meaning of development is a shift to industrialization or a shift from an economy dominated by primary sector to an economy in which industry and services play an essential role, whether with respect to production, employment or export. However, the relevance of this concept to development has now diminished only because of the shift to the knowledge based economy. It has become the aim of economic policy in all societies. Sen, Amartya K. (1990) viewed development as the expansion of human capabilities. One argument in favour of the capability approach is the need to re (focus) on people, who are the ultimate beneficiaries of real development. In the opinion of Desai, V. and Potter, R.B. (2000, p. 7) development is a certain amount of intervention or change in an existing condition by means of imitative process. Development may be between poor and strong condition of two aspects, e.g., underdeveloped and developed. Change takes place on undeveloped surface and below developed surface.

However, lower and upper limit of the surface on which change takes place is not fixed because sometimes change may take place even on upper surface or even beyond developed surface and sometimes it may take place even below the lower limit in the form of negative one. Development is generally meant for upward growth in existing condition of economy, society, quantity and quality. The main cause of development is uneven distribution of resources at different spatial units as it creates gap between two situations and development is meant for abridging this. When changes take place, the previous identity of the region is changed or transformed up or down in the system. Therefore, development is a revolution against or departure from existing or static situation or condition. Singh, K. (1999, pp. 19-25) considered development as a subjective and value-loaded concept, and hence there can not be a consensus as to its meaning. The word 'development' is used differently in diverse context. It is basically meant for unfolding or revealing or opening up something which is latent. In context of human beings, it is meant for unfolding or opening up their potential powers. Normally, development implies a change that is desirable.

Since what is desirable at a particular time, place and in a particular culture may not be desirable at other places or at other times at the same place and in the same cultural environment, it is very difficult to think of a universally acceptable definition. In context of society it can be conceptualized as social objective which a society can achieve irrespective of its culture, religion and spatial location. Development, according to him, is not only economic growth. It must encompass more than the material and financial sides of people's lives. It should, therefore, be perceived as a multidimensional process, involving the reorganization and reorientation of both economic and social systems. In addition to improvements in the level and distribution of incomes and output, it involves radical changes in institutional, social and administrative structures at any spatial level. Development is both a cause and a consequence of change. There is a two way relationship between them. Development influences, and is influenced by a change (physical, technological, economic, social, cultural, attitudinal, organizational, political, etc.).

According to Pushpesh Pant (2005, pp. 1-2) development is generally meant for economic development and western model of industrialization and urbanization. Gandhi was in favour of development but not in favour of reckless industrialization and urbanization. The rise and fall of political power in the nation or region greatly reflects the development process. For Mahatama Gandhi, development means unshackling of the poor and the downtrodden from bondage and providing access to opportunities for all round development of their personality. Development also means liberation or freedom from any kind of constraints such as hunger, bondage, illiteracy, poverty, infirmities, distress, ignorance and fear of exploitation. In other words, development means creation or making provisions of new opportunities for rational utilization through which people would be able in liberating themselves from problems. Development should also be eco-friendly. Nature is full of resources (the means of development), and the environmental resources should be harnessed properly for sustainable development.

Holler, G.P. (1988, pp. 233-235) equated development with economic growth measured by annual increases in both total and per capita GNP and changes in a country's economic structure from primary to secondary and tertiary activities. Development generally focuses on reduction in poverty, unemployment, inequality. It also focuses on creating a situation in which a region can be self-reliance. It should be culturally relevant. It also implies for a condition in which human personality can be fully realized. In fact, development can be considered as a creation of such social, cultural, economic, political and environmental climate in which human potential (knowledge, skills, talents, energies, and other competence) of each person must be fully realized and utilized in socially useful productive processes for the well-being of the people in a society. Holler further explained that any kind of development is a result of spatial inequality across geographical or politically appropriate subdivisions of the national territory in terms of physical, social, cultural, economic and political aspects. Almost everywhere there is inequitable distribution of both the intangible and tangible resources.

Deve Manjula (1991, p. 19) also joins with the similar meaning. According to her development is a multi-dimensional phenomenon. There is hardly any consensus on the meaning of development among the planners and social scientists. The meaning of development differs from person to person and from region to region and invariably changes with the times. Development is much more than mere increase in the income and earning capacity of the people. Development also includes an attainment of higher cultural values. Real development upholds the supremacy of man as a member of the human community which aims at promoting individual welfare. This is possible by way of creating conditions in which an individual's mental, spiritual and physical potential can be realized to the best advantage of the society as a whole. Similarly, Bell, M. (1988, p. 126) equated development with welfare and said that development is meant for welfare and welfare is meant for development. Human welfare, quality of life and level of living have become prominent terms in the concept of development.

Buchanan, Keith (2003, pp. 369-370) looks development as a process of economic growth and social change. Development is mainly meant for increasing economic efficiency. Others say, development is primarily a matter of increasing the rate of environmental exploitation. According to Blaut, J.M. (2003, p. 3009) development must be a matter of internal change with external aid. Improvement of human condition is the common goal of development theories. Development is after all the natural human condition. Krishna, Gopal (2000, p. 3) focused on planned development of India and defined it as an effective strategy for not only raising the standard of living of the people but also for removing regional imbalance.

Author opines that the word 'development' appears to be very simple but the concept of it is very complicated. It has a very vast canvas and includes every aspect of life of the people of an area. The term 'development' simply refers to a creation or a generation or a formation or building of a use value of any description. While crating or forming something there is need for both the actually and potentially available resources. Actually available resources are those which have already been created or achieved whereas potential resources are to be formed or developed. Once such resources are developed in a usable form, become an addition to the stock of resources (already formed or achieved). In this sense, a net addition to the stock of already achieved wealth or infrastructure can be considered as a positive change (a result of a wide range of factors of production) and is conceived as development. Development needs and involves some sort of direction, guidance and regulation to general forces of expansion or a positive change. Positive change in a use value of any description may be of quantitative or qualitative nature or of both. It means creation or formation of a use value (an asset or wealth or a resource) may be in material or in immaterial form. A use value or any object of material category is statistically quantified and measured in length, weight, height, number etc. All values or wealth of material category are tangible, say for example, rock, mineral, soil, sand, liquid material, money, machine, tool, implement, rail, road, air plane, constructed dam, reservoir, embankment and so on. In fact, all those materials or things which are created or constructed by human beings (with aid, advice and consent of the nature as well as with the action and application of hands and minds of the people) and its use either by individual or group of persons or collective people at local, regional, national or at international level in right direction with a sense of positive purpose in favour of satisfying human needs are development. Construction or creation of any useful qualitative value or wealth is socially, culturally, economically, politically and environmentally very vital for the people of a region.

The qualitative category asset or wealth can not be directly measured or counted or weighed and statistically quantified as qualities (actually or potentially available either in a person or in a material) are intangible. Qualitatively useful values may be assessed in terms of grade or level. Such qualitatively useful values or wealth may be in the form of intellectual or physical energies, capacity, capability, knowledge, skills, talents, attitude, aptitude and interest etc. in an individual or individuals. Similar useful qualitative values in terms of properties are also made available in material components too. In fact, quality is always found in quantitative objects of living or non-living groups and in no case quality can be separated from quantity. Naturally both are inalienably related to each other and creation or formation of a qualitatively use value or wealth of any description is always possible in living or non-living quantitative existence. Therefore, development is a result of creation or formation and utilization of any thing, in any form, any where, at any level and at any point of time.

Development approach or strategy plays a great deal in development. Stohr, W.B. and Taylor, D.R.F. (1981, pp. 1-12) focused on the two approaches of development or welfare. These are 'top-down or from above' and 'bottom-up or from below'. The former stands for action from above or from top to bottom. It may be from national to individual level through state, district, C. D. Block, village and family. It may also be from national to regional to local level. In this approach everything is exercised from centralized direction or from centralized control of investment. This approach generally does not allow for self sufficiency because help comes from out side. The latter stands for action from below or from bottom to top, i.e. from individual to national level through family, village, C.D. Blocks, district and state or from local to regional and to national level. In this approach everything is exercised, mobilized or controlled from local administrative bodies to regional and national. In this system local or indigenous resources, culture and technology are used in development model. This helps in greater self reliance because strength comes from within without depending on foreign or out side help or aid. This is also known as territorial approach. The 'top-down' here can be considered as an improved model or western model or modern approach and 'bottom-up' as indigenous or traditional model or local approach. The development model or development approach varies from country to country. The application of either 'top-down' or 'bottom-up' model in a country mainly depends on the strength or status of availability of its actual or potential resources.

The Prime minister of India, Dr. Manmohan Singh, laid much more emphasis on Human Face approach to development. While addressing the nation at 7.30 P.M. on 24.06.2004 on Indian Door Darshan (television) he said that development is not an end or aim in itself. Human face relates those aspects of human life which are felt essential or desirable at the minimum for bare existence of life of the mass of the people at spatial and time scale. The management of essential aspects such as health, education, drinking water, food, employment, environment etc will help increase human welfare functions and quality of life of an individual or a family or a group of people at local, regional and national level. In broader sense, 'human face consists of trying to provide the tens of millions of Indians who have no jobs or are on the verge of starvation for a large part of the year because of long stretches of unemployment' (Bagchi, Amiya Kumar, p. 9). The fulfilment of the basic needs will depend on the target groups of population such as the poor and the down trodden, vulnerable population, diseased and illiterate people, the child and the mother, etc.

Bureau E N. (2004, p. 1) the Prime Minister of India, Dr. Manmohan Singh identified seven sectors to be the pillars of development to ensure higher economic growth and more equitable social and economic development. These are Agriculture, Water, Education, Healthcare, Employment, Urban Renewal and Infrastructure

Development approach may be spatial or administrative, sectoral, social, cultural, economic, political and environmental. Spatial approach may be at local, regional and national level. Administrative approach of development may be at village, community development Block, district, state and country level. Sectoral approach focuses on different economic sectors such as agricultural and non-agricultural (construction, industrial, trade and commercial, transport and communication, and service sectors). Socio-cultural and economic approaches focus on different social, cultural and economic aspects of population with a view to raise the peace, comfort ant happiness. Political and environmental approach stresses on the formulation of appropriate plans and policies and fair allocation and equitable distribution of national resources for enhancing and maintaining the quality of life and the quality of environment. All these approaches in common integrate different elements of different sectors at different levels towards the best interest of the people of an area.

Development can be known as rural development, urban development, agricultural development, industrial development, human development or human resource development, social and cultural development, economic and political development, household level development, sustainable and un-sustainable development, environmental development, local development, regional development, national development and global development etc.

Human Capital (human resource) is central among all types of development and comprises the stock of health, nutrition, education, skills and knowledge of individuals; access to services that provide these, such as schools, medical services, adult training; the ways individuals and their knowledge interact with productive technologies; and the leadership quality of individuals. Human capital formation or human resource formation (the process or strategy of enhancing knowledge, skill, talent and other mental and physical energies or functional capabilities of person or persons) views human beings as means rather than an end. Human beings are more than material or capital goods in any kind of production process.

21st century is the century of emerging knowledge and innovations and can be fully realized with the process of human development because it will hold the key to sustainable development and national well-being. Human development can meet all the challenges to come in the future. It is defined as a capability building in terms of developing necessary skills, acquiring technical knowledge through education and training. It entails overall improvement in the quality of life of each individual. Similarly, social development is another important type of development and has much broader concept than human development. It is considered as a process of social change. Social development includes demographic parameters, health situation, educational attainments, basic social amenities, incidence of unemployment and poverty, and deprivation related indicators (Council for Social Development, pp. 216-219). Social development may be considered as the core of development because it makes the people free from several socio-economic bindings and enables to live a life of peace and comfort. Munasinghe, M. and Reid, W. (2005, p. 29) stated that social development signifies improvements in both individual well-being and the overall welfare of society resulting from increases in social capital. Similarly,

Demeny, Paul and Mc Nicoll (1988, p. 1) described economic development in terms of structural transformation in the economy and society that takes place along with growth in per capita income. Such transformations include those in the structure of production, consumption, investment, trade, income distribution, labour allocation, education, urbanization.

Part IV: Population-Environment-Development Inter-linkages

Population, environment and development are complex systems and their interrelationship is also inconstant, dynamic and complex. Relationship between human being and natural environment starts right from the inception of human-nature existence on the earth. Humans have been striving hard to improve their life and surroundings by the process of development. By doing so they have been knowingly or unknowingly making interference in nature. Particularly after the advent of modernization or technological know-how humans have disturbed the environment in such a way that has become a question of their own survival. This is a result of only the irrational and unplanned activities to the development and accumulation of wealth to support their life.

1. The relationship between population and environment is very important in the living world. The following scholars have explained the linkages between population and environment. Khoshoo, T.N. (1986, p. V) stated that the growing number of population has significant bearing on the relationship between population and the environment. High growth rate of population increases pressure on human beings to invade the environment in order to meet their growing needs. Progress in science and technology and high ambitions has further encouraged human beings to alter the environment which in turn becomes a big problem for them.

Population change and increasing population density are the most important drivers of environmental change in several ways. The relationship between population factors and the environment is multidimensional and is affected by change in other sectors such as trade and commerce, agriculture, industry, other economic activities, investment, research and the development of technology. Poverty, education, health and governance systems are also closely linked to population changes and its impact on the environment.

Richard Peet (2003, p. 59) also noted that the action of man is so powerful agency that drains marshes and lakes, smoothes down the obstacles between different countries, and modifies the primitive distribution of animal and vegetable species etc. The action of man may embellish the earth, but it may also disfigure it. According to the customs and social condition of any nation, it contributes either to the degradation or glorification of nature. Man moulds into his own image the country which he inhabits.

According to Fernie, J. and Pitkethly, A.S. (1985, p. 9) the theme of man's relationship with his environment is an old one, but in the recent decades it has acquired a new twist from the view that man might ultimately destroy his environment, and hence himself, unless urgent action on population, resources and environment issues is taken. Similarly, Ryabchikov, A. (1975, p. 6) also explained that the environment changes much faster under the influence of the forces of production. The size of population and the tremendous advances in science and technology allow to exploit the environment and to bring changes in that. Therefore, there should be rational development and harmless utilization of the environment.

Gordon MacDonald (2001, p. vii) was of the opinion that the environmental change, both natural and those resulting from a variety of societal activities, will lead to changes in demography. Successively demographic changes could influence environment. This is a common concept that an increase in population will adversely affect the environment.

2. The relationship between population and development is a complex one. Development is always meant for welfare maximization for the human population. Some favour population growth as a necessary condition for economic and other development whereas some others consider population growth as an impediment to any kind of positive development. Newbold, K. Bruce (2002, pp. 151-153) explained the similar facts regarding the relationship between population and development. According to him population growth and economic development are much debatable issues because population growth is considered as a favourable condition in some parts of the world and as an obstacle in some other parts of the world. In Europe and North America population growth and declining mortality level are thought to have stimulated economic development and the industrial revolution.

However, a different perspective is noticed in the developing world. The developing world has even far greater rate of population growth but does not follow the lead of economic growth of the developed countries. This is mainly because of higher fertility rate of population which causes lower standard of living and poverty. In developing countries the lower standard of living, poverty and appreciably high fertility rate add larger number of new persons in its population size and hence impede the ability of government or individuals to invest on the needed infrastructure. For development, the rate of capital investment should also increase with the rate of population growth. The same was opined long back by Malthus too. He stated that if the rate of population growth exceeds the rate of capital investment, the country would remain unable to invest in its population and to provide the needed infrastructure. It is apparent that high rate of population growth has negative effect on development. Rapid population growth dampens the growth of per capita GDP (the total value of goods and services produced in a country). Fast population growth normally increases dependency ratio, child population, cost on health and education, government expenditure, under and unemployment, poverty, illiteracy and reduces household saving, job opportunities, wages and earnings, etc. Conversely, declining population and fewer children enable household to invest more on education and increases savings.

Generally, rapid population growth threatens resources by placing more pressure on them. In fact, rapid population growth and high fertility rate seemingly have the greatest negative impact in the poorest countries where national institutions are weak. McNicoll, G. (1982, pp. 519-523) also noted that a high mortality, high fertility and low population growth rate was the characteristics of primitive or traditional society whereas low mortality, low fertility and stationary population growth are the characteristics of modern development and modern society. The population transition theory clearly explains the pattern of population growth and socio-economic development. Khan, A.R. (1988, p. 143) also observed that the rate of population growth has an overwhelmingly powerful effect on the entire course and pattern of development because all types of developmental programmes are affected by the rate of population growth.

3. Environment and population have very deep relation. Hagget, P. (1972, 591) overstated that environment plays a major role in determine the behaviour of man on the surface of the earth. The renowned environmentalists such as Carl Ritter (in Erdkunde), Demolins (in Essai de Geographie Sociale and Comment la route cree le type Sociale), Ellen Semple (in Influence of Geographic Environment) have given much more emphasis on environment and stated that environment controls or influences all aspects of life of population in space and time.

Similarly, the renowned scholars such as Febvre, Blache, Brunhes, Bowman (the sympathizers of possibilism) have given much importance to human population and its activities and elaborated that man is a geographical agent or an active factor of change in the domain of environment. Everything on the earth is for man and man by his habit, culture, understanding and skills change the environment. However, it does not mean that man can change the entire environment. Due to several physical barriers man can not change the environment to the extent he wishes. Man can modify or change the environment only to the extent nature permits to do so. In fact, there is intimate relation between man and environment. Both are integral parts of the ecological system. The distribution of population and human activities, location of social and cultural attributes, mental and physical energies, overall health, etc. have some relation with the environment. Chappell, J. E. (1989, p. 163) rightly pointed out that environment does not influence only material phase of life but also affects our minds and habits. These facts reveal that both population and the environment are equally important in the universe. Environment in all sense is the source of resources and human populations are meant to utilize the environmental resource in proper and justified manner for their social, cultural, economic and political development

4. Environment has its profound effect on development. Council of Europe (1993, p. 6) gave emphasis on the role of environment in development. Environment in terms of floods, mud flows, landslides, erosion and avalanches are not to be controlled solely by technical means. They impose strict limits for settlements, infrastructures, and tourist development projects and they preclude any uncontrolled regression of farming and forestry. This statement tends to indicate that any kind of cultural landscape (the result of development) of an area is highly influenced by its environment. Environment influences not only the cultural landscape but also the development of human resources and each and every sector of both the rural and urban economy.

5. Similarly, the interaction between development and population of an area is of great concern. Every aspect of life of the people largely depends on the level and pattern of development and in the same way development also depends on the status of demographic characteristics of an area. High fertility and high mortality among the populations of an area are the consequences of overall poor performance of development. In the similar sense, illiteracy, poverty, un-employment and under-employment, low standard of living, poor health, social crimes and other social and economic problems are also the result of un-development and under development of the concerned area. Less development of the concerned area works as a push force and leads to out-migration of skilled and semi skilled labourers. This ultimately harms the area of out-migration. Therefore, to raise the standard of living and per capita income, level of health and education and to reduce poverty and un-employment, and social crimes and other social and economic problems there is need for sustainable development at local, regional and national level.

6. According to Thirlwal, A. P. (2003, pp. 399-400 and 421) thc cnvironment is essential and very vital for human activities and development. Right from the 2nd half of the 20th century there has been a growing concern about the impacts of economic activities on the environment. Economic growth causes serious

environmental damage. This will constrain economic development in future. The developing countries largely depend on natural environment for their livelihood and that is why, the relationship between the economic growth and environment remains more important than that of the developed countries. It is observed that unconstrained economic growth will lead to the exhaustion of non-renewable resources and damage the environment. This will seriously affect economic production and the quality and existence of life. Kontturi, O. (1990, p. 30) noted the impact of development on land environment. He explained that socio-economic development consumes vast amount of land everyday. This trends needs to be controlled if the wastage and indeed permanent loss of good quality land is to be avoided.

7. Population, environment and development are completely inter-linked together and the interactions among them are quite complex. This is due to dynamic process of change in population and in generation and exploitation and consumption of resources in the environment. The linkages among them are quite obviously observed in the work of O'Neill, B.C.; Mackellar, F.l. and Lutz, W. (2001, pp. 172-174). They pointed out that 'no phrase has brought population, environment and development linkages home to policymakers more forcefully than environmental refugees'. Environmental refugee is related with the condition of environmental constraints under which people of an area feel their inability to cope with natural forces and decide to leave their original homeland to protect themselves from environmental problems. The environmental constraints may be drought, soil erosion, desertification, and other environmental problems which compel the people to move to another suitable place in search of generating resources (development) for their livelihood. People who can no longer earn a secure livelihood in their erstwhile homelands because of as such ecological push move to seek for better quality of life. This leads to the conservative and innovating as well as normal migration and shows the relationship with population, environment and development. Similarly, Das Gupta, S.P. (2002, p. 2) also focuses on population, environment and development linkages and highlights that human being always tries to get benefits by accumulating greater amount of wealth in the form of development from the available natural endowments and while doing so human being creates immense misery and grievous injury to the environment. Rapid development of resources for the benefit of mankind disturbs the pristine environment. This kind of human induced environmental change causes environmental refugees and in turn human happiness and quality of life are disturbed.

Pudasaini, Som, P. (1997, pp. 307-311 & 318) worked on population, environment and sustainable development and described that these are interlinked together and are complementary aspects of sustainable development. Pudasaini noted that population growth in the world in general and rapid population growth in the developing countries in particular is a cause of great concern. However, world wide efforts are under way to conserve resources, protect environment and pursue sustainable development. Such efforts in population, environment and development are positive but still require greater commitments and concerted actions from both the developed and the developing countries. This is because of the fact that people are at the centre of development and environmental concerns. To make population, environment and development relation friendly, population regulation, environmental protection and management as well as judicious development are essential. Without population regulation and environmental protection development efforts can not succeed.

Similarly, without development, environment also can not be fully protected. Therefore, to make a balanced relation among population, environment and development, population must be controlled, environment must be given due attention to improve its quality and development must be rational. Demeny, Paul and Mc Nicoll (1988, pp. IX and 2) also observed that the growth of population and economies are major forces for change in the contemporary world. Both have consequences for human well-being. Each also impinges on other. Declining mortality started population explosion; declining fertility will eventually halt it. Economic development hastens both of these declines. Rapid population growth in turn slows the pace of development and may exacerbate the environmental damage. The Size and rate of growth of populations have profound effects on human societies and their governance as well as on their environment. In fact, resource scarcity, environmental crisis and population growth are deeply implicated. Population-resource interactions in some circumstances lead to environmental degradation due to increasing demand of resources.

An Overview: Population is an agent of creation or change (development) and creates or builds something for its own interest and while doing so human beings bring changes or interference in the status of environment which may be positive as well as negative. Every aim or intention of development is positive (for the betterment of the society) but human interference leads to disturb the eco-system by polluting and degrading the quality of environment. This in turn becomes the means of suffering for human population. This is observed everywhere and all the times in the world.

Murthy, K.R. (2003, p. 385) rightly pointed out that both the development and underdevelopment coupled with unprecedented population growth cause environmental degradation. Everywhere and all the times human population continues to generate and develop resources from the nature but did not pay much attention to its resourceful environment and disturbs the ecological system. Therefore, an approach of friendly population-environment-development relationship must be encouraged towards better quality of life of the people. Sinha, Dilip (1998, p. 3) also expressed the similar views on population-environment relationship. In his words nations must strike a balance between development and environment. They must strive for an economic growth that is sustainable so that mankind is saved from total ruin. Environmental problems can not be solved by legislative measures alone. Broad awareness among the mass of the people at all levels can be a positive step to meet the exigency. Since the environment is now a global concern, it should be tackled at all levels such as local, regional, national and international level. Not much could be achieved in isolation.

In spite of much growing concern for the environment very few scholars in the world have paid attention to our social, cultural, economic and political environments which are in no case less important than physical or natural environment. Generally, we think only for physical or natural environment and our socio-cultural environment gets a back seat. Since socio-cultural environment is equally important, scholars must pay equal attention to this also with a view to make a better society for peace, comfort, freedom and happiness. Therefore, one should respect the power of all types of environment and apply it for the benefit of human kind. We should give highest priority on health, safety and environmental protection in the use of our products. Environmental protection and sound resource management are the essential parts of development planning and are of the utmost importance for the living world at the global level.

Human development or human resource development has close link with the population, environment and sustainable development. Without a human resource of right quality and right quantity in right time no kind of progress is possible. Better human development or human resource development will have efficient and strong coordinated response to the problems of population, environment and sustainable development. Pudasaini, Som, P. (1997, p. 318) and Ginkel, H. V.; Barret, B.; Court, J.; and Velasquez, J. (2003, pp. 12-14) have also stressed on the requirement of human development for sustainable and friendly relation among the population, environment and development. Therefore, to promote a balanced relation among population, environment and development human development/human resource development, particularly in the developing countries, must be taken into consideration as one of the priority areas because the core concept of all types of development lies in human resource development. For this people must be provided with adequate facilities of health and education. They must also be provided with food and nutrition, potable water, housing, clothing, full employment and other essential welfare amenities. All these will help increase human knowledge, skills, awareness, energies, attitude, interest etc. which in turn will contribute a lot to friendly and balanced population-environment-development relationship for the well-being of the society.

It is well known fact that population, environment and development interact in a variety of ways. Population change and socio-economic development occur simultaneously with the environmental damage. The global challenge in the era of economic liberalization, privatization, commercialization, industrialization, urbanization and increasing globalization is to improve the standard of living and quality of life of population through rational development and by safeguarding the total or all types of environment. Therefore, the 21st Century should be a century for check on steady growth of population (especially in the developing countries) and on environmental pollution (air, water, soil, deforestation, etc.). Generation, conservation and rational utilization of environmental resources for sustainable social, cultural and economic development must be a priority goal of this century and it is possible by developing human values and human resources. All these will help increase human welfare, quality of life and well-being of the people.

References

Al-Ebraheen, Yousef, H. (2003) Education and Human Resource Development in the knowledge Based Economy, In Human Resource Development in a knowledge Based Economy, The Emirates Centre for Strategic Studies and Research, Abu Dhabi, UAE.

Al-Suwaidi, J.S. (2003) Human Resource Development in a knowledge Based Economy, In Human Resource Development in a knowledge Based Economy, The Emirates Centre for Strategic Studies and Research, Abu Dhabi, UAE.

Amanda Banks (1994) Man-Environment Conflicts in the Tara National Park (Australia) In Conference Abstracts, IGU Regional Conference on Environment and quality of Life in Central Europe: Problems of Transition, Praguc, August 22-26, 1994.

Aperyan, V. (1976) Man Power Resources and Population under Socialism, Progress Publishers, Moscow.

Bagchi, Amiya Kumar (9 July 2004) Economic Reforms with a Human face?, The Statesman, Kolkata, India.

Bell, M.: Welfare, Culture and Environment, In Pacione Michael (1988) The Geography of the Third World: Progress and Prospect, Routledge, London.

Bhattacharya, B. (1991) Defilement of the Environment, Its Restoration and Management, In Jana, M.M. (1991) Environment Degradation and Development Strategies in India, Ashish Publishing House, New Delhi.

Blaut, J.M. (2003) Theory of Development, In Richard Peet (2003) Radical Geography,

Rawat Publications, Jaipur, India.

Buchanan, Kith (2003) Reflection on a "Dirty World", In Richard Peet (2003) Radical Geography, Rawat Publications, Jaipur, India.

Bureau E N (2004) In Employment News, Vol. XXIX, No. 21, 21-27 August 2004, New Delhi.

Chandna, R.C. (1999) A Geography of Population, Kalyani Publishers, Ludhiana, India.

Chapman, Keith (1979) People, Pattern and Processes: An Introduction to Human Geography, Arnold-Heinemann, London.

Chappell, J. E. (1989) 'Environmental Causation', In Themes in Geographic Thought (edited by Harvey Holly) reprinted by Rawat Publications, Jaipur, India.

Clarke, John. I. (1965) Population Geography, Pergamon Press, Oxford, London.

Clive, Potter (1994) Environmental Change, Population and Society in Poland In Conference Abstracts, IGU Regional Conference on Environment and quality of Life in Central Europe: Problems of Transition, Prague, August 22-26, 1994.

Coates, B. E.; Johnston, R. J.; Knox, P. L. (1977) Geography and Inequality, Oxford University Press, London.

Council for Social Development (2006) India Social Development Report, Oxford University press, New Delhi.

Das Gupta, S. P. (2002) Human Rights Vis-a-vis Environmental Issues, In Indian Journal of landscape System and Ecological Studies, Vol. 25, No.2, December 2002, Kolkata.

Daubenmire, R.F. (1974) Plants and Environment, Wiley, Eastern Pvt. Ltd., UK.

De, N.K. and Bose, A.K. (1991) In Jana, M.M. (Ed.) Environment Degradation and Development Strategies in India, Ashish Publishing House, New Delhi.

Demeny, Paul and Mc Nicoll (1988) Population and Development, Earthscane Publications Ltd., UK.

Desai, V. and Potter, R.B. (2000) The Companion to Development Studies, Arnold, London.

Deve Manjula (1991) Urban Ecology and levels of Development, Rawat Publications, Jaipur.

Dikshit, K.R. (1984) A Prologue to the Symposium on Geography and Teaching of Environment, Department of Geography, University of Pune, India.

Doroa, R.S. (1990) Man, Development and Environment, Ashish Publications, New Delhi.

Fernie, J. and Pitkethly, A.S. (1985) Resources: Environment and Policy, Harper and Row Publishers. London.

Ghosh, B. N. (1985) Fundamentals of Population Geography, Steerling Publishers Pvt. Ltd., New Delhi.

Ginkel, H. V.; Barret, B.; Court, J.; and Velasquez, J. (2003) Reflections on Human Development and the Environment In Human Development and the Environment: Challenges for the United Nations in the New Millennium. Rawat Publications, Jaipur and New Delhi.

Goel, R.L. (1998) Economics of Growth and Planning, Meenakshi Prakashan, Merrut, India.

Gordon MacDonald: Foreword In O'Neill, B. C.; Mackellar, F. l. and Lutz, W. (2001, p. vii) Population and Climate Change, Cambridge University Press, UK

Gosal, G.S. (1996) Human resource development In Transactions, Vol. 18, No. 1, Indian Institute of geographers, Pune, India.

Grigg, D.B. (1984) An Introduction to Agricultural Geography, Hutchinson, London.

Hagget, P. (1972) Geography: A Modern Synthesis, Harper and Row, London.

Hartshorne, Richard (1968) Perspective on the nature of Geography, John Murray, London.

Henk, Reitsma; Ton, Dietz and Leo, De Huan (1992) Netherlands Geographical Studies 146: Coping with Semiaridity, Geographical Society, Department of Geography, University of Amsterdam, Netherland.

Hirenmath, G.K. (2005) Policies for Human Development in the Global Libralized Scenario In Hirevenkanagoudar, L.V.; Manjunath, L.; Hanchinal, S.N.; Angadi, J.G. and Chandargi, D.M. (Eds.) Extension Strategies for Human Resource Development, Agrotech Publishing Academy, Udaipur, India.

Holler, G. P.: Regional Development In Pacione Michael (1988) The Geography of the Third World: Progress and Prospect, Routledge, London.

Human Development Report (1998), The United Nations Development Programme (UNDP), Oxford University Press, Delhi.

Ion, M. A. C. (1994) Nature, Environment and Development in Latin America, In Conference Abstracts, IGU Regional Conference on Environment and quality of Life in Central Europe: Problems of Transition, Prague, August 22-26, 1994.

Jeanne, X. K. and Roger, E. K. (2001) Global Environmental Risk, United Nations University Press, New York.

Johnston, R.J. (1994) The Dictionary of Human Geography (third edition) Blackwell Publishers, Oxford, UK.

Kayastha, S. L. (1989) Environment and Development, In Rural System, Vol. VI, Pt. 1.

Khan, A.R. (1988) Population Growth and Access to Land: An Asian Perspective In Lee, R.D.; Arthur W.B.; Kelley, A.C.; Rodgers, G. and Srinivasan, T.N.: Population, Food and rural Development, Clarendon Press, Oxford.

Khoshoo, T.N. (1986) Environmental Priorities in India and Sustainable Development, Indian Science Congress Association, New Delhi.

Kontturi, O. (1990) Finnish Eskers In Naturopa , Vol. 65, Council of Europe, Strasbourg Cedex, France.

Krishna, Gopal (22-24, December, 2000) Presidential Address on: Development, Environment and Decentralized Planning , XXII Indian Geography Congress of National Association of Geographers, India, held in the Department of Geography, Karnataka University, Dharwad, India.

McNicoll, G. (1982) Population and Development, In Ross, J.A.: International Encyclopedia of Population, Vol. 2, The Free Press, New York.

Michael, A. (2000) A Handbook of Human Resource Management Practice, Kogan Press, London.

Mitra, N. (1991) In Jana, M.M. (Ed.) Environment Degradation and Development Strategies in India, Ashish Publishing House, New Delhi.

Mondal, R. B.; Vyanga, Joseph; Prasad, H. (1989) Introductory Methods in Population Analysis, Concept Publishing Company, New Delhi.

Munasinghe, M. and Reid, W. (2005) The Role of Ecosystems in Sustainable Development In Sengupta, N.; Bandyopadhyay, J.: Biodiversity and Quality of Life, The Indian Society for Ecological Economics, Macmillan, New Delhi.

Murthy, K.R. (2003) Interface between Population, Ecology and Environment: the Needs for Sustainable Development, In Ersheng, G.A.O.: Reproductive Health, Gender and Development, B.R. Publishing Corporation, New Delhi.

Nag, P.; Kumar, C.K. and Sengupta, S. (2001) Environment, Population and Development, Concept Publishing Company, New Delhi.

Naturopa , No. 72, (1993) Council of Europe, Strasbourg Cedex, France.

Newbold, K. Bruce (2002) Six Billion Plus: Population Issues in the Twenty first Century, Rowman and Littlefield Publishers, Inc., Oxford.

Newman, L. James; Matzke, E. Gordon (1984) Population - Patterns, Dynamics and Prospects, Prentice Hall, INC. Engle Wood Cliffs, New Jersey.

Odum Eugene P. (1971) Fundamentals of Ecology, W.B. Saunders Co, London.

Pacione, Michael (1988) The Geography of the Third World: Progress and Prospects, Routledge, London and New York.

Park, C.C. (1980) Ecology and Environmental Management, Butterworth, London.

Park, J.E. and Park, K. (1983) A Textbook of Preventive and Social Medicine, Banarsidas Bhanot, Jabalpur, India.

Premi, M. K.; Ramanamma, A.; Bambawale, V. (1983) An Introduction to Social Demography, Vikash Publishing House Pvt. Ltd., New Delhi.

Pudasaini, Som, P. (1997) Population, Environment and Sustainable Development in a Global Perspective, In Ahmad, Aijazuddin; Noin, Daniel; and Sharma, H.N.: Demographic Transition-the Third World Scenario, Rawat Publications, Jaipur and New Delhi.

Purohit, Shammi and Agrawal (2004) Environmental Sciences: A New Approach, Agrobios, Jodhpur (India).

Pushpesh Pant (2005) Gandhi and Development, In Employment News, Vol. XXX, No. 27, 1-7 October 2005, New Delhi.

Ramakrishna, V. (2002) Health Education in India: Challenges to be met for Effective Implementation, In Mahadevan, K. (Ed.): Health Education for Quality of Life, B.R. Publishing Corporation, New Delhi.

Richard Peet (2003) Radical Geography, Rawat Publications, Jaipur, India.

Richard, Peet (2003) Radical Geography: Alternative Viewpoints on Contemporary Social Issues, Rawat Publication, Jaipur, India.

Robin, F.W. (1994) Environment and Society and Economic Development, In

Conference Abstracts, IGU Regional Conference on Environment and quality of Life in Central Europe: Problems of Transition, Prague, August 22-26, 1994.

Rubenstein, J. M. and Bacon, R. S. (1990) The Cultural Landscape: An Introduction to Human Geography, Prentice-Hall of India Pvt. Ltd., New Delhi.

Ryabchikov, A. (1975) The Changing Face of the Earth, Progress Publishers, Moscow.

Saxena, H.M. (1999) Environmental Geography, Rawat Publications, Jaipur.

Sen, Amartya K. (1990) Development as Capability Expansion, In Griffin, K. and Knight, J. (Eds.) Human Development and the International Development Strategy for the 1990s, MacMillian, London.

Singh, Katar (1999) Rural Development: Principles, Policies and Management, Sage Publications, Delhi.

Singh, S. N. and Yadav, K. N. S. (1982) Dimension of rural-urban migration in India and their impact on some socio-economic and demographic features. In : Urbanisation and Regional Development (ed. by Mondal, R.B. and Peters, G. L.), Concept Publishing Company, New Delhi.

Singh, Savindra (2004) Environmental Geography, Prayag Pustak Bhavan, Allahabad, India.

Singh, Savindra and Dubey, A. In Singh, L.R. (1983) Environmental Management: Some New Dimensions in Environmental Management, Allahabad Geographical Society, India.

Sinha, Dilip (1998) Development Should be Balanced with Environment, The Statesman (late City) August 3, Calcutta.

Sonnenfeld, J. (1972) Geography, Perception and the Behavioural Environment, In English, P.W. and Mayfield, R.C. (eds.) Man, Space and Environment, Oxford Uni. Press , London.

Stohr, W.B. and Taylor, D.R.F. (1981) Development from Above or Below?, Wiley Chichester, UK.

Strahler, A.N. and Strahler, A.H. (1977) Geography and Man's Environment, John Willey and Sons, New York.

Swarup, R., Mishra, S.N. and Jauhari, V.P. (1992) Encyclopaedia of Ecology, Environment and Pollution Control: An Introduction to Man and His Environment, Mittal Publications, New Delhi.

Thirlwal, A. P. (2003) Growth and Development with special reference to the Developing Economies, Palgrave MacMillan, New York.

Thyagarajan, M.T. and Khan, B.A. (2002) Social Marketing of Health and Population Innovations, In Mahadevan, K. (Ed.): Health Education for Quality of Life, B.R. Publishing Corporation, New Delhi.

Trewartha, G. T. (1969) A Geography of Population: World Patterns, John Willey and Sons, INC., New York.

Turk, Jonathan (1985) Introduction to Environmental Studies, Saunders College Publishing, New York.

Valentei, D.; Kvasha, A. and Ivanovs (1986) Population and Socio Economic Development, Progress Publishers, Moscow.

Valentey, D. I. (1978) The Theory of Population: Essays in Marxist Research, Progress Publishers, Moscow.

Weeks, J.R. (1998) Population: An Introduction to concepts and Issues, Wadsworth Publishing Company, Belmont, CA.

World Commission on Environment and Development (1988) Our Common Future, Oxford University Press.

Zelinsky, W. (1966) A Prologue to Population Geography, Prentice Hall, INC., Engle Wood Cliffs, New Jersey.

Part I: Population Dimensions

1

Four Traditions of Population-Poverty Analysis: A Way Out of the Cul-De-Sac?

Nanda R. Shrestha, Norman Johnson and Wilbur I. Smith

Introduction

Population is a defining barometer of any society as it permeates virtually every facet of life. Population, in other words, is engaged in a two-way relationship with the process of social and economic development: it shapes a society's progress which, in turn, shapes the people's socio-economic conditions in that society. One result of this interactive process is that where there is population, there is poverty.

People are at once the source of poverty and prosperity, in that they create the socio-economic institutions, including market mechanisms that reside at the heart of poverty and prosperity. And it is the people who define and attack the problem of poverty, either individually, collectively, institutionally, or through market mechanisms. Although poverty is specific to certain social classes, few seem to be able to escape its societal ramifications and wrath. It is, metaphorically speaking, a social edifice that imprisons everybody—rich or poor, prince or pauper. The question is whether one is inside the prison bars of poverty (poor), hoping to find a way out, or outside the bars (rich) keeping a close watch on those inside. It is precisely because of this socio-historical dualism that the rich in every society have feared the poor, especially since the French Revolution. Consequently, poverty has prompted the rich to develop a barricade mentality in an attempt to insure their physical and material security either through various social policies or geographical distance.

Since few deny the need to address the entrenched problem of poverty, the questions of what causes poverty and how to deal with it abound, often imbued with political slants and ideological biases. It is, therefore, hardly surprising to discover that the debate over the relationship between population and poverty is intensely polarized. Arguably, it was Reverend Thomas Robert Malthus who heightened the debate about poverty into what Boulding (1959) calls the "Utterly Dismal Theorem," as the reverend proclaimed miseries and deaths to be the fait accompli of—as well as the only lasting (universal) solution to—overpopulation, namely, poverty.

Karl Marx (1973) was not far behind. In his economic notebooks drafted in 1857–1858, Marx escalated the debate's tenor as he criticized Malthus on theoretical and socio-historical grounds, poking holes in almost every aspect of his "Utterly Dismal Theorem." Soon, the two ideologues found themselves on opposite ends of the population-poverty debate, thereby setting in motion what eventually transpired into a heated divide between the Malthusian and Marxist camps. The lively debate was further invigorated when Malthus' descendants, commonly known as Neo-malthusians, emerged on the scene in the 1950s. Armed with their own stories of pending population horrors, the Neo-Malthusians joined the debate in the true spirit of their progenitor, Malthus, extending the debate's parameters beyond poverty to include environmental degradation. Then came neo-liberals or revisionists as Kelley (1999) refers to them. Concerned with the economics of demography, neo-liberals entered the fray in the early 1980s. Led by Julian L. Simon (1981), an ardent advocate of the new breed of neo-liberal demography, they have espoused an optimism regarding the positive role of population growth in economic and technological progress that contrasts sharply with the Neo-Malthusianism position. The contemporary drama of population and poverty is, in other words, being played out as a tri-polar ideological debate, one in which Malthusians/Neo-Malthusians, Marxists, and neo-liberal have staked out distinct outposts, casting a gaze at each other's motion and movement, both on theoretical grounds and in the policy arena.

With this synoptic entry, our primary objective is first to provide a selective review of what we call the four leading traditions of population-poverty analysis: Malthusian, Marxist, Neo-Malthusian, and Neo-liberal. These traditions represent, "a mode of thought or behaviour followed by a people continuously from generation to generation; a set of customs and usages viewed as a coherent body of precedents influencing the present" (*American Heritage Dictionary*, 1982: 1284). We are cognizant of the question that may arise regarding the separation between the Malthusian and Neo-Malthusian traditions, for they stem from the same roots. Nonetheless, their separate treatment in this study offers a greater degree of conceptual clarity, especially for those who may be relatively new to the debate.

Our review of the four traditions draws into view two related pictures of the debate. First, it reveals the ideological nature of the population-poverty debate and how it has evolved over time since the days of Malthus. Second, it shows that the debate is still mired in a historical cul-de-sac, with no viable outlet to reconcile opposing views. In light of this ideological quagmire, we lay out in the concluding section a framework for finding a way out of the cul-de-sac that continues to diminish the policy value of the debate. Put simply, the framework attempts to synthesize what we consider to be the constructive components of the different entries in the ongoing population-poverty debate.

An Overview of the Population-Poverty Debate

Throughout history, population has been viewed either as a problem to be tackled or as a resource to be exploited to further military, social, political, or economic goals. This general perspective seems to have changed little in contemporary times as politicians and policymakers continue to hold such dichotomous views. In this "either-or" scenario, population is both the *problem* and a *resource* as it reflects the inherent duality of humanity: *a pair of hands* vs. *a mouth*. While the *hands* in this metaphor signifies production (i.e. the physical capacity inherent in people), the *mouths* represent consumption. It is precisely this duality of the *hands* vs. the *mouths*, presumed to be two antithetical embodiments of population that has historically defined the moral of the ongoing population-poverty debate. Although the human *mind* has been injected as an additional feature of population, it too is juxtaposed against the *mouths*, thus perpetuating the prevailing dichotomies.

From a societal perspective, the *hands/minds* and the *mouths* are the inseparable bedrock of every human society and its social and organizational development. Although the *hands/minds* form the foundation of the entire process of socioeconomic production, they alone cannot engage in production without the assistance of nature. This means that labour (human resources) and nature (natural resources) constitute the twin pillars of production whose cumulative outcome invariably defines human progress.

In addition, population is the primary creator of tools and technologies, the other two means of production necessary to augment the productivity of both land and labour. As such, population assumes primacy in this symbiotic relationship, for it is the human efforts that create the "need-and-want" satisfying goods and services that increase a society's standard of living. But the story does not end at the point of production. There would be no need for production if there were no *mouths* to feed in the first place: the physiological imperative of consumption. Production cannot be, therefore, separated from consumption, with the population acting as the common denominator of these two primary economic functions as well as societal existence (see Marx, 1973). The basic question surrounding the population-poverty debate is: Which dimension of population has greater impact on human destiny, the *hands/minds* (as producers) or the *mouths* (as consumers)?

The Malthusian Tradition of Population-Poverty Analysis

Unlike his father Daniel Malthus, a modestly prosperous English landowner with a background in economics, who believed in the perfectibility of "mankind," young Thomas Robert Malthus foresaw in population nothing but the multitude of *mouths*, engendering misery for "mankind" (Boulding, 1959). To Malthus, therefore, over-population was an ever-lurking spectre, ready to doom human progress and prosperity into a vast pool of poverty. What stirred the public imagination about the Malthusian spectre was the simplicity and lucidity of his postulation that cantered on the disparity between the rate of population growth and the rate of increase in food production, i.e., the carrying capacity of land. To quote Boulding (1959: viii):

What gave the essay on *Population* its extraordinary impact and makes it still well worth reading is the eloquence and almost agonizing moral passion with which the theme is worked out, and the clear political conclusions, especially in regard to the Poor Law, which emerge (*sic*) from the argument. (What Malthus contemplated was) a system which seemed to promise man perpetual misery on earth, and to place him in the grip of implacable forces which no mere institutional changes could assuage...he stands like a prophet of doom—reform society as you will, he seems to say, population will catch up with you; give all you can to the poor, and their poverty will not ultimately be relieved. Science and technical improvement, Christian love and generous impulses alike seem to be washed away down the stream of history on the awful flood of population" (parenthetical words supplied).

In short, relying on the mathematics of geometric and arithmetic progression, Malthus (1959: 9) postulated that "the human species would increase in the ratio of 1, 2, 4, 8, 16, 32, 64, 128, 256, and subsistence as 1, 2, 3, 4, 5, 6, 7, 8, 9…In two centuries and a quarter, the population would be to the means of subsistence as 512 to 10: in three centuries as 4096 to 13…" According to Malthus, at some point along the march of history, the ruthless mathematics of geometric population growth would outstrip the arithmetic expansion of food supply, thus violating the equilibrium between the two. "The poor," Malthus (1959: 10–11) pronounced, "consequently must live much worse, and many of them be reduced to severe distress. The number of labourers also being the proportion of the work in the market, the price of labour must tend toward a decrease…" So the crucial principle embedded in Malthus' formulation was that there must be some limit to the number of people in relation to the environment and its carrying capacity. As the logic dictated, in the absence of "preventive checks" such as birth control—a scenario of which Malthus seemed unconvinced—"positive checks" such as diseases and famines were deemed inevitable. Succumbing to these "positive checks," the poor would be reduced in number, restoring a presumed parity between population and the earth's carrying capacity (for a detailed discussion, see Shrestha and Patterson, 1990). "No wonder that after he read Malthus, Carlyle called economics 'the dismal science'" (Heilbroner, 1967: 71).

A quick historical glimpse of human population growth seems to reveal trends that resemble the mathematical ruthlessness of the Malthusian projection. At the dawn of the Christian era, the world was estimated to be populated by roughly 250 million people. Now, at the opening of the twenty-first century, we have 6.3 billion people inhabiting earth. Within a span of 2,000 years, the world has, in other words, witnessed an increase of more than 6 billion people, with over 80 percent occupying what is commonly referred to as the under-developed world where one also finds the greatest concentration of the "wretched of the earth"—the hungry and malnourished, the sick and feeble, vacillating between bare subsistence and destitution (see United Nations, 2003; World Bank, 2001).

It is this ever-unfolding drama of population that serves as a parable of pauperization (and prosperity). It is actually a meta story, a story with many plots, with many twists and turns. Its script first played out most poignantly following the Industrial Revolution of the 1760s, which unleashed a powerful engine of growth, resulting in an unparalleled surge of poverty, on the one hand, and prosperity, on the other. The degree and rapidity with which such a glaringly polarized trend of poverty and prosperity occurred had never been experienced in the annals of human history until then. Contrasts could not be any sharper as urban-industrial growth made the face of poverty and unemployment look much grittier than ever before, especially when contrasted against growing prosperity among the capitalist class (see Meek, 1954; Patterson and Shrestha, 1988). In short, the rapid pace of industrial growth and general economic improvements brought on by the Industrial Revolution (see also Basu, 2003; Nardinelli, 2004) failed to alleviate poverty and resultant social problems. Consequently, to Malthus, increased amiseration was a visible indication of over-population.

In other words, as poverty bared its jaws in British urban centres, the most visible cultural landscapes of industrial triumph as well as the gravitational centres of rural migrants and jobless masses, population growth was regarded as the culprit and, hence, the ready-made subject of scorn by those who saw it as a gathering threat to their own material and social standing in society. The parallel growth of poverty and prosperity resulting from rapid industrial progress was untenable. Furthermore, as poverty was invariably equated with social ills, it was viewed as a direct threat to the prosperity of the few in the form of social unrest and protest, a scenario which, by implication, called into question the organizational efficacy of industrial society under the capitalist relations of production. The situation, in fact, reached an ominous point where Cecil Rhodes, a diamond magnate and ardent advocate of British imperialism and after whom Northern and Southern Rhodesia as well as Rhodes scholarship were named, pressed for greater colonial expansion as a necessary solution to Britain's population and poverty problems:

I was in the East End of London (working-class quarter) yesterday and attended a meeting of the unemployed. I listened to the wild speeches, which were just a cry for 'bread,' 'bread!' and on my way home I pondered over the scene and I became more than ever convinced of the importance of imperialism. . . . My cherished idea is a solution of the social problem, i.e., in order to save the 40,000,000 inhabitants of the United Kingdom from a bloody civil war, we colonial statesmen must acquire new lands to settle the surplus population, to provide new markets for the goods produced in the factories and mines. The Empire, as I have always said, is a bread and butter question. If you want to avoid civil war, you must become imperialists (quoted in Lenin, 1969: 93-94; emphasis added).

Although rapidly industrializing England with an annual population growth rate of around 1.5 percent (see Patterson and Shrestha, 1988)—a rate not that different from what the world is currently undergoing—served as the immediate observational laboratory of that rapidly unfolding drama, the vexing vision of mass poverty was projected across the world, thus universalizing the presumed causality between population growth and poverty. The poor were blamed not only for their poverty, but for general food and resource scarcity as well. The stage, as the logic went, was set for environmental deterioration, degradation, and destruction, a doomsday syndrome that has now become the pet theme of Malthus' modern day wards: Neo-malthusians.

In the womb of the Industrial Revolution was thus conceived the *stepchild of history*—the population and poverty debate—with Malthus as its surrogate father. At that time, the world's total population was still well below one billion, a milestone that was not reached until 1804 (United Nations, 2003). None of this mattered to Malthus; he was bent on turning the stepchild of history upside down to force the issue of population into the public arena. As the eighteenth century drew to a close, the population-poverty debate attracted tremendous attention from both policymakers and scholars. The meta story of population and poverty soon turned into a mega debate of public policy—a debate that continues to this day (Magdoff, 2004; Reining and Tinker, 1975; Sen, 1993, 1994, 2000).

Although history had sporadically seen "positive checks," with the Irish famine providing some corroboration of Malthus' postulates, there has been a considerable distance between his theoretical promulgation and the socio-historical reality. With his correct observation of the class character of poverty, Malthus himself revealed the crack in the cornerstone of his theory that population growth causes poverty. In his diagnosis of the English reality, he wrote:

One half of the nation appears to act as Helots to the other half, and the misery that checks population falls chiefly, as it always must do, upon that part whose condition is lowest in the scale of society (p. 15). I believe...of the number of children who die annually, much too great a proportion belongs to those who may be supposed unable to give their offspring proper food and attention, exposed as they are occasionally to severe distress and confined, perhaps, to unwholesome habitations and hard labour (p. 25).

Furthermore, in his criticism of Adam Smith's discussion of the relationship between the wealth of a nation and the prosperity of its labouring class, Malthus ironically recognized how an increment in the national wealth, controlled as it was by the dominant classes, often went hand-in-hand with an increase in the misery of the labouring class (masses)—a kind of development that would be generally inconceivable according to the logic rooted in his universalistic principle of population. That is, as his following statement testified, poverty had less to do with population growth than with the vicious dualism that allowed the dominant classes within a society to pursue self-serving, maligned economic policies:

It has been asserted with confidence that the enclosure of common fields has frequently had a contrary effect, and that large tracts of land which formerly produced great quantities of corn, by being converted into pasture, both employ fewer hands and feed fewer mouths than before their enclosure. It is, indeed, an acknowledged truth, that pasture land produces a smaller quantity of human subsistence than corn land of the same natural fertility, and (because of) the increased demand for butchers meat of the best quality, a greater quantity of good land has annually been employed in grazing (thus leading to) the diminution of human subsistence...The increasing price of butchers meat is a natural and inevitable consequence of the general progress in cultivation; but I cannot help thinking, that the present great demand for butchers meat, and the quantity of good land that is in consequence annually employed to produce it, are the chief causes, that have prevented the quantity of human food in the country, from keeping pace with the generally increased fertility of the soil (pp. 110–111).

However, Malthus' admissions of the socio-historical reality of poverty did little to mitigate the fundamental drawbacks of his population theory; nor did they succeed in muting the voices of his critics, most prominently, Karl Marx. It mattered little whether Malthus was merely an intellectual apologist or honest accountant for the socio-historical reality (see Heilbroner, 1967: Chapter 4). His discussion of the land enclosure movement only served to expose the ideological biases under-girding his theory.

The Marxist Tradition of Population-Poverty Analysis

No matter how appealing his theory might have seemed, Malthus could not escape attacks. Besides being attacked by his contemporary David Ricardo, a renowned British political economist, biting assaults were mounted, some 60 years later, by Karl Marx. A German immigrant, Marx was no stranger to bitter poverty in industrial England as he lived, with his family, in a two-room flat in a London slum. His wife Jenny had to beg money from a neighbour to buy a coffin to bury one of their three children whose death was indirectly caused by poverty (quoted in Heilbroner, 1967: 136).

Yet overpopulation never surfaced on Marx's conceptual plane as a cause of poverty. Dismissing the *mouths* as a source of poverty, Marx emphasized the *hands* as labour and how it was deployed as a fundamental means of production, specifically in the context of class relations. Marx (1973: 100) argued that "...the population is an abstraction if I leave out, for example, the classes of which it is composed." Since there exists a dialectical relationship between population and social development, the question of poverty—to extend Marx's logic—demands a careful analysis within the context of the prevailing social classes of production. Especially important is the specific stage of social development of a society because, to quote Marx (1967: 19), "the law of population" is not "the same at all times and in all places...Every stage of development has its own law of population." The logic of the argument is that every nation or geographical area has its own stages of development and that every stage of development has its own social class relations of production with their own specific "law of population"—historically valid for that particular stage and geographically limited to that particular nation. In other words, the law of population in the agrarian stage of development in Society X is not the same as the one in Society Y (i.e., geographical difference); nor is it the same as the law of population during the capitalist stage of development (i.e. temporal difference).

According to this Marxist postulation, the debate over population-poverty relations is essentially futile if it is conducted in isolation from the changing trends of social development and class relations of production. Nor is there any prospect of coming up with a set of viable solutions to the problem of poverty under such circumstances that are devoid of any contextualization of the problem to a specific phase of social development. Logically, then, what Malthus propounded in his theory is static and generalized across time and space—

without taking into account geographical and temporal variations in terms of stages of social development as determined by both the relations (class) and forces (technology) of production. As Marx (1973: 605) said, "The amount of overpopulation posited on the basis of a specific production is just as determinate as the adequate population. Overpopulation and population, taken together, are *the* population which a specific production basis can create. The extent to which it goes beyond its barrier is given by the barrier itself, or rather by the same base which posits the barrier" (emphasis in original). Furthermore, Marx (1973: 605–607) continued:

Malthus' theory,...whose fame he appropriated through the clerical fanaticism with which he pronounced it...is significant in two respects: (1) because he gives brutal expression to the brutal viewpoint of capital; (2) because he *asserted* the fact of overpopulation in all forms of society. Proved it he has not, for there is nothing more uncritical than his motley compilations from historians and travellers' descriptions. His conception is altogether false and childish (1) because he regards *overpopulation* as being *of the same kind* in all the historic phases of economic development; does not understand their specific difference, and hence stupidly reduces these very complicated and varying relations to a single relation, two equations, in which the natural reproduction of humanity appears on the one side, and the natural reproduction of edible plants (or means of subsistence) on the other, as two natural series, the former geometric and the latter arithmetic in progression. In this way he transforms the historically distinct relations into an abstract numerical relation, which he has fished purely out of thin air, and which rests neither on natural nor on historical laws...He would find in history that population proceeds in very different relations, and that overpopulation is likewise a historically determined relation, and that overpopulation is likewise a historically determined relation, in no way determined by abstract numbers or by the absolute limit of the productivity of the necessaries of life, but by limits posited rather by *specific conditions of production*. As well as restricted numerically...Ricardo immediately and correctly confronted him with the fact that the quantity of grain available is completely irrelevant to the worker if he has no *employment*; that it is therefore the means of employment and not of subsistence which put him into the category of surplus population. But this should be conceived more generally, and relates to the *social mediation* as such, through which the individual gains access to the means of his reproduction and creates them; hence it relates to the *conditions of production* and his relations to them...The overpopulation, e.g. among hunting peoples, which shows itself in the warfare between the tribes, proves not that the earth could not support their small numbers, but rather that the condition of their reproduction required a great amount of territory for few people. Never a relation to a *non-existent* absolute mass of means of subsistence, but rather relation to the conditions of...the production of these means...to the mode of producing them.

In essence, the Marxist perspective (see Marx, 1973: 604–610) is that the notion of overpopulation is merely a reflection of social development, a composite index of *the social relations of production* (which reflect the social distribution of the means of production or class relations in general) and the *forces of production* (loosely defined here as the state of advancement of production technologies).

So, for Marx, overpopulation is only a surplus population relative to the social conditions and technological state of production. To Marx, therefore, the Industrial Revolution showed that poverty was a predictable product of the capitalist relations of production, which required a surplus labour force—the "industrial reserve army" as he called it—in order to keep the labour cost manageable. What Malthus labelled overpopulation in industrial England was merely a relative surplus of population, i.e. relative to employment opportunities under the capitalist mode of production.

Although one may find the theoretical underpinning of the Marxist tradition logically tenable, it falls far short of its promise.

First, it is not only counterintuitive to the observed reality that rapid population growth invariably exacerbates poverty; it is also myopic to summarily downplay the negative impact of population growth on the process of development of a given society. Few would dispute that every phase of development has its own law of population, but that does not mean those phases do not experience excess population. Population growth in excess of absorptive capacity strains environmental resources and capital investment and tends to undercut the bargaining power of labour. Consequently, unemployment climbs and the price of labour tends to stagnate, a form of development that seldom serves labour in its ongoing struggle with capitalistic forces (see Shrestha and Patterson, 1990). And the expected transition from a lower level to a higher level of social development is stalled or postponed.

Second, because of its counterintuitive tendency, Marxist position has found little popular appeal in the population policy arena. "Socialist" societies have seldom formulated national polices on population growth. However, a rare socialist application occurred in Mao's China where population control was discouraged despite its enormous population base and growth, but the policy was abandoned in the mid-1970s, particularly following Mao's death, in favour of family planning, including coercive practices.

The Neo-Malthusianism Tradition of Population-Poverty Analysis

As a tradition, Neo-Malthusianism is a post-World War II extension of the Malthusian orthodoxy, an old argument with a new twist, as its advocates carry on the torch that Malthus ignited more than 200 years ago. The conclusion of the war signalled the end of Europe's colonial control in Asia and Africa. The emergence of these nations from the yoke of colonialism not only exposed their mass poverty but was also accompanied by accelerating population growth in many of them (see de Castro, 1977).

The human population underwent an explosive growth in the twentieth century. For instance, the world recorded two billion people around 1930. The numbers then climbed to over 3 billion in 1960 and nearly 4 billion by 1970, with the vast majority of this unprecedented rise confined to Asia, Africa, and Latin America. With nearly 80 million people being currently added to the world each year, over 95 percent of the total growth occurs in underdeveloped countries due to their dramatic declines in mortality, particularly infant mortality, coupled with large numbers of young people in the productive-age cohorts (Population Reference Bureau, 2003; United Nations, 2003).

It is precisely this explosive growth trend that sounded a loud population alarm worldwide, especially during the decades of the 1960s and 1970s (Norton, 2002; Sadava, 2002). In view of such rapid population growth, Malthus—who was often overshadowed during his days by his close friend and intellectual nemesis, David Ricardo (Heilbroner, 1967: Chapter 4)—emerged as a doomsday prophet in the post-World War II era. His theory became the dominant population paradigm of the day, with Neo-malthusians evoking the ghastly image of what Paul Ehrlich (1971) termed *The Population Bomb*, reminiscent of devastating atom/nuclear bombs (see also Barkley and Seckler, 1972). Then there was *The Limits to Growth*, a headline-making report put out by the Club of Rome under the authorship of Donella H. Meadows et al (1972), one in which humanity faced an imminent global disaster. There was a proliferation of literature espousing such a scenario. Malthusianism, reborn with a new vigour as Neo-Malthusianism, had an immense impact, especially in the policy arena, where population control was urged in underdeveloped countries (Ng and Mudd, 1965; Reining and Tinker, 1975). Even such internationally renowned and respected scholars like Kenneth Boulding (1959) and Arnold Toynbee (1965) lent a voice to the Malthusian cause. Boulding (1959: v) paid homage to Malthus by quoting Keynes who wrote "if only Malthus, instead of Ricardo, had been the parent stem from which nineteenth-century economics proceeded, what a much wiser and richer place the world would be today!"

Whether "wiser and richer" or not, the world is now deeply immersed in

Malthusian thinking. Although the Neo-malthusians rarely recite Malthus' mathematical verse of population growth and food production, they subscribe to the fundamental prophecy of Malthusianism. They have expanded the parameters of the ever-raging population-poverty debate to include what Sadava (2002: 6) describes as *ecological Malthusianism*, i.e. environmental degradation (see also Ehrlich, Ehrlich, and Daily, 1993; Ehrlich, I. and Lui, 1997; Escobar, 2003; Ives and Misserli, 1989; Martine, 1996). As Norton (2002: 4) summarizes:

Rapid population growth has at least three adverse effects on human well-being. First, it increases poverty—the number of people that are impoverished, the proportion of the community that is impoverished, and the severity of the impoverishment. Second, it increases environmental degradation—the misuse of natural resources—with adverse consequences on many dimensions of human well-being. Finally, it prevents environmental enhancement by holding back the savings and investment that would permit environmentally sustainable economic growth and retards the agricultural productivity that would encourage environmentally friendly agriculture and conservation (see also Ahlburg, 1994; Cipolla, 1962; Coale and Hoover, 1958; Frederiksen, 1975).

Population growth, accordingly to the Neo-malthusians, is the self-destructive human menace that devours everything. Nowhere is this imagery more vividly portrayed than in the 1972 movie *Soylent Green*, a futuristic crime thriller. The year is 2022 and the setting is the city of New York. Packed with 40 million inhabitants, the city is ripe for pestilence. While a few live in luxury, there is a severe shortage of all necessities basic to human survival. There is enormous crowding. Ice is precious and a single raw steak is more prized than gold. Here enters soylent green, a high-energy product (chips) made out of kelp from the oceans. Manufactured by the food giant Soylent Corporation, the product is presumably an answer to growing population and hunger. But there is not enough soylent green to sustain the city's population as the demand far exceeds its supply. But that's not the end of the drama surrounding *Soylent Green*. Late in the movie, an old man walks into a beautiful "death chamber," where people can go to die a peaceful death rather than live on in misery. That is when *Soylent Green* comes together as the old man's dead body is transported to the factory where soylent green is produced. The truth unfolds.

In depicting "high-tech cannibalism," the movie can be treated as a replica of Ester Boserup's (1965, 1981) theory that population pressure is the motor of technological innovations no matter how depraved a form it may take. The movie is, in essence, a peep into what may lie ahead for humanity: a Neo-malthusian nightmare. And that is the plot line that has dominated much of the population-poverty debate for more than half a century as the imprints of the Neo-malthusian tradition are almost everywhere, particularly in terms of national economic policies, including their environmental dimension.

As notions from the Neo-malthusian tradition swept across the underdeveloped world, emphasis was placed on family planning programs—invariably made available free of charge—to control the growth of *mouths.* [1] The objective was to avert impending disasters resulting from increasing poverty and environmental degradation and to set underdeveloped countries on the path of economic development. The seminal study by Coale and Hoover (1958) was instrumental in justifying "...birth control as a part of United States foreign policy" (Piotrow, 1973: 15). Subsequently in 1965, President Lyndon B. Johnson promised to "assist family planning programs in nations which request such help." Organized and implemented through its Agency for International Development (AID), the US was then the largest supporter of efforts to curb population growth in the underdeveloped world (see Ravenholt, 1975). Also prominent among the ardent advocates and underwriters of family planning programs in many underdeveloped countries were the United Nations, the Population Council, and the Ford and Rockefeller Foundations; their roles were far-reaching and profound in both formulating and implementing those programs (see Caldwell and Caldwell, 1986; Donaldson, 1990; Harkavy, 1995; Piotrow, 1973).

In view of its enormous population and incidence of poverty, it was hardly surprising that, within the underdeveloped world, India emerged as an early leader in promoting family planning as an integral part of the national development policy. A year after President Johnson's announcement, the Indian prime minister declared, "We must press forward with family planning. This is a programme of the highest importance" (both quoted in Davis, 1975: 27). Determined to bring the rate of population growth down, some advocates of family planning programs went so far as to advocate coercive measures such as induced abortion, forced sterilization, and denying public health services (see Davis, 1975). For example, one advocate stated: "Public health measures which can save millions of lives should not be practiced in China on a nationwide scale" (G. Winfield quoted in Frederiksen, 1975). In the case of India, Prime Minister Indira Gandhi implemented in the mid-1970s compulsory sterilization, a policy which became so unpopular that it led to her electoral defeat in 1976 (Sen, 1994; see also Connelly, 2003; Hartmann, 2003; Rao, 2003; Seamus, 2003).

The Neo-liberal Tradition of Population-Poverty Analysis

Population control is firmly grounded as it remains a leading mantra of development policy and poverty reduction efforts in many underdeveloped countries. However, challenges have been mounted to Malthusian thinking from time to time by what Allen C. Kelley calls "population revisionists"—mostly economists with a neo-liberal bent—who generally downplay the negative impact of population growth on economic development (for a detailed discussion, see Kelley, 1999). However, as the neo-liberal challenge to Malthusianism/Neo-Malthusianism was generally sporadic and scattered, it failed early on to emerge as a distinct tradition of population-poverty analysis. The decisive swing occurred in the early 1980s. Although there appears to be no particular global event or national movement triggering the rise of the Neo-liberal tradition, it is generally tied to Julian Simon, a prominent economic demographer. When Simon declared population as *The Ultimate Resource* (1981), it was a decisive stance against Neo-Malthusianism, built around a relatively strong theoretical foundation. The book "attracted enormous attention to the population debate. This was due both to his conclusion that in the immediate-run, rapid population growth was likely to exert a *positive* impact on economic development in many Third World countries; and to the effectiveness of the book's highly accessible exposition and 'debating style'" (Kelley, 1999: 17). Also instrumental in its sudden upsurge was the ability of Simon's argument to influence the Reagan administration's population policy, both domestically and globally.

Similar to the Marxist criticism of Malthusian theorization of population, Simon's assault on Neo-Malthusianism was waged on both paradigmatic and policy grounds, thus giving the Neo-liberal tradition of population-poverty analysis a firm footing. It was a well-argued two-pronged analysis with some empirical basis. On the one hand, Simon's analysis represented a theoretical positioning of neo-liberal economic demography. On the other hand, it exposed some of the empirical vulnerabilities of Neo-malthusian *environmentalism*, one in which population growth is routinely branded as a source of worldwide resource depletion as well as ecological declines and disasters. In essence, Simon (1993) methodically extended the human *hands* vs. *mouths* dichotomy of the ongoing population-poverty debate to include human *minds* as a knowledge pool, an engine of inventions and innovations, along with increased resource productivity and price-induced resource discoveries and substitutes (i.e. overall more efficient resource utilization), all leading to economic development and prosperity.

To Simon (1995), "population growth is our greatest triumph." "The most important benefit of population size and growth," he proclaimed, "is the increase it brings to the stock of useful knowledge. *Minds* matter economically as much as, or more than, *hands* and *mouths*. The progress of civilization is limited largely by the availability of trained workers. The main fuel to speed the world's progress is the "stock of human knowledge" (Simon, 1993: 6; emphasis added).

He then went on to add that:

There is only one important resource which has shown a trend of *increasing scarcity* rather than *increasing abundance*. That resource is the most important for all human beings. Yes, there are more people on earth now than ever before. But if we measure the scarcity of people the same way that we measure the scarcity of other economic goods—by how much we must pay to obtain their services—we see that wages and salaries have been going up all over the worlds, in poor countries as well as in rich countries. The amount that you pay to obtain the services of a barber or a cook has risen in India, just as the price of a barber or cook—or economist—has risen in the United States over the decades. This increase in the price of peoples' services is a clear indication that people are becoming scarcer even though there are more of us (Simon, 1994: 7; emphasis added).

Not done, he attacked Neo-Malthusianism environmentalism with a theocratic zeal, relying on market price trends and on resource discoveries and substitutes:

Every resource economist knows that all natural resources have been getting more available rather than scarcer, as shown by their falling prices over the decades and centuries...Every forecast of the doomsayers has turned out flat wrong. The famous Famine 1975 forecast by the Paddock brothers—that we would see millions of famine deaths in the U.S. on television in the 1970s—was followed instead by gluts in agricultural markets. Paul Ehrlich's primal scream about "What will we do when [gasoline] pumps run dry?" was followed by gasoline cheaper than since the 1930's. The Great Lakes are not dead; instead they offer better sport fishing than ever. The main pollutants, especially the people which have killed people for years, have lessened in our cities...The wrong forecasts of shortages of copper and other metals...have helped cause economic disasters for mining companies and for the poor countries which depend upon mining...Because of increased demand due to population growth and increased income, the price of whale oil for lamps jumped in the 1840's, and the U.S. Civil War pushed it even higher, leading to a whale oil "crisis." *This provided incentive for enterprising people to discover and produce substitutes.* First came oil from rapeseed, olive, linseed, and camphene oil from pine trees. Then inventors learned how to get coal oil from coal. Other ingenious persons produced kerosene from the rock oil that seeped to the surface, a product so desirable that its price then rose from US$ .75 a gallon to US$ 2.00. This high price stimulated enterprisers to focus on the supply of oil (Simon, 1994: 1, 7 & 13; emphasis added).

Typical of neo-liberalism, however, the logical basis of Simon's contention regarding the economics of population, poverty, development, and environmental degradation is rooted in *market determinism.* As it claims the market to be the remedy to social and economic ills such as poverty and environmental degradation, it is no less ideologically one-sided in its policy application than the Neo-malthusian belief that population control is the panacea or the Marxist utopia of classless society; So, to neo-liberal revisionists, the only element lacking to release the pressure valve of unbounded progress and prosperity is market freedom. "The world's problem is not too many people, but lack of political and economic freedom...the extent to which the political-social-economic system provides personal freedom from *government coercion...*The market-directed economies have performed much better economically than the centrally-planned economies (Simon, 1994: 14; emphasis added).

While few would question Simon's statistical information, his cure-all *market determinism* is as counterintuitive as Marxist *class determinism.* No doubt, the free market economy (i.e. capitalism) is wonderful when it comes to economic production. But what Simon and many other Neo-liberals fail to see, or elected to ignore, is that market "efficiency" in finding price-induced economic growth and production efficiency does not mean that population growth does not contribute to poverty and environmental degradation. Since the bottom line of the market economy is profit, [2] the market often sidesteps its social and environmental costs. Economic history is, in fact, replete with examples of market-generated negative externalities with gross social and ecological consequences (for a detailed discussion, see Mishan, 1969). One of the legacies of economic growth and population growth is air and water pollution, which has now emerged as a serious public health crisis in cities across the world, from Kathmandu to Kuala Lumpur, Cairo to Cape Town to Quito, Bangkok to Bombay, Shanghai to Sao Paulo. For example, "Polluted air in 36 Indian cities killed some 52,000 people in 1995. China (a socialist state with a booming capitalist enterprise that has consistently recorded for about two decades a high rate of economic growth and where the per capita income has more than doubled during the same period) reported at least 3 million deaths from toxic urban air from 1994 through 1996" (CNN, 1999: 1; parenthetical words added). In a BBC news report, Kirby (2004a: 1) noted that "Two-fifths of the world's people already face serious water shortages, and water-borne diseases fill half its hospital beds."

Moreover, contrary to Simon's market logic, poverty is on the rise in many countries, and all this in the face of the market economy's global proliferation. Harrison (1989: 35) writes, "Hunger is the painful focus of absolute poverty...Absolute poverty has been increasing, both in total numbers and in the proportion of the population affected." The telling sign of the gravity of this situation is that the World Bank, a powerful global policy advocate of the market economy in the underdeveloped world, has been preoccupied with poverty alleviation in many countries (World Bank, 2001; see also Kirby, 2004b; Magdoff, 2004).

The free market economic system may be the best productive economic machine ever devised, but it alone cannot cure poverty. For example, in the United Sates—the shining star of market triumphs—some 35 million citizens are mired in poverty in rural fringes as well as urban trenches, with millions of children denied access to adequate health care and quality education. No matter, how one regards Simon's theory, he is the foundational touchstone for the Neo-liberal tradition of population-poverty analysis and has had a noticeable influence on population policy, especially in the US. His anti-population control stance and neo-liberal demography was adopted as a centre piece of the Reagan administration's population policy. As a result, the Reagan administration reversed the course of US financial support for population control programs as an instrument of its foreign policy, a policy in place since the 1960s. Subsequently, it either cut off or drastically reduced its funding of various family planning programs, both domestically and globally. As Kelley (1999: 4) remarks, "the elevated influence of the ideas of Julian L. Simon (1981) on the Reagan Administration's population policies, which were unsupportive of family planning, in part triggered the commissioning of the 1986 National Academy assessment of population consequences. This assessment was undertaken almost entirely by economists, the revisionists...By numbers, then, the economist/revisionists have exercised exceptional influence in the debates over the last decade." After a short hiatus during the Clinton administration, the anti-population control policy is in vogue, once again, under the current Bush administration, thus keeping the Neo-liberal tradition at the forefront of the population-poverty debate.

Concluding Remarks and a Policy Synthesis

With the above review of the four principal traditions of population-poverty analysis and their ideological underpinnings, we have come full circle. The questions remain: What causes poverty— population growth as Malthusians and Neo-malthusians claim, unemployment and the social class structure as Marxists espouse, or the absence of market freedom (neo-liberal market policies) as Simon expounds? And what is the policy remedy for poverty? In exploring these two interrelated questions, we now put forward a set of propositions with the objective of finding a way out of the ideological cul-de-sac surrounding these traditions. We focus on three key issues: the unit of analysis of population-poverty relations, explanations of what causes poverty, and policy formulation for attacking poverty.

The Unit of Analysis of Population-poverty Analysis in Relation to Policy Formulation: One drawback common to all four traditions is the unit of analysis, which is macroscopic as they tend to present a sweeping picture of population-poverty relations, often recommending a one-size-fits-all singular policy, irrespective of national, historical, geographical, social, developmental, or cultural variations. What is missing from such a macro analysis is the basic empirical fact that population growth and poverty are local phenomena with their own local dimensions and characters, thus demanding solutions that are locally suitable. In light of the geographical specificity of population-poverty relations, our proposition is straightforward: what is required is society-specific analysis of population-poverty relations in the context of that society's demographic, social, and economic realities (see, for example, Shrestha, Conway, and Bhattarai, 1999). Without such an analysis, it is nearly impossible to paint a picture of the demographic, social, and spatial nuances of poverty—a picture that would help to formulate a policy that is locally suitable.

Explanations of What Causes Poverty: Is population growth a *development asset* (*hands* and *minds*: a source of human labour as well as human capital, including technological inventions and innovations) or a *development liability* (*mouths*: an agent of resource drains, undermining economic growth and development as well as human capital formation)? This is the kind of dichotomy we observe in all four traditions. Our answer is both positions have merit, depending upon the temporal stage of social development or the demographic composition of specific societies in relations to their social and economic conditions and resource base (see also Magdoff, 2004).

Take, for example, the United States of America on one end of the geographical and social development spectrum and Bangladesh on the other. It would be foolhardy to claim that poverty in the US, a country endowed with vast amounts of resources, is a function of Malthusian/Neo-malthusian population growth or its numerical size. And the US certainly does not suffer from the absence of Simonian economic freedom and technological advancements. So any attempt to tie the gritty profile of US poverty to any one explanation, Malthusian, Simonian, or Marxist, would be conceptual folly and historical fallacy. Nonetheless, it is clear that market mechanisms, along with great strides in technological advancements, have failed to overcome poverty in the US (Yates, 2004).

Some could argue that one element perpetuating poverty in the US is poverty itself. Although seemingly tautological in nature, the argument is that entrenched poverty tends to engender what may be called the "culture of poverty"—a phenomenon that may break "the spirit of self-help," often stunting individual drive and motivation to pull oneself up by one's own bootstraps. Resultantly, intergenerational poverty and associated social problems set in. The problem becomes further compounded as the rich and powerful build social, political, and geographic barricades to distance themselves from the poor. And the free market response to the socio-spatial entrapment of poverty proves to be hardly any less punitive. Businesses desert poor areas—some out of fear and discrimination and others due to increased operating costs and decreased business volumes. And jobs move to outer spaces, leaving the poor spatially trapped in urban trenches and rural fringes. While one may pronounce such a scenario as a sign that the market is working efficiently as it protects its profit interests, poverty is intact, bound to certain spaces, classes, races, and gender. In other words, poverty, once a consequence, becomes a cause, thus setting in motion the cycle of effect-cause-effect on the one hand and intergenerational entrapment on the other.

It is a different story in Bangladesh, a country about the size of Wisconsin with more than 130 million people distributed over a mere 55,000 square miles. It is a country with limited resources and technological advancements, where 77 percent of the population lacks adequate food (AFP, 2004). It would be conceptually myopic to deny that population growth aggravates poverty in Bangladesh. As usual, suffering most from the deepest wounds of poverty are the poor, who, ironically, tend to have relatively larger family sizes and minimal or no access to even basic health services and educational opportunities and for whom gainful employment is scarce (see Shrestha, 2000).

So it would be naive to overlook the live exhibition of the Malthusian and Neo-malthusian drama of population growth and poverty in countries like Bangladesh. Whenever population growth runs ahead of the market demand for labour, wages may be depressed and unemployment/underemployment may increase. As wages constitute the primary source of income for the poor, the situation tends to become quite onerous for them and collectively detrimental to the national economy because it stunts disposable income and, hence, effective demand and capital investment, both required to stimulate economic growth and expansion (Norton, 2002). In addition, as Neo-malthusians point out, "Rapid population growth strains the fixed capacities of basic human services—education, health, and nutrition (all basic human needs, and necessary for building a good social infrastructure and stock of human capital). Fixed levels of basic infrastructure essential for survival...are spread over greater numbers of people and hence the per capita delivery of services is reduced. In short, "non-pecuniary measures of poverty also increase", (Norton, 2002: 6; see also Ahlburg, 1994; parenthetical words added). Consequently, the development of human capital and its innovative and inventive energy and capacity are severely sapped, thus reinforcing the vicious cycle of poverty.

Under such circumstance, there is little doubt that population growth is a development liability. In countries like Bangladesh, poverty is actually more than the personification and daily reminder of how population growth impacts the poor as well as the physical environment. It is also directly attributed to the entrenched social class structure as Marx argued and the absence of well-established economic freedom and technological advancements as Simon advocated. The complexity of alleviating poverty in such countries matches the complexity of its causes. Nonetheless, as history reveals, socioeconomic development, although by no means adequate to eliminate Marxist class disparities, often goes a long way in creating employment opportunities as well as reducing the rates of population growth that Neo-malthusians desire. Both of these outcomes tend to mitigate poverty or at least keep it from rising.

Population is not all *mouths*, however, ready to devour and deplete resources, thus condemning humanity to a state of misery. As *hands* and *minds* (brains), it is the prime asset of every society; without it, production (development) is neither possible nor necessary. So population is the axis of every aspect of production, along with its raison d'être. That is to say people are the sole agency capable of effectively attacking poverty—either individually or collectively, independently or in concert with the market forces and institutional apparatus such as state policies and civil society organizations. There is no denying that population is a foundational resource necessary to nurture and nourish societal progress and prosperity. This is a conclusion that both Marx and Simon reached, based on social development trends through time and space, although their policy solutions to poverty are patently different in view of their bipolar perspectives on historical materialism.

Policy Formulation to Attack Poverty: Now that we have unmasked the multifaceted aspects of population-poverty relations, we now turn to the issue of policy synthesis to attack poverty. Beforehand, we explore the nature of poverty that lies at the core of our proposition.

Poverty can be broadly categorized into two types: *relative* and *absolute* poverty (Harrison, 1989; Independent Commission on International Development Issues, 1989). By definition, relative poverty is, as the terms suggests, *relative*; it is a matter of *degree* rather than an issue of *survival* or *viable existence*. At any given moment, people are poorer or richer *relative* to others irrespective of class, society, or social development. As the issue of eliminating relative poverty tends to veer toward the utopian realm of socialism, a vision perhaps worthy of human pursuit but historically proven impractical, it falls outside the domain of our present proposition. We only address absolute poverty, poverty characterized by the deprivation of basic human needs or of income/economic opportunities necessary to satisfy such needs (Harrison, 1989; World Bank, 2001).

What we discern from the above discussion is that, regardless of the historically bifurcated debate on population-poverty relations—*hands/minds* vs. *mouths*—poverty is an outcome of multiple forces. Specifically, poverty can be treated as an ecosystem, one in which it is engaged in a complex system-wide relationship with other elements in a cause-effect-cause manner (see also World Bank, 2001). While poverty may not have a singular cause or effect, breakdown at any of the nodes within the ecosystem could aggravate it or undermine policies to attack it.

Our ecosystem framework contains three agencies. *Individuals*, the first agent, represent the Malthusian beings, in that they have the ability to make decisions to direct, if not determine, the course of their fate. As such, they can exercise substantial control over their behaviour. For example, just as they can choose to have more children, they can choose to delay their marriage or have fewer children in accordance with their economic plans and aspirations. In the meantime, however, one needs to be cognizant that certain social environments, state policies or institutional setups, and market forces can induce or inhibit individual behaviours. In this sense, every opportunity should be made available for individuals to enhance the stock of their human capital and to induce individuals to behave responsibly and productively in order to tear down the trap of their poverty. Without full participation and determined efforts on the part of individuals/families, no external measures are likely to have lasting effects on reducing poverty just as many individual efforts are likely to fall by the wayside in the absence of institutional support and incentives. Irrespective of the contextual rationality or irrationality of one's behaviour, individuals occupy a critical position in the trilogy of our ecosystem framework.

The state/institutions are policymaking and policy implementation agencies. These institutions are the organizational entities endowed with the regulatory power over matters of governance as well as social, political, and economic responsibility to its citizens. As such, it can minimize the negative impact of social class stratification on poverty. As the World Bank (2001: 38) notes, "The state—because of its power to raise revenues and use them as an instrument of redistribution—has a central role, especially in providing basic social services and infrastructure." The state has the authority to set and execute policies that address competing interests, based on a system of rewards and punishments to induce positive *market* as well as *individual* behaviours so that they contribute toward finding ways to serve the greater good of society and reduce poverty. The principal role of the state in our framework is to reduce social inequalities that the World Bank (2001: 38; parenthetical words added) claims, "affect both the pace of (economic) growth and the distribution of its benefits. The distribution of growth benefits matters, not least because distributional conflict can undermine the stability needed for overall growth (and, hence, for creating economic opportunities to attack poverty)." What lies at the heart of state policies, however, is leadership. To apply Barrington Moore's (1987) argument, it is the leadership, not the political system that is fundamental to effective policy implementation. Without the leadership bent on serving the society and citizens it rules, free of specific class interests and imperatives, the state's effectiveness in solving poverty is greatly impaired.

Nonetheless, in addition to civil society and various social institutions, the state actions can be complemented by the *market*, the third incarnation in the trilogy of the proposed framework. As it directly reflects Simon's view on population and poverty, the market here refers to a free enterprise system where economic freedom to pursue business opportunities exists. Today the market is a fixture of human organization in every society. The primary role of the market is to produce not only goods and services, but also gainful employment, thus allowing individuals to harness and enhance their human capital stored in *labour*. Since the market has historically demonstrated an ingrained tendency to become predatory, the state must exercise its authority in a balanced manner. It must steer the market to act socially responsible while staying clear of constrictive policy measures that suffocate the market's growth potential and its subsequent contribution to poverty alleviation.

To conclude, our policy framework accepts as received truth that all three components—individuals, the state, and the market—have converged time and again in every society to produce one of the ugliest villains of human history: poverty. In this sense, all three ideological perspectives—Malthusian/Neo-malthusian, Marxist, and Simonian (Neo-liberal)—can separately stand firm on their respective grounds, taking solace that they are correct in their diagnosis of poverty, while denouncing each other's position through their narrow ideological prism, thereby failing to find a common policy ground to effectively attack poverty. However, such a sense of ideological satisfaction offers little comfort in terms of finding a viable solution to poverty. Nor is it practical to devise a one-size-fits-all, singular policy solution to class- and place-specific poverty. Many such universalistic policies have failed. A successful frontal attack on poverty, therefore, demands an integrated strategy that is methodically designed and delivered.

Since the three ideological positions underlying the four traditions of population-poverty analysis have merged to produce poverty, we must mobilize them together, carefully removing ideological demarcations separating them in order to form a collective antidote to poverty. And our proposition does just that as it represents an attempt to synthesize their key roles in order to set a coherent and integrated policy to attack poverty. The task is challenging, for our proposed strategy involves bringing three contradictory ideological positions together for a common cause. As shown in Table 1.1 and discussed above, our policy synthesis proposes a triangular strangulation of poverty through a coordinated attack, launched simultaneously from three different fronts, without undercutting the fundamental tenets and spirit of the three ideological positions. Our fundamental argument is that all three ideological positions—Malthusian/Neo-malthusian (preventive checks on population growth), Marxist (reduced social class impact and disparity), and Neo-liberal (enhanced economic freedom and responsible market behaviour)—not only explain poverty, but they can also uniquely contribute to solving it. Simply put, they must be conjoined into a nexus of policy coordination, emphasizing the greater good of society. Short of such a multi-pronged and coordinated strategy, the socio-historical villain named *poverty* will continue to haunt everybody everywhere—rich and poor, paupers and princes. And, when poverty strikes, perhaps the only question left to ask is whether one is inside the bars of a social prison (poor), hoping to find a way out, or is sitting outside the bars (rich), constantly keeping a vexing watch on those inside in order to preserve his/her material prosperity and insure physical safety.

Table 1.1: An Overview of Four Traditions of Population-Poverty Analysis

Malthusian Tradition: Although promulgated in the late 18th century, it continues to permeate every population debate or policy. **Leading Advocate:** Malthus (1798)		
Basic Premises/Arguments	**Policy Implications/ Recommendation**	**Principal Strengths/Shortcomings**
▪ Malthusian theory postulates that population grows geometrically and food production arithmetically, thus leading to disequilibrium between the two: the 'Malthusian trap' or 'poverty trap.' In short, population growth retards economic growth and causes poverty.	▪ Public policy should pursue reduction in population growth through preventive checks on the birth rate through 'moral restraint' (postponement of marriage) or positive checks on the death rate through 'misery and vice' (the periodic outbreak of wars, pestilence, and disease stemming from overpopulation: the Malthusian trap). ▪ No public intervention to offer welfare to the poor, for that would only perpetuate poverty.	▪ Brings attention to population growth as an issue in the economic and social development of societies. ▪ Unrealistic assertion of overpopulation in all societies and all phases of economic development. ▪ Assumption of the natural laws of population growth and food production. ▪ No consideration of technological progress. ▪ Ideologically biased.
Marxist Tradition: Marx's treatise on population resulted from his criticism of Malthus. **Leading Advccates:** Harvey (1974), Marx (1973, Meek (1954)		
Basic Premises/Arguments	**Policy Implications/ Recommendation**	**Principal Strengths/Shortcomings**
▪ Surplus population (overpopulation) is not a function of food supplies. Sufficient supply of food is completely irrelevant to workers with no employment. It is unemployment and lack of access to the means of production that creates surplus population (poverty).	▪ Public policy should generate employment. ▪ Public policy should provide access to the means of production (i.e., redistribution of the means of production). ▪ Public policy should promote socialist ideals in which socioeconomic classes would wither away; no property owners (or capitalist class), no proletarians—hence, no overpopulation, no poverty.	▪ Employment is an issue in any population debate. ▪ Social class distribution of the means of production is central to the question of poverty. ▪ Consideration of technological progress. ▪ Disregard for population growth as an important contributor to poverty. ▪ Reliance on socialism as a solution to poverty. ▪ Ideologically biased.

<table>
<tr><td colspan="3">Neo-Malthusian Tradition: Surfaced as a ruling population order in the 1960s and 1970s. Continues to dominate the debates.
Leading Advocates: Brown (1973), Ehrlich (1971), Hardin (1968)</td></tr>
<tr><th>Basic Premises/ Arguments</th><th>Policy Implications/ Recommendation</th><th>Principal Strengths/Shortcomings</th></tr>
<tr><td>▪ Extending Malthusian theory, Neo-malthusians argue that population growth (pressure) results in environmental degradation and economic retardation, and poverty perpetuates.
▪ Dramatic portrayal of the multifront doomsday syndrome as if it were imminent.</td><td>▪ Public policy should promote family planning through use of birth control technology.
▪ Promotion of agricultural technology to increase food production.</td><td>▪ Consideration of population growth as factor in analyzing poverty.
▪ Consideration of technology and innovation as an ingredient in solving poverty.
▪ Too much reliance on technical solutions.
▪ Little consideration of social class distribution of production means as a serious source of poverty.
Underestimation of human resiliency and innovativeness.</td></tr>
<tr><td colspan="3">Neo-liberal Tradition: Emerged as a prominent perspective in the 1980s, challenging the Neo-Malthusian stance. Has affected US policy on population.
Leading Advocate: Simon (1981)</td></tr>
<tr><th>Basic Premises/ Arguments</th><th>Policy Implications/ Recommendation</th><th>Principal Strengths/Shortcomings</th></tr>
<tr><td>▪ Population is the ultimate resource, especially in the long run; population growth is good because it expands the stock of useful knowledge, leading to innovations and progress.</td><td>▪ Opposition to public policy promoting population control.
▪ Public policy should promote free markets and political freedom and, thereby, solve poverty.</td><td>▪ Consideration of population as a source of resource creation and progress
▪ Disregard for population growth as factor in causing poverty or socioeconomic ills.
▪ Excessive reliance on market theocracy as a panacea to poverty.
▪ No consideration of class disparity as a root cause of poverty (i.e. socioeconomic inequality treated as a given).
▪ Ideologically biased.</td></tr>
</table>

Notes

1. Actually national policy measures, urged by such agencies as the USAID, UN, Ford Foundation, and Rockefeller Foundation, were often two-pronged: *family planning* to control population growth and *agricultural development* to increase food production. At the centre of the latter measure was what is commonly known as the Green Revolution, a biogenetic technological revolution, involving the development and application of high-yielding varieties of seeds—namely maize, wheat, and rice—all intended to greatly increase agricultural productivity per unit of land (Harrar, 1965).
2. In recent years, the concept of *triple bottom line* has come into vogue. Championed by the World Resources Institute, it can be described as a guiding principle, whereby businesses are encouraged—or even mandated in some cases through regulatory requirements—to be not only mindful of their *economic performance* (profit/shareholder value), but also demonstrate *environmental responsibility* and *social equity or responsibility* (see www.wri.org).

References

AFP (2004) "77 Percent of Bangladesh's Population Lack Food: Poverty Map", Accessed February 27, 2004. <http://news.yahoo.com>.

Ahlburg, Dennis (1994) "Population Growth and Poverty", In Cassen, Robert, ed. Population and Development: Old Debates, New Conclusions. New Brunswick, NJ: Transactions Publishers.

Barkley, Paul W. and David W. Seckler (1972) *Economic Growth and Environmental Decay: The Solution Becomes the Problem*. New York: Harcourt.

Basu, Kaushik (2003) The Economics of Child Labour", *Scientific American*, 289: 4, 84–91.

Boserup, Ester (1965) *The Conditions of Agricultural Growth*, Chicago: Aldine.

——(1981) *Population and Technological Change*. Chicago: University of Chicago Press.

Boulding, Kenneth E. (1959) "Foreword", In Malthus, Thomas Robert. *Population: The First Essay*. Ann Arbor, Mich.: University of Michigan Press, v–xii.

Brown, Lester (1973) *In the Human Interest*, New York: Norton.

Caldwell, John C. and Pat Caldwell (1986) *Limiting Population Growth and Ford Foundation Contribution*, Dover, NH: Francis Pinter.

Cipolla, Carlos (1962) *The Economic History of World Population*, Middlesex: Penguin Books.

CNN.com (2004) "Cities May Be Key to Saving Environment", <http://www.cnn.com>.

Coale, Ansley J. and Edgar M. Hoover (1958) *Population Growth and Economic Development in Low-Income Countries*, Princeton: Princeton University Press.

Connelly, Mathews (2003) "Population Control Is History: New Perspectives on the International Campaign to Limit Population Growth", *Comparative Studies in Society and History*, 45: 1, 122–147.

Davis, Kingsley (1975). "Population Policy: Will Current Programs Succeed?" In Reining, Priscilla and Irene Tinker, eds. *Population: Dynamics, Ethics, and Politics*. Washington, D. C.: American Association of the Advancement of Science, 27–36.

De Castro, Josué. (1977) *The Geopolitics of Hunger*, New York: Monthly Review.

Donaldson, Peter J. (1990) *Nature Against Us: The United States and the World Population Crisis 1965–1980*, Chapel Hill, NC: University of North Carolina Press.

Ehrlich, Isaac and Francis Lui (1997) "The Problem of Population and Growth: A Review of the Literature from Malthus to Contemporary Models of Endogenous Population and Endogenous Growth", *Journal of Economic Dynamics and Control*, 21, 205–242.

Ehrlich, Paul R. (1971) *The Population Bomb*, London: Pan.

Ehrlich, Paul R., Anne H. Ehrlich, and Gretchen C. Daily (1993) "Food Security, Population, and Environment", Population and Development Review, 19: 1, 1–60.

Escobar, Arturo (2003) "Power and Visibility: Tales of Peasants, Women and the Environment", Accessed July 18, 2003. <http://www.hsph.harvard.edu>.

Frederiksen, Harald (1975) In Reining, Priscilla and Irene Tinker, eds. *Population: Dynamics, Ethics, and Politics*. Washington, D. C.: American Association of the Advancement of Science, 103–113.

Grimes, Seamus (2003) "Controlling Third World Population: A Major Theme of the UN Population Conference in Cairo", Accessed July 18, 2003. <http://www.hsph.harvard.edu>.

Hardin, Garrett (1968) "The Tragedy of the Commons", *Science*, 162, 1243–1248.

Harkavy, Oscar (1995) *Curbing Population Growth: An Insider's Perspective on the Population Movement*, New York: Plenum Press.

Harrar, J. George (1965) "The Race between Procreation and Production", New York: The Rockefeller Foundation.

Harrison, Paul (1989) "What Is Relative Poverty?" In Weisband, Edward, *Poverty Amidst Plenty: World Political Economy and Distributive Justice*. Boulder, Colo.: Westview Press, 34–37.

Harvey, David (1973) "Population, Resources, and the Ideology of Science", *Economic Geography*, 50, 256–277.

Hartmann, Betsy (2003) "The Malthusian Orthodoxy", Accessed July 18, 2003. <http://www.hsph.harvard.edu>.

Heilbroner, Robert L. (1967) *The Worldly Philosophers: The Lives, Times, and Ideas of the Great Economic Thinkers*, New York: Simon and Schuster.

Independent Commission on International Development Issues, The (1989) "What Is Poverty?" Weisband, Edward. *Poverty Amidst Plenty: World Political Economy and Distributive Justice*, Boulder, Colo.: Westview Press, 30–34.

Ives, Jack D. And Bruno Messerli (1989) *The Himalayan Dilemma*, London: Routledge.

Kelley, Allen C. (1999) "The Population Debate in Historical Perspective: Revisionism Revisited", Unpublished manuscript; an earlier version of this paper was presented at the Nobel Symposium in Economics, December 5–7, Lund, Sweden.

Kirby, Alex (2004a) "Why World's Taps Are Running Dry", Accessed March 11, 2004. <http://newsvote.bbc.co.uk>.

——(2004b) "Poverty 'Is World's Worst Threat", Accessed March 11, 2004. <http://newsvote.bbc.co.uk>.

Lenin, V. I. (1969) *Imperialism: The Highest Stage of Capitalism*, Peking: Foreign Language Press.

Magdoff, Fred (2004) "A Precarious Existence: The Fate of Billions?" *Monthly Review*, 55: 9, 1–14.

Malthus, Thomas Robert (1959) *Population: The First Essay*. Ann Arbor, Mich.: University of Michigan Press.

Martine, George (1996) "Population and Environment in the Current Development Scenario", Working Paper Series Number 96.02, Harvard Centre for Population and Development Studies, Harvard University.

Marx, Karl (1967). *Capital* (Vol. 1) New York: International Publishers.

——(1973) *Grundrisse: Foundations of the Critique of Political Economy*, New York: Vintage Books.

Meadows, Donella H. et al. (1972) *The Limits to Growth: A Report for the Club of Rome's Project on the Predicament of Mankind*. New York: New American Library.

Meek, Ronald L. (1954) *Marx and Engels on Malthus*, New York: International Publishers.

Mishan, E. J. (1970) *Technology and Growth: The Price We Pay*, New York: Praeger.

Moore, Barrington, Jr. (1987) *Authority and Inequality under Capitalism and Socialism*, Oxford: Clarendon Press.

Nardinelli, Clark (2004) "Industrial Revolution and the Standard of Living", In *The Concise Encyclopaedia of Economics*, The Library of Economics and Liberty. Accessed January 15, 2004, <http://www.econlib.org/library/Enc/IndustrialRevolutionandtheStandardofLiving.ht

Ng, Larry K. Y. and Stuart Mudd, eds. (1965) *The Population Crisis: Implications and Plans for Action*, Bloomington, Ind.: Indiana University Press.

Norton, Seth W. (2002) "Population Growth, Economic Freedom, and the Rule of Law", PERC Policy Series, Issue Number PS-24.

Patterson, John G. and Nanda R. Shrestha (1988) "Population Growth and Development in the Third World: The Neo-colonial Context", *Studies in Comparative International Development*, 23:2, 3–53.

Piotrow, Phyllis T. (1973) World Population Crisis: The United States Response, New York: Praeger.

Population Reference Bureau (2003) "Human Population: Fundamentals of Growth, Population Growth and Distribution", Accessed October 31, 2003. <http://www.prb.org>.

Rao, Mohan (2003) "An Imagined Reality: Malthusianism, Neo-Malthusianism and Population Myth." *South Asia: E-Journal*, Accessed July 18, 2003, <http://www.hsph.harvard.edu>.

Ravenholt, R. T. (1975) "AID's Family Planning Strategy", In Reining, Priscilla and Irene Tinker, eds. *Population: Dynamics, Ethics, and Politics*, Washington, D. C.: American Association of the Advancement of Science, 53.

Reining, Priscilla and Irene Tinker (1975) *Population: Dynamics, Ethics, and Politics*, Washington, D. C.: American Association of the Advancement of Science.

Sadava, David E. (2002) "Human Population Growth: Lessons from Demography", In Chrispeels, Maarten J. and David E. Sadava, eds. *Plants, Genes, and Crop Biotechnology*, Accessed January 15, 2004. <http://www.plantbiotech.jbpub.com/pdf/chrispeels_Ch01_001-021.pdf>.

Sen, Amartya (1993), "On the Darwinian View of Progress", *Population and Development Review*, 19: 1, 123–137.

——(1994) "Population Policy: Authoritarianism versus Cooperation", *Social Change*, 24: 3/4, 20–35, <http://www.hsph.harvard.edu>.

——(2000) "Will There Be Any Hope for the Poor?" *Time*, May 22, 2000, 94–95, Accessed July 16, 2003 <http://proquest.umi.com>.

Shrestha, Nanda R. (2000) "A Personal View of Child Labour", *Education About Asia*, 5: 3, 47–49.

Shrestha, Nanda R., Dennis Conway, and Keshav Bhattarai (1999) "Population Pressure and Land Resources in Nepal: A Revisit, Twenty Years Later", *Journal of Developing Areas*, 33: 2, 245–268.

Shrestha, Nanda R. and John G. Patterson (1990) "Population and Poverty in Dependent States: Latin America Considered." *Antipode: A Radical Journal of Geography*, 22: 2, 121–155.

Simon, Julian (1981) *The Ultimate Resource*, Princeton, NJ: Princeton University Press.

——(1993) "Population Growth Is Not Bad for Humanity", Accessed August 10, 2003. <http://www.uwmc.uwc.edu/geography/malthus/NORTON02.txt>.

——(1994) "More People, greater Wealth, More Resources, Healthier Environment" Accessed August 10, 2003, <http://www.uwmc.uwc.edu/geography/malthus/NORTON02.txt>.

——(1995) "Population Growth Is Our Greatest Triumph ?" Accessed August 10, 2003, <http://www.uwmc.uwc.edu/geography/malthus/NORTON02.txt>.

Toynbee, Arnold J. (1965) "Man and Hunger: The Perspectives of History", In Ng, Larry K. Y. and Stuart Mudd, eds. *The Population Crisis: Implications and Plans for Action*. Bloomington, Ind.: Indiana University Press, 133–148.

United Nations (2003) "The World at Six Billion", Accessed December 10, 2003. <http://www.un.org/esa/population/publications/sixbillion/sixbilpart1.pdf>.

Weisband, Edward (1989) *Poverty Amidst Plenty: World Political Economy and Distributive Justice*, Boulder, Colo.: Westview Press.

World Bank (2001) *World Development Report 2000/2001: Attacking Poverty*, New York: Oxford University Press.

Yates, Michael D. (2004) "Poverty and Inequality in the Global Economy", *Monthly Review*, 55: 9, 37–48.

2

Greying of the Baby Boomers in America: Problems and Prospects

Samuel Thompson

Introduction

There is a striking demographic change occurring in the United States. This change is connected to a phenomenon known as the greying of America, which is dominated by the population cohort of Baby Boomers. Every seven seconds, another baby boomer turns 50 years old. The baby boom generation refers to births between 1946 and 1964, totalling 76 million children. According to the 2000 U.S. Census, there were 35 million Americans aged 65 or over. Paradoxically, projections indicate that by the year 2030, one in every five Americans will be 65 years or older (Himes, 2000, 3). In essence, the proportion of the elderly will continue to increase for many decades. The two main factors responsible for the increasing elderly population are longevity and declining fertility rates. People are living longer due to innovations in medicine coupled with a declining young population, and the result is greying in America. As the number of baby boomers increases, there are going to be issues that require proper planning for the long-term, especially in the realm of retirement, housing, transportation, and healthcare.

Retirement of the Baby Boomers

In 1935 President Franklin D. Roosevelt signed into law the Social Security Act, representing part of an overall effect to stimulate the U.S. economy during the Great Depression. The Act specified the age of 65 as the point at which people will be eligible to receive their Social Security or old age insurance benefits. Since the enactment of the Act, Americans have looked forward to reaching that pivotal age so that they can spend the rest of their lives in leisure. Some spend their golden years in recreation vehicles travelling across the 48 contiguous states. While some retirees play golf every morning, others choose to spend their days in rocking chairs on their front porch. However, as the masses of baby boomers are reaching the age of 65 (Table 2.1); the public's perception of retirement will undoubtedly be transformed.

Table 2.1: Total Population and Proportion of 65 Years or Older in the USA: 1930-2040

Population in Thousands		
Year	Total	Age 65+
1930	122,755	6,634
1940	131,669	9,019
1950	150,697	12,270
1960	179,323	16,560
1970	203,212	20,066
1980	226,546	25,549
1990	248,710	31,242
2000	281,422	34,992
2010 (Projection)	299,862	45,501
2020 (Projection)	324,927	53,733
2040 (Projection)	377,350	77,177

Source: US Census Bureau, 2003.

Since baby boomers make up 52 percent of the entire working population (Caudron 1997), the assumption is that their exodus from the labour force will create a large vacuum in the labour force, to the detriment of employers. As baby boomers retire, these occupations are predicted to lose the largest number of workers, including secretaries, truck drivers, elementary school teachers, janitors and cleaners, secondary school teachers, registered nurses, engineers, and accounting and auditing clerks (Dohm 2000).

However, the most likely scenario is that aging baby boomers will work, in some capacity, well beyond the age of 65. Current and future jobs will be more dependent on brainpower than physical strength, thus allowing older Americans capable of working to work until very late in life. Supporting this trend is the fact that baby boomers are well educated, are much healthier, and have longer life expectancies than their preceding generation (Wellner 1999). Overall, they would rather fulfil their retirement by contributing to society in some positive way- may be volunteering or reading to children.

There is also the recognition that retirement is not a panacea for all seniors. There are legitimate reasons some baby boomers will likely work past the conventional age of retirement. They may be forced to work due to financial difficulties. Many baby boomers have the false impression that they will have plenty of money saved to fund their retirement. But it is believed that many of them are not accounting for the very real possibility that they may live past the age of 100, often referred to as centenarians. In essence, without adequate financial preparation, many baby boomers will continue to work in their old years.

There is speculation that Social Security funds will be exhausted by 2030, and many companies will not be able to afford the pensions expected by their baby boomer employees (Caudron 1997). Currently, Social Security is a massive program providing benefits to more than 45 million people (Table 2.2). About 63 percent of the beneficiaries are retired workers; 7 percent are the spouses and children of retired workers. Similarly, 11 percent of the beneficiaries are disabled workers who are out of the labour force, especially for medical reasons; 4 percent represent the spouses and children of disabled workers. Lastly, there are 15 percent representing the spouses and children of deceased retired workers.

Table 2.2: Social Security Beneficiaries: December 2000

Type of Benefit	Number of Recipients (in thousands)	Percent
Total Benefits	45,417	100
Retired Workers	28,506	63
Spouses and Children of Retired Workers	3,255	7
Disabled Workers	5,036	11
Spouses and Children of Disabled Workers	1,639	4
Survivors of Deceased Retired workers	6,981	15

Source: Social Security Administration, 2001.

With so many individuals counting on the benefits of the Social Security System, the viability of the program is in doubt in terms of funding. In an attempt to streamline the system, the Congress of the United States amended the program to shore-up the Social Security Trust Funds. One of the changes is a gradual increase of the retirement age to 66 by the year 2005 and 67 by the year 2022 (Wiatrowski 2001); the original retirement age is 65. Since the years 2005 and 2022 are future prospects, there are no data to measure the effect of increasing the age on old age insurance benefits and the Social Security Trust Fund. Obviously, it boils down to the fact that baby boomers are saving too little and living too long to realistically expect a life of leisure in their senior years.

Another scenario is that retired baby boomers will take a short break and then change careers. Popular late-life career choices will include consulting, teaching, joining a small company, or starting their own business (Kuhn 1995). Being employed by small companies will appeal to baby boomers because they will be able to use their experience for the betterment of the companies. Many also gravitate toward small companies because they offer flexible schedules and less stressful work environment. It is also expected that a large number of baby boomers will return to school after retiring from their current jobs, either to train for a new career or just for personal enrichment (Caudron 1997). In 1998, 48 percent of Americans over the age of 55 were volunteers.

This percentage is expected to increase as more of the aging baby boomers appear on the retirement stage. While some seniors feel very positive about volunteering, there is a different view shared by former high-ranking corporate professionals who want to volunteer only to be assigned menial duties. Such was the case when Don Spieler, ex-president of Kodak's Mexico operations, retired and wished to volunteer for the United Way in his hometown. Because he had served on national boards for Junior Achievement and the Special Olympics, and was a two-term president of the American Chamber of Commerce in Mexico, he expected the United Way would be thrilled to capitalize on his experience and expertise. The director of the local United Way interviewed him, and when he was invited to join the agency, Don expected to be asked to head an important committee. Instead, he was asked to do for raising fund. Don was insulted and taken a back, and did not accept the assignment (Tanz 2000). It is obvious that baby boomers who are interested in volunteering after retirement will have to realize that their past high-ranking jobs are irrelevant when it comes to assigning volunteers to complete needed tasks.

When baby boomers do eventually make the decision to cease working, they overwhelmingly wish to retire gradually by first going from full-time to part-time employment (Caudron 1997). Part-time jobs and job sharing programs were developed at DuPont in Wilmington, Delaware, for young employees with families. But in recent years, employees in their 50s are taking advantage of the programs (McCune 1998). Even if they change employers, many boomers are expected to trade in their high-powered full-time careers for part-time jobs that are less stressful (McCune 1998).

Often, the average life span is divided into three segments: first, there is education, then work, and lastly leisure. But as baby boomers reach retirement age, they are expected to revolutionize the definition of a retiree, just as they have revolutionized every other stage of life, as they passed through it. Education, work, and leisure will be interspersed throughout the entire life span, as many boomers go on sabbatical after retiring from their initial career, return to school to upgrade knowledge base, and then work once again in a new field. Retirement for them will be much more active and much more involved in society than it was for their parents.

Housing for the Elderly

In the past decade, the number of nursing home residents has decreased by about 10 percent, even though the number of people over age 75 has increased by 27 percent (Shapiro 2001). This decrease in nursing home residency is expected to become even more apparent as the baby boom generation reaches the elderly cohort. Housing choices for the boomers range from retrofitting current homes to elaborate continuing care communities. It is anticipated that baby boomers will be in better health than previous elderly generations, and they probably will not need housing facilities that offer extensive nursing care.

When elderly people choose to stay at home, it is referred to as "aging in place" (Benedict 2001). Since many of the elderly own their homes in familiar neighbourhoods, hence they feel comfortable in remaining in the same homes. Often to make aging in place possible, homes must be retrofitted. The most common home construction problems require remedying to accommodate seniors that include master bedrooms on the second floor, bathrooms that are too small for a wheelchair, bathtubs that are difficult to get in and out of, and kitchens with high counters and overhead microwaves and cupboards that cannot be reached (Horvitz 1997). In addition to large-scale construction to retrofit seniors' homes, specialized appliances and furniture can be installed, such as bathtub grab bars and lever faucets and doorknobs. Baby boomers are expected to drastically increase the demand for retrofitting services, which will drive down the cost of these improvements (Horvitz 1997).

As baby boomers age, they are not likely to follow the Floridization phenomenon, a reference to the migration of retirees from the Northeast and Midwest to the Sun Belt states. The new trend is that aging baby boomers are staying in the same houses and neighbourhoods where they raised their families, often referred to as "naturally occurring retirement communities" (Perry 2001). These communities are proliferating in the country, bringing to an end the trend to move to Florida after one's retirement.

Cities across the country are recognizing the growth in their elderly population, and they are making improvements to cater to their elderly. For example, a neighbourhood in Los Angeles, California, is extending stoplight times to give seniors in the area more time to cross-busy streets and in Atlantic City, New Jersey, casino taxes are being used to help fund the retrofitting of homes owned by seniors (Perry 2001).

In 2000 a study by the AARP (formerly American Association of Retired Persons) found that 82 percent of people 45 years and older intend on staying in their current homes until the end of their lives (in Benedict 2001). However, there are a handful of baby boomers who intend on spending their golden years in a new home that is larger and plusher than their current homes; they desire large airy homes, with high ceilings and many windows, low-maintenance exterior and modern appliances (National Association of Home Builders 2002). Conversely, some future seniors will seek homes with small lots that are easy to maintain, in diversified neighbourhoods where they are surrounded by people of all ages (Otto 1999). Baby boomers will not be interested in living in neighbourhoods where residents are primarily of old age, the way that their parents have, because they will mostly want to live in neighbourhoods that do not remind them that they are getting older (Perry 2001).

While staying at home is anticipated to be the housing of choice for the majority of aging baby boomers, assisted living is currently a very popular option for individuals requiring a low level of care. It is estimated that there are more than 30,000 assisted living facilities in the United States and more than one million individuals live in them (Benedict 2001).

Assisted living facilities usually resemble studio apartments. Facility employees are there to help residents with bathing, dressing, eating, and taking their medications. But there are no nurses or other medical professionals on staff. This can pose quite a problem. Seniors with cognitive disorders and other medical problems are increasingly planning on moving into assisted living facilities. The bigger problem with assisted living facilities is that staff often is not trained to handle people with some of these medical problems such as dementia or Alzheimer's.

Assisted-living appeals to many seniors because they help the resident remain independent, they offer abundant social interaction, and they have a homelike feel. Unfortunately, there are often hidden fees for things like laundry service and meal delivery to the room and the costs can increase without notice (Shapiro 2001).

The typical cost for keeping someone in an assisted living facility is over US$2,100 a month. Although this is cheaper than a nursing home, government controlled medical coverage such as Medicare[2] or Medicaid[3] can only be applied to nursing homes (Horvitz 1997). However, it seems the cost of assisted living will decrease as more of these facilities are built to accommodate the aging baby boomers (Shapiro 2001). It is common for elderly individuals to splurge and live in an assisted living residence, assuming they will stay there until their death. But more than 75 percent of assisted living residents are forced to eventually leave for the elevated level of care a nursing home provides (Shapiro 2001). After exhausting their savings on the assisted living, they often find it hard to pay for the nursing home later in their life.

To make assisted living more affordable for the elderly, local housing authorities must explore how to provide rental assistance to residents of assisted living facilities (Shafer 2001). A final housing option for the elderly that is expected to gain popularity with the aging baby boomers is continuing-care communities. These communities offer a mixture of three levels of care, so that as residents they can stay in the same community. Usually they have a country-club atmosphere, with healthcare facilities nearby but out of sight so that the residents are not reminded of how they are aging (Horvitz 1997). Continuing-care communities appeal most to elderly couples, because they can purchase apartments in the community. But the apartments are very costly, averaging US$ 110,000 to purchase a two-bedroom. Then there are monthly fees for the services, which is in average US$ 2,000 (Shapiro 2001).

There was a time when these types of communities were notorious for not being financially sound, when a number of them went bankrupt in the 1980s. But now they are required by states to keep large cash reserves to prevent residents from being left homeless. Also, there is now a Continuing Care Accreditation Commission to protect consumers of homes in these communities (Shapiro 2001). Baby boomers have dealt with the numerous housing options for the elderly when caring for their parents and it is expected that because many of them have seen their parents in nursing homes, they will wish for alternative housing options as they age. The majority of them will probably work to stay in their own homes. But for those who do not, assisted living and continuing-care communities will be the choice, as these facilities become affordable.

Transportation and the Elderly

Based on recent studies, increasing numbers of elderly people will have a huge impact on transportation policy in the United States (Coughlin 1997 & 1999; McKnight 2001). Transportation is how people remain physically connected to each other. For every generation, transportation provides the connection to jobs, to activities, to volunteering, to stores and marketing services, and to healthcare facilities. Historically, walking was the main form of transportation, and old people could walk to the corner store. Each shopping store was close enough to encourage walking, and the road condition was good enough for old pedestrians. Since Post-World War II, people started to settle around the suburbs, where stores and other facilities are miles away. Their main transportation changed to automobiles. Now, most of the elderly people depend on the car for meeting daily needs, while traffic conditions for elderly pedestrians are not efficient.

Driving may not remain a lifelong option of the elderly because of diminished capacity. Many elderly people may live in communities with inadequate sidewalks, short-duration traffic signals, and hard-to-read signage that can cause problems for older pedestrians. Transportation could be a dangerous proposition for old people. For driving automobiles, aging affects how people drive. Drivers over 75 years old cause the second highest fatality rate on the nation's roads; second only to drivers aged 16 to 24 years old. A recent study conducted for the Department of Health and Human Services and the Department of Transportation suggests that fatalities of drivers over 75 years old could top 20,000, nearly tripling today's number of deaths on the road (Wisconsin Traffic Safety Reporter 2000).

As a result of aging, elderly people lose the physical abilities required for driving. Their eyes struggle to make out detail, absorb light, handle glare, and adapt to darkness. Almost one third of those over 65 years have significant hearing loss, and it jumps to 75 percent at 75 years of age (McKnight 2001). For reaction time, mental sharpness can remain the same, but the pace slows. It takes longer to process information, especially from several sources. The older people get, the more prescription and over-the-counter medication they tend to take. These can cause drowsiness and disorientation, which may even require additional medication to control. A heart disease or the aftermath of a stroke can cause disorientation, dizziness, fainting, blurred vision, and weak limbs.

It is not easy finding ways to meet the travel needs of people for whom the car is no longer available as the primary mode of transportation. This population includes people who choose to curtail their driving, those whose licenses are restricted in some way, and those who are not able to drive at all. Today, public transportation is structured primarily to accommodate suburban commuters, and the distances involved and the absences of pedestrian facilities along many streets often preclude travel for older persons. Other obstacles to use of public transit include unfamiliarity with routes and schedules, remoteness of stops, exposure to weather, need for assistance, and fear of harm.

To determine who can still drive safely, or who should be restricted in their driving, everyone should be tested. Drivers who do not recognize their ability are part of the problem for transportation safety. There is general acceptance of the need to require older drivers, at some point, to demonstrate that they really can drive safely, although acceptance by many of the older drivers themselves is more in principle than in personal practice.

In almost all states, there is an age at which drivers must begin appearing at a licensing office for a renewal examination. The Maryland Motor Vehicle Administration is evaluating a screening program, which ultimately might be integrated into the license renewal system. The screening process takes less than 15 minutes and includes tests for visual acuity, scanning, visualization of spatial relationships, visual search and sequencing, as well as tests of memory, and head and neck mobility.

Technological development can make cars easier and safer to drive. For example, sophisticated cruise control systems are also reaching the market place that will automatically keep cars at a safe following distance. Ultraviolet systems for displaying critical elements of the scene ahead in a way that enhances their visibility, particularly at night or in heavy rain are in development. Also, modifications in airbag designs that adjust the rate of inflation to the severity of impacts will help reduce the chances of injury from the airbag itself. Although such advances may be of considerable benefit to the elderly, there is some concern about how well this population will adapt to new technology. On the other hand, there is some justification for optimism. As the years go on, many of the older population would have had enough experience with computers and other electronic devices to ease the transition to the new automobile technologies.

Healthcare for the Elderly

The impact of the aging U.S. population on the healthcare system is receiving increasing attention. In the future, a relatively small population will be forced to care for the elderly, and this will require a shift in the emphasis of healthcare. Historically, the emphasis in healthcare has been on acute care of younger people. Long-term care of older citizens was of secondary importance, even when it is clear that a demand exists.

The healthcare labour force is aging along with the general population. The average age of the hospital staff nurse was 40 in 1991 and reached 45 in 2000. Since aging workers have different needs than younger workers, benefit packages will need to be reconfigured to reflect employees' concerns about retirement and healthcare. Hospitals will also need to figure out how to attract and retain older workers due to the relative shortage of young entry-level staff. There will also be increasing numbers of women filling the roles of physician and hospital administration staff (Friedman 1991).

With the expected growth of the female population in the United States, there are several issues that will impact healthcare. First, the majority of females will be concentrated in the upper ages, because they are likely to outlive their husbands. Second, women tend to marry men older than themselves. This means that 75 percent of most elderly men will have a spouse living with them, compared with 44 percent of most elderly women. Third, women are more likely to live alone as a result of divorce, death of a spouse, or simply choosing to stay single. Fourth, elderly women are more likely than elderly men to live in poverty. Thirty percent of those over 85 years have incomes below the poverty level, and the risk is even higher for minority women. The reason is that women in this age group have either outlived their resources, or have expended them on long term care for themselves or their spouses. Finally, women tend to report poorer health than men of the same age group and so require more healthcare services. Women average 1.4 more physician visits per year than men do and constitute 77 percent of nursing home patients (Friedman 1991).

A change in attitude toward aging is needed. A society that celebrates youth and fears aging will lead to chronic labour shortages, a skewing of healthcare priorities and a mismatch between medicine and patients. A better balance between the traditional culture of youth and the demographic realities of the next century is necessary. The rising cost of healthcare at all levels is a concern and Medicare in particular. It is not surprising that a disproportionate share of the healthcare services goes to the elderly. About 12 percent of the population accounts for one-third of the total healthcare expenditures (Schulz 2001).

Differences among the aged are important to note. Many are healthy and use only a moderate amount of services, while others require extensive help. For example, 9 percent of the elderly accounted for 70 percent of all Medicare payments in 1982. At the same time, about 40 percent of the elderly received no Medicare benefits (Schulz 2001).

Regardless of the level of usage of Medicare, there were concerns about the funding of the program. In 1999 Congress acted to improve the situation by increasing the deductible for Medicare (Schulz 2001). However, this is not expected to fully defray the effects of the aging baby boom population.

Conclusion

One thing is clear; the aging of America is inevitable. Over the last two hundred years the median age has more than doubled from 16 years in 1800 to 35.3 in 2000—the age at which half of the population is young and the other is old. As modern medicine and other healthy lifestyle changes continue to prolong life expectancies of the elderly and, without a corresponding increase in fertility, the median age will continue to increase in the United States. This will alter social life and social institutions at all levels, with implications in the realm of retirement, housing, transportation, and healthcare. Many boomers are to be out of the work force due to retirement, but the prediction of huge vacancies will not materialize. Many boomers will postpone retirement, work part-time, or perhaps start a new carrier. These activities will fill the void created by those who embark on full retirement.

It is obvious that boomers will have many choices in terms of housing. Many are going to be as independent as possible because they do not want to be restricted to nursing homes. The housing industry is preparing to satisfy the needs of the retiring boomers; many of them are better off economically than their parents. Conversely, there is a need for city planners, traffic engineers, and land developers to work out designs that will transform cities into pedestrian friendly areas. Finally, there will be an increase in old age diseases as the population ages. The challenge for policy makers is the availability of healthcare workers, and also making healthcare affordable for all the elderly. In the end, proper planning now will go a long way in alleviating potential problems as more Americans become old and fray in the coming years.

Notes:

Social Security Act: The Social Security Act allows workers and employers to be taxied (a percentage of the workers' wages, matched by a similar percentage employer contribution) and the money is kept in a Social Security Trust Fund. The Social Security Administration began payment in 1940 and today continues to make monthly Social Security payments to eligible contributors.

Medicare or Medicaid: In 1965 these two programs were created to alleviate the medical cost burdens of the elderly and poor. Medicare was specifically designed for the elderly, while Medicaid applied to the poor of all ages, including the elderly poor.

References

Benedict, Elizabeth (2001) When Baby Boomers Grow Old, *American Prospect*, V.12, n.9: 20-25.

Caudron, Shari (1997) Boomers Rock the System, *Workforce*, V.76: 42-44. Coughlin, F Joseph (1999) Technology Needs of Aging Boomers, *Issues in Science and Technology*, Fall: P53.

——(1997) Ten Myths About Transportation for the Elderly, *Transportation Quarterly*, Winter: P91-101.

Dohm, Arlene (2000) Gauging the Labour Force Effects of Retiring Baby-Boomers, *Monthly Labour Review*, v.123, n.7: 17-25.

Friedman, Emily (1991) Healthcare's Changing Face: The Demographics of the 2181 Century, Hospitals: *The Journal of the American Hospital Association*, 65:7 36-40.

Himes, Christine L. (2001) Elderly Americans. *Population Bulletin*, v. 56, n.4, 1-39.

Horvitz, Leslie Alan (1997) Aging America is Big Business, *Insight*, n.45: 38-39.

Kuhn, Susan E. (1995) Retire Today: Find a New Job Tomorrow, *Fortune*, v.132, n.2: 102-106.

McCune, Jenny C. (1998) The Future of Retirement. *Management Review*, v.87, n.4: 10-16.

McKnight, A James (2001) Too Old to Drive? *Issue in Science and Technology*, Winter:

P63-69.
National Association of Home Builders (2002) Shades of Gray. *Builder*, V.25, n.1: 178-180.
Otto, Laura (1999) Old? No Way! *Journal of Property Management*, V.64, n.3: 66-69.
Perry, Joenen (2001) For Most, There's No Place Like Home, *U.S. News & World Report*, V.130, n.22: 66.
Schulz, James H. (2001) "The Economics of Aging" 7th edition. Westport Connecticut, Greenwood Publishing Group, Inc. pp 171-204.
Shafer, Dee Naquin (2001) Coming of Age, Journal *of Housing and Community Development*, V.58, n.3: 33-38.
Shapiro, Joseph P. (2001) The Assisted-living Dilemma, *U.S. News & World Report*, v.130, n.20: 64-66.
——(2001) Growing Old in a Good Home, *U.S. News & World Report*, v.130, n.20: 56-61.
Social Security Administration (2000) *Fast Facts and Figures About Social Security*. www.ssa.gov/statistics/fast_facts/2001
Tanz, Jason (2000) Candy Striper, My Ass! *Fortune*, V.142, n.4: 156-160.
Wellner, Alison Stein (1999) Workplace 2018: Retirement Boom or Bust? *Training*, V.36, n.8: 54-59.
Wiatrowski, William J. (2001) Changing Retirement Age: Ups and Downs. Monthly Labour Review, V. 124, n.4, 3-12.
Wisconsin Traffic Safety Reporter (2000) Bureau of Transportation Safety, Wisconsin Department of Transportation. July/August.

3

Global Aging and the Rural Health Divide: An Analysis of Physician Geographic Maldistribution

Christopher Cusack

Introduction

Across the globe, societal aging firmly establishes its social and economic presence as a demographic phenomenon. While many demographic issues are more commonly associated with geographic regions, such as sub-replacement fertility rates in Europe or skewed sex ratios in Southeast Asia, the aging of populations serves as something of a demographic unifier. Increased life expectancies and reduced mortality rates are appropriately viewed as positive trends, though the magnitude and rapidity of these trends necessitates analysis of the problems and prospects of such change. As this change is global in nature, with countries around the globe facing similar trends of aging populations, opportunity for broad application of case study analysis is inherent. Policy makers can readily learn to anticipate problems and enact population policies and programs based on the successes and failures of other nations around the globe.

Even the wealthiest countries with the greatest means at their disposal are not immune to difficulties brought about by growing elderly populations. Social and economic burdens associated with an aged population can be considerable and can strain, in particular, the provision of quality health care. The National Research Council (2001) has noted that aging populations are apt to include increasing numbers of disabled persons and result in heightened demands on health care systems. Meeting the needs of the elderly requires more than an adequate amount of health resources; it necessitates a distributive model of these resources that encompasses the disparate needs of a potentially and geographically dispersed population. The imbalance between populations in need and available physicians is known as "physician geographic misdistribution" and is one of the more pressing issues associated with societal aging (Council on Graduate Medical Education 1998, 1).

This problem is not isolated to any single country and is a growing concern around the globe. In their study of the maldistribution of physicians in Japan, Kobayashi and Takaki (1992) found that rural areas were often faced with a shortage of physicians. Using census data to analyze the distribution of general practitioners, Wilkinson (1999) likewise found that capital cities are oversupplied and the more rural and remote areas are undersupplied in every State and Territory of Australia. South Africa not only needs more doctors in totality, but it needs them at the right places—rural regions and black townships (Kale 1995). A comparative study of dementia in East Asia identified rural areas as lagging in the provision in health services while containing a disproportionate elderly population (Ineichen 1998). This disparate distribution of health resources is well documented, and puts at particular risk the aging populations in rural or other less developed areas of countries.

Physician geographic maldistribution can be analyzed by using the United States as an exemplar of a prosperous country facing constraints in health care provision. Indeed, large numbers of Americans, including the elderly, have only limited access to health care and many Americans have no health care insurance. A principal problem facing the elderly is a maldistribution of health care resources. Many elderly reside in rural regions of the country while most health care providers are located in more affluent metropolitan areas.

The purpose of this study, then, is threefold. First, the demographic shifts and global distribution of aging populations are reviewed to highlight the universality of this trend. Next, a case study analysis of the causes and consequences of physician geographic misdistribution in the United States is explicated. Finally, the potential for cross national applicability of policies and programs addressing inequitable distributions of health care resources and an outlook to the future are provided.

Global Elderly

The United Nations (UN) designated 1999 as the 'International Year of Older Persons' serves as an excellent indication that population aging is a worldwide happening (Tonn et al., 2001, 852). Reinforcing such recognition, the newsmagazine *U.S. News and World Report* depicted 'The Global Aging Crisis' on its March 1, 1999 cover. Justifying such exposure, the world's median age is projected to age at a far more rapid rate over the next 50 years than it did during the previous half century. From 1950 to 2000, the median age increased less than three years—while it is expected to increase nearly 10 years between 2000 and 2050. Also by the year 2050, nearly 16.3 percent of the world's population is projected to be 65 years or older—as compared to only 6.9 percent in 2000 (United Nations Population Division 2001).

Life expectancies are rising, particularly in the developed world, as male and female life expectancies exceeded 75.0 years in 19 and 57 countries respectively in 2000. From the top 10 countries for life expectancy at birth, only Japan and Australia are not European countries (Lopez et al. 2001).

The European continent is indeed at the vanguard of global aging. Among major world regions, Europe has the highest percent of population aged 65 and over (National Research Council 2001, 32). In Germany, the median age in the year 2025 is projected to be 46 years. Median ages for Greece and Bulgaria are projected to reach 47 (Eberstadt 2001). Similarly, the United States is expected to continue to age rapidly, with its population over the age of 65 increasing from 39 million in 2010 to 79 million in 2050 (Tonn et al. 2001, 851). In 1950, the proportion of children in regions of the more developed world was 27 percent while that of older persons was 12 percent. By 2000, the proportion of older persons in the more developed regions had surpassed that of children and, in 2050, the proportion of older persons is expected to be more than double that of children.

Yet, the developed world does not face this issue alone. In fact, older populations of developing countries are growing at a more rapid rate than those in Europe and North America (National Research Council 2001, 33). This demographic trend poses a dilemma, as it is likely to inhibit the potential for development and serve to encumber fledgling economies. As noted by Eberstadt (2001), "current developed countries grew rich before they grew old; many of today's low-income countries, by contrast, look likely to become old first." China's projected population aged 65 and over will surpass 300 million people in the year 2050—more than the current size of the US population. Likewise, even the 'youngest' regions of the world, including Latin America and Africa, will have substantial elderly populations. Aging populations, that are likely to be at odds with the potential for economic prosperity will also intensify social and ethical debates.

Throughout both the developed and developing worlds, the issue of population aging is understood to potentially be one of the most important long-term economic liabilities. While developing countries have perhaps more pressing demographic concerns, they too are likewise affected by global aging due to the interconnectivity of the global economy. Rising old-age dependency and slow- or no-growth of workforce populations in the world's largest economic engines will impact national economies worldwide (CSIS 2002, 1). Stagnant or contracting workforces faced with the need to support ever-increasing aged populations will experience serious economic repercussions. Of particular concern is the ability to provide necessary resources to cover rising costs of health care provision for a growing and increasingly aged dependent population.

These trends are only to become more relevant as, demographically, the world is likely to experience: further decreases in mortality at the expense of increased morbidity; increased instances of incapacitating, costly, and as yet untreatable health related illnesses; and, an augmented need for long-term care of the 'illderly' (World Health Organization 1995). Issues associated with a growing elderly population include reduced tax revenues, economic security concerns, distinct housing and transportation needs, and an increased burden on health resources. Already, expanding elderly age cohorts in Europe are necessitating many governments to undergo a difficult reassessment of their provision of medical and other benefits for the aged—similar actions are beginning to be proposed in other parts of the developed world as well (Peterson 1999).

Aging in the United States

The United States provides an appropriate geographic unit of study with broad, and potentially cross-national, applicability of the problems and prospects of an aging society. Although Social Security solvency is widely recognized as a primary concern for the elderly, health care is the real 800-pound gorilla facing the US economy regarding the aging issue. Federal spending on the three principal programs associated with the elderly—Social Security, Medicare, and Medicaid—is also rising rapidly, from 20 percent of the federal budget in 1970 to a projected 68 percent in 2030 (Altman and Shactman 2002, 3). A primary concern is that without fundamental changes to the system, the medical costs of the aged will require an ever-increasing portion of what will soon be an insufficient public budget. The principal health care coverage for the elderly is particularly susceptible to the foibles of an arrangement in which costs will soon be outpacing inputs.

Yet, future bankruptcy of the Medicare program is not the only health related concern for the elderly population, as already there are serious shortages of health care provision in certain regions of the country. While many elderly choose to retire to communities in the Sunbelt states of California, Arizona, and Florida, there are also high concentrations of elderly in the more rural counties of America's interior. The elderly constitute their most significant percentages in the counties ranging from the Dakotas south to Texas. With only a few exceptions—highlighted by counties in Florida—the counties comprised of considerably higher (greater than one standard deviation above the mean) persons aged 65 years and over are found in the central Plains region of the country. This settlement pattern of the oldest-old is closely aligned with America's 'Heartland'—a region growing ever older, Whiter, and demographically more stagnant (Frey 2002, 353).

The Heartland receives relatively little in-migration, and much of its youthful population is migrating out of the region in search of job opportunities and economic advancement. There is widespread evidence of counties in this region with increasingly concentrated aged populations and diminishing workforces. States and counties experiencing declining population densities due to out-migration tend to be less urbanized and stretch from the northern Great Plains to the Appalachian states of Kentucky and West Virginia (Manson and Groop 2000, 497; Fonseca and Wong 2000). While the younger population moves away from the Heartland, an increasing number of elderly are choosing to remain within the region. These demographic decisions are resulting in the phenomenon known as "aging-in-place" (Taylor etal. 2002, 7).

Rural counties experiencing this aging-in-place are likely to experience the greatest difficulties in terms of requirements to meet the needs of their aged population. Rural areas, which already possess a higher concentration of elderly than their urban counterparts are further constrained by the challenge of serving a geographically disperse population. As such, service and health care provision is frequently less comprehensive and less accessible in comparison with more urbanized areas. The greatest problems are in those rural communities totalling fewer than 10,000 people and lacking adjacency to metropolitan areas. In these areas the supply of physicians is slightly higher than it was more than half a century ago, while the ratio of physicians to the general populace has been more than doubled in urban areas since 1960 (Council on Graduate Medical Education 1998, 25).

Aging populations in America's rural heartland are therefore often faced with fewer treatment options, fewer health care providers, and greater distances to travel in order to access health care services (Rogers 2002). The growth in the specialization of physicians serves as a principal contributor to the geographic maldistribution of physicians. Consequently, nearly one in five persons in the United States who live in rural areas is served by fewer than one in ten of the nation's physicians (Council on Graduate Medical Education 1998). This situation could worsen for rural communities. The physician manpower appears to be swinging from a perceived surplus to a perceived deficit. The smaller and more remote communities are likely to be the first to feel the effects of a physician shortage (Pong and Pitblado 2001).

Yet, it would be too simplistic to merely associate the relatively large elderly populations in the Heartland with inadequate health care provision. In fact, the majority of populations is either served by local health resources or is economically able to travel to receive health care, or both. Thus, the high rates of elderly do not necessarily correlate with the areas of greatest need. Rather, additional information is required in order to make that determination. First, since elderly populations in rural areas are most at risk, the definition of 'rural' must be made clear. The Office of Management and Budget (OMB) provides one of the most readily agreed upon definitions of 'rural.' According to the OMB, all counties not identified as 'metropolitan' are designated as 'rural.' The distinction between metropolitan and rural counties is determined by the presence or absence of 'cities' as well as the proportion of residents commuting to jobs in cities (National Advisory Committee on Rural Health 2001).

While rural–urban comparisons can be somewhat limited by geographic mobility of patients and doctors, they remain effective in highlighting the overall disparity in the availability of physicians (Pong and Pitblado 2001). Consequently, these classifications are widely utilized not only by policy analysts and decision makers but by other governmental agencies as well. The Bureau of Primary Health Care identifies the country's Health Professional Shortage Areas. Counties or other geographic units receive this designation if the population-to-primary care physician ratio is greater than 3500:1 (Pong and Pitblado 2002). Not surprisingly, there are more than twice as many rural health professional shortage areas than metropolitan shortage areas (National Advisory Committee on Rural Health 2001). With 1,847 shortages, rural areas comprise more than 67 percent of all shortage areas designated by the Bureau of Primary Health Care.

Though representing an increased burden, designation as a shortage area does not necessarily indicate a severe health service problem for a community. For many, commuting to primary health care facilities or taking advantage of improving telemedicine technology provides solutions. Yet, for many others, such opportunities are either limited or virtually non-existent. Counties most at risk are those counties designated as rural health shortage areas that also contain elevated elderly poverty rates. In the United States, 187 counties can be identified as rural health shortage areas with high rates (greater than one standard deviation) of elderly poverty. These counties, located primarily in the south and southeast, represent the true problem of physician geographic maldistribution. Perhaps not surprisingly, many of these counties also have significant minority populations. In fact, 43 of the 187 counties or 23 percent have the majority of either Black or Hispanic population.

The problem of physician geographic maldistribution in no other states is as much as in the state of Mississippi. The shortage of health care professionals in the smaller states and in more isolated communities has already been noted (Hart-Hester and Thomas 2003). Yet, Mississippi is simply the core of a region at risk that extends from the Tex-Mex border to the heart of Appalachia. The average per capita income of persons aged 65 and over in these counties is only slightly more than 77 percent of the national average. Thus, the region of greatest concern is not that which contains the greatest per capita elderly population; rather it is the region represented by an amalgamation of variables that result in a true health provision problem. It is not simply having a substantial elderly population, or high poverty rate, or a rural designation, or a lack of local health resources. Instead, it is the synthesis of all of these factors that allow for the identification of those counties with an inability to serve at risk the elderly population.

Throughout the United States, access to health care provision proves a real problem in rural communities. In comparison to their urban counterparts, rural Americans are more likely to be poor, old, and of poor health. Rural Americans are also less likely to have access to an automobile or public transportation or to even have a telephone (National Advisory Committee on Rural Health 2001). However, even in rural America, distinctions can and should be made on the basis of severity of the health resource problem. Rural counties contain high rates of impoverished elderly and are designated as health care shortage areas and pose particular dilemmas. A majority of these 187 rural counties possess three principal factors that make counties difficult to staff with physicians; extreme and persistent poverty, a lack of conventional physical and cultural amenities, and populations that consist primarily of groups that are ethnic or racial minorities within the United States (Council on Graduate Medical Education 1998, 22). Despite enactment of a variety of federal health care workforce programs to address the issue, physician geographic maldistribution remains a persistent problem—and as the rural population of America ages, it will grow ever more acute.

Outlook to the Future

In the United States, and around the globe, the problem of physician geographic maldistribution is a growing concern. Despite government's concern over the future solvency of health benefits for the elderly a greater proportion of the aged population faces serious limitations in their ability to access needed health resources. The inaccessibility of health resources for the rural aged is to increase, as mortality rates decrease and life expectancies increase throughout the world. Indeed, the elderly have their own entity. The persons who are of 85 year and above are known as the 'oldest-old.' On a per capita basis, the oldest-old exact twice the hospital care and twenty times the nursing-home care as the young-old (Treas and Torrecilha 1995; Peterson 1999). The oldest-old represents the fastest growing segment of the elderly population. The increased demands of this population for services and budget shares will only intensify in upcoming years.

Globally, the number of persons of 60 years or above will be more than triple by 2050, while the number of persons of 80 years or above is expected to undergo more than a five-fold increase (United Nations Population Division 2000). This ever-increasing aged population is likely to have significant socio-economic consequences—particularly in the realm of health care provision. Though, people are living longer lives and life expectancies continue to rise around the globe, increasing numbers of elderly are living on ill and impaired (Treas and Torricilha 1995, 63). The problem is that the elderly population is increasing most dramatically in the less developed regions of the world. By the end of the 1990s, the world's elderly population was increasing by more than 750,000 persons each month – with 80 percent of this change occurring in the developing world (National Research Council 2001, 33). Growth of the elderly population, in tandem with their geographic distribution, will pose one of the most pressing conditions of economic and ethical issues in the societies.

Getting the necessary health resources to the populations most in need has already been subject to a number of potential solutions. The United States alone has enacted an array of programs over the past 30 years to address this issue. These programs can be grouped around five main strategies:

1. Deployment of health professionals to areas of need.
2. Establishment of clinics for the direct provision of care.
3. Educational intervention designed to increase the flow of health professionals to underserved areas.
4. Economic incentives to induce health professionals to practice in underserved areas.
5. Research and consultation aimed at specific problems associated with maldistribution.

For the most part, these programs have had only limited success, as the problem of physician geographic maldistribution has not abated with time. An additional contributing factor to the maldistribution is the increase in the number of female physicians—who overwhelmingly choose urban areas in which they live and practice. New programs that support women willing to work in underserved rural areas are now being proposed (Council on Graduate Medical Education 1998, 17).

Besides a draconian measure of compulsory service in rural areas, the development and utilization of telehealth is another potential option. Telehealth represents the utilization of telecommunications between health care providers and patients when face-to-face consultation is not viable. Telehealth technology becomes more powerful and affordable. This helps increase long distance interaction between physicians and patients and could thus alter rural medical service delivery substantially (Pong and Pitblado 2001). Yet, telehealth requires a certain level of income and instruction and, mirroring the current digital divide, thereby limiting its application in the more remote regions of poverty. Certainly there are no easy solutions for this problem that will only increase in time. Government programs are in place to alleviate as best they can the problem of physician geographic maldistribution. In the United States and around the globe, however, the issue will continue to require not just government resources but also filial responsibility and an ethos of care by society at large.

References

Altman, Stuart H. and David I. Shactman (eds.) (2002) Policies *for an Aging Society*, Baltimore: The Johns Hopkins University Press.

Centre for Strategic and International Studies (2003) Meeting *the Challenge of Global Aging: A Report to World Leaders from the CSIS Commission on Global Aging*, Washington D.C., the CSIS Press.

Council on Graduate Medical Education (1998) Physician *Distribution and Health Care Challenges in Rural and Inner-City Areas*, Washington D.C., U.S. Department of Health and Human Services.

Eberstadt, Nicholas (2001) The Population Implosion, Foreign *Policy* 123: 42-54.

Fonseca, James W. and David W. Wong (2000) Changing Patterns of Population Density in the United States, The *Professional Geographer* 52(3): 504-516.

Frey, William H. (2002) Three Americas: The Rising Significance of Regions, *Journal of the American Planning Association* 68(4): 349-355.

Hart-Hester, Susan, and Charlotte Thomas (2003) Access to Health Care Professionals in Rural Mississippi, Southern *Medical Journal* 96(2): 149-154.

Ineichen, Bernard (1998) Responding to Dementia in East Asia: Developments in Japan, China, Taiwan and South Korea, Aging *& Mental Health* 2(4): 279-285.

Kale, Rajendra (1995) New South Africa's Doctors: A State of Flux, British *Medical Journal*, 310: 1307-1311.

Kobayashi, Yasuki and Haruyoshi Takaki, (1992) Geographic Distribution of Physicians in Japan, Lancet 340(8832): 1391-1393.

Lopez, Alan D., Omar B. Ahmad, Michel Guillot, Mie Inoue, Brodie D. Ferguson, and Joshua A. Salamon (2001) *The Global Burden of Disease 2000 in Aging Populations: Research Paper No. 8*, Cambridge, Massachusetts: Centre for Population and Development Studies.

Manson, Gary A. and Richard E. Groop (2000) U.S. Inter-county Migration in the 1990s: People and Income Move Down the Urban Hierarchy, the *Professional Geographer* 52(3): 493-504.

National Advisory Committee on Rural Health (2001) Medicare *Reform: A Rural Perspective*, Rockville, MD: The National Advisory Committee on Rural Health.

National Research Council (2001) Preparing *for an Aging World: The Case for Cross-National Research*, Washington, D.C.: National Academy Press.

Peterson, Peter G. (1999) *Gray Dawn: How the Coming Age Wave Will Transform America and the World*, New York: Random House, Inc.

Pong, Raymond W. and J. Roger Pitblado (2001) Don't Take 'Geography' for Granted! Some Methodological Issues in Measuring Geographic Distribution of Physicians, *Canadian Journal of Rural Medicine* 6(2): 103-112.

Pong, Raymond W. and J. Roger Pitblado (2002) Beyond Counting Heads: Some Methodological Issues in Measuring Geographic Distribution of Physicians, *Canadian Journal of Rural Medicine* 7(1): 12-20.

Rogers, Carolyn C. (2002) Rural Health Issues for the Older Population, Rural *America*17 (2): 30-36.

Taylor, Melissa, James Carroll, John Seebach, and Irakli Khodeli (2002) The Changing Population in the U.S.: Baby Boomers, Immigrants and Their Effects on State Government. *Trends Alert: Critical Information for State Decision-Makers*, Lexington: The Council of State Governments.

Tonn Bruce E., Greg Waidley, and Carl Petrich (2001) The Ageing US Population and Environmental Policy, Journal *of Environmental Planning and Management* 44(6): 851-876.

Treas, Judith and Ramon Torrecilha (1995) The Older Population, In, *State of the Union: Social Trends*, edited by Reynolds Farley, pp. 47-92, New York: Russell Sage Foundation.

United Nations Population Division (2001) World *Population Prospects: The 2000 Revision*, New York: Population Division, United Nations.

Wilkinson, David (2000) Inequitable Distribution of General Practitioners in Australia: Analysis by State and Territory Using Census Data, Australian *Journal of Rural Health* 8: 87-93.

World Health Organization (1995) The *World Health Report 1995: Bridging the gaps*, Geneva: WHO.

4

Impacts of Undocumented Aliens: A Case Study of the Organ Pipe National Monument

George M. Pomeroy and Richard McQown

Introduction

Organ Pipe Cactus National Monument in south-western Arizona's Pima County was once an out of the way Sonoran Desert preserve famous, in part, for its namesake flora. In 1976 its pristine ecosystem and sound land management practices were recognized through being awarded the honour of biosphere reserve status. Two and a half decades later the National Park Rangers Lodge of the Fraternal Order of Police conferred another distinction upon Organ Pipe—"the most dangerous National Park in America" (Dinan 2002). The extent of this transformation was illustrated in August of 2002 when an AK-47 bullet, fired by a pair of Mexican citizens who had crossed unabated over our southern border, passed through the bullet-proof jacket of 28-year-old park ranger Kris Eggle. The murder of this young ranger served as an exclamation point on a situation which has spun out of control. In an interview conducted shortly after Mr. Eggle's death, Organ Pipe's chief ranger stated, "The typical park ranger doesn't sign up for this…What we have here is a war" (Fialka, 2003).

The large-scale influx of illegal migrants crossing the southern border of United States is having a disastrous impact upon both the preservation and enjoyment of public lands in this region. Due in large part to U.S. Border Patrol crackdowns in more populous border areas, the 83-mile length of the Arizona-Mexican Border that contains Organ Pipe is now the crossing point most frequently used by illegal migrants (Bustos, 2002). In 2001, Organ Pipe estimated the number of illegal visitors passing through its wilderness was 100 times the number of roughly 3,000 people who legally obtained backcountry permits (Becherer, 2002). The greater the levels of illegal usage of the park, the less likely it becomes that law abiding user groups will utilize this land held in trust for them.

Within this section of the border region, the sheer numbers of human traffic alone is sufficient to cause grave ecological damage. Additionally, the impact from smuggling and other criminal activities threatens the property and safety of residents, public land users and park rangers. Taken in combination, the vast numbers of traffic and the criminal activity perpetuated by a number of these persons pose a serious challenge for the operations of National Parks and other public lands in border regions. Clearly, action is needed to improve the current situation where both the ecological and recreational integrity of Organ Pipe are in serious jeopardy.

The Organ Pipe National Monument and Vicinity

Organ Pipe National Monument (referred to as Organ Pipe) established in 1937 encompasses over 330,688 acres of Sonoran Desert Ecosystem. The Sonoran Desert extends from South-eastern California and Baja California in the west to South-western Arizona and the Mexican State of Sonora in the east. Roughly 120,000 square miles of this area lies within the United States. The park was established in large part to protect fauna and flora distinctive to the Sonoran Desert and takes its name from the Organ Pipe cactus which is prevalent within the parks's domain and distinctive to the area. The Organ Pipe sector of the Sonoran Desert contains several mountain ranges interspersed with lowland plains and valleys. The most significant mountainous areas in Organ Pipe N.M. are the Ajo, Puerto Blanco, Bates and Diablo ranges.

Climatic patterns for the Sonoran Desert show precipitation occurring primarily during the summer monsoon period and in winter events with Pacific maritime influence. This bimodal pattern of precipitation enables an unexpected level of biological diversity in this hottest North American desert. Trees on the range are predominantly Little-leaf Palo Verdes, Desert Ironwoods, Catclaw and Saguaro with an under story of sagebrush, woody shrubs and mesquite. Freemont Cottonwoods, Arizona Ash and Willows are often found in riparian areas. Perhaps most conspicuously, the ecosystem supports a number of cacti including the park's namesake the rare Organ Pipe. Common park animals include Coyotes, Javelinas, Bighorn Sheep, Jackrabbits, Kangaroo, Rats and Rattlesnakes.

Border Issues and Park Management Concerns

A good starting point for discovering the causes for the flow of illegal immigrants into Organ Pipe and the extent to which it is occurring is Michelle Malkin's *Invasion: How America Still Welcomes Terrorists, Criminals, and Other Foreign Menaces to Our Shores* (2002). The author, herself the daughter of legal immigrants, describes the depth to which our government has been negligent in defending its borders on a number of fronts. For the Arizona-Mexican border she describes the inadequate resources of the border patrol to police remote areas and discusses how many of the measures taken after the September 11th terrorist attacks are directed more towards placating the Mexican government and ensuring the welfare of the illegal immigrants than actually stemming the tide. She also points out the dangerous nature of many of the migrants by detailing crimes such as home invasion robberies and auto thefts that are rampant along the migrant routes. Additionally, she tells of the increased numbers of illegal crossings on the Mexican border by middle-easterners and armed drug smugglers. Due to lawlessness on the southern border the armed Mexican troops have increasingly entered the United States and have even fired upon and pursued Border Patrol agents and park rangers. In summary, she paints a portrait of an out of control border guarded by an agency lacking the resources, or the willpower, to enforce it.

Researchers have become aware of the detrimental environmental impacts of undocumented aliens. Most recently, McIntyre and Weeks (2002) examined impacts to the Cleveland National Forest in Southern California, quantifying the estimated environmental impacts on a per 1,000 aliens basis. There findings were that for every thousand undocumented aliens there were 772 meters of new trails, 656 square meters of "disturbed area," 50 kilograms of litter generated, and 11 campfires. They concluded that efforts to interdict illegal crossings through the "Operation Gatekeeper" program merely led to a spatial redistribution of those crossing to areas such as the National Forest. This has implications for other managed lands, including Organ Pipe.

Despite the need for addressing the impacts of undocumented aliens, the management literature of the National Park Service (NPS) contains little to address this serious problem. This lack of attention is evident at both the park-level and system-wide. The NPS does have a valuable guide and management source (Anderson, Lime and Wang, 1998) for identifying factors that are detrimental to both the parks' ecosystems and the enjoyment of visitors and providing a range of strategies and tactics managers can use to address these unacceptable impacts. However, this guide does not speak to issues surrounding undocumented aliens. Specific to Organ Pipe N.M., but also offering little in regard to the impacts of undocumented aliens is the 1997 *Final Supplemental Environmental Impact Statement Re-analysis of Cumulative Impacts on the Sonoran Pronghorn* and *Organ Pipe Cactus National Monument General Management Plan Final Environmental Impact Statement* (National Park Service). While both are comprehensive and well-prepared documents, they are surprisingly devoid of content appropriate to the impacts of undocumented aliens.

Environmental Damage in Organ Pipe National Monument

The remoteness of Organ Pipe along with its proximity to the border has made it an attractive crossing point for multitudes of undocumented aliens. William Wellman, Superintendent of Organ Pipe, estimated that, in the year 2000, 40,000 to 80,000 illegal migrants passed through Organ Pipe (Clynes, 2002). Only one year later, due to increased border enforcement in more populous areas, park officials estimated that roughly 200,000 migrants had taken this route (Butts, 2002). This flood of persons has had grave consequences for the park's natural resources. One of the ways that the migrants degrade the parks natural resources is their creation of dozens of new trails across the park. Park officials estimate that over 100 miles of commonly used unplanned footpaths are now in Organ Pipe (Blinkly, 2000). These unplanned and unwanted trails destroy vegetation, disturb wildlife, cause soil compaction and erosion and can damage stream banks. Often these disruptions seriously impede efforts to restore threatened or endangered species, such as the Pygmy Owl and Sonoran Pronghorn, and efforts to repair damaged habitat can take decades in this delicate ecosystem.

These problems are compounded when these "wildcat" trails are used as roadways. Organ Pipe management has attempted to prevent cross-country vehicle travel by placing 12-foot-long, 5,000-pound concrete highway barriers along routes frequented by migrants. These efforts have been ineffective as the illegal motorists either drive around them, further damaging the ecosystem, or use chains to remove them.

A problem associated with these illegal thoroughfares is the prevalence of abandoned vehicles. In 2001 alone, Organ Pipe officials found 150 abandoned vehicles on their property (Custred, 2000). Many of the vehicles used by smugglers or migrants are unsuited for the harsh conditions found on these trails. When they become unable to proceed further due to mechanical failure or terrain the vehicles are abandoned and often times set on fire. The detrimental physical presence of these abandoned vehicles in wilderness areas of the park along with the threat of escaping fluids necessitate performing the difficult and expensive task of removal as soon as possible.

An immense amount of trash is left behind in the park by the migrants particularly in areas commonly used by legitimate park visitors and in wilderness regions. Food containers, plastic, burlap bags and clothing are among the most prevalent trash. Additionally, improperly disposed human waste is problematic along heavily used paths. The most obvious effect of both of these problems is aesthetic. The sight and smell of refuse in what was intended as a pristine natural area is contrary to the park's land management goals. Just as seriously, this matter has a detrimental effect on environmental quality and can present a health risk.

The threat of wildfire is a serious concern for land managers in this arid region. Battling wildfires is both costly and dangerous and even under the best of circumstances significant resources are allocated to their suppression. In border areas, however, natural ignition sources and careless legitimate visitors are less of threat than that presented by the use of campfires by undocumented aliens. It isn't possible to determine that wildfires caused by campfires were set by immigrants, U.S Forest Service records show a disproportionately high number of human induced fires start in areas along popular migration routes (United States Forest Service, 1998). Additionally, attempts to reduce fire dangers by performing prescribed fires on public lands are inhibited by the difficulty of ensuring that the area is unoccupied.

Not directly related to the monument's environmental features, but also of concern is crime associated with undocumented aliens. Crimes ranging from petty theft and vandalism to life threatening have become a common occurrence in Organ Pipe. Federal lands are not immune to the host of transgressions that are rampant in many southern border regions. Numerous instances of the breaking and entering of park buildings and employee residences have been reported with a serious loss of government equipment and property. Mitigation efforts such as alarms and physical barriers such as window and door bars have failed to reduce property crimes on public buildings (Immigration and Naturalization Service, 2002). Unattended buildings are subject to repeated robberies and vandalism. In other federal lands in Arizona, the situation has actually grown so serious that buildings have had to be abandoned. The San Bernardino National Wildlife Refuge in the south-western part of the state was reduced to levelling a large maintenance workshop after a government dump truck was stolen from it and used to destroy fences along the path back to Mexico (Immigration and Naturalization Service, 2002).

A more serious danger presents itself when narcotic smugglers utilize these migration routes. This region of Arizona is recognized as possessing some of the greatest potential for border and narcotics-related violence on the entire United States/Mexican border. Evidence collected by federal agencies has indicated that the organizations involved in this illicit activity have targeted individual federal employees who disrupt their shipments. Murder of Organ Pipe Ranger Kris Eggle was instrumental in an apprehension that resulted in the confiscation of hundreds of pounds of narcotics only days before his death (Fialka, 2003). Some smugglers are escorted by heavily armed scouts who are equipped with automatic assault weapons, encrypted radios, night vision optics, and even thermal imaging devices.

Park visitors and residents of neighbouring communities have expressed concern about encountering undocumented aliens or drug smugglers, who often mix in with groups of undocumented aliens. Due to this some park neighbours will not hike in the park or even visit it. There have been relatively few encounters and the vast majority of visitors are unlikely to see any illegal activity, but the potential for serious encounters is high.

A third set of impacts is upon park visitors and employees. The effects of large numbers of undocumented aliens and the smugglers who take refuge in their midst has been detrimental to both park users and federal workers. At minimum, the influx of these persons takes away from the wilderness experience sought by visitors. It also creates a situation where the public is hesitant to use areas of the park where this traffic primarily occurs or even avoid the park altogether. Park rangers spend a significant amount of time apprehending undocumented aliens, providing them with emergency medical services and disposing of abandoned vehicles. Park employees are compelled to plan their work in a way that minimizes their chances of encountering those involved in illegal activities. This disrupts optimal scheduling for many work activities such as resource management and science projects, and in some cases has resulted in certain projects not being carried out. Park employees also devote time to picking up litter and repairing damaged fences.

The ability of park staff to perform their duties is also reduced by this situation. Safety concerns have forced resource management personnel to go to the field in teams rather than individually. This redistribution of the limited number of persons available for this task reduces the effectiveness of the work and adds significantly to costs. Even more significantly, the danger levels have led to a reduced presence of rangers in certain park areas in order to reduce the potential conflicts. The situation has led to a number of resignations in park personnel and reluctance for qualified rangers to accept assignment there.

The reduced workforce is also forced to spend a significant portion of their time and resources on assisting the border patrol. National Park Service Rangers have the authority to enforce Federal Immigration laws which, in turn, requires them to detain undocumented migrants until agents of the U.S. Border Patrol arrive. The isolated location of Organ Pipe and the limited number of Border Patrol agents mean that any incident involving illegal migrants will occupy the ranger for, at minimum, one hour until they arrive. They also must perform contraband searches and provide humanitarian services until the Border Patrol assumes custody. This places a serious burden upon the ability of the ranger to complete the tasks assigned to his patrol.

Law Enforcement and Safety

The influence of large numbers of undocumented aliens is a serious hamper on the effective management of park resources and safety of visitors and staff. The migrant presence must be taken into account when planning any resource management or visitor use activities. The following section addresses methods by which park staff can best attempt to perform the duties of which they were entrusted.

The creation of a situation where Organ Pipe can be used and managed without fear of criminal activity must be the primary focus. While the shifting of available resources towards addressing the law enforcement issue and away from traditional environmental and cultural park activities, the reestablishment of control over park lands is the surest way to prevent their further degradation. The most basic way to regain a sense of lawfulness in the park is to increase the presence of security personnel. Additional rangers, properly trained and outfitted, are the first step towards regaining the public's confidence. Although funding this may take away from other park activity budgets, it is the most important measure available to park managers.

A step towards improving law enforcement activities in Organ Pipe and other public lands in Arizona and New Mexico was the signing of a memorandum of understanding (MOU) in March 2001 among the National Park Service, Border Patrol, Bureau of Land Management, U.S. Fish and Wildlife Service and the Natural Resources Conservation Service (Immigration and Naturalization Service, 2002). The focus of this agreement was to further inter-agency cooperation and to provide a more standardized level of training for organizations traditionally not in the role of border security. An increased presence by members of these organizations could serve to curtail the current deficiency of available park rangers. The synergistic utilization of regional law enforcement personnel would also be furthered by adopting similar equipment and communications procedures. Another mitigation measure is to evaluate the design and management of park areas and facilities. The use of lighting and fencing could serve to discourage illegal activities at high-risk sites. Alternatively, these sites could be relocated in safer areas or temporarily restricted or closed to the public.

Natural Resource Protection

Observing the Park Service's conservation goals has been difficult in the current park-operating environment. To gain an understanding of the extent of the damage incurred, a thorough resource inventory should be undertaken. Through a comparison of this data to previous studies the effects of resource protection measures can be determined. The key proactive resource protection action is tied to law enforcement patrol locations. When the resource inventory determines the most sensitive and endangered areas, an increased presence by park rangers or other enforcement personnel can reduce the migrant traffic and further environmental damages in these places. For restoring areas already damaged, a systematic program of rehabilitation could take place behind the heightened protective measures. For actions such as removal of accumulated trash, trail and riparian area rehabilitation and restoration of vandalized natural features, park employees could be aided by volunteer groups or seasonal hires. More intensive measures like abandoned vehicle removal and road repairs could be aided by employing private contractors to a greater extent.

Conclusions

The situation in Organ Pipe N.M. is only one part of a larger problem in South-western public land management. Public land managers and rangers are forced to confront situations such as border defence and counter-drug operations which should be managed and performed by other agencies. However, until legislators and policy makers create an environment where these agencies can conduct these tasks properly and thoroughly, these non-traditional tasking simply cannot be ignored by park managers. Through the wise use of their available resources and those of cooperating entities, the Organ Pipe management can prioritize and address the most critical threats to the park. In the long term, park managers must make their plight more widely known both to the government and especially to the public in order to ensure the preservation of Organ Pipe's unique natural and cultural resources for future generations.

References

Anderson, Dorothy H.; David W. Lime; and Theresa L. Wang (1998) Maintaining *the Quality of Park Resources and Visitor Experiences: A Handbook for Managers,* prepared for the Cooperative Park Studies Unit, Department of Forest Resources, University of Minnesota, St. Paul: University of Minnesota.

Bercherer, Max (2002) "Perilous Parks: Border's Sensitive Areas are Trampled", Arizona *Daily Star*, September 9.

Blinkly, Gail (2000) "Migrants Leave Trail of Trash", High *Country News*, October 9.

Bustos, Sergio (2002) "Arizona Tops for Border-Crossing", *the Arizona Republic*, December 28.

Butts, Mike (2002) "Drug Runners, Migrants Crushing Wilderness along Mexican Border", *The Arizona Republic*, June 13.

Clynes, Tom. (2003) Arizona Park Most Dangerous in U.S.", National *Geographic News*, January 13.

Custred, Glenn. (2000) "Alien Crossings", the *American Spectator*, October.

Dinan, Steven. (2002). "Arizona Site of Killing Rated as Most Dangerous," The *Washington Times*, August 13.

Fialka, John (2003) "The Death of a Ranger Shows Venerable Job's New Hazards", *The Wall Street Journal*, January 22.

Immigration and Naturalization Service (INS) (2002) *Report to the House of Representatives Committee on Appropriations on Impacts Caused by Undocumented Aliens Crossing Federal Lands in Southeast Arizona*, Phoenix: U.S. Immigration and Naturalization Service.

Malkin, Michelle (2002) *Invasion: How America Still Welcomes Terrorists, Criminals, and Other Foreign Menaces to Our Shores,* Washington DC: Regnery Publishing.

McIntyre, David L. and John R. Weeks (2002) "Environmental Impacts of Illegal Immigration on the Cleveland National Forest in California", *Professional Geographer*, 54:2(392-405).

National Park Service (NPS), United States Department of the Interior, World Wide Web available at http://www.nps.gov/orpi/.

National Park Service (NPS), United States Department of Interior (1997) *Organ Pipe Cactus National Monument General Management Plan Final Environmental Impact Statement,* Ajo AZ: National Park Service.

National Park Service (NPS), United States Department of Interior (1997) *Final Supplemental*

Environmental Impact Statement-Re-Analysis of Cumulative Impacts on the Sonoran Pronghorn, Ajo, AZ: National Park Service.

United States Forest Service (USFS), United States Department of Agriculture (1998) *Border Agency Fire Control, USDA*, San Diego: United States Department of Agriculture, United States Forest Service.

Wellman, William (the Superintendent of Organ Pipe National Monument, May 2003) Telephone interviews.

5

Changing Geography of Health and Health Care in Romania in the Last Decade of the 20th Century

Liliana Dumitrache

Introduction

The WHO defines health as a state of complete physical, mental and social well-being and not merely by the absence of disease. The health state of the population should be a major concern of every country, its preservation being an essential requirement for a productive life. In other words, only a healthy population can warrant the economic and social progress; only a healthy population can offer the premises for macroeconomic changes.

The determinants of health status involve *economic factors* such as personnel income or nutritional status; *health care* in terms of access and quality, *health behaviour*, that is: diet, bad habits (like smoking, drinking,) and *social and physical environment*, social condition, stress, exposure to pollutants, professional risks.

The economical condition is correlated to the population health state, the poverty state being associated to a damaged health condition all the time. The law incomes can affect the access-(meaning limitation) to resources such as food, living facilities, treatments and medicine; in this case, health care and social policies should take into account the unfortunate social class condition.

Health expenditures are also influenced by the level of the development that is generally speaking, the richer a country is, the higher health expenses grow.

The access to sanitary services, their quality and competence of the medical staff, even if they don't have a determinant role, are also affecting the population health condition, while a higher level of training and an adequate infrastructure are determining a regain of health their inadequate situation is considerably reducing this opportunity.

The health behaviour or the lifestyle plays an important role in the etiology of some diseases; some unhealthy habits such as smoking, alcohol consumption, sedentary life and obesity are contributing to the worsening of illnesses.

The quality of the environment can drive a positive or a negative impact even if indirect or secondary on human health. The assessment of this impact is very difficult; generally it is considered that its dimension depends on the type of the pollutants and its lasting, but the human response to them isn't homogenous, some people being more sensitive than others.

Each of these determinants could influence the Health State in a certain degree but the health problems are generated by their common action most of the time. The health state depends not only on the volume and quality of the current inflows, but also on the health inherited from a previous period. However, the current inflows can influence the future Health State in terms of appreciation -if the balance of the flow is positive- or depreciation- if the balance of this flow is negative.

The illness is limiting the individual autonomy, is reducing his work capacity and efficiency; to provide a good population health means to extent the working time limit and also to reduce social costs and public expenses.

Health was entirely neglected during the totalitarian period and as result, the Romanian population has inherited a precarious Health State having to face a major health problem like high infant mortality rates, reduced life expectancy and high incidence of infections diseases in 1990.

Since the Revolution of 1989, Romania has gone through a period of rapid and major changes in every sector. The reform in each sector (administrative, social, health, education) is being undertaken against a background of economic crisis, with a steep fall of GDP and a rising inflation associated to a sharp increase in unemployment.

The difficulties associated to the period of transition expressed by the decrease of the living standards and the proliferation of poverty, the low efficiency of the medical assistance, the lack of equipment and medicine have led to a continuously deterioration of the Health State situation reflected by the values of health indicators.

In order to show the particular situation of Romania, the health indicators, were comparatively and evolutionarily analyzed, where possible, in a European Context.

Evaluation of Health Status

General Mortality rate: Table 5.1 shows the evolution of the general mortality rates in selected European Countries. One can notice a visibly higher mortality rate in the Eastern European Countries in comparison with the Western ones.

Moreover, starting with 1990, the values of this indicator are decreasing in the Western European Countries, while, in the Eastern ones, the values show continuously increasing differences (5‰) in mortality between West and East.

During 1995-2000 Bulgaria, Hungary and Romania had registered the highest mortality rates in Europe (Table 5.1).

The steady increase of general mortality in Romania represents an effect of the scarce attention accorded to the people's health in the communist regime, but it also represents a sign of the present depreciation of Health State.

Table 5.1: General Mortality Rate in Selected European Countries

Country	1970-1975	1990-1995	1995-2000
Romania	9.4	11.1	12.7
Bulgaria	9.7	12.7	13.4
Hungary	11.8	14.6	14.1
Poland	8.3	10.5	10.0
France	10.6	9.8	9.2
Italy	9.8	9.9	9.6
Netherlands	8.3	8.8	8.9

Source: World Resources 1996-1997, Human Development Report, 2001.

As far as the structure of deaths by the main causes is concerned, Romania follows the tendency of other European Countries' but with more important differences.

The main cause of deaths in European Countries-was the *circulatory system diseases* (Table 5.2).

However, one can notice important differences between the Western European Countries and the Eastern European Countries and especially between the latter countries and Romania.

The mortality due to such diseases is considerably lower in the Western European Countries, while in the Eastern ones, its level keeps higher; Romania registered the highest specific death rate at the time.

The second death cause in all European Countries was tumours (cancer). The differences between the values of cancer mortality in the countries of the region are less spectacular; Romania and Bulgaria registered the lowest mortality rates, but only because of their incomplete or delayed detection of the disease.

The respiratory system diseases represent a less frequent death cause than the circulatory system diseases or cancers. However, in Eastern Europe, their frequency is still high. Mortality values place Romania again on the first position, followed by Bulgaria and Hungary.

The mortality due to *digestive system diseases* also shows differences between Western and Eastern European Countries, Hungary and Romania holding the leading places.

Table 5.2: Major Causes of Deaths in Selected European Countries (Cases per 100000 Inhabitants)

Diseases	Romania	Bulgaria	Hungary	Poland
Circulatory system diseases	815	764	726	653
Cancers	172	173	304	234
Respiratory system diseases	87	60	67	44
Digestive system diseases	68	36	114	38

Contd...

Diseases	France	Italy	Netherlands
Circulatory system diseases	273	378	346
Cancers	233	234	238
Respiratory system diseases	60	53	67
Digestive system diseases	43	45	32

Source: Comisia Nationala de Statistica, Bucuresti

In Romania, the level and the structure of mortality show a deterioration of the health situation, expressed by the increasing number of deaths due to cancer or digestive system diseases. However, an encouraging fact is the decreasing tendency of the mortality due to respiratory system diseases, which is a result of mass vaccinations and of the reducing exposure to pollutants, taking into account that many pollutant enterprises were closed down. The distribution of these death rates at national level emphasizes the important differences among Romanian counties.

The circulatory system diseases present a higher frequency (over 1000 cases/100,000 inhabitants) in the Western parts of the country, especially in Arad, Bihor, Salaj and also in South-Western counties (Giurgiu, Mehedinti, Dolj). The main risk causes of the circulatory system diseases are hypertension, cholesterol and smoking. Other related factors are obesity and sedentary life. Some of these factors such as consumption of fats, hot spices, food and spirits are typical for these regions.

A high frequency of *tumours*-over than 200 cases/100,000 inhabitants are also registered in the Western parts of Romania, counties as Timis, Arad, Bihor being again on the top of the list.

High values of mortality due to tumours characterize some counties from Transylvania-Cluj, Maramures, Alba or Mures. The lifestyle (smoking and drinking), the reproductive behaviour and genetic factors are also incriminated to increase the risks of cancers.

The deaths rates due to *respiratory system diseases*, even if they have decreased lately, still show higher frequencies rates in some counties from the Southern or Eastern parts of Romania, especially in Teleorman, Giurgiu, Calarasi, Botosani, Neamt, Vaslui.

The mortality rate due to the *digestive system diseases* still remains high in the Southern part of Romania, especially in Giurgiu, Calarasi and Buzau counties.

Infant Mortality: This is an indicator which reflects not only the level of general development, but also the efficiency of medical assistance. The value of the infant mortality rate proves again the Romania's particular situation in the communist regime as well as in the actual period.

Table 5.3 shows the important differences in the level of the infant mortality between the Western and Eastern European Countries. During 1970-1975 Romania had registered the highest infant mortality rate in Europe—40 percent. After 1990, even if its level has significantly decreased—19 percent, Romania's position still remains stable in the top. However, we have to mention that the actual values of the infant mortality rates do not necessarily reflect the decrease in the numbers of the infant deaths, but it might as well be a result of the decreasing number of births (Table 5.3).

Table 5.3: Infant Mortality Rate in Selected European Countries

Country	1970-1975	1990-1995	1997	2000
Romania	40.0	23.0	22.3	18,6
Bulgaria	26.0	14.0	15.8	14
Hungary	34.0	15.0	10.9	9
Poland	27.0	15.0	12.1	9
France	16.0	7.0	5.0	5
Italy	26.0	8.0	6.2	6
Netherlands	12.0	7.0	5.4	5

Source: World Resources 1996-1997; Human Development Report, 2001; Anuarul Demografic al Romaniei, 2000.

The analysis of the distribution of infant mortality values on the Romanian territory shows that differences still keep high, the value of 30‰ being often exceeded in: Ialomita, Calarasi, Bihor counties.

More deaths are also caused by congenital anomalies and pneumonia .If anomalies are determined by internal factors, difficult to be controlled, deaths by pneumonia are due to socio-economic and sanitary factors, which vary according to the social environment.

Life expectancy

The high rates of general and infant mortality have a negative influence on longevity, thus, Romania and Hungary show the lowest levels of life expectancy. While in the Western European Countries the very high values had already dropped, in Romania, no important change has been noted since 1960, the values orbiting around 69 years.

At present, the difference in life expectancy level between Romania and the Western European Countries is about 8 years. In comparison to the Eastern European Countries, Romania shows the lowest life expectancy in males, while female life expectancy is closer to the Eastern European average. This indicator varies between 66 and 72 years, lower values being characteristic for the North-West and South-East counties.

Incidence of infectious diseases: An alarming fact in Romania is the increasing incidence during 1990-2000 of certain infection diseases as tuberculosis or hepatitis and AIDS. The occurrence of local cholera epidemics, infections with Salmonella and Trichina should also represent a major and urgent concern for the Romanian authorities.

The analysis of the health indicators in the European Context reveals the precarious Health State of the Romanian population in comparison both to Western Countries and to the countries which are living through a transition phase themselves.

Health Index: The values of Health Index show the oscillations over the years of the health status of the population. Considering only the values of the Health index at the beginning and at the end of the period, 1990-2000 one can say there are insignificant changes in the population health state, the value of health index being 0,438 in 1990 and respectively 0,431 in 2000. By knowing that the population Health State improves as the index value gets closer to "0", we can conclude that health state of the population improved. However, the only 0.007 small differences between these two indices show that this improvement is not significant.

The health index of the Romanian population also shows significant regional differences; in 1997, the values of this index varying between 0.689 and 0.239 with an average of 0.465.

The counties can be grouped as follows:

- Counties with severe health problems, their index value exceeding 0.500.
- Counties with a frail Health State their index value is between 0.465-0.500.

- Counties with a good Health State, including the former ones where the index values are lower than 0.465.

  One can notice some differences in 2001 than in 1990
- The extension of the areas having serious health problems, associated to the reduction of the areas being on good health.
- The deterioration of the population Health State in the areas which were registered in 1990 as having a frail Health State: Olt, Arad, Mures, Buzau.

Fortunately, an inverse situation exists: the counties which in 1994 were identified as having severe health problems or a frail Health State, improved their Health State: Satu Mare, Maramures, Bistrita Nasaud in the North of the country, Hunedoara, Galati, Constanta.in the South. The improvement of the population Health State in these counties is a result of the decreasing rates of death due to respiratory system diseases, as much as, to the decreasing of the infant mortality rates.

The considerably decreasing of the respiratory system diseases in these areas might be a consequence of closing down the industrial pollutant enterprises.

The reduced rates of infant mortality in these counties reflect a general trend of decreasing the natality.

In fact, the reduced value of the Health Index a 0.465 in 1997, compared to 0.482 in 1994 should be considered an improvement of the general Health State.

Analysis of Health Care Status

After all, health care systems reflect the norms and the values of the society they were set in. A better organization of health care systems and a more efficient resource distribution may be the premises of higher quality in the health systems, and finally, in the health state of the entire population.

The Structure of the Romanian Health Care System

Romania has had a long tradition in organizing health care. Between the First and Second World War there was a social insurance system based on the Bismarkian sick -fund model. In 1949, the "Law on State Health Organization" was passed and there was a gradual transition to a Semashko health system. The main features of the Romanian Health Care System during these four decades were: government financing, central planning, rigid management and a state monopoly over health services. The absence of a private sector and the fact that all professionists in the health system have the status of salaried civil servants were also to be noted.

This centralized organization, the lack of competition or individual initiative, a persistent under funding, inefficiency and inflexible norms and inadequate health care equipment have increased the sanitary system crisis, leading to an increasing pressure for change. The sanitary reform began in the 1990 and had, as a principal objective the decentralization of the health care system by introducing the Health Insurance Law.

Among its other objectives were: to restructure the primary care system and to separate it from the secondary care (polyclinics) and tertiary care (hospitals) system; to change the physician-patient relationship by introducing the family-doctor and to improve the quality and the efficiency of medical assistance.

Seven years later, the health system still keeps state owned and it is coordinated by the Ministry of Health through 42 district health directorates which, consist of a network of hospitals, polyclinics, dispensaries and other health institutions. A certain number of specialized or single specialty hospitals, medical institutes and institutions for continuing education of health professionals are directly responsible to the Ministry of Health.

One can notice the existence of around 4,000 private surgeries of 2,800 dentist's and over 3,000 pharmacies. However, private practice in the primary and secondary state's health care provide only a very small percentage of medical care, the privatization process having been more active in dentistry so far.

The allocation of financial resources may encounter many difficulties, Romania still being a country that applies general tax systems in order to finance Health Care. The Law of Social Insurance hasn't been put to work since the Houses of Insurance, meant to collect the money obtained from insurance payments, are totally absent, and therefore, all funds are directed to the State Budget, which, in its turn, spares only small shares for Health Services (around 8-9 percent of total government expenditure).

The total State funding for health are distributed both to the Ministry of Health and to the other Ministries with Health networks as "budgetary items". This means that funds are allocated for specific purposes and may not be transferred between spending categories.

Other external sources of finance as the local Special Funds for Health (deriving from a monthly 2 percent contribution from individuals' and enterprises' gross income, a 10 percent tax on tobacco and alcohol advertising expenditures and a 1 percent tax on tobacco and alcohol sales) are supplementing the Ministry of Health Budget.

At present, even if the *Houses of Insurance* have been set up, it is not so easy to supply their health providers with the corresponding funds. The funds continued to be collected by the Ministry of Finances, which have difficulties in transferring the money to the health providers, in time, this situation generating many scandals and discontentment. Moreover, taking into account the high percentage of indebted persons (represented by the retired and the unemployed), we might as well find out that the collected funds are not so great after all, and a subsequent change of funding through social insurance will not necessarily supply the immediate resources for health investments, since they have to be supplemented on by budgetary funds.

As regards the dispensaries that have to perform primary medical functions and provide urgent treatments, we should mention that they have scarce infrastructure, because they work on out dated equipment, they are discontinuously supplied with sanitary materials and medication and they lack well-trained personnel.

As result, the population would rather go in for secondary care services, even if they cost more.

People's scarce information on the role of the family doctor lead the first attempt of implementing this kind of system at a national scale, to failure in 1997, although the 1992 experiment in some selected counties ran successfully. Therefore, it is obvious that the implementation of the sanitary reform will still take a lot of time and its result will be long waited for.

The Level of Health Care Services

Romania, as many other Eastern European Countries, has shifted its focus on healing the ailments, rather than on their foreseeing and that is why, primary health care has been taken over by the secondary ones. This trend is clearly suggested by the great number of specialists and hospital beds. In Romania, there were 486 inhabitants per physician in 2000, that is even more than in developed countries, but instead there were fewer hospitals. For this reason, hospitals are poorly equipped and they may often fail in providing good health care since they lack reactive and chemicals. Unfortunately, there is no hope of improvement since the financial resources distributed to Health Care Systems are highly deficient (Table 5.4).

For instance, both actual expenditures and GDP shares of the Health Care System have constantly decreased ever since 1990, so that in 1997, they have received only a 2.6 percent share of the GDP (20 USD/person/year) and around 3 percent in 2000

By considering the number of physicians and the number of medical units, the specialists appreciated that the level of the sanitary services couldn't exceed the medium limit in the Eastern Region. However, at the national level, there are many disparities which are reflected by the variations of the Health Index by county.

Table 5.4: Some Indicators of Health Care in Selected European Countries (1997-2000)

Country	Inhabitants per hospital bed	Inhabitants per physician	Health expenditures as percent of GDP		
			1990	1997	2000
Romania	132	486	3.9	2.6	3
Bulgaria	67	389	5.4	4.7	3,8
Hungary	97	280	6.0	6.9	5,2
Poland	180	431	5.1	4.6	4,5
France	109	357	9.1	9.7	7,3
Italy	131	208	8.3	8.5	5,6
Netherlands	170	400	8.7	8.8	6

Source: World Resources 1996-1997 and Comisia Nationala pentru Statistica, Bucuresti.

In 1997, the values of Health Service Index were ranging from 0.181 to 0.578 around an average of 0.300.

Taking into account that a reduced value of this index asks for a higher level of sanitary services, the counties can be grouped as follow:

- Areas with a low level of medical assistance, when the values of Health Services Index exceeds 0.300;
- Areas with a medium level of medical assistance, when the values of the Health Services Index ranges between 0.200 to 0.300;
- Areas with a high level of medical assistance, when Health Index values are smaller than 0.200.

The analysis of the distribution of these areas shows a predominance of the medium level medical assistance.

However, one can notice a number of 13 counties in South and South-Eastern Romania with a low level of medical assistance, while only 4 counties-Cluj, Iasi, Sibiu, Covasna and Bucharest registered a higher level.

The highly ranges of Health State levels lead to uneven funding of health care systems. This fact can obviously be identified in areas with serious health problems, or in areas with low-quality health care systems, but it doesn't necessarily imply that there is any connection between them. However, poor health care systems will still be prevalent as long as there is no sizeable funding.

The Health Index-Health Service Index relationship warns that improvements of sanitary conditions will not necessarily lead to significant improvements in population's health state and therefore, other non-medical steps are required.

Conclusion

This paper has analyzed changes in the state of Health of the Romanian Population and the provision of health services in the post communist period. It is clear that the state of health has been continuously deteriorating and that the Romanian population is less healthy than both other communist countries of CEE and countries of Western of Europe.

The structure of health care system has not been significantly modified since the collapse of communism and it struggling to cope with current health problems.

Health services have not adapted to changing conditions, primary care services are inefficient and the distribution of medical personnel is inadequate. However, this analysis has suggested that reform of health care system, for example through increased funding, may not alone be sufficient to improve the health state of the population. Instead, efforts need to be taken to educate the population about more healthy patterns of behaviour, while issues of socio-economic status (particularly poverty) also need to be urgently addressed.

References

Enăchescu, D. and Vlădescu, C. (1995) '*Politica socială în domeniul sănătății'*, România în context european, Editura Alternative, Bucureşti.'

Guvernul României (1995) "*Raportul Dezvoltării Umane în România*", Bucureşti.

I.M.C. (Institute for Mother and Child) (1993) *Reproductive Health Survey- Romania*; Preliminary Report, Bucharest'

Mihăilă , V.and Bejan, T. (1995) '*Analiza cluster aplicată studiului inegalităților în asistența sanitară în județele României*, caiet documentar nr.14, I.N.S.S.C., Bucureşti.'

Ministerul Sănătății (1995) '*Raport privind activitatea desfăşurată în perioada nov.1992-oct.1995*, Bucureşti.

O.M.S. (1995) *Rapport sur la Santé dans le Monde*, Genève.

O.M.S. (1995) *Promotion de la santé et action communautaire en faveur de la santé dans les pays de l'O.M.S.*, Genève.

Popa, I. and Enăchescu, D. (1990) '*Indicatori agregați ai stării de sănătate şi aplicabilitatea lor în sănătatea publică.*' I.N.S.S.C., Bucureşti.

Tinu, A.M. (1995) *Women's Health Profile: Romania (Country Report)*, prepared for Conference on the Health of Women in Central and Eastern Europe, Vienna.

U.N.I.C.E.F. (1995) *Statistică socială, culegere de date*, Bucureşti.

6

State of Health of the Hungarian Population in the Period of Transition

Eva Edit Kiss

Introduction

During the decades of socialism (1945-1989) major changes took place in the social and economic development of Hungary that have also influenced the population's state of health. During the first two decades, after 1945, the favourable trends dominated. In this extensive period a significant social and economic progress can be observed. A series of towns and industrial plants were established without consideration to the impact on the physical environment. Economy, mainly heavy industry, developed at a fast rate. The socialist transformation of agriculture was completed, housing conditions improved, the network of public health services was extended and no rural region was left without local doctors. Therefore, living conditions along with the state of health of the Hungarian population improved (Orosz, 1985). However, from the mid-1960s some negative effects upon the way of life and living conditions could also be observed. The reasons of such negative effects are industrialisation of rural regions, huge social and regional mobility, transformation of the settlement structure. The continuous deterioration of the quality of environment (Enyedi, 2000), on the one hand, has contributed to the poorer state of health. On the other hand, in the 1980s those intentions and ecological movements were strengthened which had pressed the formation of state environmental protection politics and put the environmental issues to the forefront. In spite of this, essential changes did not take place. Neither the population's state of health nor the quality of settlement environment were improved.

In the history of Hungary the 1989 was a significant year when the socialist system collapsed and market economy began to take shape. As a consequence of the change in the political system radical social and economic reforms affected all walks of life. Many of them involved favourable changes and an increasing emphasis was put on environmental protection. In spite of these, the state of health of the Hungarian population further worsened, even at an accelerated rate. As a result, today the poor state of health is considered as a big problem in

Hungary. According to a representative national survey (Bernát, 2002) 75 percent of the inquired persons have selected housing conditions, environment pollution, education, suicide, livelihood, public security as the factors, while in 1988 it was only 50 percent. This means that the situation is worst in case of the state of health of the population. The reasons of such condition are very complex. However, the two basic causes—the unfavourable heritage of socialism and the negative impacts of the change in the political system lead to emergence of unemployment, frequent price rises, an increase in poverty, widening of social and income differences, decline in public health services. These have directly or indirectly affected health conditions. Not only has the population's state of health deteriorated in consequence of change in the political system, but the previously hidden symptoms have also been exposed. They even aggravated the former systems of damaging effects.

The basic aim of this paper is to demonstrate some characteristics of the state of health of the Hungarian population. How and why it changed in the period of transition. The paper is based on latest statistical data, however, some experiences of a survey carried out in the less developed rural settlements (Sarud, Tiszakeszi, Tiszaszentimre, Újszentmargita) situated in the Mid-Tisza Region in 1998 are also included to confirm national trends and to indicate some special features particularly of rural state of health. Originally this survey was carried out in 1998 in order to reveal the changes in the rural living circumstances (Kiss, 2001), but part of the results regarding the state of health are used here also. On the other hand, they are still valid and suitable (despite their relatively low rate) for indicating some phenomena and trends because since then no significant changes comparable to those in the beginning of the 1990s occurred. In Sarud 44 households (189 persons), in Tiszakeszi 44 households (174 persons), in Tiszaszentimre 58 households (270 persons) and in Újszentmargita 49 households (211 persons) were interviewed and they represented 7.6 percent of the households in Sarud, 4.6 percent in Tiszakeszi, 5.8 percent in Tiszaszentimre and 8.2 percent in Újszentmargita. In this way, information on 10-12 percent of the population's state of health was made available in each settlement except for Tiszakeszi where the households surveyed represented only 6.4 percent of the population (of the four settlements this is the largest one with more than 2000 inhabitants).

After the introduction some major indicators of state of health are introduced with particular reference to the main causes of death. Then, in the second section the effects of the changes and challenges of the transition period on the spatial and social variations in the state of health are evaluated. Finally some perspectives are outlined.

Major indicators of State of Health

Number of population: State of health occupies a central place among the quality features of population because it determines economic activity, tolerable loading and relationship of the population to their work. It is evident that a healthy man can concentrate better, he is capable of more long-lasting efforts and generally greater achievements than an unhealthy man. State of health depends on numerous factors such as way of life, income situation, social and economic development, demographic conditions, standard of health services as well as other objective and subjective elements. That is why, it is extremely difficult to evaluate it and it is usually possible with taking many factors into consideration. The most frequently used indicators of the population's state of health are demographic data, number and composition of acute and chronic diseases, number of patients hospitalised, number of disabled people etc. Among them the number of population is one of the most important.

Since 1981 the population of Hungary has constantly been decreasing. It was not expected -according to the statistical estimations- that there will be essential improvement in the near future. The number of population of the country declined to half a million (from 10.7 millions to 10.2 millions) between 1980 and 2001. Today it is not only the population of many villages but also the population of majority of the towns is dwindling. The negative balance of natural increase is the main reason as for some years 20-40000 more people died than were born. The number of deaths increased in the 1970s, and then from 1980 it has become stable on a permanently high level. In the beginning of the 1990s Hungary occupied the last place among the European countries in terms of the number of live-births (12.80) per 1000 inhabitants but in terms of the number of deaths per 1000 inhabitants (14.3) was the first. During the last decade there was no significant change in such unfavourable conditions (Tables 6.1 and Table 6.2).

What is the reason for it? This is primarily explained by the increasing death rates of men, though lately the death rate of women has also increased. It is extremely unfavourable that in the 1990s the deaths of young and middle aged adults had increased. Between 1980 and 2001 the rate of deaths of 30-39 years old men from all deaths has increased from 1.6 percent to 2.2 percent and the rate of 40-49 years old from 3.3 percent to 9.5 percent. Similarly, in case of women an increase of almost similar size is experienced because the rate of 30-39 year age group women has increased from 0.7 percent to 0.9 percent and of the 40-49 year age group women from 1.7 percent to 4.2 percent. In spite of this, the dominance of women in the older age groups still exists. During the last decade the mortality of old people did not essentially change, although the ageing which has begun since 1960s has continued. This represented 76 percent of the deaths in

1980 and 78 percent in 2001. Between 1980 and 2001 the rate of population growth of less than 14 years of age decreased from 22 percent to 17 percent, but the rate of people of 60 year old and above increased from 17 percent to 20 percent. The mortality of men also exceeds the mortality of women within the category of 60 year old and above in the population. This can be fundamentally traced back to the physiological reasons (Table 6.1).

Table 6.1: Some Major Demographic Data of Hungary

Year	Number of population in Thousands	Gender		Life expectancy at Birth		percent of 0 -14 year old population	percent of 60 & + year old population
		male	female	male	female		
1949	8204	4423	3781	59.3	63.4	24.8	11.6
1960	9961	4804	5157	65.9	70.1	25.4	13.8
1970	10322	5004	5318	66.3	72.1	21.1	17.1
1980	10710	5189	5521	65.5	72.7	21.9	17.1
1990	10375	4985	5390	65.1	73.7	20.5	18.9
2000	10199*	4851	5348	67.1	75.6	17.1	19.6

*Data from 2001.

Source: Yearbook of Health Statistics, 2000 and Statistical Yearbook of Hungary, 2001.

Table 6.2: Main Data of Vital Statistics of Hungary

Demographic Attributes	Year				
	1970	1980	1990	1995	2000
Live births	151819	148673	125679	112054	97597
Deaths	120197	145355	145660	145431	135601
Natural increase or decrease (-)	31622	3318	-19981	-33377	-38004
Infant deaths	5449	3443	1863	1195	900
Live births per 1000 Population	14.7	13.9	12.1	11.0	9.7
Deaths per 1000 population	11.6	13.6	14.1	14.2	13.5
Infant deaths per 1000 live births	35.9	23.2	14.8	10.7	9.2

Source: Yearbook of Health Statistics, 2000.

In the past decades the most favourable development was in the form of a decline in the mortality rate of infants. This was noticed due to an improvement in the health care facilities of infants and mothers. The percentage of deaths of one year old infants in 1980 was 2.70 percent, while in 2001 this figure came down to 0.6 percent. This is still higher on an international comparison. This is also confirmed by the high number of deaths (8.2 percent) per 1000 live-births of under one year age in 2001. This figure indicates slightly better position than that of some former socialist countries such as Rumania, Russia, and Bulgaria. It is also a remarkable achievement that the death rate of childhood population particularly of boys has decreased in 2000 (Table 6.2).

Deaths and Their Causes: The death rates of the Hungarian population have always been below the death rates of other European countries over the 20th century. This is especially true for the decades between 1965 and 1995 because the favourable processes of the former decades were broken in the 1960s. This is also reflected in the average life-expectancy at birth primarily of men. There was a decline of 1.6 year in the life expectancy of men between 1960 and 1990. But especially from the mid-1990s it shows a slow increase and now it is about 67 years. At the same time average life-expectancy at birth for women increased by 5.5 years over the same period and now it is almost 76 years. However, the data of average life-expectancy at birth of the Hungarian population are still the worst among the European countries (Table 6.1).

For many years the effects of leading causes of death remains the same and their proportions in total deaths have not changed considerably except for the rate of deaths caused by neoplasm. Deaths caused by the diseases of the heart and circulatory, cerebrovascular systems are still on the first place. About 53 percent of total deaths in 1980 and 50 percent in 2001 were caused by them. During 1980-2001 the rate of deaths caused by diseases of neoplasm increased from 19 percent to 26 percent and this placed on second order. During the last decade the rate of deaths (4.8 percent) caused by liver disease occupied third position. Their number has doubled between 1980 and 2001, but the increase was particularly spectacular at the end of 1990s. Now their number exceeds 6000. All three leading groups of causes of death amount to almost 81 percent of deaths. According to the number of deaths per 1000 population we are still in the forefront among the developed countries, which is very unfavourable. Deaths by accident occupy the fourth place as their proportion has decreased from 4.9 percent to 4.7 percent. Their number (8760) was the highest in 1990. Besides these, the rate of deaths caused by suicides and chronic diseases of the respiratory system (excluding tuberculosis) are considerable, although the number of both has spectacularly decreased during the last ten years (Table 6.3).

Table 6.3: Major Causes of Deaths in Hungary

Major Causes of Death	Year			
	1980	1990	2000	2001
	145355*	145660*	135601*	132000*
Malignant neoplasms	27550	30871	33280	33500
Heart-diseases	38501	38908	38656	37500
Cerebrovascular diseases	24851	21347	19839	18700
Arteriosclerosis	9709	11408	7550	6800
Bronchitis, emphysema, asthma	7043	4800	3732	3100
Diseases of liver	3040	5570	6883	6400
Accidents	7158	8760	5875	6200
Suicide and self-injury	4809	4133	3289	3100

* Total Deaths by all Reasons
Source: Statistical Yearbook of Hungary, 2001

The most frequent causes (diseases) of deaths are widespread in Hungary. Numerous factors such as improper way of life, unhealthy food, malnutrition, unsatisfactory physical exercise, heavy smoking and consumption of alcohol, permanent stress, unfavourable social and economic circumstances, heavily polluted environment etc. are very complicated and their cumulative effects manifest even in an increased degree. Generally exact information on such factors is not always available. Here, it has to be mentioned and emphasized that the transition period which came to its end involved grave social conflicts and tensions. This has indirectly also contributed to the development of the factors mentioned above and played the role in deteriorating the state of health. Even today, quite a lot of people suffering from diseases of the heart and circulatory, respiratory and digestive systems and of neoplasm also receive medical treatment in the shorter or longer term.

In the studied rural settlements 26-29 percent of the inquired have reported about regular problem of their health. The majority of them are women. Most of their complaints concerned the heart and circulatory system, headache, nervous system, respiratory and digestive systems and to locomotor disorders. This order accords with the most widespread diseases and with the leading causes of death. With a view to this there were no major differences between genders.

Turnover of Some Health Establishments: The turnover of patients in the polyclinics, in different clinics and hospitals is still high though a decline in this and an improvement in health status have been noticed since 1990. This may be due to the reform of the health services, cessation of the health service without payment, the spreading of naturopathy and introduction of the free choice of physicians. Pulmonary dispensaries clearly demonstrate that decreasing turnover of patients does not always mean fewer patients. In these establishments the turnover of patients between 1990 and 2001 decreased from 2077 thousands to 2035 thousands, however, the number of new T.B. patients increased from 3330 to 3598 (Table 6.4).

Table 6.4: Some Major Data of Dispensaries in Hungary

Patients or Dispensaries	1980	1990	2000
Number of TB patients	15548	11176	3314
Number of new TB patients	5412	3330	3598
Number of registered non-TB patients with pulmonary	115264	177565	390772
Number of new psychiatric patients taken in care	18644	19719	22432
Number of registered patients of psychiatric dispensaries	107698	127884	130762
Number of registered alcoholics in dispensaries	49950	64416	40867
Turnover of pulmonary TB-clinics (thousands)	2476	2077	2035
Turnover of psychiatric dispensaries (thousands)	731	921	1262
Turnover of addictology dispensaries (thousands)	227	209	178

Source: Yearbook of Health Statistics, 2000.

The turnover of psychiatric dispensaries has increased by 27 percent during the last decade. In other words, in 2000 more than 1.26 million people appeared in these establishments. These data are very important because they indicate that the changes took place in all walks of life over the whole country after 1989. It means spiritually a huge burden. Facing such problems is also an enormous stress and as it is very difficult to cope with it they often lead to the development of neurotic symptoms and diseases of nervous system. This explains the increase of new and registered psychiatric patients.

In the less developed villages the turnover of local health establishments (surgery, pharmacy) is high because of poor state of health of the inhabitants. In each village most of the inquired go to general practitioners at least twice a month. As a result the turnover of local pharmacies remained also high. This was

61 percent in Sarud, 73 percent in Tiszakeszi, 68 percent in Tiszaszentimre and 67 percent in Újszentmargita. Such percentages of the inquired were observed mainly because of their monthly visit to the local pharmacy. This suggests relatively high medicine consumption. After 1989 the prices of medicines have increased even though the people consume more medicines (their choice has also widened) and thus spend a few thousand fortnights (USD 10-20). Besides the local health establishments most of the inquired also go to a clinic located in a larger settlement, usually in a town. Going to a hospital is less frequent; however, in each village few persons reported that they have to visit a hospital regularly. Approaching other kind of health establishments was not typical in the villages studied.

Smoking and alcohol or drug consumption occupy a significant place among risk factors as they play an important role in the development of various diseases and in addition they also increase the turnover of health establishments. Hence, it is necessary to analyse them in more detail. However, these risk factors or bad habits are not only causes but also consequences of various kinds of social-economic and other problems.

In the period of transition the number of regular smokers and consumers of alcohol further increased although public health government using different means (e.g. wide range of information activity) tried to make them aware of abandoning these harmful habits, but no success was achieved. In 2001 the rate of the population smoked regularly was estimated at 30-35 percent while in the 1980s their rate was only about 10-25 percent. In the less developed villages the rate of regular smokers was also high. According to the1998 survey they were 33 percent in Sarud, 19 percent in Tiszakeszi, and 29 percent in Tiszaszentimre. The majority among them were men. The rate of occasional smokers was also considerable just like as the passive smokers. The joint proportion of occasional and regular smokers can be estimated at 40-50 percent at national level. This is also a matter of great concern. Much more people suffered from the damages caused by the smoke of tobacco which can lead to various diseases of the respiratory and circulatory systems. It is also worth mentioning that the majority of smokers spend quite a lot of money for cigarettes (according to the survey about USD 25-60 per month). This also means that usually they cut expenditure on the amount for food, clothes and other items. This is especially tragic, since incomes are quite low (net average salary USD 300-400 per month) in these settlements and lots of families have livelihood problems.

Hungary still belongs to the leading countries in per capita alcohol consumption, though the amount of alcohol and bear consumed per capita has decreased since 1990. This may be probably because of rise in prices. But the consumption of wine has slowly increased. This can be explained by the widespread viticulture traditions and easily production of wine at home. Due to high alcohol consumption the estimated number of alcohol addicted persons is rather considerable. Between 1980 and 2001 their number has increased fourfold. The rate of increase was especially fast in the 1990s and nowadays their number exceeds 820000. The three-quarters of them are men. This is about 8 percent of the Hungarian population. In the villages under study only 3-6 percent of the inquired have admitted that they consume alcohol regularly. This relatively low rate can be due to the fact that regular alcohol drinking is considered as a larger sin than smoking and people are ashamed of admitting it. The rate of alcohol consumers was occasionally much higher (21-25 percent) in the four settlements. Alcoholism with severe health damage was not only the problem of public health at the end of the 20th century, but of the whole society as it affects various fields of life (e.g. transportation, crime, work).

In Hungary before the change in the political system drug consumption was not widespread. After 1989 this appeared as a concomitant of the socio-economic transformation. Particularly, it is popular among young and male population. Drug consumption is often the consequence of various (family, private life, working place, school etc.) problems. At the turn of millennium almost 13000 drug consumers were registered in Hungary. Most of them lived in the capital city. In 2000 280 deaths were caused by drug consumption.

Disabled People: The number of disabled people may also be a relevant indicator of the population's state of health. During the past few decades their number continuously increased but increase was evidently more in the beginning of 1990s. There were 43000 disabled persons in 1985, 65000 in 1990 and 135000 in 2001. This is partly a consequence of the fact that many people take advantage of their illnesses and apply to the Medical Expert Committees to declare them officially disabled in order to qualify for disability benefit from the government. The closer of their work places has also been another reason of disability. Some of them also pretend to suffer from chronic disease(s) and thus ensure some support 'as a salary' in the future too. In case of Hungary, the sudden growth of disabled people does not indicate unambiguously the impairment of state of health, because a considerable part of the disabled people would still able to work, but because of some reason they do not want to work or they do not find employment. That is why it is thought that the best solution is that if they become disabled pensioners. This is a certain kind of way out of difficulties.

New Challenges after 1989

In the course of analysis of some indicators of state of health we have to consider that sharp differences can be experienced in the state of health of different social groups and of the population living in different regions of the country.

In the beginning of 1990s the state of health of population deteriorated much, which was partly because of the new phenomena and processes appearing in the last decade. In the beginning of 1990s almost 700 hundred thousand people had lost their job, prices had suddenly increased but wages did not follow them, livelihood become more and more difficult. Nowadays according to an estimate 30-35 percent of the population lives under the minimum of existence. Income and social differences have sharpened and they can be observed in space too. Because of increasing insecurity, strengthening blighted prospects and because of the lack of fast adjustment to new challenges the considerable proportion of the society have increased the camp of 'the losers of the change in the political system', whose living conditions and state of health have strongly deteriorated. At the same time 'the winners of the change in the political system' have formed only the narrow layer of the society, but the state of health of this group has not considerably improved either because they had to work much harder and undertake larger risks and responsibility for the better living conditions and higher incomes. Tensions and stress pressing on them have also increased. Thus, Hungarian society has paid a high price for the social and economic reforms.

Social status makes a significant difference in the state of health. Generally, those having better health have higher education and higher income. Such persons are intellectual workers and live in better housing circumstances or better settlement environment. The changes occurred after 1989 were quite unfavourable and afflicted agricultural workers, the unemployed, the pensioners and the gypsy population living on the periphery of the society. According to the latest census only 200000 gypsies lived in Hungary or at least so many people admitted their ethnic identity. The real number of the roaming population is probably much larger than this. It can be estimated at about 5-600000. After 1989 they were the first to lose their jobs. They are less qualified, their living conditions are poor, and their income is low. They live mostly in backward regions, in the periphery. As a result their state of health remains poorer than the national average (Losonczi, 1997). In fact, these social groups are those which could not adjust to the challenges, to the new conditions and circumstances of the transition period. Their disadvantageous social status and defencelessness have increased in the last decade, and along with the inherited unfavourable state of health have resulted in further deterioration. The living circumstances— such as housing conditions, infrastructural provisions of settlements and environmental pollution—have favourably changed during the last decade.

The political, economic and social changes that took place since 1989 have equally and profoundly affected households and individuals. No such radical change has happened in Hungary for a long time. Naturally, these effects displayed temporal and spatial variations and they have affected their life to a rather different extent. They have meant serious challenge and required great adaptability. Those, who could not follow the events have been increasingly pushed into the background, meanwhile others have enjoyed significant advantages. This has led to the sharpening of contrasts in living standards and to a growing social inequality on local levels too (Kiss, 2001).

Besides the social differences, the changes in the political system have also made spectacular regional differences in the field of state of health of the people coming from different geographical locations of their residence. The social and economic changes took place have further sharpened such differences. There are major variations in the development levels between the Western and Eastern parts of the country. The former, called Transdanubia, is closer to the Western border. Its infrastructural provision, transport and geographical location are more favourable. The population in this region is 'the winners' of the change in the political system. The living circumstances and housing conditions are better and the built environment is less polluted. Latter is the Eastern part. It is not the same in comparison to the former one. Despite decreasing differences the state of health is still more favourable in urban settlements where about two thirds of the Hungarian populations live. Thanks to the better living conditions and public health services.

'The big losers' of the change in the political system are those regions (e.g. north-eastern part of the country) where earlier heavy industry (mining, metallurgy, machinery industry) had dominated. After 1989, the state of health of their population has suddenly deteriorated because of loss of working places and their livelihood. The other 'losers' are those regions which were or are still underdeveloped. In 1995 26 percent of the settlements belonged to this group (Kiss, 1995). Researches carried out in the beginning of 1990s show that the state of health of people living in periphery, less developed regions is not good in comparison to the average health condition of the country. This can be explained not only by the poorer living circumstances but also by the unfavourable demographic features which are not only reasons but also consequences (Kiss, 1993, 1995). According to the survey carried out in the less developed rural settlements in 1998 it was found that health condition of the people did not favourably improve during the last decade as 59 percent of the inquired in Sarud, 39 percent in Tiszakeszi, 22 percent in Tiszaszentimre and 37 percent in Újszentmargita reported that their living conditions were not good in the 1990s.

This is primarily explained by the decreasing number of local working places. If people do not have a job and income they cannot take advantage of the local infrastructural provisions developing relatively fast. Probably, this can also be the reason why 60-79 percent of the inquired who had taken everything into consideration have reported that their life has become worse.

In the four villages the changes and challenges after 1989 have significantly affected the inhabitant's state of health (Kiss, 1993). This is in a close connection with the changes in their lifestyles and living conditions. The majority of the participants of the survey have reported unfavourable changes in their life and living conditions caused by the transformation in the political system. One of the most essential changes was that the duration of working hours has increased whereas time for leisure decreased. Not only the high prices but also the lack of time is the reason why people go for a summer holiday in lesser numbers. Most of the inquired have stated that they work more and sleep less than before 1989. Partly, this is the reason why 34-41 percent of them reported that their state of health has deteriorated over the last decade. As a consequence it is not a miracle at all that the personal consumption of medicines has increased by 14-34 percent in the studied villages. This can be explained by several reasons. Some of them are increased stress stemming from the changed working conditions, feeling less protected and more uncertain, the fear of losing job, the everyday problems of subsistence.

In the studied villages the transformation in the political system has changed most radically the life of those who became unemployed or entrepreneurs, and it is quite difficult to adjust to it physically and mentally. In case of the former group the lack of salary makes this situation much more serious. A lack of sufficient time for being together with the family and for leisure activities and the increased working hours of family members are also the source of tension, especially in case of the latter group. Probably these are also the reasons why the number of people struggling with complaints of the nervous and neurotic systems. Physic complaints have increased in these settlements in the period of transition. The percentage of inquired having regular complaints of the nervous system at the time of the survey was 4.8 percent in Sarud, 3.4 percent in Tiszakeszi, 3.4 percent in Tiszaszentimre and 5.7 percent in Újszentmarrgita.

Conclusions

Despite an indisputable social and economic progress Hungary has inherited a heavily polluted environment in settlements and a population with deteriorating state of health from the socialist period. In addition, after 1989 this unfavourable situation has aggravated as radical social and economic reforms have strongly affected the population's state of health. The state of health of the Hungarian population has deteriorated and this has been reflected in the major indicators of state of health. The rate of deterioration was fast especially in the first half of 1990s when the social and economic transformations were the most intensive.

During the last decade the social and spatial differences have suddenly increased. The state of health of the unemployed and pensioners is not good. Such persons belong to the 'losers' of the change in the political system. Most of them live not only on the periphery of the society but also in the 'periphery of the country'. Such areas are the declining regions or in the less developed rural regions. Despite the unfavourable changes, it seems that from the beginning of the 21st century (which means the end of the transition period) the state of health of the Hungarian population has begun to improve. Some certain indicators show this trend. However, it is also true that a much longer period is necessary for a spectacular improvement in the state of health of the Hungarian population.

References

Bernát, Á. (2002) 'Az egészségi állapot a legnagyobb probléma (The state of health is the biggest problem)', Népszabadság, November 25.pp15.

Enyedi, G. (2000) Bevezetés: a településkörnyezet (1), In: Glatz F. (ed.) Magyarország településkörnyezete. (Settlemen environmnet of Hungary) MTA. Budapest, pp.1-9.

Kiss, É. (1993) 'Az egészségi állapot néhány jellemzője a Közép-Tiszavidék elmaradott térségében (Some features of the state of health in the underdeveloped Mid-Tisza Region)', Népegészségügy Vol.74.pp.22-30.

Kiss, É. (1995) 'Az elmaradott területek és a nem-normatív támogatások (The underdeveloped regions and non-normative supports)', Földrajzi Értesítő, Vol. 3-4. pp.213-243.

Kiss, É. (2001) 'Falvaink sorsa az ezredfordulón: a közép-tiszavidéki tapasztalatok Future of our rural settlements:the esperiences of the Mid-Tisza Region)', Tér és Társadalom. Vol.1. pp.131-153.

Losonczi, Á. (1997) 'A magyar népegészség romlásának társadalmi okairól. (On the social reasons of the impairing of the Hungarian population's state of health)' *INFO-Társadalomtudomány* Vol.40. pp. 11-31.

Orosz, É. (1985) Az egészségügyi infrastruktúra területi egyenlőtlenségeinek vizsgálata (Study of regional inequalities in the health services) MTA RKK. Pécs 201p.

7

Education for Surging Population

Rameshwari Pandya

Introduction

In recent years population growth has become one of the most crucial human problems. The number of people in the world is growing at a staggering rate. Today every tick of the clock adds 3.3 people to the population. This rate will increase to 4.4 in near future if the same rate continues. The picture is not very rosy to conceive. If the crisis has not yet arrived it is just round the corner. Every seventh person in the world is an Indian today. In India there has been a phenomenal rise in the population in the last few decades.

Most of the countries of the world experienced rapid population growth after World War II but not as a result of an increase in the birth rate, as was the case in the United States and certain other western countries, but as a result of a commendable decline in the death rate. Death rates are continuing to come down as they should, while birth rates in the majority of the developing countries remain very high. It is now obvious to all people working in the field of population that the rising aspirations of the world's people can never be achieved unless population growth and economic development are brought into balance. Furthermore, this desired reduction in fertility will not be achieved by appealing only to the adult generation but also to the young people. Those young people who are educated recognize a small family quite proper and desirable.

The aim of education is to increase knowledge and ways of knowing, to develop understanding and awareness, and hopefully, to help us to achieve wisdom in the conduct of our lives, both as individual and a collcctive group. These aims are shared by the new field that has come to be called population education.

Population Education

Population education in a broad way can be defined as 'an educational programme which provides for a study of the population situation in the family, community, nation and the world, with the purpose of developing in the students a rational and responsible attitude and behaviour towards that situation'. Under this widespread umbrella many things can be included in population education but the selection of content, the emphasis and the methods of treatment will obviously vary from place to place, culture to culture and the stage of the development of a particular country. It is, therefore, necessary that there is no rigidity about the content or emphasis of population education. However, a few major areas are clearly identifiable which could form the core of population education. The specific objectives of helping the young, eventually to make more rational decisions concerning their own behaviour on population matters should be framed.

The goals of population education are to develop understanding the impacts of population characteristics and processes on national development both in the short and long run, as well as their impacts on the individual and his family. Thus, population education deals with society at both the macro and micro levels. As such, it serves a dual purpose. First, it serves to develop an informed citizen capable of understanding population characteristics and processes as they affect society, and capable of making responsible decisions with regard to public as it might affect, and be affected by these processes. Second, population education aims at developing informed individuals who will, as a result of the knowledge and understanding achieved through their education, make responsible decisions, concerning their own reproductive behaviour. This is the beginning of wisdom and represents the moral and ethical purpose of population education.

Population education seeks to bring about a realization of the individual, family, social and environmental effects of the explosive increase in human population, the rapid shifts in concentration and distribution of people, the implications of changing age and other demographic patterns and the conceivable options that may be open to mankind to cope with the consequent problems. It is not only confined to a particular age group but also to the students who will become the principal child-bearers within one or two decades.

Obviously, it is not easy to reduce the content and objectives of such a broad area of learning into a concise definition. Population education is a relatively new concept and it seems more logical to explain it in terms of objectives rather than by a single definition. One of the best such enumeration was compiled by Bhatia in 1969. He framed six primary objectives of population education. These are:

1. Basic understanding of population dynamics including the growth rate and structure of population of a country in the context of world population.
2. Appreciation of the significance of the population characteristics for the present and future quality of life including economic development and the attainment of a high level of health, education, housing, diet and other amenities of life.

3. Realization that the size of the family can be easily planned for the benefit of individual families and that large families are not necessary in the present day.
4. Understanding of the health risks involved for the mother and the child.
5. Appreciation of the small family as a setting in which a high quality of life for each person is more likely to be attained.
6. Understanding of the Governments Family Planning Programme in relation to the country's need.

Need for Population Education

1. Rapid population growth 'is a threat to economic development, especially with respect to the per capita economic growth. The greater the population the less there is to distribute to the people. In India the growth of economy is just being 'eaten up' by even more rapid growth of population. The Indian economy continues to be an economy of shortages. This is mainly due to the country's excessive population growth. This means that the population increases rapidly as a result of death control but the increase in the production of food and other necessities does not keep pace.
2. The second crucial problem which the country faces is that of providing adequate food for more and more people. While the achievements of the green revolution have been spectacular for the welfare of the millions of Indians, it is still modest, in terms of actual needs.
3. Rapid population growth in the last half century has also affected the structure of our population. Almost half of the population of the country today is less than 16 years of age whereas the median for most advanced countries is 30 to 35 years. A young population requires a particular kind of expenditure to support it; a proportionately large outlay is required for supporting the social services needed for it, like education, health and other facilities etc.

The most immediate problem to be tackled is related to the reproductive age group population. In this regard it would be worthwhile to remember Sloan Wayland's very emphatic remarks, "as countries around the world have been working to bring the population increase into a balance with the general effort at economic and social development. From this one learns a lesson. The lesson is that the dramatic success experienced in reducing death rates in a short period of time cannot be duplicated in action to decrease the birth rate". The whole business of family planning and reduction of birth rates is not "once for all" affair nor is it concerned with only the population currently capable of bearing children. Perhaps more vital problem is that of young people who will constitute the 'adult population of the world in the next three decades. Over 45% of our population is under 15 years of age. This group will strongly influence the demographic in the cultivation of a desire amongst the youngsters to adopt family planning as a way of life. If the future population behaviour resembles to that of their parents, today's population problem will be regarded by comparison, only as a minor one. If on the other hand these young people become cognizant of the factors of their population situation and recognize that it warrants more decisions on an ever more rational basis which is of vital importance for developing responsible parenthood. Perhaps the quintessence of "Responsible Parenthood" is their capacity and the desire to take "rational decisions in regard to one's own family size. In other words, responsible parenthood and responsible fertility behaviour are very close.

These can be achieved only when we catch the young and through proper education develop right attitudes amongst the vast population which has yet to enter fertility age group and thus strengthen and enlarge the area of commitment towards checking population growth.

Population education becomes relevant as a motivational instrument which will prompt the younger generation with a desire to adopt small family norm. This desire should grow out of both the concern for over population and quality of life.

Thus, population education is not only concerned with population awareness but also with developing attitudes and values so that quality and quantity are taken care of.

When Population Education Should be Given

1. At School Level: The rapid growth of population presents an issue of momentous significance for man and no educational programme that makes any claim of relevance to human issues can ignore it.

In considering the potential content of population education, it is proposed to adopt the approach of looking at it in a total perspective that would bring within it whatever appears to be logically related to it. Five broad areas with which the content appears to fall may be demarcated.

A. The Collection and Analysis of Population Data: A detailed break-up of the content under this head would be as follows:

1. Methods of collecting population data
2. The demographic processes of birth, death & migration
3. Calculation of birth, death and growth rates
4. The age structure of population, and the causes
5. Underlying different kinds of age structures

6. Determinants of fertility, morbidity & mortality
7. Trends of population growth refined indices of fertility and mortality

B. Population Growth and Human Development: At the macro-level of the nation, the topics to be considered would be the relationship between population growth and such variables as land and natural resources, agriculture, food, housing, employment, economic development, educational development and the development of health services.

At the micro level of the family, the topics to be considered would be the impact of family size on the quality of life in the family and aspects of development of the individual.

C. Population Planning: The objective of a course such as that outlined above would be to give the learners an insight into the totality of issues connected with population ranging from the nature, measurement, causes, determinants and consequences of Population growth as well as of urbanization both at the micro-level of the family and at the macro-level of the community. Hopefully, the acquisition of such an insight may succeed in providing the learners with a sound cognitive and attitudinal basis that would contribute to rational decision making both as an individual and as a member of society, when occasions for such decisions arise.

An obvious situation in which a personal decision will be involved will arise many years later in adulthood when the learner would be faced with the process of decision making in relation to reproductive behaviour, not in the insulated atmosphere of a class room but in an emotionally charged social, psychological context in which both individual urges the role expectations, as a husband or wife, and as an adult member of a social group he/she would powerfully affect decision making and action. While it would be idle to pretend that exposure of a decision that is productive of both individual and social good, it is reasonable to expect that the probability of a rational decision from a person who has such educational experiences is much higher than from a person who has not had an orientation of population issues.

It is recognized that much of the current interest in population education has arisen from the need to reduce the rate of population growth in many areas of wide adoption of a small family norm in the hope that reproductive behaviour would be in accordance with such a norm. Educators have, however agreed that the best educational preparation for the achievement of this objective is to promote the development of an insight into the impact of population growth on the quality of life by means of a programme that is untarnished by any kind of crude propagandist emphasis. Stephen Viderman says, "the aims of education are to increase awareness and hopefully to help us achieve wisdom in the conduct of our lives both as individuals and collectively". These aims are shared by the new field that has come to be called population awareness education.... Population education aims at developing an informed individual who will as a result of the knowledge and understanding achieved through their education, make responsible decisions concerning their own reproductive behaviour.

Over and above any pragmatic objective related to the small family norm or the limitation of population growth, population education in the hands of an imaginative teacher sensitive to the analysis of dynamic relationships between interconnected variables opens up interesting possibilities- of examining the inter play between variables and sharpening the insights of students. Population growth is a function of fertility, mortality and migration, each of which in turn depends on a number of determinants. The nature and magnitude of the determinants produce variations in fertility, mortality, migration and finally in the size of the population and its growth rate.

The age structure of a population depends on the pattern of increase or decrease in fertility, mortality and migration and affects them in turn. Discussions of the basic weaknesses of crude birth rates and death rates and the dangers involved in generalizing from them would lead to the development of a critical attitude towards numerical relationships. An understanding of standardization as a method of ensuring comparability and of the calculation of age specific fertility and mortality rates, standardized rates and reproduction rates, a method of obtaining more and more refined measures to describe the phenomenon will provide an effective illustration of the purposive activity of the human mind in its search for more and more meaningful ways of comprehending the processes that go on around it. It will be these examples of the educational possibilities of population studies that in the hands of an acknowledgeable and imaginative teacher, population education could have distinctive educational uses to warrant its inclusion in the school curriculum, apart from any pragmatic purpose that may be achievable in the long run and for which a sound cognitive and attitudinal basis may be laid in school.

2. At College Level: The objective of population education is to enable the students to understand that the family size is controllable, that population limitations can facilitate the development of the higher quality of life in the nation and that a small family size can contribute materially to the quality of living for the individual family.

Students at all levels have a right to accurate information about the effect of changes in family size and in national population on the individual, the family and the nation so that this body of knowledge is utilized to control family size and national population with beneficial impact on the individual families.

Also to give the learner an insight into the totality of issues connected with population, ranging from nature, measurement, causes, determinants and consequences of population growth as well as of urbanization at both the micro level of the family and the macro level of the community, the nation, or world at large to the dynamics of the reproductive process and finally to the possibilities of planning family size and population growth.

A. Contents for College Level: The objectives laid down for population education depend on the contents and the relevant concepts drawn from different academic disciplines such as demography, economics, civics, geography, sociology, ecology, biology, health education etc. The approach, therefore, is necessarily interdisciplinary. The curriculum specialists who would be responsible for developing the college program shall have to work closely with various specialists from demography, behavioural sciences and biological sciences and also with specialists working in the area of family planning. Core concepts relevant to population education thus chosen would form an outline of the course content to be incorporated in the total school program. For incorporation, it would be necessary that the course is properly articulated and properly graded according to the suitability of concepts and information for different levels of education.

On the basis of overall objectives laid down, the following six major areas have been identified which are not exclusive to particular disciplines but draw from several social sciences and biological sciences. They also have a wide scope for encompassing most of the concepts related to population education at the college level. These areas are:

1. The population growth (determinants & demographic situation)
2. Economic development and population growth (consequences)
3. Social developments and population growth (consequences)
4. Health, Nutrition and population
5. Biological factors, family life and population
6. Population programs: national and international

3. At the Post-graduate Level: There can not be much scope for any formal inclusion of matters regarding population education in the theory papers for the M.A. or M.Ed. courses. Perhaps some could be mentioned in the paper on philosophy of education. In the elective papers Curriculum Development and Educational Administration and supervision may provide some scope for the inclusion of relevant matters. Dissertations that usually form a part of these courses usually could provide good opportunities for useful investigations and studies and demographical and allied studies. Some relevant areas may provide some scope for useful research work at the Ph. D level also.

By Whom Should it be Taught?

1. Teachers: Unless and until our teachers and would be teachers are exposed to the problem of population education and unless faith is created in their mind about the great intensity of the problem vis-à-vis the future prosperity of the country, not much success can be achieved in the proper orientation of the school going children.

It is well known that the main purpose of including small doses of population as an integral part of the elementary and secondary syllabus is to slowly but surely inculcate in the young minds a gradual consciousness of the patent fact that the material resources of a country can only be stretched to a certain extent.

It is also a patent educational truth that the success of any educational scheme, plan or project does not depend merely on the administrators or planners at the top but largely depends on the efforts of the individual class teacher.

Population Education has to be included in all our teacher education programmes both for elementary and secondary school and college teachers in a big way.

India's population increase must be curbed otherwise no real improvement in the standard of living of people is possible. The problem has to be tackled through different angles and the participation of every person is necessary. One of the important features of our country's population is the predominance of young people. About 45 percent are below 15 years of age and a significant number from among them will become parents after a few years. Thus, in recent years a large number of educationists have supported the idea that young children should be made aware of population problems. They feel that a massive program of population education should be started in the schools and colleges so that students could take right decisions about the size of their future family.

Only teachers can give the education of population at school and college level. The teacher can develop the proper attitudes among students so that they could also take a wise and rational decision about the family size when they become adults. But for that the teacher should have proper knowledge and for this they should go under foreign service programme for population education.

The objectives of in-service program for population education are listed below:

1. To develop an understanding in teachers about the population situation and its implications on social and economic life of the country.
2. To make the teachers aware about the trends of population growth in the developing and the developed countries and its comparison with India.
3. To develop an understanding about the different biological factors responsible for population growth and relationship of population and environment.

4. To impart the knowledge about some of the problems which are the product of population growth e.g.: social tensions, crimes etc.
5. To develop an attitude among the teachers so that they could take a wise and rational decision about the family sue.
6. To develop in teachers the skill of locating the areas related to population education and to weave the contents of population education effectively in their teaching subjects.
7. To develop the ability of collecting and analyzing the demographic data and interpreting the charts, graphs etc. related to population.

2. Parents: Parents are the first teacher who gives education to their children about population. They can set the examples of themselves to their kids and compare the past and present population growth. During ancient period the people were unknown about the methods of family planning but now-a-days so many methods/techniques are available to reduce the family size, so the parents can make their kids aware about all new techniques and methods of family planning. At the time of marriage of their kids they can give the knowledge or information about family planning devices to the newly wed couples. The siblings can also give the education to their youngsters about family planning.

3. Formal: Progress on population education should fit in very well into co-curricular programmes arranged by a college education. These programmes usually include items like debates, stage-plays, one-act plays, symposia etc. Items can always be found out to, in a suitable manner, highlight the urgent necessity of restricting population in order to have a better standard of individual and national growth. Trainees may be encouraged to study demographic literature as a preparation for essay writing contests and debates. Poetry competitions and plays could also suitably lead to this orientation. Extension lectures on the relevant subjects could be given by family planning experts and demographers and may provide useful initiation.

The problem of educated unemployed and the problem of the ever-increasing size of school and college classes are items of immediate interest to teachers and students alike and they can be directly linked with the work in any college of education. At elementary level, the program of curricular and co-curricular work is more or less on similar lines. The course should be of 2 years. In a two year course some content matters are also included and as such added opportunities could be found to include suitable material on population education at proper places.

4. Non-formal Education: Adult Education programs also provide useful information regarding family planning and allied programs. Mostly trained teachers are put in charge of the Adult Education programs either on a whole time or on a part time basis. Suitable orientation of the Adult Education workers/Teachers is, therefore, necessary.

Here the work will have more direct bearing on the subject of Family Planning. The twin purpose of this is proper mental preparedness as well as practical acquaintance with the family programs. Help could be taken from the health authorities through their Family, Planning personnel while training teachers for the adults.

Role of Home Scientists in Imparting Population Education

1. Academician: As we say, if a man is educated, he is educated individually but if a woman is educated, the whole family is educated. The Home Scientist can give population education, teach them about family planning devices / methods and explain their advantages, importance and uses.

As an academician she can teach the students about population growth, birth rate, death rate, migration, reasons and consequences of the population growth. Like this she can give the education to the students as a part of the curriculum and she can also take up research and action project related to family planning. She can also teach all these things to her family and also to her neighbours. She can impart education to her child at the time of his/her marriage and let them know about different safe methods of family planning.

2. Communicator: As a communicator the home scientists can also impart population education. In the rural areas as well as in the urban communities the home scientists can arrange talks, discussions for family planning. They can teach about methods, devices of family planning to the people, number of children one should have in the family, spacing between the two children etc. The population education can be effectively given by using teaching aids like charts, posters, flashcards, flannel boards, video films, etc.

3. Non-formal Educator: Home Scientists can play a very important role by:

1. Continuing to develop and refine the objectives, scope and content of population education at various levels.
2. Helping in stimulation and orientation of various concerned agencies is another major task that home scientists can undertake starting with Ministries of Education and Educational Administrators and including all types of educators and teachers. It is most important to present them with the relevant facts and convince them of the importance of population education as a part of their teaching experience.
3. The third area of work for Home Scientists lie in the sphere of conducting pilot programmes in schools, colleges, in teacher training activities among out-of-school groups.

4. Home Scientists can take studies and research and can provide invaluable help by carrying out attitudinal, cultural and other studies to help evolve the content and methodology so essential for a new and unprecedented programme dealing with human relations and humanity.
5. Teachers can also arrange role plays, street plays, bhavai, puppet shows for giving information to the people.

Conclusion

Population education is a new area and no model exists which could be adopted to suit the conditions prevailing in our country. We have to tread a new ground keeping in view our cultural background and present needs and future aspirations. The essence of the program should be to give the learner an insight into the totality of issues connected with population including the nature, causes, determinants, consequences of population growth, both at the micro and macro levels, the nature and dynamics of the reproductive process and finally the possibilities of planning family size and population growth.

Hopefully, the acquisition of such an insight may develop an understanding and attitude that contribute positively to rational decision making, both at an individual level and as a member of society when occasion for such decision making arises.

To quote Stephen Viederman, 'the aims of education are to increase awareness and hopefully to help us achieve wisdom in the conduct of our lives, both as an individual and collectively. These aims are shared by the new field to be called Population Awareness Education. Population education, as a result of the knowledge and understanding achieved through their education make responsible decisions concerning their own reproductive behaviour'.

Research and Programme evaluation should be included as a part of the development of a national programme from the very beginning. Knowledge of the nature of population learning and the developmental stages of population learning are obviously of the greatest importance to teachers and curricula developers.

Thus, population education is no less sensitive than any thing else that we may teach in schools. It may be relevant to the students' own life, both now and in the future.

References

Anthony, A. (1974, et al.) Population Growth and Development, Indian Social Institute, New Delhi.

Chalam, K.S. (1981) Promoting Family Planning through Non Formal Education, Indian

Journal of Adult Education, Vol. 42, No. 1-2. Jan-Feb., pp. 25-28.

Jain, S.P. (1977) Indian Population and Development.

Jersild, A.T. (1974) The Psychology of Adolescents, Mc Gram Hill Book Company, New York, pp. 278.

Kothari, Prakash (1991) Sex education mist, Times of India (Delhi) 5th Feb., p.4.

Kakar, V.N. Communication in Family Planning - India's Experience, the National Institute of Health and Family Welfare, New Delhi.

Mehta T.S. (1972 *et al.)* Population Education Selected Reading, Population Education Cell, National Council of Educational Research and Training, New Delhi.

Moses, S and C. Praveena (1983) A Study on Sex Education: Its need and attitude of adolescent. Journal of Family Welfare, 30 Vol. Dec., p 34.

Nair, G.R. (1987) Towards Zero Population: Communication Revolution in Family Planning, Social Welfare XXXIV, No.9, Dec., pp. 32-34.

National Baseline Survey of Population Education in India (1980) National Council of Educational Research and Training, New Delhi.

Pandya, K. (1990-91) Development of a question bank of sex education unit of science syllabus of IX std. at the Rural Secondary Schools of Baroda, M.Sc. (Home) dissertation, Faculty of Home Science, M.S.U. Baroda.

Sen, A.K. (1982) Population growth and nutrition problems: A case study for population Education, Indian Journal of Adult Education, Vol. 43 No.3, March 1982 pp. 1O-13.

8

Geographical Analysis of Health Care in the Catchment Area of Raul Targului River, Romania

Aurel Gheorghilas

Introduction

The basin of the Raul Targului River is totally included in Arges county, where it occupies a surface of 2,91,017 acres (1,17,773 ha), that is 17.2 percent of the whole county surface—16,86,781 acres (6,82,631 ha). Among the 99 villages registered in the entire county, 19 of them (19.2 percent) are situated in the Raul Targului River. Also, among the six cities in the Arges County, two (Campulung city and Mioveni city) are situated at the extremities of the Raul Targului River. 1,49,270 (23.3 percent) of the total population of the Arges County live in these two cities.

The delimitation of the Basin of Raul Targului River on geographical and human criteria implies small differences for the natural limits as there is overlapping of the natural and the economic limits. This is noted as a quite rare coincidence. Therefore, drawing the human-geographical limits includes the administrative extremities of the villages, which, as a whole, overlap the surface of the basin limited by the waters. Taking into consideration that the human and geographical reality is based on essential components of a human settlement, that is the population, the homes and the economic space. Most of the processes and phenomena have been analyzed at the level of the administrative space regarding the limits of the nineteen rural villages and the two urban cities (Campulung, Mioveni) in the basin of the Raul Targului River.

Next to the basin of the Raul Targului River, there is a surface which overlaps almost perfectly over a space with traditional spiritual symbolic importance to the civilization—that is *the muscelean space*—which has been considered as an attractive subject for scientific research in different spheres. This is also indirectly tackled by geographers under the physic-geographical and the social grounds. Throughout the political, social and geographical aspects it has been emphasized that the evolution of this region took place where the transformations have taken very different shapes. The antropical evolution has included new elements to the natural environment by transforming the existing elements; it has determined new relations, which conferred to the geographical space a great social-economic efficiency. Besides the population, the economic activities have represented a pressure element which is very relevant for the structural evolution of the whole territory. In this matter, the transformations that have been taking place over the last decade have been manifested as a continuous restructuring of the economic activities, especially the industrial ones. This led to a differentiated influence over the geographical components.

History of Medical Services and its Evolution in the Muscelean Space

The medical assistance in Romania was first created for the poor people and for the invalids. In the Muscel area, starting from the consolidation of the feudal state, documents signed by the lords stated the right of the poor people to be fed and to be taking care of by the people in Matau village. This favour allows them for some exemptions from taxes. The poor and the invalids who were mentioned in these documents had their homes in the southern part of Campulung city, where the church and the mill was placed (today, this area is known as *the field of the knaves*).

The institute of social and sanitary assistance was founded in 1775. *The Community Administration* (*Epitropia obstilor*), which dealt with caring of the orphans, the invalids and the old people was also established. The Constitutional Rules, created in 1831, stated some medical rules. The establishment of civil registers and the obligation of providing smallpox vaccines are under that rule. Yet, considering the small amount of medical products and the thin medical networks, a result of the permanent threatening caused by epidemics, the administrative counsellors in Muscel County tried to have a well knowledge of the medical state of the people in the villages. Recurrently, reports were made and kept at the Prefecture so that the activity of the doctor and his assistance could be marked and campaigns of vaccinating children and of providing public health could be organized.

Yet, health state of the population was satisfying; the medical personnel were treating diseases such as: pellagra, paluster fever, the diseases of the digestive pipe and the respiratory system. The control reports [1] written by doctors during the inspections in villages have also stated that some dwellings were not built properly because of their position on bent ground. Therefore, the mud quickly surrounded them. Also, most of the dwellings are consisted of only one room in which eight-ten persons and animals live together.

For the improvement of health condition in rural villages, the doctors proposed the following during his speech made in front of the County Council of Muscel in 1890: "it should be pleading at the Government for building of the rural ambulances, which had satisfying results for the sick people; it should also be pleading for building of rural hospitals in this county, because, as we know, the only county hospital which exists is insufficient considering the number of people and their necessities; the mayors and teachers should execute the orders given by the doctors regarding the prevention of sickness; the teachers should be thought to vaccinate children in case the medical personnel is insufficient; the people should not wash their clothes in wells; the people should not melt the hemp in the village; the dwellings should be aired; the swamps in the yard should be buried with sand; the rural pharmacies should be provided with more drugs, in case they exist". [2]

The first real hospital was established in 1864. But it was placed in an old building which needed a year of repairing and improvements (the rooms permanently needed painting and repairing, the medical supply was incomplete, and, also, the clothes, the sheets, the kitchen etc. was not sufficient). After three decades, in 1890, an initiation of building a new county hospital was taken. This was a result of several reports of the County Sanitary Service. The report stated that "the county hospital was almost ruined and any repairing expenses would be useless". [3]

The proper medical activity in Campulung city was facilitated with some important doctors such as Nicolae Jugureanu, Gheorge Costea, Haralambie Makerie, Petre Georgescu, Nicolae Falcoianu etc. The sanitary service has gravitated around the old county hospital, which was named after Nicolae Kretulescu [4], a son of Muscel and also one of the promoters of the Romanian Medicine.

Organization of the Sanitary System at the Present Time

After the war, there was one hospital for adults, one for children, a maternity, several medical circumscriptions (on neighbourhoods), a hospital for TBC, a nursery, an orphanage and three pharmacies in Campulung. After 1960, there was a rising in the number of sanitary units because of the opening of medical clinics in the rural space and inside the factories. The state politics stated that every village must be provided with special conditions for medical assistance and with at least one clinic and one pharmacy in the public sector. On the other hand, the clinics for working people (inside the factories) allowed a faster accessibility to the medical services for the working men, a better report of their health condition, having a preventing prophylactic and healing role.

In the present time, there are 2 hospitals in Campulung city. The first one is a territorial one and another one treating lung diseases. These two hospitals have 557 beds, 3 clinics (of which one is specialized in stomatology). There is one orphanage with 150 beds. There are three pharmacies and seven medical clinics in the public sector, and ten pharmacies (among which five are mixed), one pharmaceutics storehouse, four medical rooms, 13 dentist rooms, two medical laboratories, and five dental laboratories in the private sector. In Mioveni, there is one hospital (in Racovita neighbourhood) with a capacity of 65 beds placed in an old building (not corresponding with the needs and require urgent notice for improvements), one clinic, three human surgeries and one pharmacy. In the private sector, there are four medical rooms (of which, three are dentist) and two pharmacies.

At each village level there is a territorial village surgery functions but the medical services offered here are of a low quality because of the insufficient number of medical personnel. In rural environment the private medical sector is not so much. The only private units found in rural environment are the pharmacies (one unit for each village in: Aninoasa, Boteni, Darmaresti, Leresti, Mihaiesti, Stalpeni), two private medical rooms (in Stalpeni) and one private dentist room (in Leresti).

The number of employees in the sanitary system is differently structured on life levels (urban-rural) and on property levels. Therefore, at the basin level 94.5 percent of the total number of public sector doctors and 96.7 percent of the total sanitary personnel are found. The private sector is weakly represented. This constitutes approximately 6 percent of the total number of private sector doctors and 4.6 percent of the total number of the medical personnel. The percentage of doctors who work on life grounds in urban environment is 76.60. The total number of doctors is 141 and from among them 112 are in Campulung and 29 in Mioveni. Only 23.4 percent doctors work in the rural environment. The total number of sanitary personnel working in urban environment is 489 (83.6 percent) and from among them 403 personnel are in Campulung and 86 in Mioveni. Only 16.4 percent sanitary personnel work in the rural environment.

Village level distribution of doctors shows that four doctors each work in Leresti and Hartiesti, three doctors in Berevoiesti, Mihaiesti, Poienarii de Muscel, Titesti and Valea Mare Pravat. Rest of the settlements (63 percent) is provided with the services of one or two doctors. The medium sanitary personnel are better represented in Hartiesti town and Valea Mare Pravat (13-11 employees). Other nine towns namely Albestii de Muscel, Balilesti, Berevoiesti, Godeni, Leresti, Mihaiesti, Poienarii de Musacel, Schitu Golesti, Stalpeni have 5-6 employees. Rest of the towns (42 percent) has 2-4 employees.

Number of villagers who correspond to an employee in the sanitary system at the basin level varies much, i.e. 72.2 in Campulung) and over 1000 in Bughea de Jos, Darmanesti. 47.3 percent of the rural towns such as Aninoasa, Berevoiesti,

Boteni, Davidesti, Godeni, Leresti, Poienarii de Muscel, Stalpeni, and Valea Mare Pravat register numbers between 400 and 600. Other 31.5 percent of the rural towns such as Albestii de Muscel, Mioarele, Schitu Golesti, Mihaiesti, Balilesti, Titesti register a number from 600 to 800. Due to a large number of personnel in the sanitary system the number of village patients per employee in Mioveni city, in Valea Mare Pravat and Hartiesti town has visibly decreased compared to that of other rural towns (with numbers less than 400).

Table 8.1: The Sanitary Personnel, 2005

Nr. Crt.	Settlements	Total	Doctors		Medium sanitary personnel	
			Spb	Spv	Spb	Spv
1	Campulung	530	112	3	403	12
2	Mioveni	125	29	2	86	8
3	Albesti	6	1	-	5	-
4	Aninoasa	6	2	-	4	-
5	Bălilesti	7	2	-	5	-
6	Berevoiesti	8	3	-	5	-
7	Boteni	5	2	-	3	-
8	Bughea de Jos	3	1	-	2	-
9	Davidesti	5	2	-	3	-
10	Darmanesti	3	1	-	2	-
11	Godeni	7	2	-	5	-

Contd...

Nr. Crt.	Settlements	Total	Doctors		Medium sanitary personnel	
			Spb	Spv	Spb	Spv
12	Hartiesti	17	4	-	13	-
13	Leresti	11	3	1	6	1
14	Mihaiesti	9	3	-	6	-
15	Mioarele	3	1	-	2	-
16	Poienari	9	3	-	6	-
17	Schitu Golesti	7	2	-	5	-
18	Stalpeni	9	2	1	5	1
19	Titesti	7	3	-	4	-
20	Valea Mare	14	3	-	11	-
21	Vladesti	6	2	-	4	-

Spb = public sector; Spv = private sector.

The situation is more dramatical in terms of the number of patients corresponding to one doctor. The only town where the value of the parameter remains at a normal level is Campulung city (372.2 villagers for one doctor), thanks to the existence of a town hospital with a large capacity including a large number of medical experts. In the rural environment eleven towns (i.e. 58 percent of the rural towns) show 1500 villagers for one doctor, however, three towns from among them show very large numbers. These are Albestii de Muscel (4,652), Darmanesti (3,725), and Bughea de Jos (3,027). Rest of the villages (also Mioveni) where 2-4 doctors work, the number of villagers varies from 1,000 to 1,500.

Quality of Sanitary Services

The quality of sanitary services has been analyzed on the basis of information collected from the field and after synthesizing the results of the opinion test, applied on a considered sample at the level of micro chain, on life environments – neighbourhood for urban, village for rural, in the entire component town in the Basin of Raul Targului River. After the field research it has been noticed that the life environment is an element which generates differences at the level of health care in the Basin of Raul Targului River. After analyzing the final results one may say that the sanitary services in Campulung town are of high quality as this town is well represented by sanitary units and specialized personnel. Only 2 percent of the interrogated people were totally unsatisfied with the medical care in the town while 40 percent declared themselves satisfied.

However, the condition of Mioveni city is different as 43 percent of the villagers were found partially satisfied and even unsatisfied. The main inconvenience is that there is small number of sanitary units and of specialized personnel. The condition of town hospital in Racovita neighbourhood is not good as here the number of beds is less. There is degradation of the building and there is lack of medicines and current services. Deficiency in ruling the funds of the health insurance is also noticed.

The rural environment confronts with major problems at the level of organizing and unfurling the medical services. The villagers generally manifest their dissatisfaction concerning the medical services. They identified the lack of specialized personnel, insufficient number of special units, lack of medicines and of other supply in the village surgeries. Alarmingly, the quality of sanitary services in over 56 percent of the rural villages is low or very low. Generally, the small villages such as Bratia, Otelu, Malu, Putina, Draghescu, Chilii, Colnic, Cocenesti, Grosani, Vacarea, Pitigaia, Dealu Frumos, or the communities of rudders (Gamacesti, Gura Pravat, Pojorata, Valea Manastirii etc.) are in isolated condition.

In some larger villages (28 villages—31 percent of the rural towns), the majority of 41 percent of the questioned people were partly satisfied considering the conditions of a limited representation of sanitary units and of trained personnel. The medical services provide a part of the necessary work. Nine villages (Vladesti, Balilesti, Bughea de Jos, Godeni, Poienarii de Muscel, Matau, Boteni, Davidesti and Titesti) from among them are placed along the main affluent of Târg River (Bratia, Bughea, and Argesel). Some other medium villages such as Valea Pechii, Valea Popii, Livezeni, and Valea Stanii are placed along the main Campulung-Pitesti road. Albesti, Candesti and Bilcesti are on the northern part of the Campulung Depression.

The quality of medical services in 13 villages (14.3 percent of the rural towns) is of medium quality. Over 20 percent of the questioned people declared themselves satisfied with the local medical service. These are larger villages, which, in time, achieved a social and economic progress. In the sanitary domain several territorial village surgery works are governed by the agricultural societies or by the state industries such as Berevoiesti, Aninoasa, and Schitu Golesti (examine-centers). Mihaiesti, Hartiesti, Vulturesti, Leresti, Voiesti, Valea Mare Pravat, Bughea de Sus, Stalpeni villages are with a complex economic and agro-industrial profile.

In conclusion, the sort of accessibility facilities such as sanitary assistance, the technology and the more complex equipments of the urban medical centers influence health of both the rural and urban people. The medium and the young age population have better health status in the rural environment. The rural population tends to avail less medical services due to isolation, lack of roads or transportation, as well as due to high costs of movement to the nearest city. In this condition, the rural populations are treated too late or sometime they are not at all treated.

Notes

1. In a report written by the mayor doctor of Muscel county, handed to the County Prefecture in 1886, he stated that Sanitary Services was led by the mayor doctor, three doctors and three medical agents; 760 inspections were made and 3 509 consultations at home were made. Diseases such as: scarlet fever, dysentery, typhoid fever, diphtheria, measles, convulsive cough were found in 45 villages, from 870 sick persons 79 died. Also, none of the villages was missed by the disease called paludism, brought by the spring rains—1876 cases had been treated

2. Sima Violeta, Pintilie D., (1983) Aspects regarding the sanitary situation in Muscel county at the end of 19th century, Studies and Communications, Campulung Muscel Publishing Museum.
3. For building a new place for the county hospital 2000 lei was allotted from the budget for creating the project, the building being finished with lent money from the Deposition and Registration House (100 000 lei). The county hospital had also received another donation from Minister Dionisie Aninosteanu from Câmpulung in 1882, 15000 lei, and later on, in 1909, another donation of 15 000 lei from Elena Rucareanu (born as Baldovin)
4. Founder of Small Surgeon School at Coltea Hospital, in 1842, the first school of medicine in our country, also author of the first book of medicine written in Romanian language (Book of Descriptive Anatomy); Nicolae Kretzulescu has also been an important political and cultural figure of the 19th century. He has participated at the Revolution in 1848, as a reviser in several counties, he was three times called prime-minister between 1862 and 1866, he held several ministry portfolios and he represented the country as a minister in Berlin, Petersburg, Rome, and Paris. Culturally speaking, he contributed to the creation of the Romanian Academy, of the University of Bucharest and Iasi, of the Romanian Athenaeum, of beautiful Art Schools and the Music Conservator in Bucharest–Dumitru Baciu (1980).

References

Aricescu C.D., (1856), *History of Campulung*, Buharest.

Dumitrache Liliana, (2004), *The health status of the Romanian population.A geographical approaching,* Edit. Univers Enciclopedic, Bucharest;

Erdeli G. (coord.), (1999), *Dictionary of Human Geography*, Edit. Corint, Bucharest;

Erdeli G., Dumitrache Liliana, (2001), *The geography of population*, Ed. Corint, Bucharest;

Sima Violeta, Pintilie D., (1983), *Aspects concerning the medical situation of Muscel County at the end of the 19th century*, Studii & Comunicari, Edit. Muzeului Campulung Muscel.

Part II: Environmental Aspects

9

Cancer and the Environment: A Multi-level Analysis

Ann Novogradec

Introduction

In 1964, the World Health Organization (WHO) noted that "the majority of human cancer is potentially preventable" (Doll and Peto, 1981: 1197). A recent publication by the WHO continues to re-iterate that cancer is still in fact "one of the most preventable non-communicable chronic diseases" (WHO, 2007:3). It is plausible then to question why cancers are still occurring at such alarming rates and what strategies should be put forth to decrease future occurrence. Just over "10 million new cancer cases occur each year, 4.7 million are in the more developed countries and nearly 5.5 million are in the less developed countries" (WHO, 2002: 17).

In order to truly combat cancer, it is proposed that more attention needs to be made not only to targeting risk factors on an individual level, but to also address these and other deeper rooted issues and influences which are part of our micro and macro environments.

Cancer can be broadly defined as "a single condition, which actually consists of more than one hundred different diseases, all characterized by the uncontrolled growth and spread of abnormal cells" (Antman and Taub, 1995). The process by which normal cells are transformed into cancerous cells (carcinogenesis) occurs as a result of carcinogens [1] found in one's micro environment(s). "Carcinogens can induce cancer in an organism, and as such, the biological environment and physical resources (*i.e. genetics, aging, sex, etc.*) play a role in the degree of vulnerability to the carcinogen(s) in question" (Novogradec, 2007b: 214). Forces from the macro environment play key roles in both cancer causation and prevention. These environments, as well as individual resources are explored in more detail.

A Multi-Level Analysis for Understanding the Connections between Cancer and the Environment: An Environment and Cancer Framework

There are several environments which must be considered when examining cancer causation and preventative measures that can be taken to decrease cancer risk. A multi-level analysis is proposed which brings to light both the micro and macro environments as well as an individual's resources.

There are many *contexts* which individuals can be impacted by, and within which they can make an impact on – these broadly are captured in both the *living and working environments* which, more specifically, encompass the (a) home (i.e. residence) (b) work (i.e. workplace), (c) social (i.e. bars, nightclubs, coffee shops, movie theatres, etc.) and (d) other environments (i.e. parks). "Context may affect exposure to risk and the individual's response strategies" (Kuh et al., 2003: 780). It is therefore suggested that the proposed framework be used to promote and adopt positive changes aimed at achieving good health. This framework can also be re-worked to identify cancer risk factors and to implement strategies geared towards cancer prevention on a community level. This would be particularly relevant in light of cancer clusters or other ill health effects which impact a community at large. Although the primary focus of this paper is on individuals, similar analysis and strategies could be implemented on a community level provided that the framework is re-worked to address communities rather than individuals. The proposed framework will aid in the identification of an individual's strengths and weaknesses through the analysis of their resources, which are then compared to the opportunities and threats faced in the micro and macro environments in order to decrease cancer risk and aid in cancer prevention. This framework could essentially also be used to decrease the risk of other ill health effects apart from cancer.

The environment and cancer framework captures one point in time. It is recognized that people's lives are forever changing, therefore it is suggested that this framework be applied both retrospectively and on an on-going basis as new knowledge, developments, and changes take place. It is also acknowledged that resources, environments, and forces that were once relevant, may no longer play a role later in life—however, it is imperative to recognize that what has happened in the past is relevant to current health, especially in light of the fact that cancer causation has a latency effect. The application of the proposed framework can be used in conjunction with the **S**trengths, **W**eaknesses, **O**pportunities, **T**hreats (S.W.O.T.) analysis to assess and make the necessary changes required in order to decrease the risk of cancer and other ill health effects.

Individual Resources (Level 1)

Based on the proposed framework, "resources" are the characteristics that distinguish individuals from each other. In essence, it is what makes individuals and their circumstances unique. "Resources" can be approached as five parts: (1)

personal, (2) physical resources/biological environment, (3) human, (4) economic, and (5) other resources. The factors which make up these parts will be explored to determine how an individual's strengths and weaknesses posed by their resources pertain to the causation and prevention of cancer as identified through the use of the S.W.O.T. analysis, which is discussed further in Section 4.0.

Personal Resources: Personal resources can be thought of as the resources which are imbedded in one's identity. It includes one's mind frame; personality; culture; ethnicity; spirit/soul; feelings; gender roles, attitudes; experiences; capabilities; knowledge (both formally learned via education or acquired elsewhere); skills, judgment, morals, etc. In terms of the S.W.O.T. analysis, personal, and all other resources can be regarded as both strengths (a means to decreasing cancer risk or preventative measures which can be taken), as well as weaknesses (i.e. factors contributing to increased cancer risk). For instance, the feeling of stress can induce unhealthy lifestyle choices made within the microenvironment such as an increase in smoking, alcohol use, and unhealthy dietary choices which could lead to changes in ones physical resources/biological environment, such as increased body mass index and/or gastroesophageal reflux disease (GERD), all risk factors for esophageal cancer (Novogradec, 2008a). On the contrary, stress could also be channelled towards making positive changes, such as turning a stressful situation into something positive (i.e. networking with others facing similar situations). In this instance, individuals may tap into their human resources to assist in social organization and change (societal forces). We can see an example of this when cancer patients, caregivers, friends, and/or family members of cancer patients take a stressful situation and try to "do good" by means of participating in a cancer walk (societal forces which also impacts the human resources' physical resources/biological environment (i.e. physical activity)) to raise funds for cancer research (economic and technological-industrial forces respectively)—this illustrates how individual resources are impacted in relation to the macro environment.

To illustrate another example of how personal resources can be viewed as both strengths and weaknesses, and how they interact and influence other resources and environments, let's further consider the factor of stress by exploring personality type. Personality type can be considered a weakness when, for instance, one possesses the characteristics inherent of a Type C personality, or if one perceives that they have a lack of control over stressors and environmental factors. On the flip side, strengths would include not possessing a Type C personality, and having perceived control over stressors and environmental factors which are said to reduce stress as well as the physical resources/biological environments affected as a result; as suggested by the stress-diathesis model. Elaboration on Type C personality type, the stress-diathesis model, and perception of control are interconnected and could potentially influence whether or not the S.W.O.T. analysis would even be considered as a strategy (i.e. the practicality of it) that could influence changes within one's life. As such, these concepts are explored in more detail below.

Attributing cancer causation to personality is not a new phenomenon. "In AD 200-300, Galen argued that there was an association between melancholia and cancer" (Ogden, 2000:304). Further, in 1901 Sir William Osler reported the spontaneous shrinkage of metastases from breast cancer in two women, claiming that it is often much more important to know what patient has the disease, than what kind of disease the patient has (Osler, 1906). Over the past two decades there has been growing interest in the relationship between personality and cancer, commonly referred to as the "Type C" concept (Tomoshok, 1987; Eysenck, 1985). Eysenck (1990) suggested that individuals who react to stress with hopelessness and helplessness, and who repress emotional reactions to life events are characteristics of a "Type C" personality.

Hafen et al., (1996) note that some researchers believe that personality may play a key role—as do diet, accidents, early childhood experiences, and genetic make-up; these factors create what is referred to as 'weak links' which determines how stress will affect a person. "Psychoanalyst Herbert J. Freudenberger points out that these weak links, which are part of our personality, are for the most part "learned and reinforced behaviours" (Hafen et al., 1996: 106-107) which also plays a role in how one deals with stress. Ogden (2000) suggests that the issue of control over stress plays a role in feelings of helplessness in the face of stress.

Seligman (1975) describes 'helplessness' as a psychological state which frequently results when events are uncontrollable. Levy and Heiden (1990:259) describe 'hopelessness' as a concept which is closely related to helplessness. "It includes the feeling that a situation or condition is without solution." To demonstrate these concepts in relation to stress related to negative life events (all attributes of 'Type C' personality), it is important to understand the "life events theory" which was developed "to examine stress and stress-related changes as a response to life experiences" (Ogden, 2000:233). A meta-analysis examining psychological factors in the development of malignant disease was conducted by LeShan (1959). His analysis was based on the premise that if the 'life events theory' was valid, then cancer mortality rates should be highest for widowed, next highest for divorced, and lowest for married and then single persons. The results found that some of the data were consistent with this hypothesis showing that "the most relevant psychological factor was the loss of a major emotional relationship prior to the first-noted symptoms of neoplasm" (Cooper, 1988: 374).

However, the study of personality's role in cancer etiology has been fraught with inherent difficulties. These are briefly discussed before examining the attributes of a "Type C" individual.

First, much research examining cancer-prone personality traits are retrospective in design, making it impossible to determine whether patients develop cancer because they have the particular personality attributes of a "Type C" personality or whether these certain personality factors develop as a consequence of the cancer experience (Taylor, 1999; Cooper, 1988). Although the role of personality traits in the development of cancer is inconclusive, prospective longitudinal studies examining the role of individual predispositions avoid some of these methodological problems (Taylor, 1999). Second, "it may be possible that because some studies are done in the hospital setting prior to diagnosis (already suggesting that there is a health problem), traits and characterisitics that are identified by researchers may be biased" (Eysenck, 1996:195). Third, assuming that 'Type C' personality exists, "it may be that the link between cancer and personality [personal resource] is indirect; people with a cancer-prone personality may smoke more, drink more, and have a more unhealthy type of diet [other environments]" (Eysenck, 1996: 195). Fourth, "it is also possible that cancer, even before diagnosis, causes feelings of hopelessness and helplessness, or has other influences on personality, thus reversing the assumed causal relationship (Eysenck, 1996:196). Lastly, the speculation that personality can produce cancer can be destructive not only scientifically but also psychologically (Taylor, 1999).

Nevertheless, Hafen et al., (1996) claim that stress can cause physical illness which is due partly to physiology, (the biological environment/physical resource) and partly to personality (personal resource). Further, their theory proposes that everyone has the same network; sets of hormonal switches and cycles and that these control how we respond in different situations, including stressful ones. Based on this theory, everyone has the same physiological make-up and there is no explanation of why individual reactions impact the body differently. According to Bennett (2000), the stress-diathesis model is designed to attempt to explain individual differences. This model shows that "stress places some degree of strain on bodily systems such as the central nervous system, immune system, or both. However, whether and where this is translated into a disease process is a function of biological factors such as genetic phenotype [2] [biological environment/physical resource] or previous exposure to particular pathogens [3] [which can be found in the micro environment]" (Bennett, 2000:40).

"It has been argued that a lack of control over stressors and environmental factors may be related to an increase in the onset of cancer" (Ogden, 2000:305). Endler et al., (2000:246) contend that "control over a specific situation (situational control) is often investigated by making available or eliciting a response that a person can use to affect the event (for example by self-administering a stressor, making a decision, or obtaining more detailed instructions)".

Further, "perceptions of control alone are sufficient to reduce stress (the control does not actually have to be present or realized but merely perceived to be present)" (Endler, 2000:246). Consistent with this, the administration of a decision-making tool often used in the field of business will be brought to light as a solution to increasing individual control through the recognition of individual strengths and weaknesses as well as opportunities and threats posed by the environment.

Physical Resources/Biological Environment: Physical resources, also referred to as the biological environment encompasses all genes, as well as cellular structure, organization, function, mechanisms of action and molecular interactions within and between cells. The biological environment takes into account all genetic and cellular processes which occur during development (beginning in-utero) until death.

Additionally, it includes body functions and movement (i.e. bending, posture, etc.), physical activity, routes of entry (i.e. inhalation, ingestion, oral contact, dermal absorption, etc.,), transmission (i.e. mother to infant, sexual, parenteral, etc.), physiology, as well as physiological differences resulting from differences in sex (including pulmonary function, metabolism, body composition, renal structure, hormones, etc.), and includes all systems (i.e. immune, nervous, gastrointestinal, endocrine, etc.) aging, weight, etc. (Novogradec, 2006).

The field of molecular epidemiology has provided some of the answers researchers are looking for in understanding why cancer incidence occurs amongst specific populations. One of these includes the role of heredity as implicated in familial cancer. In this regard, the role which genetics plays in cancer causation can illustrate both the strengths and weaknesses attributed to the biological environment/physical resources.

Some common forms of childhood cancers have been linked to genetics. For instance, the biological environment has proven to play a significant role for both retinoblastoma and Wilm's tumour (also known as nephroblastoma)—these would be regarded as weaknesses within the biological environment/physical resources in relation to the application of the S.W.O.T. analysis. More specifically, the Rb1 gene has been linked to retinoblastoma incidence (Dyer and

Bremner, 2005; Perera, 1997; Mitchell, 1992). Similarly, genes such as WT1, WT2 and WT3 have been implicated in the etiology and progression of Wilm's tumour (Perotti et al., 2005; Rivera and Haber, 2005; Guertl et al., 2003; Tay, 1995; Williamson and Van Heyningen, 1994). Twin studies can help shed some light on whether cancer risk can be attributed solely to genetics, or whether there is a gene-environment relationship which exists. "Since identical twins have the same genetic makeup (i.e. genotype), differences in cancer incidence between twins cannot be attributed to genetics alone, but must necessarily involve differential environmental exposures (conversely, similarities in cancer incidence between twins will support the genetic basis of cancer)" (Novogradec and Ali, 2004: 21). Various twin studies conducted by Lichtenstein et al., (2000), Verkasalo et al., (1999), and Harris (1997) emphasize the importance of studying the environmental context (factors that fall within the realm of the micro environment) in combination with genetic predispositions (Novogradec, 2006).

For example, the genetic polymorphism associated with either the CYP1A1*2 or GSTM1*2/*2 genotypes by themselves have not shown to have any significant effect on the risk of cancer development (Autrup, 2004). However, since these genetic traits "influence the metabolic activation or detoxification of carcinogenic chemicals" (Perera, 1997:1069), the microenvironment needs to also be considered (Novogradec, 2006). For instance, a review conducted by Bartsch et al., (2000:3) found that "some CYP1A1/GSTM1 0/0 genotype combinations appear to predispose the lung, esophagus, and oral cavity of smokers to an even higher risk for cancer or DNA damage". However, the authors noted that confirmation of these findings were still required.

To elaborate further on gene-environment interactions, consider the role of alcohol (social environments) in relation to genes (biological environment). When consumed, alcohol (also known as ethanol) enters cells and is broken down into a toxic compound known as acetaldehyde (Rutherford, 2002), better classified by The International Agency for Research on Cancer (IARC) (1999) as a Group 2B [4] carcinogen. What happens to acetaldehyde in our system mainly depends on whether or not the aldehyde dehydrogenase-2 (ALDH2) gene has an alteration or not. This alteration is also known as a "polymorphism". In a system where no alterations of this gene exist, the acetaldehyde is easily converted into acetic acid, commonly known as vinegar, and is readily used by the body to provide energy (Rutherford, 2002). Conversely, a polymorphism in the ALDH2 gene will render the enzyme inactive, making it impossible for the system to make the conversion; such people should avoid alcohol at all costs because the diminished activity of this enzyme dramatically increases the risk for certain cancers such as that of the esophagus (Muto et al., 2000; Yokoyama et al., 1998).

The condition of the ALDH2 gene can determine the risk for certain cancers. Along these same lines, the ALDH2*2 gene plays a role on human tastes toward alcohol. Alcohol consumption is reduced among those individuals who carry one or two ALDH2*2 alleles. This is the case because ALDH2*2 generally serves as a strong protective factor against alcoholism by making the taste of alcohol unpleasant (Higuchi et al., 1995). Therefore, according to Yokoyama et al., (1998) it is very likely that ALDH2*2 protects against alcohol-induced cancers in the normal population. However, in drinkers, it potentiates the carcinogenic effects of alcohol exposure. Genetic testing can determine whether or not certain people have the ALDH2 polymorphism (Rutherford, 2002). If tested positive for the ALDH2 polymorphism, reduction in alcohol consumption should be made to potentially reduce the risk of developing alcohol-related cancers [5] such as those of the upper aero-digestive tract (Lewis et al., 2008).

As illustrated above, genetics in combination with micro environments can act as both strengths and/or weaknesses in relation to cancer. To illustrate this point further, consider the gene-environment interplay as it relates to lung cancer risk. Hall (1997:71) states that "lung cancer risk is strongly associated with exposure to cigarette smoking, however, only a fraction (10 percent–20 percent) of the life time smokers develop lung cancer, suggesting that genetic factors may affect an individual's susceptibility to lung cancer." Similar remarks are made by Kiyohara et al., (2002:241) who contend that "lung cancer is a multi-factoral disease and as such requires an improved understanding of the interplay of environment and genetic polymorphisms". Shields (1999:S7) confirms this when noting that "numerous gene-environment interactions for lung cancer risk have been demonstrated, whereby genetic polymorphisms [6] in carcinogen metabolizing genes have been shown to modify the effects of carcinogen exposure on cancer risk and DNA adducts." In essence, some individuals may be predisposed to certain types of cancer because of the effects that carcinogens have on their particular DNA. The effects that some carcinogens may have on one person may be very different in comparison to another person. Furthermore, both genetic factors and environmental effects play important roles in an individual's "threshold limit value". [7]

Human Resources: Human, economic and other resources act as surrogates for a set of other factors pertaining to either the causation or prevention of ill health, including cancer. In relation to human resources, this would include factors such as: valuable political connections, social support, social ties, networks, etc.. To illustrate the role that human resources play in the prevention of cancer (classified as a strength in the S.W.O.T. analysis) consider a study conducted by Kang and Bloom (1993) whose objective was "to examine the relationship between social support and the use of cancer-screening tests among older Black Americans" (Kang and Bloom, 1993: 737). Their study found that "social support seemed to be associated with increased use of mammography and occult blood stool examinations among older Black Americans" (Kang and Bloom, 1993: 737). The suggested implications of this would be to design interventions which would increase the utilization of social networks as an effective means of increasing the use of cancer screening, with the ultimate goal of reducing cancer mortality (Kang and Bloom, 1993). This example illustrates how human resources aid in the means towards preventative measures made available by more macro technological-industrial forces. If social organization were to occur on a large scale it would also influence societal forces which could change societal knowledge, perceptions, and expectations on cancer prevention via screening. On the contrary, an example of how human resources can act as a weakness might include the misuse of valuable political connections to create lax policies surrounding risk assessment and management, allowing for unsafe levels of carcinogens to be produced by industry, which in turn may result in the increase of cancer incidence. In this light, human resources are being unethically used on an individual level, to impact larger political-legal forces on a macro level, thereby influencing the micro environments.

Economic Resources: Economic resources include factors pertaining to monetary value and worth (i.e. assets such as property), the availability of and access to money, wealth, inheritance, etc. The role that economic resources have in the causation and/or prevention of cancer or ill health can be direct or indirect. For instance, in a population-based case-control study conducted by Baris et al., (2000), it was found that elevated risks of multiple myeloma was associated with lower income among both Blacks and Whites residing in the United States. In countries where the health care system is not subsidized by the government, one's economic resources can mean the difference between life and death either directly (i.e. access to health care), or indirectly (i.e. the quality of food purchased and consumed, overall nutritional habits, housing, sanitation, etc.) and can affect both the prevention and causation of cancer. On the flip side, access to more money could also result in risky behaviours such as more money to purchase and consume alcohol, cigarettes, etc. (which is related to personal resources, explained above).

Other Resources: Other resources consist of factors not belonging to any of the other categories described above, and also includes those factors that are overlapping and complex such as socioeconomic status (SES), social class, occupational status, and poverty. For instance, socioeconomic status draws on personal resources (i.e. knowledge gained via education), economic resources (i.e. income) and other resources (i.e. occupation). To illustrate this point further, let us revisit the study noted above by Baris et al., (2000). This study also showed that other socioeconomic measures such as occupation-based SES and education were also found to be associated with increased risks of multiple myeloma. Further, another case-control study evaluating the independent influences of individual and community SES on the risk of breast cancer suggested that "there was something about living in high-SES communities that resulted in an increased risk of breast cancer independent of individual-level SES" (Webster et al., 2008: 1128). The associations between socioeconomic status and breast cancer risk are not well understood. More research needs to be conducted in this vein to identify deeper rooted issues and associated risk factors.

These examples illustrate that both low and high socioeconomic status are associated with increased risks to different cancer sites. Factors such as low socioeconomic status and class are complex because they are said to act as surrogates for a set of other factors such as poor housing, living in worse communities, unemployment, workplace hazards, stress, poor nutritional status, etc., (Isaacs and Schroeder 2004; Pickens and Orringer, 2003; Brown and Devesa, 2002; Brown et al., 2002a; Fitzpatrick, 2001; Gorey and Vena, 1994). Furthermore, factors pertaining to SES can also play a role in the prevention of cancer, as illustrated in a study carried out in Scotland conducted by Power et al (2008) which examined the intentions and action in colorectal cancer screening. Their study found that "socioeconomic deprivation and poor health distinguished attenders vs. non-attenders at screening" (Power et al., 2008: 292). This suggests that resources, economic and other, can act as a proxy for other deeper rooted issues, which can ultimately affect prognosis—particularly if a person waits until the cancer is at a late stage before seeking medical advice.

Micro Environment (Level 2)

The microenvironment consists of environments that are not part of the broader or macro environment, but rather, includes the surrounding environments which directly affect the individual. As such, the microenvironment can be divided into four parts and comprise (1) natural environment and microbes (2) built, (3) social, and (4) other environments.

Recall the various living and working contexts as noted in Section 3.0 (home, work, social and other), which are embedded in the microenvironment. There is connectedness between individual resources, the microenvironment, and the macro-environmental forces—as such it is often difficult to refer to one without discussing the others. Combined with the microenvironment, routes of entry play an important role in cancer causation. More specifically, body burden—or the total sum of carcinogens in the body—is a concept which takes into account all routes of entry (i.e. inhalation, ingestion, dermal absorption, etc., (physical resources/biological environment)) as well as all sources of carcinogens (i.e. food, air, water) found within the microenvironment (Novogradec and Ali, 2004).

Natural Environment and Microbes: The natural environment consists of the ecosystem in which we are a part of (i.e. air, water, soil, etc.) and functions as a system. When this system is out of balance, all species and microbes living within it are in danger (Novogradec, 2006). The "natural" environment includes all beneficial and harmful attributes of our natural environment, including all aspects that are part of our ecosystem (plants, animals, microbes, etc.), the earth, and its atmosphere (Novogradec, 2006). Human intervention with the natural environment is connected to the built environment where its various by-products (i.e. pollution, waste, etc.) can be potentially carcinogenic or harmful to health. Microbes that live in the natural environment and human body (i.e. bacteria, viruses, protozoa, etc.) as well as the natural environment itself, have shown to play roles in cancer etiology (Novogradec, 2006).

Since animals and humans often share the same environment, is not uncommon that they also may suffer the same fate. Consider the high-risk esophageal cancer regions of China and the high frequency of esophageal cancer among chickens in the same regions. Ghadirian et al., (1988) and Yang (1980) suggest that the existence of "common" carcinogens in food sources and the natural environment are plausible explanations for this occurrence since these are the environments that are shared amongst chickens and their owners. Often times, the first sign that there is something harmful in the environment surfaces in the natural environment. For instance, in Quebec's St. Lawrence estuary, exposure to polycyclic aromatic hydrocarbons (PAHs) originating from nearby aluminium smelters was found to be the cause of increased cancer rates amongst beluga whales (Martineau et al., 2002a; Fox, 2001; Watanabe, 2000; Steingraber, 1998; Colborn et al., 1997). Evidently, "the human population living in proximity of the beluga habitat is affected by rates of cancer higher than those found in people in the rest of Québec and Canada, and some of these cancers have been epidemiologically related to PAHs" (Martineau et al., 2002a: 285). According to Martineau et al., 2002b, "further support for PAH carcinogenicity in humans has been provided by epidemiologic studies such as those carried out in aluminium workers of the Saguenay-Lac Saint-Jean region of Canada (Tremblay et al., 1995; Armstrong et al., 1988; Theriault et al., 1984). In these studies, the epidemiologic association between exposure to PAHs and lung and urinary bladder cancers has been strong enough to warrant the compensation of affected workers by the Quebec Health and safety Workers Compensation Board" (Martineau et al.,

2002b: A562).

There is also a microbial role in cancer causation. To demonstrate the interplay between various forms of transmission and the microbial connection to cancer causation, consider how microbes, more specifically viruses, are involved with the development of cervical cancer. Nearly all cervical cancers contain DNA from the human papillomavirus [8] (HPV). There are many strains of HPV; HPV 16 and 18 are considered to be high-risk strains (Novogradec, 2007a). Although some HPV infections resolve on their own, those that do not are usually high-risk strains that occasionally develop into a persistent infection, potentially leading to the development of cervical cancer if left untreated, implicating HPV as a necessary cause of cervical cancer (Novogradec, 2007a; Walboomers et al., 1999; McNeil, 1997; Bosch et al., 1995). HPV infection is the most common sexually transmitted viral disease, and women who engage in sexual activity at a young age and who have a number of different partners will most likely acquire HPV infection over their lifetime. Furthermore, their partners' sexual histories also play a role; the more sexual partners one has, the increased risk they face. Other risk factors for cervical cancer include becoming sexually active at a young age and smoking (Novogradec 2007a; Franco and Ferenczy 2002). Infection with genital HPV has also been associated with other cancers such as those of the penis, anus, vagina, and vulva (Burchell et al., 2006; Muñoz et al., 2006).

The more we know about what causes certain cancers, the more equipped we will be to prevent them from occurring in the first place. Hence, it is clear that an upstream approach, one which focuses on prevention and which considers individual resources and the micro and macro environments, needs to be taken in order to ultimately decrease the risk of various cancers. With reference to the above discussion, risks of HPV infections can be minimized through various different measures—the application of the S.W.O.T. analysis in combination with the environment and cancer framework is recommended in this effort. Depending on the individual's resources and environments, these goals and objectives will differ. Nevertheless, to illustrate some goals that may be set in an attempt to decrease the risk of HPV one may strive to: i) never smoke or quit smoking ii) abstain from sexual activity at a young age, iii) when choosing to be sexually active to a) use condoms, b) select partners who have had minimal sexual partners themselves, c) partake in routine pap tests (active screening for cervical cancer) and d) prior to engaging in unprotected sex, consider the possibility of vaccination against high risk strains of HPV. Some controversies still exist in the literature on whether or not mandatory vaccination against certain strains of HPV amongst 9-12 year old girls is warranted (Gostin and DeAngelis, 2007; Markowitz, 2007). These controversies illustrate the macro technological and industrial forces at play.

Other viruses, protozoa, and bacteria have also been implicated for their roles in various different cancers. For instance, chronic infection with either or both Hepatitis B and C has been associated with the development of hepatocellular carcinoma (HCC) [9] (Novogradec, 2007a). Since infection with Hepatitis B often occurs at an early age but the occurrence of HCC usually does not appear until decades later, researchers suggest that there are also other microenvironments which also need to be considered, such as exposures to naturally occurring aflatoxins (which are produced in some dietary staples such as peanuts and maize), as well as alcohol consumption and co-infection with Hepatitis C (Kirk 2006; Herrera, 2005). Epstein Barr Virus (EBV) is yet another example of a virus implicated for its role in cancer causation. According to the International Agency for Research on Cancer (1997), infection with EBV is associated with risk for Burkitt's lymphoma, Hodgkin's disease, Non-Hodgkin's Lymphoma and nasopharyngeal carcinoma (Novogradec, 2007a). Furthermore, long-term infection with S. haematobium [10] has been associated with the development of bladder cancer. Factors such as genetics, immune response, and other associated infections (i.e. Hepatitis) also play a role in the outcome of infection, and can yet again illustrate how both individual resources and the microenvironment are implicated in cancer risk (Novogradec 2007a; IARC, 1994).

Up to this point, it has been demonstrated how microbes can play a role in the causation of cancer, but they can also play a protective role. For instance, "Helicobacter pylori (H. pylori) [11] infection has been implicated for its role in the pre-cancer process (i.e. chronic gastritis) associated with gastric adenocarcinoma and gastric MALT lymphoma. [12] However, it also has been found to have a protective effect against Barrett's esophagus—a precursor for adenocarcinoma of the esophagus (a type of esophageal cancer)" (Novogradec, 2007a: 461). This illustrates the importance of recognizing that the microenvironment can act as both an opportunity (i.e. protective effect) and threat for cancer risk and other health effects. For those microbes which present as a threat, "greater awareness of the various precautionary measures that can be taken amongst high-risk populations must occur. More specifically, risk factors and methods of transmission need to be addressed through i) educational measures, ii) changes in current high-risk practices, behaviours, attitudes, and perceptions, iii) [access to] and the adoption of safer alternatives, iv) improved living and working conditions, and v) increased availability of and access to overall healthier environments" (Novogradec, 2007a: 464).

Built Environment: The built environment consists of human intervention with the natural environment resulting in various by-products such as pollution, waste, etc. It also includes human-made infrastructure, as well as the products of industrialization, which may include: synthetic chemicals (i.e. those found in cosmetics, common household items, cleaning products etc.), pharmaceuticals, radioactive substances etc. (Novogradec, 2006; Novogradec and Ali, 2004). The natural environment is not often thought of as a threat to health (i.e. contribute to the development of cancer). However, solely (i.e. aflatoxins, asbestos) or in conjunction with the built environment it is clear that this is not always the case.

Since industrialization, the line between the natural and built environments has become less clear. Consider the effects of exposure to radionuclides which may occur naturally, but can also be artificially produced. According to the U.S. Environmental Protection Agency (2007), "cancer is the major effect of concern from radionuclides. Radium, via oral exposure, is known to cause bone, head, and nasal passage tumours in humans, and radon, via inhalation exposure, causes lung cancer in humans. Uranium may cause lung cancer and tumours of the lymphatic and hematopoietic tissues". These exposures can take place in various different contexts. For instance, studies examining exposure to radon both in the context of work (i.e. underground miners) and home (i.e. residential) have been linked to lung cancer risk (Barros-Dios et al., 2002; Darby et al., 1998).

Furthermore, exposure to asbestos has been linked to incidence of mesothelioma, lung, and esophageal cancers, amongst others. Over time, a number of different "exposure" studies have been conducted from multiple perspectives examining cancer causation resulting from the microenvironment. "Since several earmarked "occupational carcinogens" (i.e. asbestos, radon, gas, and benzene) are not strictly monitored or measured in the general environment, one cannot be certain that these presumed occupational carcinogens are in fact solely the result of workplace exposures (Siemiatycki et al., 2004). This gives rise to concerns on a *micro level*, such as deciphering the totality of study findings. It also raises concerns on a *macro level* such as the implementation of stringent policies and regulatory measures as well as social responsibility" (Novogradec, 2007b:215).

Some of what we know about cancer etiology has been the result of macro level forces (i.e. political–legal and technological-industrial forces). For instance, poor industrial practices and a lack of social responsibility on the part of industry can be to blame for the illegal industrial dumping of trichloroethylene and perchloroethylene which had contaminated nearby well water used by the surrounding community for drinking and bathing. This has resulted in a leukaemia cluster amongst a group of children living in a community in Woburn Massachusetts in 1972. In 1996, Jonathan Harr wrote a book entitled "A Civil

Action" which recounted the difficulties surrounding the necessary scientific proof of association as required by the legal system before a company can be made liable. This illustrates the various macro-environmental issues at play.

Cancer clusters such as the one noted above, can provide better insight to causation. A cancer cluster can be broadly defined as "a geographic area, time period, or group of people with a greater than expected number of cancer cases" (Novogradec and Ali, 2004: 24). The study of cancer clusters undoubtedly presents several difficulties for researchers, clinicians, and public officials. Maheswaran and Staines (1997) point out an apparent challenge involved with cancer clusters, including the significant chance that the cluster of people exposed to a particular substance will disperse, further reducing the chances of identifying a cluster. Nonetheless, as acknowledged by Aldrich and Sinks (2002), "a set of common characteristics unique to current etiologic cluster investigations have uncovered new information about the causes of cancer and/or have demonstrated a preventable link to a known carcinogen" (Aldrich and Sinks, 2002: 810).

Cancer clusters can also emerge in the face of large scale catastrophes. Consider what research has shown in the aftermath of tragedies such as the A-bomb and the Chernobyl disaster. Since the atomic bombs were dropped in Hiroshima and Nagasaki in 1945, research has shown that nearly 'forty years after the fact, the cancer incidence among the exposed survivors (excluding leukaemia) was still increasing relative to that among the unexposed. This held true irrespective of the dosimetry systems or models used to evaluate risk' (Rotblat, 1988: 45-46). According to the National Academies (2003), 'the incidence of A-bomb related leukaemia rose almost in direct proportion to dose of radiation, where the risk was much higher for those exposed as children than for those exposed as adults. Nevertheless, incidence of radiation-related leukaemia peaked at 7–8 years after exposure' (National Academies, 2003:4). Unlike leukaemia incidence, "the increased risks of solid cancers did not diminish but lasted throughout a lifetime. There is a marked radiation effect when survivors reach the age at which cancers most often occur" (National Academics, 2003: 4). The Radiation Effects Research Foundation is an excellent source of information for both past and on-going studies related to the atomic bombings of Hiroshima and Nagasaki, providing much insight to both the short and long term effects of human exposure to radiation at different doses (http://www.rerf.or.jp/).

The aftermath of the Chernobyl nuclear accident which occurred in April 1986 may providc a more recent example. It was only several years after the disaster that evidence surfaced pertaining to the increased rates of childhood thyroid cancer. The cause was later understood to be attributed to exposure of external ionizing radiation during childhood (Moysich et al., 2002; Stephenson,

2001; N.S., 1999; Robbins and Schneider, 1998).

Radiation knows no territorial boundaries. Because of variable weather conditions in the days following the accident, radiation also spread over large parts of Scandinavia, Poland, and the Baltic States, as well as southern Germany, Switzerland, northern France and England. The dense clouds of radioactivity were widely dispersed over Europe, with caesium and iodine directly contaminating the lichen eaten by Lapland's reindeer, the grass of Wales and parts of Ireland and the flora and fauna of the French and Italian Alps" (Chernobyl Children's Project International, 2008). Technological-industrial forces led to the development of the nuclear reactor in the first place, but also was responsible for the accident and the damage thereafter. Following the accident, the built environment (radiation) combined with natural forces (weather conditions) impacted the health of various populations, as well as the surrounding natural environment and microbes. However, it did not end there. The intersect of the natural and built environments were also impacted (i.e. tainted food sources) which turned this tragedy into a global catastrophe, hence impacting the social environment of various people across different geographies (i.e. voluntary vs. involuntary exposures). Soon after the accident, dangerously irradiated food (i.e. tainted powered milk from Poland and tainted produce from countries in Europe) was exported from Europe to many parts of the third world where controls and safety checks were inadequate (Chernobyl Children's Project International, 2008). This brings to light the interplay between macro political-legal and economic forces at hand.

Over twenty years after the Chernobyl accident, cancer's latency effect is now being realized amongst affected populations. 'Cancer of the thyroid gland is rising sharply in New York State, and while there are no data on the rates among different ethnic groups, doctors with patients that are émigrés from the Former Soviet Union believe that this population accounts for a significant part of the rise, which can be traced back to the Chernobyl nuclear accident' (Pérez-Peña, 2006; Bracken, 2006). A group of doctors in New York have recently organized a conference with the United Nations, urging immigrants from the Ukraine, Belarus, and Russia and physicians alike, to screen this population for thyroid cancer, with the ultimate goal being to diagnose and treat thyroid cancer early. If caught early enough, thyroid cancer has a good prognosis (Pérez-Peña, 2006; Bracken, 2006). This illustrates how the use of technological-industrial forces can help detect (i.e. screening via biopsy, annual sonograms etc.) and treat thyroid cancer once identified. Furthermore, it demonstrates how societal forces can impact political-legal forces. For instance, New York doctors recognized that other American doctors may not necessarily think in terms of Chernobyl and radiation exposure when seeing immigrant patients from these areas, therefore they have come together to educate and bring awareness to policy makers, colleagues, and patients alike (Bracken, 2006).

Ill health as a result of exposures is an on-going matter of concern. Consider both the short and long-term health effects following the recent collapse of the World Trade Centre which took place on September 11, 2001. "A large number of people sustained potential exposures to smoke, dust, particulate matter, and a variety of toxins, including asbestos, pulverized concrete, glass fibres, polycyclic aromatic hydrocarbons (PAHs), and polychlorinated furans and dioxins. Additionally, many had exposure to psychological traumatogens. The most common effects seen to date are respiratory and mental health consequences. The long-term consequences of exposures are not yet known" (Moline et al., 2006: 294). There remains concern about the potential for late-emerging diseases such as cancers, which will not become apparent still for decades (Samet al., 20007; Herbert, 2007; Moline et al., 2006). In a follow-up to Samet et al.'s (2007) article, Dr. Robin Herbert [13] discusses some of the troubling findings which are beginning to surface such as the handful of cases with multiple myeloma presenting in very young individuals; multiple myeloma is a condition that almost always presents later in life. Dr. Herbert remarks that the reality is that we will never know the full range of what the World Trade Centre responders were exposed to—and this brings to light the concern of synergistic effects at play (Herbert, 2007).

These examples demonstrate cancer clusters which result from acute exposures. Nevertheless, some environment and health issues and problems are said to be the result of chronic, low-level exposures. This topic is hotly debated amongst scientists – particularly in light of the fact that it goes against the very principle guiding the field of toxicology which notes that the dose makes the poison. However, there is growing evidence that low level exposures to endocrine disrupting chemicals can result in a multitude of health effects such as reproductive problems, learning disabilities, behavioural problems and various cancers (Colborn et al., 1997). [14] Since certain hormones have been implicated for their role in various hormone-related cancers such as those of the breast and prostate, it is plausible that those chemicals which mimic these hormones may also play a role in increased risk to certain cancers. The possibility that low level exposures to certain chemicals can have detrimental effects on health, calls for the need of more accurate risk assessment methods; particularly in light of the fact that those currently being used by regulatory agencies are based on traditional toxicological testing (Welshons et al., 2003).

Although the role of exposures in cancer causation are very real, they can also be difficult to prove. There are several reasons that can account for these difficulties. The first can be attributed to the incomplete assessment of multiple exposure routes, types, and the dose. The second includes the difficulty of identifying the causative agent(s) and quantitatively measuring synergistic, interactive, and timing effects of exposure to a multiplicity of chemicals in the environment. Closely related to this is the latency effect, and the challenges associated with identifying and isolating exposures over one's lifetime and ruling out confounding factors. Next, is the difficulty of proving causality using statistical significance rather than practical significance. Often times nearly the entire community has to fall victim to illness or disease related to the environmental exposure(s) before any "statistical significance" is obtained. Also problematic is the limited number of cases available for study. If the sample size is not large enough, it becomes increasingly difficult to statistically show any association(s). Another difficulty in proving cancer causation encompasses the concerns regarding data quality such as recall bias, systematic errors, poor data sources, and diagnostic and coding inaccuracies which may flaw the investigation (Novogradec 2007b; Novogradec and Ali, 2004; Maheswaran and Staines, 1997; Heath, 1996). Hence, receiving compensation is not always easy, particularly when absolute proof of causation is not always supported in the literature.

For instance, there have been several studies examining the association between different cancers and the dry cleaning industry. Some studies have been successful at confirming esophageal cancer risk amongst drycleaners, attributing this association to PCE [15] as the cause (Ruder et al., 2001; Vaughan et al., 1997; Ruder et al., 1994, Blair, 1990). However, as Vaughan et al., (1997:692) point out with their own case-control studies examining this relationship, the findings linking esophageal cancer risk in the dry cleaning industry (due to the use of PCE) could easily be explained by chance. When occupational groups are identified as "high risk" for cancer, a search for the cause becomes passionately pursued by some researchers (Hansen et al., 2001; Wartenberg et al., 2000a; Wartenberg et al., 2000b; Boice and McLaughlin, 2001; Wartenberg et al., 2001; Wartenberg et al., 2002; Weiss, 1995; Apfeldorf and Infante, 1981). The victims (regardless of how, what, where, when, or why they were exposed and whether exposures were involuntary or not), are not usually compensated, since without scientific proof of the *theories* about their illness(es) and/or disease(s), "cause(s)" are merely speculation and cannot therefore form the basis of compensatory actions.

This highlights the issue that officials must recognize that there are likely many factors involved in cancer causation, hence uncovering one cause and one effect with absolute proof in accordance with the legal system may not always be realistic. Recognizing these limitations, the onus of proof should be shifted onto the proto-developer to show that no reasonable environmental harm or adverse health effects will result from their activities, instead of the conventional approach of having the affected public prove harm (Jordan and O'Riordan, 1999). This illustrates the role of both the political-legal and technological-industrial forces in causation. In the meantime, alternative and supplementary methodologies (Novogradec, 2006) and assessment measures (O'Brien, 2000) should be considered in addition to the implementation of societal forces such as mass education and social organization (which often begins on a grassroots level) to implement policy changes.

Social Environment: The social environment brings to light voluntary vs. involuntary exposures. This includes lifestyle and dietary choices, such as those that are voluntary (i.e. smoking, use of recreational drugs, alcohol use, as well as exposures from hobbies, crafts, etc.) and those that are involuntary (i.e. exposure to environmental tobacco smoke, nearby asphalt fumes, communal printer fumes, etc.). These exposures are often the result of built or natural environments. Health promotion suggests that "change" can occur by changing our reference group. Reference group theory is based on the principle that people take the standards of significant others (i.e. human resources) as a basis for making self-appraisals, comparisons, and choices regarding need and use of information. This could potentially impact the use and success of the S.W.O.T. analysis—but could also create emotional instability if disrupted. Health promotion recommends that we should avoid carcinogens found in the environment—but it begs the question of why carcinogens resulting from the built environment are there in the first place, pointing again to macro-level forces at play. Nevertheless, since there are carcinogens in the environment, preventing exposure to them can potentially prevent cancer. This has been illustrated by "the drop in male lung cancer cases from the reduction in tobacco smoking or the drop in bladder cancer among cohorts of dye workers from the elimination of exposure to specific aromatic amines. This provides evidence that preventing cancer is possible when we act on what we know" (Clapp et al., 2008:1). In this sense, so long as change is practical (i.e. one's livelihood is not in jeopardy as a result of change), individuals will be more receptive to take a pro-active approach. In this light, societal forces can aid in challenging the very system which allows for those carcinogens originating from built environments to exist.

Other Environments: Other environments are simply those environments which do not fall under the purview of the natural environments and microbes, the built, or social environments.

Macro Environment: (Level 3)

The macro-environment encompasses the broader forces that are affected by, and which also affect, individual resources and microenvironments. As such the macro environment consists of six different forces, which include: (1) political-legal forces; (2) technological-industrial forces; (3) economic forces; (4) societal forces; (5) natural forces; (6) other forces. As demonstrated, there is much interconnectedness between individual resources, the microenvironment, and macro-environmental forces.

Political-Legal Forces: Political-legal forces would include the outcomes of elections, and the implementation of legislation, policies, and decisions rendered by various commissions and agencies at every level of government (Wright et al., 1998). It would also include regulations, laws, court judgments, etc. Political-legal forces can act as both opportunities and threats. In order to reach set goals and objectives, individuals draw on the strengths and weaknesses of their resources to optimize on opportunities and minimize threats posed by their micro and macro environments. To illustrate how political-legal forces can ultimately impact health, consider what might occur if the government in country X legislates that all fresh fruit is to be genetically modified beginning on June 22, 2000. This would substantially impact the individuals who purchase only organic fruits from that point forward. Further, fruit imported from other countries will have their own regulations and will need to meet country X's new standards. Under new government policy, individuals will no longer have access to organic fruit via supermarkets, farmers and/or any other government regulated fruit source/outlet, therefore individuals seeking to consume only organic fruits will have to search for alternatives. This may include growing their own organic fruit drawing on their economic resources, obtaining it from their human resource(s), purchasing organic fruit from a non-government regulated farm, etc. These options are pending on access and availability and are determined by individual resources. Individuals with common goals can draw on societal forces to advocate and try to change policy, or may start a system or organization where organic fruit could be available by honing in on their own resources. Conforming to the new norm and simply purchasing what is available in government-regulated markets and the other sources which supply only genetically modified fruits, would result in failing to reach set goals and objectives. The difference between consuming organic vs. genetic modified fruit may ultimately affect individual health.

Technological-Industrial Forces: Technological-industrial forces include all factors pertaining to technology and industry, hence, it is intertwined with the built environment. It includes scientific improvements, innovations, technological advancements, research and development, and the availability of goods and services as a result of industry and/or technology. Technological-industrial forces include the power of industry and technology on society as a whole, and on individuals. Sometimes these forces bring to light tragedy (whether intended or not) and sometimes they can better health. They are often driven by economic forces. The advent of technological advancements such as the invention and use of those aspects pertaining to the built environment (i.e. nuclear weapons, chemicals, planes, etc.) have created a venue for small and large scale technological-industrial related disasters affecting populations at large, as evidenced by the aftermath of the A-Bomb, Chernobyl and collapse of the World Trade Centre. Technological-industrial forces could also affect a smaller group of people as demonstrated by the cancer cluster in Woburn Massachusetts.

Technological-industrial forces can impact health and the environment both positively and negatively. For example, scientific improvements in cancer treatment can provide an opportunity for better prognosis for cancer patients. An example of a threat would be the use of a pharmaceutical product that results in serious adverse health effects such as cancer. For example, "during the 1940s to the mid 1970s, several pregnant women had been prescribed the synthetic drug estrogen diethylstilbestrol (DES) in order to prevent miscarriages (Mericskay et al., 2005). It was not until some twenty years later that studies found that the maternal intake of DES has resulted in an increased risk of clear-cell adenocarcinoma of the vagina and cervix amongst female offspring (Veurink et al., 2005; Palmer et al., 2002; Hatch et al., 2001; Hatch et al., 2000; Swan, 2000; Hatch et al., 1998; Herbst, 1979; Herbst and Scully, 1970)" (Novogradec, 2006:4). In recent years, the link between in-utero DES exposure and breast cancer risk has also been studied amongst women living in the United States and findings have suggested that women over forty years of age who have had prenatal exposure to DES are at an increased risk for breast cancer (Palmer et al., 2002; Palmer et al., 2006).

Economic Forces: Economic forces include but are not limited to governmental, technological, industrial, and agricultural spending and profits. It includes economic gain as well as fundraising efforts for the greater good. Government and business operations have a significant impact on economic forces and vice versa. Economic forces include factors such as the impact of growth or decline in gross domestic product, increases and decreases in interest rates, taxes, inflation, the value of the dollar, etc. (Wright et al., 1998). Therefore, economic forces influence, and are influenced by cycles and trends in the economy (i.e. depression, recession, boom, or trough). To illustrate the interconnectedness between individual, micro, and macro environments consider instances when government regulations (political-legal forces) have allowed for the sale of products with carcinogens in them (built environment impacting individual and environmental health) resulting in industrial profit, ultimately driving the economy (economic forces). Economic forces can also be used to provide relief through subsidized programs, infrastructure etc. such as government funding spent to aid in housing, education, and research. In these instances, economic forces can act as opportunities.

Societal Forces: Societal forces consist of societal knowledge, perceptions, and expectations. It includes social responsibility or lack thereof, and can be described as the arrangements (institutional and other) that exist within society. In this light societal forces are intertwined with political-legal and technological-industrial forces as they take into account the relationship between industry, government, and citizenry. Societal forces include social organization which often, but not always, originates on a grassroots level. Social organization can take place to promote research, education, and change and as such can be viewed as opportunities for cancer prevention. On the contrary, societal forces can also be viewed as threats if they are used to promote actions, behaviours, exposures, etc. related to cancer causation. For instance, as noted by Hofrichter (2000) a "toxic culture" may exist within society when social arrangements which encourage and excuse the deterioration of the environment and human health exist.

Societal forces impacts, and are impacted by, individual resources as well as the micro and macro environments at large. It may include societal traditions, values and rights, trends, and ethnic and cultural practices and customs. Wright et al. (1998) describe traditions as the defining societal practices that have lasted for decades or even centuries. For instance, consider traditions that families (human resources) have over Christmas—this could play a role in cancer causation if it leads to over-consumption of alcohol and smoking, exposure to environmental tobacco smoke, and unhealthy eating habits (social environment), but may also act as an opportunity (i.e. physical activities—physical resources/biological environment). Values and rights on the other hand, refer to concepts that society as a whole holds in high esteem which may or may not be included in codes of ethics, conduct, charters, etc. This could include the freedom of speech—which may impact efforts associated with socially organizing for cancer prevention (societal forces). Societal trends on the other hand present various opportunities and threats or constraints to industry, government, and individuals (Wright et al., 1998). For example, in the 1930's the spread of cigarette smoking, particularly amongst women, was one of the most visible signs of a change in trend that developed as a basis of a social attire, expression, acceptance, and/or belonging.

The latency effects of this trend show a substantial rise in lung cancer mortality rates approximately thirty years after the rise in smoking prevalence (Weiss, 1997). Ethnic and cultural practices as well as customs can also be implicated for their role in cancer causation. For instance, 'some ethnic practices, such as those pertaining to cooking (i.e. inhalation-exposure to cooking fumes, the consumption of charred meat, the consumption of pickled or moldy foods, etc.) have been associated with various different cancers (Anderson et al., 2005; Kim et al., 2002; Franco and Rohan, 2002). Furthermore, in certain regions of Iran, the custom of eating opium dross as well as the consumption of contaminated bread containing large quantities of silica fibres originating from extraneous seeds used in the bread, have been suspected as the "initiating" carcinogenic factors for esophageal cancer (Ghadirian et al., 1988)' (Novogradec, 2007b). On the contrary, ethnic and cultural practices and customs may also act as opportunities when they promote healthy lifestyles and behaviours in relation to cancer prevention.

Natural Forces: Natural forces include events occurring in the physical world. They may consist of changes in climate, weather patterns and cycles, ocean temperatures and wind patterns, rain and ice storms, floods, heat waves, droughts, wild fires, mudslides, hurricanes, tornados, typhoons, etc. As with all other forces, natural forces are also connected to other micro and macro environments and individual resources. This was demonstrated by the role that weather patterns had on the spread of Chernobyl's nuclear fallout—had the weather patterns been different perhaps less people would have been affected globally. To further demonstrate the intricacy of natural forces with other environments, consider the occurrence of global warming which "is the result of the accumulation of greenhouse gases in the atmosphere, occurring both naturally (i.e. water vapour, carbon dioxide, methane, ozone etc.) and as a result of human activity (i.e. the burning of fossil fuels, deforestation, the use of chlorofluorocarbons and fertilizers, etc.)" (Novogradec, 2008b:865). Human activity or intervention with the natural environment (built environment) can also result in changes to natural forces, as seen with global warming. Furthermore, the built environment can also threaten natural forces and human health—for instance, the burning of fossil fuels can lead to air quality problems which are associated with poor respiratory health. Natural forces can act as a mode of transmission of sources, exposures, and contaminants associated with ill health —consider the health effects resulting from the Elbe flood which took place in 2002 in Central Europe. Stachel et al., (2004) note that the flood was responsible for the spread of various water-borne diseases via fecal-contaminated waterways and drinking supplies, and exposure to toxic pollutants from nearby industrial sites and municipal sewage (Novogradec, 2008b). Exposures to industrial pollutants can inevitably also lead to cancer clusters in nearby communities. Natural forces therefore can act as an opportunity or threat to health.

Other Forces: Other forces are simply those forces found in the macro environment which do not fall under the purview of political-legal, technological-industrial, economic, societal, or natural forces.

Recommendations: S.W.O.T. Analysis

There are many factors which play a role in both cancer causation and prevention. Those factors which are unpredictable and unforeseeable are certainly far more difficult to avoid—such as preventing carcinogenic exposures immediately following the Chernobyl disaster or the collapse of the World Trade Centre. In spite of this, through education, awareness, and research it is possible to identify and act on this knowledge in order to minimize or eliminate various risk factors associated with different cancers, and other illnesses. In this light, the environment and cancer framework can be applied in relation to the S.W.O.T. (strengths, weaknesses, opportunities, threats) analysis to help achieve this.

The S.W.O.T. analysis is a technique commonly applied to business organizations in order to excel at achieving their goals and objectives. However, it is proposed that the S.W.O.T. analysis can also be applied at an individual or community level to achieve goals and objectives pertaining to cancer prevention and the promotion of environmental and human health. To date, applying the S.W.O.T. analysis in this manner has not been suggested.

"Goals" represent the desired general ends toward which efforts are directed" (Wright et al., 1998:65). For instance, a goal may be to minimize the risk of lung cancer or to decrease the level of indoor air pollution at work and in the home. Each set goal will have a set of objectives, as well as their own anticipated outcomes—by identifying and avoiding risk factors that cause lung cancer—the risk of other illnesses may consequently also be decreased. "Objectives are often quantified versions of goals; they are verifiable and specific since without these characteristics, objectives will not be able to provide a clear direction for decision-making or assessment of performance" (Wright et al., 1998:65). For example in order to achieve the goal of decreasing indoor air pollution in the work and home, baseline measures must first be taken in order to accurately assess whether or not the goal was met by means of satisfying the set objectives. Once a baseline measurement is taken, specific set objectives should be established. These objectives should be specific and quantifiable—for example, this may be achieved by specifying how much of what contributors to indoor air pollution should be reduced by when. To attain this, first an assessment of the strengths and weaknesses posed by the individual and the opportunities and threats posed by the micro and macro environments must be completed. An example of an objective might be to eliminate all exposures of second hand smoke by January 23, 2009. In certain countries, political-legal forces have already banned indoor smoking in workplaces (opportunity), but have not yet banned smoking in residences (threat only if smoking is still taking place in the home). There are many other factors which must also be considered, such as the sale of cigarettes, which are still rampant (threat: technological-industrial forces; built environment; economic forces) and the accessibility and social stigma attached to cigarette smoking. This is not an exhaustive list—there are also other factors which must be identified—these will vary on an individual level and are often driven by macro forces. Goals and objectives are achieved at their maximum potential when an individual's strengths and weaknesses are matched with the opportunities and threats posed by their micro and macro environments.

Through set goals and objectives, the S.W.O.T. analysis allows for the systematic identification of issues and factors pertaining to cancer causation and prevention by honing in on individual strengths and the opportunities posed by the micro and macro environments. It also allows for the recognition and (corrective) action pertaining to individual weaknesses, and the avoidance, minimization, or active participation necessary to combat the threats posed by the micro and macro environments. In combination with the environment and cancer framework, the S.W.O.T. analysis provides individuals with the necessary tools to recognize and minimize or avoid risk factors such as those surrounding the social environment (i.e. unhealthy nutrition over a prolonged period, smoking, physical inactivity, excessive use of alcohol, etc.) as well as aid in preventative measures (i.e. lobbying for the creation of legislation that prevents industry from producing products with carcinogens in them). An excellent book by Armstrong et al., (2007) is strongly recommended to assist in setting goals and objectives geared towards cancer prevention.

Concluding Remarks

In order to attain the goal of preventing cancer, an upstream approach must be taken which considers the individual as well as their micro and macro environments. The proposed environment and cancer framework accompanied by the S.W.O.T. analysis, aids in systematically deciphering the various factors involved in cancer causation and prevention. Through education, research, awareness, and action, various changes can take place on every level in order to decrease cancer risk. Efforts should not only be aimed at changing at-risk perceptions, attitudes and behaviours, but also at adopting precautionary measures and safer alternatives for improved and healthier living and working environments. Nevertheless, addressing the deeper-rooted issues embedded in the micro and macro environments must also be targeted. In order to achieve cancer prevention on a population level, social organization must be aimed at targeting the systemic issues and problems inherently driving cancer risk, such as those connected with lax policies and legislation which enable run-away industries. Furthermore, changes need to be made that address what Hofrichter (2000) refers to as the "toxic culture" which exists in society. That is to challenge the very social structure, system and arrangements which encourage and excuse the deterioration of environment and human health (Hofrichter, 2000). Changes need to occur on a macro level such that cancer prevention is on the political radar. In light of cancer causation, practical significance should be considered as an adequate means for legal accountability. Furthermore, alternative and supplementary methodologies and assessment measures must be developed (or adopted) and implemented. Political and legal forces alike need to ensure that there is accountability for poor industrial practices, and poor judgment calls from those in positions of power and social responsibility must form the fabric of these efforts. Through social and community organization, as well as individual endeavours, cancer can truly become a preventable disease.

Acknowledgement

The author of this paper is supported by the Canadian Institute of Health Research (CIHR): Canada Graduate Scholarship Doctoral Award.

Notes

1. Carcinogens are cancer-causing agents. The most recent description of the "categories of *agents*", according to the International Agency for Research on Cancer (IARC), includes: "both "specific" as well as "groups" of related chemicals, complex mixtures, occupational or environmental exposures, cultural or behavioural practices, biological organisms, and physical agents" (WHO and IARC, 2006). Carcinogens are agent(s) capable of initiating development of malignant tumours. (On-line Medical Dictionary, 2003).
2. The total characteristics displayed by an organism under a particular set of environmental factors, regardless of the actual genotype of the organism. Results from interaction between the genotype and the environment (On-line Medical Dictionary, 2003).
3. Disease producing organisms that can exist in many different places (for example: air, dust, counter top surfaces, the body, etc.) (On-line Medical Dictionary, 2003).
4. According to the International Agency for Research on Cancer (2004), a Group 2B carcinogen is an agent that is *possibly carcinogenic to humans*.

5. Alcohol was recently evaluated in 2007 by the IARC as a Group 1 carcinogen, meaning that the agent is *carcinogenic to humans*.
6. The regular and simultaneous occurrence in a single interbreeding population of two or more alleles of a gene, where the frequency of the rarer alleles is greater than can be explained by recurrent mutation alone (typically greater than 1percent). The concept includes chromosome polymorphism. (On-line Medical Dictionary, 2003).
7. In this context, threshold limit value refers to the maximum amount and duration of exposure to a chemical substance or other environmental exposure without suffering from cancer or other ill health effects.
8. HPV are small, double stranded DNA viruses.
9. A type of liver cancer.
10. A form of protozoa. A blood fluke which matures in the veins that drain the human bladder.
11. Helicobacter pylori (H. Pylori) is a bacterium.
12. Two different types of stomach cancer.
13. Dr. Robin Herbert is the co-director of the World Trade Centre Medical Monitoring Program at Mount Sinai Medical Centre in New York.
14. A synthetic estrogen.
15. PCE is a solvent used in the dry cleaning industry; it is also used in other industries.

References

Aldrich, T., and Sinks, T. (2002) Things to know and do about cancer clusters. *Cancer Investigations* 20(5-6), 810-6.

Anderson, K.E., Kadlubar, F.F., Kulldorff, M., et al., (2005) Dietary Intake of Heterocyclic Amines and Benzo(a)Pyrene: Associations with Pancreatic Cancer. *Cancer Epidemiology Biomarkers & Prevention* 14, 2261-2265.

Antman, K.H. and Taub, R. (1995)Cancer. In D.F. Tapley, T.G. Morris, L.P. Rowland, J.Lapook, R.J. Weiss *Complete Home Medical Guide 3rd Edition,* The Columbia University College of Physicians and Surgeons, CMPCnet, Chapter 17. http://cpmcnet.columbia.edu/texts/guide/hmg17_0001.html# (accessed July, 2003)

Apfeldorf, R. and Infante, P.F. (1981) Review of epidemiologic study results of vinyl chloride related compounds. *Environmental Health Perspectives* 41, 221-6.

Armstrong B, Tremblay C, Thériault G. (1988) Compensating bladder cancer victims employed in aluminium reduction plants. *Journal of Occupational Medicine* 30(10), 771–775.

Armstrong, L., Dauncey, G., Woodsworth, A. (2007) *Cancer: 101 Solutions to a Preventable Epidemic*, New Society Publishers, Canada.

Autrup, H. (2004) Gene-Environment interaction in environmental carcinogens In Nicolopoulou-Stamati, P; Hens, L; Howard, C.V; Van Larebeke, N. Cancer As An Environmental Disease. Kluwer Academic Publishers, Dordrecht, The Netherlands. Pp. 71-101.

Baris, D., Brown, L.M., Silverman, D.T., et al., (2000) Socioeconomic Status and

Multiple Myeloma Among US Blacks and Whites. *American Journal of Public Health* 90(8), 1277-1281.

Barros – Dios, J.M., Barreiro, M.A., Ruano-Ravina, A., Figueiras, A. (2002) Exposure to Residential Radon and Lung Cancer in Spain: A Population-based Case-Control Study. *American Journal of Epidemiology* 156(6), 548-555.

Bartsch, H., Nair, U., Risch, A., Rojas, M., Wikman, H., Alexandrov, K. (2000) Review: Genetic Polymorphism of CYP Genes, alone or in combination, as a risk modifier of tobacco-related cancers. *Cancer Epidemiology, Biomarkers & Prevention* 9, 3-28.

Bennett, P. (2000) *Introduction to Clinical Psychology*. US: Open University Press.

Biggart, Bill (2007) Bill Biggart Photographer (1947-2001). September 11, 2001. http://www.billbiggart.com/911.html (accessed October, 2008).

Blair, A., Stewart, P.A., Tolbert, P.E., et al., (1990) Cancer and other causes of death among a cohort of drycleaners. *British Journal of Industrial Medicine* 47, 162-8.

Boice Jr, J.D. and McLaughlin, J.K. (2001) Errors in TCE analysis. *Environmental Health Perspectives* 109(3), A108.

Bosch, F.X., Manos, M.M., Muñoz, N., et al., (1995) Prevalence of human papillomavirus in cervical cancer: a worldwide perspective. *Journal of the National Cancer Institute* 87, 796-802.

Bracken, K. (2006) New York Times: Metro: Chernobyl's Legacy http://video.on.nytimes.com/index.jsp?fr_story=5b04b37c2678c35dbd369bab57f98a296da98b44&rf=fr_std (accessed October, 2008)

Brown, L.M., and Devesa, S.S. (2002) Epidemiologic trends in esophageal and gastric cancer in the United States. *Surgical Oncology Clinics of North America* 11, 235-256.

Brown, L.M., Devesa, S.S., Fraumeni Jr., J.F. (2002a) "Chapter 1: Epidemiology of Esophageal Cancer" *In Posner, M.C., Vokes, E., Weichselbaum, R (eds) Cancer of the Upper Gastrointestinal Tract, BD Decker Inc.,*

Burchell, A.N., Winer, R.L., de Sanjosé, S., Franco, E.L. (2006) "Chapter 6: Epidemiology and transmission dynamics of genital HPV infection," *Vaccine* 24(Supp3), S3/52–S3/61.

Chernobyl Children's Project, Ireland (2003). http://www.chernobyl-ireland.com/home/default.asp (accessed June, 2003)

Chernobyl Children's Project International (2008) Information Sheets: Schools/Education. http://www.chernobyl-international.com/school_education/information_sheets.461.html#sequence (accessed October, 2008)

Clapp, R.W., Jacobs, M.M., Loechler, E.L. (2008) Environmental and Occupational Causes of Cancer: New Evidence 2005-2007. *Reviews on Environmental Health* 23(1), 1-37.

Colborn, T., Dumanoski, D., and Myers, J.P. (1997) *Our Stolen Future*, First Plume Printing, New York.

Cooper, L.C. (1988) Personality, Life Stress and Cancerous Disease. In Fisher, S; Reason, J. *Handbook of Life Stress, Cognition and Health.* Toronto: John Wiley & Sons Ltd., pp. 369-381.

Darby, S., Whitley, E., Silcocks, P., et al., (1998) Risk of lung cancer associated with residential radon exposure in south-west England: a case-control study. *British Journal of Cancer* 78(3), 394-408.

Doll, R., and Peto, R. (1981) Avoidable risks of cancer in the US, *Journal of the National Cancer Institute* 66 (6), 1194-1308.

Dyer, M.A., and Bremner, R. (2005) The search for the retinoblastoma cell of origin. *Nature Reviews Cancer* 5(2), 91-101.

Endler, N.S., Speer, R.L., Johnson, J.M., Flett, G.L. (2000) Controllability, Coping, Efficacy, and Distress. European Journal of Personality 14, 245-264.

Eysenck, H.J. (1985). Personality, cancer and cardiovascular disease: A causal analysis. *Personality and Individual Differences* 5, 535-537.

Eysenck, H.J. (1990) The Prediction f Death from Cancer by means of Personality/Stress Questionnaire: too good to be true? *Perceptual Motor Skills* 71, 216-218.

Eysenck, J.H. (1996) Personality and Cancer. In Cooper, L. Cary. *Handbook of Stress, Medicine, and Health.* New York: CRC Press, Inc., pp. 193-215.

Fitzpatrick, R. (2001) Social Status and Mortality. *Annals of Internal Medicine* 134(10), 1001-1003.

Fox, G.A. (2001) Wildlife as sentinels of human health effects in the Great Lakes - St. Lawrence Basin, *Environmental Health Perspectives* 109 (S6), 856-861.

Franco, E.L., and Rohan, T.E. (2002) *Cancer Precursors: Epidemiology, Detection and Prevention*, Springer-Verlag Inc., New York.

Franco, E.L. and Ferenczy, A. (2002) Cervix. In Franco, E.L., and Rohan, T.E. *Cancer Precursors: Epidemiology, Detection and Prevention*, Springer-Verlag Inc., New York, pp. 249-286.

Ghadirian, P., Vobecky, J., Vobecky, J.S. (1988) Factors Associated with Cancer of the Oesophagus: An Overview. *Cancer Detection and Prevention*, 11, 225-234.

Goncalves, E. (2001a) The Nuclear Body Count. *Earth Island Journal*, 26-28.

Goncalves, E. (2001b) The Secret Nuclear War. *The Ecologist* 31(3), 28- 34.

Gorey, K.M., and Vena, J.E. (1994) Cancer differentials among US blacks and whites: quantitative estimates of socioeconomic related risks.*Journal of the National Medical Association* 86, 209-215.

Gostin, L.O., and DeAngelis, C.D. (2007) Mandatory HPV Vaccination: Public Health vs. Private Wealth. *Journal of the American Medical Association* 297(17), 1921-1923.

Guertl, B., Ratschk, M., Harms, D., et al., (2003) Clonality and loss of heterozygosity of WT genes are easily events in the pathogenesis of nephroblastomas. *Human Pathology* 34(3), 278-281.

Hafen, Q.B., Karren, J.K., Frandsen, J.K., Smith, N.L. (1996) *Mind/Body Health: The Effects of Attitudes, Emotions, and Relationships.* US: Allyn & Bacon.

Hall, O. (August 13, 1997) *Cancer susceptibility genes and molecular epidemiology.* Plenary Session: Gene replacement for lung cancer: Molecular Genetics of Lung Cancer, University College, Dublin, Ireland.

Hansen, J., Raaschou-Nielsen, O., Christensen, M. et al., (2001) Cancer incidence among Danish workers exposed to trichloroethylene. *Journal of Occupational and Environmental Medicine* 43, 133-139.

Harr, J. (1996) *A Civil Action*, Vintage Books, New York.

Harris, E.L. (1997) Importance of heritable and non-heritable variation in cancer susceptibility: evidence from a twin study, *Journal of the National Cancer Institute* 89 (4), 270-272.

Hatch, E.E., Palmer, J.R., Titus-Ernstoff, L., et al., (1998) Cancer risk in women exposed to diethylstilbestrol in utero. *Journal of the American Medical Association* 280(7), 630-634.

Hatch, E., Herbst, A.L.., Hoover, R., et al., (2000) Incidence of squamous neoplasia of the cervix and vagina in des-exposed daughters. *Annals of Epidemiology* 10(7), 467.

Hatch, E., Herbst, A.L., Hoover, R.N., et al., (2001) Incidence of squamous neoplasia of the cervix and vagina in women exposed prenatally to diethylstilbestrol (United States). *Cancer Causes and Control* 12(9), 837-845.

Heath, Clark W. (1996) Investigating causation in cancer clusters. *Radiation and Environmental Biophysics* 35, 133-136.

Herbert, R. (2007) Interview with Robin Herbert on the health effects of the World Trade Centre dust (By: Rachel Gotbaum). Supplement to: Samet JM, Geyh AS, and Utell MJ. The Legacy of World Trade Centre Dust. New England Journal of Medicine 2007;356(22):2233-2236. http://content.nejm.org/cgi/content/full/356/22/2233/DC1 (accessed October, 2008)

Herbst, A.L., and Scully, R.E. (1970) Adenocarcinoma of the vagina in adolescence: A report of 7 cases including 6 clear-cell carcinomas (so-called mesonephromas). *Cancer* 25, 745.

Herbst, A.L. (1979) DES-associated clear cell adenocarcinoma of the vagina and cervix. *Obstetrical and Gynecological Survey* 34(11), 844.

Herrera, L.A., Benitez-Bribiesca, L., Mohar, A., Ostrosky-Wegman, P. (2005) Role of Infectious Diseases in Human Carcinogenesis, *Environmental and Molecular Mutagenesis* (45/2-3), 284-303.

Higuchi, S., Matsushita, S., Murayama, M., Takagi, S., Hayashida, M. (1995) Alcohol and aldehyde dehydrogenase polymorphisms and the risk for alcoholism. *American Journal of Psychiatry* 152, 1219-1221.

Hofrichter, R. (2000) "Critical Perspectives on Human Health and the Environment." In R. Hofrichter (Ed) *Reclaiming the Environmental Debate: The Politics of Health in a Toxic Culture.* Cambridge, Massachusetts: MIT Press. Pages 1-15.

International Agency for Research on Cancer (IARC) (1994) *IARC monographs on the evaluation of carcinogenic risks to humans. Volume 61: Schistosomes, Liver Flukes and helicobacter pylori.* Lyon: IARC http://monographs.iarc.fr/ENG/Monographs/vol61/volume61.pdf (accessed October 2008)

International Agency for Research on Cancer (IARC) (1997) *IARC monographs on the evaluation of carcinogenic risks to humans. Volume 70: Epstein-Barr Virus and Kaposi's Sarcoma Herpesvirus/Human Herpesvirus 8.* Lyon: IARC http://monographs.iarc.fr/ENG/Monographs/vol70/volume70.pdf (accessed October 2008)

International Agency for Research on Cancer (IARC) (1999) *IARC monographs on the evaluation of carcinogenic risks to humans.* Volume 71. *Re-evaluation of Some Organic Chemicals, Hydrazine and Hydrogen Peroxide.* Lyon: IARC.

International Agency for Research on Cancer (IARC) (2004) *IARC monographs on the evaluation of carcinogenic risks to humans. Complete List of Agents evaluated and their classification.* Lyon: IARC. http://monographs.iarc.fr/ENG/Classification/index.php (accessed October, 2008)

International Agency for Research on Cancer (IARC) (2007—in press). *IARC monographs on the evaluation of carcinogenic risks to humans.* Volume 96. Alcoholic beverage consumption and ethyl carbamate (urethane). Lyon: IARC.

Isaacs, S.L., and Schroeder, S.A. (2004) Class—The ignored determinant of the Nation's Health. *The New England Journal of Medicine* 351(11), 1137-1142.

Jordan, A. and O'Riordan (1999) The Precautionary Principle in Contemporary Environmental Policy and Politics. In Raffensperger, C., and Ticker, J.A. (eds.,) Protecting Public Health and the Environment: Implementing the Precautionary Principle. Island Press. Pp. 15-35.

Kang, S.H., and Bloom, J.R. (1993) Social Support and Cancer Screening Among Older Black Americans. *Journal of the National Cancer Institute* 85(9), 737-742.

Kim, H.J., Chang, W.K., Kim, M.K., et al., (2002) Dietary Factors and gastric cancer in Korea: A case-control study. *International Journal of Cancer* 97(4), 531-535.

Kirk, G.D., Bah, E., Montesano, R. (2006) Molecular epidemiology of human liver cancer: insights into etiology, pathogenesis and prevention from The Gambia, West Africa, *Carcinogenesis* 27(10), 2070–2082.

Kiyohara, C., Otsu, A., Shirakawa, T. et al., (2002) Genetic polymorphisms and lung cancer susceptibility: a review. *Lung Cancer* 37, 241- 256.

Kuh, D., Ben-Shlomo, Y., Lynch, J., Hallgvist, J., Power, C. (2003) Life course epidemiology. *Journal of Epidemiology and Community Health* 57, 778-783.

LeShan L. (1959) Psychological states as factors in the development of malignant disease. *Journal of the National Cancer Institute* 22, 1-18.

Levy, M.S., Heiden, A.L. (1990) Personality and Social Factors in Cancer Outcome. In Friedman, S. Howard. *Personality and Disease.* US: John Wiley & Sons, Inc., pp.254-279.

Lewis S, Campbell S, Proudfoot E, Weston A, Cotter T, Bishop J. (2008) Alcohol as a Cause of Cancer. Sydney, Cancer Institute NSW.

Lichtenstein, P., Holm, N.V., Verkasalo, P.K. et al., (2000) Environmental and Heritable

Factors in the Causation of Cancer. *The New England Journal of Medicine* 343(2), 78-85.

Maheswaran, R., and Staines, A. (1997) Cancer Clusters and Their Origins. *Chemistry and Industry* 7, 254-257.

Markowitz, L.E. (2007) HPV Vaccines—Prophylactic, Not Therapeutic. *Journal of the American Medical Association* 298(7), 805-806.

Martineau, D., Lemberger, K., Dallaire, A., Labelle, P., Lipscomb, T.P., Michel, P., and Mikaelian, I. (2002) Cancer in wildlife, a case study: Beluga from the St. Lawrence estuary, Quebec, Canada, *Environmental Health Perspectives* 110 (3), 285-292.

Martineau, D., Lemberger, K., Dallaire, A., Michel, P. (2002b) St. Lawrence Beluga Whales, the River Sweepers? *Environmental Health Perspectives* 110(10), A562-A564.

McNeil, C. (1997) HPV Vaccines for Cervical Cancer Move Toward Clinic Encounter Social Issues. Journal of the National Cancer Institute 89(22), 1664-1666.

Mericskay, M., Carta, L., Sassoon, D. (2005) Diethylstilbestrol exposure in utero: a paradigm for mechanisms leading to adult disease. *Birth Defects Research. Part A, Clinical and Molecular Teratology* 73(3), 133-135.

Mitchell, C. (1992) Multistage carcinogenesis in paediatric and adult cancers, *European Journal of Cancer* 28(1), 296-298.

Moline, J., Herbert, R., Nguyen, N. (2006) Health Consequences of the September 11 World Trade Centre Attacks: A Review. *Cancer Investigations* 24(3), 294-301.

Moysich, K.B., Menezes, R.J., Michalek, A.M. (2002) Chernobyl-related ionizing radiation exposure and cancer risk: an epidemiological review. *The Lancet Oncology* 3, 269-279.

Muto, M., Hitomi, Y., Ohtsu, A., Ebihara, S., Yoshida, S., Esumi, H. (2000) Association of aldehyde dehydrogenase 2 gene polymorphism with multiple oesophageal dysplasia in head and neck cancer patients. *Gut* 47(2), 256-261.

Muñoz, N., Castellsagué, X, Berrington de González, A., Gissmann, L. (2006) "Chapter 1: HPV in the etiology of human cancer," Vaccine *24 Supp3, 1-10.*

National Academies (2003) Report in Brief: Health Effects of Radiation: Findings of the Radiation Effects Research Foundation. http://dels.nas.edu/dels/rpt_briefs/rerf_final.pdf (accessed October, 2008).

Novogradec, A. and Ali, S.H. (2004) Incorporating the Environmental Context in the Study of Cancer: Issues and Implications. In Nicolopoulou-Stamati, P., Hens, L., Howard, C.V., Van Larebeke, N. (ed) Cancer as an Environmental Disease. Kluwer Academic Publishers, Dordrecht, The Netherlands, p.11-38.

Novogradec, A. (July 2006) The Examination of the Causes of Cancer through an Environmental Lens. In ISBN eBook consisting of Papers presented at Inter-Disciplinary Net: Probing the Boundaries (Peer Reviewed Conference Proceedings). 5th Global Conference at the University of Oxford, Mansfield College: Making Sense of Health, Illness and Disease, p.1-16.

Novogradec, A. (2007a) "Infection" In Colditz, G.A. (ed) Encyclopedia of Cancer and

Society. Sage Publishers, Thousand Oaks, California, p.461-464.

Novogradec, A. (2007b) "Carcinogens" In Robbins, P. (ed) Encyclopedia of Environment and Society. Sage Publishers, Thousand Oaks, California, p.214-216.

Novogradec, A. (2008a) "Esophageal Cancer" In Zhang, Y. (ed) Encyclopedia of Global Health. Sage Publishers, Thousand Oaks, California, p.620-623.

Novogradec, A. (2008b) "Risk" In Philander, S.G. (ed) Encyclopedia of Global Warming and Climate Change. Sage Publications, Thousand Oaks, California.

N.S. (1999) Thyroid Cancer rose after Chernobyl. *Science News* 156(6), 95.

O'Brien, M.H. (2000) When harm is not necessary: risk assessment as diversion, in R. Hofrichter (ed.), *Reclaiming the Environmental Debate: The Politics of Health in a Toxic Culture*, Institute of Technology Press, Cambridge, Massachusetts, pp. 113-133.

Ogden, J. (2000) *Health Psychology: A Textbook 2nd Edition.* Buckingham: Open University Press.

On-line Medical Dictionary (2003) Department of Medical Oncology, University of Newcastle upon Tyne. The CancerWEB Project. http://cancerweb.ncl.ac.uk/cgi-bin/omd?query=polymorphism (accessed June, 2003)

Osler, W. (1906) *Aequanimitas.* (pp 758-759) New York: McGraw-Hill.

Palmer, J.R., Hatch, E.E., Rosenberg, C.L., et al., (2002) Risk of breast cancer in women exposed to diethylstilbestrol in utero: preliminary results (United States). *Cancer Causes and Control* 13(8), 753-758.

Palmer, J.R., Wise, L.A., Hatch, E.E. et al., (2006) Prenatal Diethylstilbestrol Exposure and Risk of Breast Cancer. *Cancer Epidemiology, Biomarkers and Prevention* 15(8), 1509-1514.

Perera, F.P. (1997) Environment and Cancer: Who are Susceptible? *Science*, 278(5340), 1068-1073.

Pérez-Peña, R (April 20, 2006) In Throats of Émigrés, Doctors Find a Legacy of Chernobyl. The New York Times: N.Y./Region. http://www.nytimes.com/2006/04/20/nyregion/20chernobyl.html?_r=1&oref=slogin (accessed October, 2008)

Perotti, D., Vecchi, G.D., Lualdi, E., et al., (2005) Wilms tumour in monozygous twins: clinical, pathological, cytogenetic and molecular case report. *Journal of Pediatric Hematology/Oncology* 27(10), 521-525.

Pickens, A. and Orringer, M.B. (2003) Geographical Distribution and Racial Disparity in Esophageal Cancer. *Annals of Thoracic Surgery* 76, S1367-1369.

Power, E., Van Jaarsveld, C.H.M., McCaffery, K., et al., (2008) Understanding Intentions and Actions in Colorectal Cancer Screening. *Annals of Behavioural Medicine* 35, 285-294.

Radiation Effects Research Foundation: A Cooperative Japan-US Research Organization (2007) http://www.rerf.or.jp/ (accessed: October, 2008).

Rivera, M.N., and Haber, D.A. (2005) Wilms' tumour: connecting Tumorigenesis and organ development in the kidney. *Nature Reviews Cancer* 5(9), 699-712.

Robbins, J., and Schneider, A.B. (1998) Radioiodine-induced Thyroid Cancer: Studies in the Aftermath of the Accident at Chernobyl. *Trends in Endocrinology and Metabolism* 9(3), 87-94.

Rotblat, J. (1988) Technical Note: The cancer risk from low doses of radiation: What can be learned from A-bomb survivors? *Journal of Radiological Protection* 8(1), 39-46.

Ruder, A.M., Ward, E.M., Brown, D.P. (1994) Cancer mortality in female and male dry-cleaning workers. *Journal of Occupational Medicine* 36(8), 867-874.

Ruder, A.M., Ward, E.M., Brown, D.P. (2001) Mortality in Dry-Cleaning Workers: An Update. *American Journal of Industrial Medicine* 39, 121-132.

Rutherford, D. (2002) *Alcohol Metabolism.* NetDoctor.co.uk http://www.netdoctor.co.uk/focus/nutrition/facts/lifestylemanagement/alcohol.htm(accessed September, 2002)

Samet, J.M., Geyh, A.S., and Utell, M.J. (2007) The Legacy of the World Trade Centre Dust. *New England Journal of Medicine* 356(22), 2233 – 2236.

Seligman, M.E.P. (1975). *Helplessness: On depression, development, and death.* San Francisco: Freeman.

Shields, P.G. (1999) Review: Molecular epidemiology of lung cancer. *Annals of Oncology* 10 Suppl 5, S7-S11.

Siemiatycki, J., Richardson, L., Straif, K. et al., (2004) *Listing Occupational Carcinogens*. Environmental Health Perspectives 112 (15), 1447–1459.

Stachel, B., Gotz, R., Herrmann, T et al., (2004) The Elbe flood in August 2002—the occurrence of polychlorinated dibenzo-p-dioxins, polychlorinated dibenzofurans (PCDD/F) and dioxin-like PCB in suspended particulate matter (SPM), sediment and fish, *Water, Science and Technology* 50(5), 309-316.

Steingraber, S. (1998) Living Downstream: A Scientist's Personal Investigation of Cancer and the Environment, Vintage Books, a Division of Random House, Inc., New York.

Stepheson, J. (2001) Chernobyl's Legacy. *The American Medical Association* 286(18), 2225.

Swan, S.H. (2000) Intrauterine exposure to diethylstilbestrol: long-term effects in humans. *Acata Pathologica, Microbiologica, et Immunologica Scandinavica* 108(12), 793-804.

Tay, JS. (1995) Molecular genetics of Wilms' tumour. *Journal of Pediatrics and Child Health* 31(5), 379-383.

Taylor. E. S. (1999) *Health Psychology, 4th Edition*. Boston: McGraw-Hill.

Theriault G, Tremblay C, Cordier S, Gingras S. (1984) Bladder cancer in the aluminium industry. *Lancet* 1(8383), 947–950.

Tomoshok, L. (1987) Personality, coping style, emotion and cancer: Towards and integrative model. *Cancer Surveys* 6, 545-567.

Tremblay C, Armstrong B, Theriault G, Brodeur J. (1995) Estimation of risk of developing bladder cancer among workers exposed to coal tar pitch volatiles in the primary aluminium industry. *American Journal of Industrial Medicine* 27(3), 335–348.

U.S. Environmental Protection Agency (EPA) (2007). Technology Transfer Network Air Toxics Web site. Radionuclides (including Radon, Radium and Uranium) http://www.epa.gov/ttn/atw/hlthef/radionuc.html#ref2 (accessed: October, 2008)

Vaughan, T.L., Stewart, P.A., Davis, S., Thomas, D.B. (1997) Work in dry cleaning and the incidence of cancer of the oral cavity, larynx, and esophagus. *Occupational and Environmental Medicine* 54, 692-5.

Verkasalo, P.K., Kaprio, J., Koskenvuo, M., and Pukkala, E. (1999) Genetic predisposition, environment and cancer incidence: a nationwide twin study in Finland, 1976-1995, *International Journal of Cancer* 83, 743-749.

Veurink, M., Koster, M., Berg, L.T. (2005) The history of DES, lessons to be learned. *Pharmacy World and Science* 27(3), 139-143.

Walboomers, J.M.M., Jacobs, M.V., Manos, M.M., et al., (1999) Human Papillomavirus is a necessary cause of invasive cervical cancer worldwide. *Journal of Pathology* 189, 12-19.

Watanabe, M.E. (2000) Research: is pollution causing cancer in beluga whales? Endangered population gets attention, but complications abound, *The Scientist* 14 (19), 19.

Wartenberg, D., Reyner, D., Scott, C.S. (2000a) Trichloroethylene and cancer: epidemiologic evidence. *Environmental Health Perspectives* 108 (Suppl 2), 161-176.

Wartenberg, D., Reyner, D., Scott, C.S. (2000b) TCE Meta-Analyses: Wartenberg et al.'s Response. *Environmental Health Perspectives* 108(2), A543.

Wartenberg, D., Reyner, D., Scott, C.S. (2001) Errors in TCE Analysis: Response. *Environmental Health Perspectives* 109(3), A108-A109.

Wartenberg, D., Scott, C.S. (2002) Carcinogenicity of trichloroethylene. *Environmental Health Perspectives* 110(1), A13-A14.

Webster, T.F., Hoffman, K., Weinberg, J., et al., (2008) Community- and Individual-Level Socioeconomic Status and Breast Cancer Risk: Multilevel Modeling on Cape Cod, Massachusetts. *Environmental Health Perspectives* 116(8), 1125-1129.

Weiss, N.S. (1995) Cancer in relation to occupational exposure to perchloroethylene. *Cancer Causes and Control* 6, 257-266.

Weiss, W. (1997) Cigarette Smoking and Lung Cancer Trends: A Light at the End of the Tunnel? *Chest* 111, 1414-1416.

Welshons, WV, Thayer, K.A., Judy, B.M. et al., (2003) Large effects from small exposures. I. Mechanisms for endocrine disrupting chemicals with estrogenic activity. *Environmental Health Perspectives* 111, 994-1006.

Williamson, K.A. and Van Heyningen, V. (1994) Towards and understanding of Wilms' tumour. *International Journal of Experimental Pathology* 75(3), 147-155.

World Health Organization (WHO) (2002) *National Cancer Control Programmes: Policies and Managerial Guidelines 2nd Edition.* Geneva: WHO Library Cataloguing-in-Publication Data.

World Health Organization (WHO) and The International Agency for Research on Cancer (IARC), *IARC Monographs on the Evaluation of Carcinogenic Risks to Humans: Preamble* January 2006 http://www-cie.iarc.fr/monoeval/preamble-new-06.pdf (accessed April 2006)

World Health Organization (2007) *Fight Against Cancer: Strategies that prevent, cure and care.* http://www.who.int/cancer/publicat/WHOCancerBrochure2007.FINALweb.pdf (accessed October, 2008).

Wright, P., Kroll, M.J., Parnell, J. (1998) *Strategic Management Concepts 4th Edition.* New Jersey: Prentice Hall Inc.,

Yang, C.S. (1980) Research on Esophageal Cancer in China: a Review. *Cancer Research* 40, 2633-2644.

Yokoyama, A., Muramatsu, T., Ohmori, T., Yokoyama, T., Okuyama, K., Takahashi, H., Hasegawa, Y., Higuchi, S., Maruyama, K., Shirakura, K., Ishii, H. (1998) Alcohol-related cancers and aldehyde dehydrogenase-2 in Japanese alcoholics. *Carcinogenesis* 19(8), 1383-1387.

10

Health of Coastal Waters and Estuaries of the United States of America

Shivaji Prasad

Introduction

Costal zone is a unique environment where water, land and air meet, and processes occur to form a landscape different from those found anywhere else. Winds and waves, tides and currents, migrating sand dunes and mud flats, a variety of plant and animal life—all combine to form our ever-changing coasts. Tremendous population and development pressures have been building in coastal areas around the world for the last four decades. Coastal waters are often horribly polluted with untreated (or partially treated) municipal, industrial and agricultural wastes. Rivers bring more pollutants, including chemicals and heavy metals, along with increasing loads of eroded sediments torn from the hinterlands. The pressure caused due to increased anthropogenic activities, urban sprawls, industrialization, roads and building constructions, land-use and land cover modifications has triggered widespread resource degradation. Coastal fisheries are chronically over-exploited in much of North America and parts of Latin America, Asia, Africa and Europe. In some cases, due to development of "dead" zones such as near the mouth of Mississippi River, the economically vital fisheries have collapsed or are in serious decline. Critical coastal resources, such as mangroves and coral reefs -among the most productive and biologically diverse ecosystems on earth provide vital habitats, feeding grounds and nurseries for literally tens of thousands of species of fish, shellfish and invertebrates. However, these resources are being plundered in the name of development. The time has come that nothing less than integrated coastal management strategies are needed: strategies that take account of population growth and distribution, urbanization trends, generation of wastes and the use (and abuse) of available resources, among others. The coastal demographics are growing too alarming. Underlining the crisis of our coasts are the escalating human population in coastal zones and their over exploitation of coastal fisheries resources.

On global scale, coastal zones comprise less than 20 percent of Earths' surface but sustain more than 50 percent of the human population. Already nearly two-thirds of humanity—some 3.6 billion people—crowd along a coastline, or live within 150 kilometres of coastline. If the present trends continue, within three decades 75 percent of humanity or 6.4 billion people will reside in coastal areas, nearly a billion more people than the current global population. Almost all of the high-population mega cities around the world are located on or near the coasts. Throughout much of the world, coasts are over-developed, over-crowded and over-exploited. Coastal zones are most viable economic zones that provide 90 percent of world's fisheries, about 25 percent of biological productivity as well as major source of off-shore oil and gas.

Out of China's 456 cities with municipal status (as of 1990), 305 of them are coastal. Many of these cities seem to be growing at more rapid rates than those in the interior of the country. In Southeast Asia, 65 percent of all major cities—those with populations of 2.5 million or more - are located along the coast. In Latin America and the Caribbean, where 75 percent of the population will be urban by the turn of the century, 57 out of 77 major cities are coastal cities. One of the most over-crowded coastlines in the world is the Mediterranean. The current population of the Mediterranean Basin countries is around 380 million, with 146 million living along the coast itself. Another 100 million tourist flocks to its shores every year during summer (Anonymous, 2003).

Mexico, the United States of America, and southern Canadian provinces adjoining U.S. border are highly urbanized and almost all of their major urban centres are located on or near to some coastline. In the United States, 54 percent of Americans now live in 772 coastal counties adjacent to the Atlantic and Pacific Oceans, the Gulf of Mexico and the Great Lakes. At present, US coastal counties already contain 14 of the country's 20 largest urban centres. Over the past 30 years, coastal populations have grown by 41 million, faster than the country as a whole. The Washington DC-based Population Reference Bureau has reported that, between 1960 and 1990, coastal population density in the United States increased from 275 to nearly 400 people per square kilometre. By the year 2025, nearly 75 percent of all Americans are expected to live in coastal counties; with population density doubling in some areas such as Florida and southern California. Florida, almost entirely coastal, is projected to have more than 16 million residents by 2010, an increase of over 200 percent from its 1960 level of 5 million. South Florida, which had 6.3 million population in 1990, is expected to have to cope with 15 to 30 million people by 2050 (Ullman, et al. 2000). Similar dramatic increases are projected for both California and Texas. Demographers think coastal areas in the U.S. will keep on growing well into the next century.

Due to increased anthropogenic interactions with water for recreational and other purposes, our coastal areas, oceans and fisheries are under enormous stress.

There is an urgent need of a concerted effort in an integrated manner to improve the quality of coastal resources and aquatic systems.

North American Coasts

North American coastlines are vast encompassing diverse landscapes and physiographic characteristics. The coastal zone extends about six miles (or 10 kilometres) out from the shore. There is enormous variability in benthic communities along the North American coasts. Some areas have high concentration and productivity of fish and invertebrates and quicker growth than other areas. The high-energy Northeast and Northwest coasts of the United States are quite different from its Southeast and Gulf of Mexico coastlines (mountainous streams in the North-East coastal region vs. streams flowing on terrain having gentle slopes in the South and Gulf of Mexico coastal region). Each coastal ecosystem has unique group of plants and animal species. To describe regional contrasts, the North American coastal water zones can be divided into the following:

A. Northeast and Northwest Coastal zones of the United States: The Northeast and Northwest are temperate, high-energy coasts, where rocky headlands have small and well-mixed estuaries surrounded by small salt marshes. These regions have usually rugged coastlines (NOAA, 1998c).

North-eastern estuaries lie in the most densely populated and highly industrialized areas along its coasts. Due to intensive use since ages, their shorelines have lost wetlands and have left some in highly degraded condition. Extensive constructions of roads, railway tracks, and dikes along these coastlines have impacted wetlands severely. A variety of pollutants and toxic compounds ranging from household sewage to chlorinated organic compounds from homes and factories discharges are flowing into estuaries and coastal waters. In the past, intensive use of petroleum products for home heating and transportation have resulted into several oil spills into these estuaries. In this context, New York Harbour, Massachusetts, Commencement Bay and Washington are worth mentioning (NOAA, 1998c).

B. Mid-Atlantic, Southwest and Gulf of Mexico (GOM) Coastal Zones of the United States: Coasts in Mid-Atlantic, Southwest and Gulf of Mexico (GOM) regions are dominated by large estuaries systems and vast wetlands. For example, Louisiana located in the GOM region alone has 40 percent area of all of wetlands present in the United States. However, lately there has been continuous degradation and loss of wetlands in this region (NOAA, 1998c). Construction of dams, levees, and canals to control flooding has led to increased rate of coastal erosion at the rate of roughly 30 square miles per year. Similarly, changes in land-use in central Florida have transformed Everglades and nearby ecosystems dramatically, and now causing drastic decline in the number of wading birds, fisheries, and threatening survival of Florida Panthers. It is praiseworthy that Federal and Florida state governments have taken strong steps to restore these ecological degradations.

Population Trends Along the US Coastlines

The total surface area of US estuaries and coastal water bodies, excluding the Great Lakes and those in Alaska, Hawaii, island territories, is about 75,000 square kilometres (NOAA, 1990). In the United States of America (USA), coastal communities were among the first settlements, and they have always accounted for a major percentage of the overall USA population. Moreover, the population in the coastal areas is increasing constantly. More than 54 percent of US total population resides in the coastal counties, and occupies about 26 percent of the total land area (NOAA, 1998a). During the last decade, 17 of the 20 fastest growing counties were located along the coast. In addition, 19 of the 20 most densely populated counties in the US are coastal counties. Further, 16 of these counties have the largest number of housing construction. These densely populated areas have been primary centres of transportation, tourism, recreation, commercial fishing and other industrial establishments (NOAA, 1998a). On the North-East coast, there is virtually one continuous urban area stretching from Boston to New York to Washington DC, containing 50 million people (Anonymous, 2003). Obviously, the North American coastlines, in general, and its Eastern coasts in particular, are under intense stress due to coastal developments and anthropogenic pollutions. Lee County in Florida which had population of 50,000 four decades ago now has a population over 410,000 (Hampson, 2000). Since 1993, the population of the hot 100 counties has grown nearly 50 percent faster than the entire US population (Ullmann et al., 2000). Some of the densely populated states are given in the Table 10.1.

Coastal Erosion

Strong wind speed, tides and storms cause high soil erosion along US coastlines. All of the 30 coastal US States and States along Great Lakes have severe erosion problems. Of these, 26 States experiencing net loss of their shores. On Southeast coast of Barrier Islands, coastline recessions of up to 25 feet per year are common. On Great Lakes, the recession rates on average are 50 feet per year. In heavily populated areas, one to two feet erosion may be very dangerous. Folly Island in South Carolina has eroded at a rate of 9 feet per year at the east end and 15 feet per year at the west end of its coasts (NOAA, 1998b).

Table 10.1: Some of the Densely Populated Coastal States of the North-Eastern Part of the United States

US State	Total area (sq. mile)	Total population (million)	Length of coastline (mile)	% of land area in coastal counties	% of population residing in coastal counties
New Jersey	7,419	7.7	127	95	99.0
Florida	53,937	12.9	1,350	93	97.4
Oregon	96,002	2.8	296	22	56.0
Delaware	2,396	0.784	28	100	100

Causes of Pollution of Coastal Waters and Estuaries

Contaminated sediments from point and non-point sources reaching coastal waters cause serious degradation of coastal ecosystems. A wide range of contaminants from agricultural, urban waste water treatment plants, industrial, road and house construction sites, and military establishments are carried to coastal waters through discharges from streams and rivers. Bi-products of petrochemical plants are known to be very harmful to the biological marine resources as well as to human health when they contaminate the sediments in coastal waters. Harbour dredging and disposed sediment materials also cause significant contamination of coastal waters. These pollutants affect biological resources of its aquatic systems. Further, apart from causing ecological problems and habitat degradation of aquatic fish and plant species, these toxic materials enter into food chain and cause significant problem to human health. Hundreds of sites in marine and estuarine waterways are contaminated at a level sufficient to cause adverse effects on aquatic organisms (Armitage, 1995). Recent studies on American coastal bays revealed that approximately 7 percent of the 4,000 square miles area spread over 23 coastal bays carried toxic sediments (Hameedi, et al. 1999) and about 10 percent of the sediments underlying U.S. waters are contaminated with toxic pollutants to a degree that poses potential risks to fish and other marine living resources and the humans who consume it (U.S. EPA, 1997, 1998). For example, in the Gulf of Mexico, an environmental "dead zone" now covers over 7,700 square miles caused by agricultural and industrial pollution discharges from vast Mississippi River basin. Another form of pollution is the introduction of exotic or non-native species into marine environments. These marine invaders are on the increase along US coastal waters due to high discharges of ballast waters and cargoes of ships from overseas.

Size of Estuary and Regional Patterns of Toxicity

National Status and Trends Program of NOAA completed a sediment toxicity assessment in 1997. The size of the study area selected ranged from a small (0.3 sq. km) to a big 1,550 sq. km. It didn't cover offshore ocean waters. Chemical analyses measured concentrations of about 80 chemical contaminants in the sediment samples (Hameedi, 1997; NOAA, 1998b). The toxicity assessments of the bottom sediments from coastal waters revealed that spatial extent of sediment toxicity varied widely from one estuary to another. Larger estuaries and bays with areas equal to or larger than 250 sq. km had a lower average toxicity of 6.0 percent compared to the estuary and bays of smaller than 250 sq. km area which showed an average toxicity level of 10.0 percent. The variations were due to the wide range of variations in the amount of contaminants from effluents, outfalls, and the volume of coastal runoffs.

In general, the severe toxicity was found in highly urbanized and industrialized tributaries, bayous, inner harbours, and marinas (Long, et al., 1996; Turgeon et al., 1998). The overall toxicity was grouped as pervasive (found in Newark Bay [New Jersey] and San Diego Bay [California]); patchy found in Boston Harbour, the Hudson-Raritan Estuary, and Sabine Lake (Massachusetts); isolated (found in Tampa Bay [Florida] and St. Simons Sounds [Georgia]), or slight in some other estuaries.

The overall average toxicity was 7.3 percent, and it ranged from 6 percent to 12 percent in different coastal regions. Higher levels of toxicity (about 35 percent) were found in the small urbanized estuaries of north-eastern and south-western (off the California coast) coast regions. In estuaries of south-eastern coastal regions, the levels of toxicity (about 3 percent) were relatively much lower. The lower toxicity was attributed to the presence of less urbanized and undeveloped farms, forests, wetlands and limited industrial developments. However, the toxicity was quite severe in isolated areas particularly near naval stations, marinas and boat harbours. Later, study was extended to cover other coastal zones such as Biscayne Bay (Florida) in Southeast; and Galveston Bay (Texas) in the Gulf of Mexico; and Chesapeake Bay, Puget Sound, and Delaware Bay on the Northeast Atlantic coastline (Hameedi, et al., 1999).

Contaminated sediments on the sea bottom may re-suspend, transport and re-deposit in areas far from the original location. Additionally, contaminants may "break free" from sediments, and mix with water making their benthic environment toxic. Thus, one of the important goals of the coastal resource management is to track and monitor sediment contamination and toxicity, and post advisory to public.

Restoration of Coastal Habitats in North America

As the American coastlines are geographically, biologically and culturally rich and diverse, the American people continue to use them more intensively than before. As a result, the anthropogenic impacts on coastal environments are expected to increase in future. Nevertheless, maintenance of healthy benthic environments and aquatic systems including wildlife habitats along American coastlines is undertaken very seriously by the United States government as well as by its citizens. Variety of coastal restoration programs at local to watershed and regional scales are in place on an on-going basis in order to tackle various ecological impacts on coastal benthic environments.

Benthic habitat restoration refers to range of activities intended to improve biological productivity or functioning of a particular benthic system. Most common objective of a habitat restoration is to apply measures that bring the ecological and or biological condition to its baseline condition – for example, a particular aquatic species of a coastal water and estuary that existed earlier prior to an adverse condition(s) inflicted on it.

Coastal habitat restoration can take any of the following forms:

Baseline Conditions: In this approach, the restoration efforts are aimed at taking measures that enable return on the original pre-existing condition of an area. For example, restoring a lost wetland, and bringing to its original status in terms of its biotic species and physiographic conditions.

Mitigation: In this case, the aim is to compensate any loss of ecological conditions caused at other place. For example, adding and adopting an exotic species in an area in order to compensate loss of that species at other place as a result of encroachment resulted from land clearing and housing development or road construction. Another example would be a restoration that seeks to compensate for wetland impacts at one location by enhancing or creating a wetland at another site. Wetland restoration is major theme in the Louisiana State which occupies 40 percent of the U.S. coastal wetlands alone (NOAA, 1998c).

Habitat Creation: This is an attempt to create a habitat at a place where it did not exist earlier. Such attempts may include development of ponds along coastline in order to provide spawning habitat and breeding stock of a fish species or aquatic plant that is not common in that coastal zone. Later, this stock is released in coastal waters and allowed to adapt to the prevailing ecological environment over time in the selected coastal zone.

Thus coastal habitat restoration can provide an effective means of mitigating anthropogenic impacts on coastal estuaries and its aquatic systems. Restoration is often aimed at the "keystone species". The Keystone species are those species whose abundance is essential to the survival of a particular biological community characteristic to the region. The keystone species are very valuable ecologically and their restoration usually helps improving an entire ecosystem of the region. For example, in the Mid-Atlantic and Gulf of Mexico, oysters are a keystone species where as Pacific salmon is the "keystone" species in the Northwest and Alaska region. Consequently, a great effort is underway through out Chesapeake Bay in restoring oysters (Chesapeake Bay Program, 1993). Similarly, Coral reefs are important in protecting and maintaining marine ecosystem. Although coral reefs cover less than 1 percent of the ocean's surface, they have created a home to over 25 percent of all known marine animal and plant species. Coral reefs help to increase in size and abundance of these species (Monsen, 2002). Coral reef structure buffers shorelines from wave action, storms, and floods, and thus helps to prevent shoreline erosion. Therefore, educating public and developing community awareness about the beauty, richness and complexity of coral reefs and their benefit to marine ecosystem is important. For example, piles of brush or woody debris, referred to a brush piles, are analogous to reefs, and create aquatic habitats.

In the United States, the Federal, the State and the other local governments including community volunteers and non-governmental organizations are pursuing coastal restoration cooperatively at every level. There are several projects such as Coastal America targeted to protect and restore coastlines (Coastal America, 1996). These programs are geared towards restoring every aspect of coastal habitats. Some of the major agencies and programs along with rules and regulations promulgated to pursue protection and restoration of coastal habitat in the United States are listed in Table 10.2 (NOAA, 1998c).

Some of the major research and conservation institutes related to coastal zone resource protection and management in the United States of America (USA) are as follow.

- Coastal Studies Institute, Louisiana State University, Baton Rouge (Louisiana).
- The Centre for Coastal and Watershed Studies of U.S. Geological Survey, St. Petersburg and Tampa (Florida).
- Wetland Biogeochemistry Institute.
- Wetland Science Institute of National Resources Conservation Service, U.S. Government.
- Department of Coastal Environments, North Carolina State University devoted to MS and Ph.D. degree program solely devoted to Coastal resources issues.

Table 10.2: Major Legislations, Agencies and Programmes Aimed at Improving Coastal Resources

Agencies and Programmes	Legislations
1. U.S. Fish and Wildlife Services (USF&W) 2. The Coastal Ecosystems Program 3. The National Coastal Wetlands Conservation Grants Program	1. Federal Water Pollution Control Act (Clean Water Act) of 1972
1. National Oceanic and Atmospheric 2. Administration (NOAA) 3. National Habitat Program 4. National Marine Fisheries Service 5. Damage Assessment and Restoration Program 6. The Office of Ocean and Coastal Resource Management 7. National Estuarine Research Reserves System 8. National Marine Sanctuary Program	1. Coastal Zone Management Act (CZMA) 2. of 1972 Special Area Management Plans (SAMP) National Estuarine Research Reserves System 3. Comprehensive Environmental Response 4. Compensation and Liability Act (CERCLA or Superfund) of 1980 and 1986 5. Oil Pollution Act (OPA) of 1990 6. Coastal Wetlands Planning, Protection and Restoration Act (CWPPRA) of 1990
1. U.S. Department of Agriculture (USDA) 2. Natural Resource Conservation Service (NRCS) 3. Water Bank Program 4. Wetlands Reserve Program 5. U.S. Forest Service (USFS)	1. Magnuson-Stevens Fishery Conservation and Management Act of 1996 2. National Marine Sanctuaries Act 3. Water Resources Development Act 4. North American Wetlands Conservation Act
1. U.S. Department of Defence (DOD) 2. U.S. Army Corps of Engineers 3. Defence Environmental Restoration Program	1. Food, Agriculture, Conservation and Trade Act 2. Rivers and Harbours Act
1. U.S. Environmental Protection Agency 2. (USEPA) 3. National Estuary Program (NEP) 4. Great Waters Program	1. Coastal Non-point Pollution Control 2. Program Guidance 3. Management Measures for Sources of 4. Non-point Pollution in Coastal Waters
1. Coastal America	2. Coastal Protection and Restoration Act

Scientists have discovered that near shore ocean currents serve as links to populations, habitats and ecosystem on the regional scale. According to Stanford biologist Stephen Palumbi, the conservation activities need to be concentrated on productive "neighbourhoods" on a neighbourhood-by-neighbourhood basis on all scales from larvae to the entire ecosystem. Palumbi used innovative devices such as Shore-based radar and computer-based mapping tools including genetic mapping of marine populations and discovered that the near shore underwater neighbourhoods are a lot smaller and cosier for benthic communities (Lazaroff, 2003).

Management Issues

For coastal zone management, development of integrated and sustainable coastal plans on both ecological and bioregional basis based on near-shore landscape and land-use and cover type characteristics are critical. In the United States, each coastal state has enacted coastal zone management plans. The Law of the Sea Convention which became effective in 1994 gives all states the right to manage its marine resources within their 200 nautical miles Exclusive Economic Zones. In my view, a coastal zone management plan should address a number of important scientific issues which should include, but not limited to, the following:

The need for a comprehensive review and evaluation of coastal management programs and projects in an effort to see what has worked and what hasn't. The aim here should be to see if there are some program elements which are common to other successful efforts.

The need for a centralized data base in each country or region, detailing, among other things: population growth and distribution trends; rates of urbanization; industrialization patterns and trends; state of coastal resources and exploitation rates; consumption patterns; pollution levels in coastal waters; and pollution and sediment loads brought in by river systems.

An overwhelming need for better data sets on the state of critical coastal resources, particularly data on the current state of mangrove forests, sea grass beds and coral reefs is felt. Utilization of GIS systems and satellite imagery in an effort to obtain more and better quality data on the actual extent of these resources and their current condition should be considered.

Coastal resource managers are learning a great deal about the coastal resources such as mangroves, sea grasses, coral reefs and fisheries from new investigations and observations. Some of the main policy issues which could benefit coastal resource managers may include:

(a) the need for states, provinces and counties sharing common resources to evolve towards a sea or river basin-wide approach to management. Further, formulation of more region-specific resource management agreements could be developed, (b) the fundamental need for national, state and local governments to build up the capacity of political, administrative and scientific institutions to formulate and implement comprehensive coastal management strategies, in close collaboration with local communities, (c) the need to try out special area management programs in selected areas in an effort to provide data and policy feedback for broadening the scope of management efforts later on.

Our coastal aquatic resources are under crisis. Therefore, management of coastal resources in a more sustainable manner should be taken at highest priority.

Summary

Due to increasing population pressures on the American coastlines, particularly on its North-Eastern coastlines of the United States of America has caused intense stress on its estuaries and coastal waters. Coastal urbanization and anthropogenic pollutions discharged to estuaries and coastal waters has considerably increased resulting high toxicity in some estuaries. There are numerous coastal protection programs and legislations are in place for coastal restoration. These programs have been implemented on local-to-regional scales to tackle various ecological impacts on coastal benthic environments. The Federal, the State and other local governments including community volunteers and non-governmental organizations arc pursuing coastal restoration cooperatively at every level.

References

Anonymous (2003) Coastal Mega cities, People and Planet, 2003.

Armitage, T.M. 91995) EPA's contaminated sediment management strategy. In Allen, H.E. (ed.), Metal contaminated aquatic sediments. Chelsea, MI: Ann Arbor Press. Pp. 273-286.

Chesapeake Bay Program, (1993) Chesapeake Bay strategy for the restoration and protection of ecologically valuable species, CBP/TRS 113/94.

Coastal America, (1996) Establishing an effective model for coastal management. Washington, DC: Coastal America.

Federal Emergency Management Agency (1997) (on-line) Hurricane background and preparedness information, FEMA Web site. URL: http://www.fema.gov/hu97/hurinfo.htm

Hameedi, M.J. (1997) Strategy for monitoring the environment in the coastal zone. In Haq, B.U., et a. (eds.), Coastal zone management imperative for maritime developing nations. Dordrecht, The Netherlands: Kluwer Academic Publishers.

Hameedi, M.J., E.R. Long and M.R. Harmon (1999) (on-line) Sediment Toxicity. In: NOAA's State of the Coast Report. Silver Spring. MD: National Oceanic and

Atmospheric Administration. URL: http://state-of-coast.noaa.gov/bulletins/html/sed_15/sed.html

Hampson, Rick (2000) A formula for disaster on the crowed coastline (Part-3). USA Today, July 28, 2000.

Lazaroff, Cat. (2003) (on-line) Marine Experts Unveil Secrets of Coastal Conservation. ENS, Washington, D.C. URL: http://ens-news.com/ens/feb2003/2003-02-19-06.asp

Long, E.R.A, Robertson, D.A., Wolfe, J. Hameedi, and Sloane, G.M. (1996) Estimates of the spatial extent of sediment toxicity in major US estuaries, Environmental Science and Technology, 30:3585-3592.

Monsen, Lauren (2002) Experts cite coastal land use as major risk to coral reef health. Washington File, Office of International Information Program (06/07/2002), pp.1-4. URL: http://usinfo.state.gov

National Oceanic and Atmospheric Administration (NOAA), (1990) Estuaries of the United States: Vital statistics of a natural resource base. Rockville, MD: NOAA, National Ocean Service, Office of Ocean Resources Conservation and Assessment, pp. 79.

National Oceanic and Atmospheric Administration (NOAA), (1998a) (on-line) "Population at risk from Natural Hazards", by Sandy Ward and Catherine Main, NOAA's State of the Coast Report, Silver Spring, MD: NOAA. (URL): http://state of coast.noaa.gov/bulletins/html/par_02.html

National Oceanic and Atmospheric Administration (NOAA), (1998b), The National Status and Trends Program for marine environmental quality, Silver Spring, MD: NOAA, National Ocean Services, National Centres for Coastal Ocean Science, pp. 32.

National Oceanic and Atmospheric Administration (NOAA), (1998c) (on-line), Restoring Coastal Habitats, Tom Ardito and Darlene Finch. NOAA's State of Coast Report, Silver Spring, MD:NOAA. URL: http://state_of_coast.noaa.gov/bulletins/html/chr_10/chr.html

Simpson, R.H. (1974), The Hurricane Disaster Potential Scale. Weather-wise, (27):169

Turgeon, D.D., Hameedi, J., Harmon, M.R., Long, E.R., McMahon, K.D., and White., H.H. (1998), Sediment toxicity in coastal waters, Silver Spring, MD:NOAA, National Ocean Service, Office of Ocean Resources Conservation and Assessment. 20 pp.

Ullmann, Owen, Paul Overberg and Rick Hampson (2000), Boom on the Beach (Part-I). USA Today, July 28, 2000. [http://www.usatoday.com/weaher/hurricane/2000/beachboom/wpart1.htm].

U.S. Environmental Agency (EPA), (1997) The incidence and severity of sediment contamination in surface waters of the United States. Vol. 1: National Sediment Quality Survey. Office of Science and Technology, Standards and Applied Science Division, Washington, DC. EPA 823-R-97-006. September (1997).

U.S. EPA (1998) EPA's Contaminated Sediment Management Strategy, Office of Water, Washington, DC, EPA 823-R-98-001, (April 1998).

11

Environmental Status of Water Resources in Kumaon Himalaya

P.C. Tiwari and Bhagwati Joshi

Introduction

The water is one of the most fundamental and critical natural resources on the earth. We depend on the water for a wide range of values and uses. It plays a crucial role in all sectors of activities, such as, domestic, agriculture, industry etc. In a large measure, the development and productivity of a wide range of natural resources depend on the availability of surface and ground water. Besides, water offers multitude of recreational opportunities that are enjoyed by us. Our awareness of the importance of water to the global environment is changing the future of water resource management around the world. Over the past decade, water, particularly the surface and ground water, have emerged as a major consideration in Global discussion on sustainable development. Since, the United Nation's Earth Submit held in Rio de Janeiro, Brazil in 1992, remarkable progress has been made in advancing the worldwide consensus on addressing water management and conservation issues. In view of increasing industrialization and mounting urbanization across the globe and the resultant increased demand of water, an increasing number of countries are viewing their water resources as a source of economic wealth and development. The management and conservation of water resources is therefore imperative for channelizing the process of sustainable development to desired destinations. The international community recognizes the multiple benefits and roles of water. Given the wide disparities between countries and social and economic priorities, finding a common definition of what constitutes sustainable water management is crucial.

The Himalaya represents one of the geo-dynamically unstable, ecologically fragile and economically most underdeveloped mountain ecosystems of the planet. The continuous uplift has led these mountain ranges vulnerable to large-scale tectonic movements and landslides and to the processes of surface removal. Till recently, the Himalayan Mountains have been considered merely as an extension of the plains of north India from the point of view of planning and management of natural resources. But, our understanding about the problems of hilly and mountainous areas and the approach to their development has undergone a drastic change during the recent years. This change is reflected in the deepening anxiety over the disruption of ecological balance in Himalaya and its attendant deleterious effects on the ecology, economy and community sustainability in the plains of north India (Maithani, 1986).

During the recent years, a variety of changes have emerged in the traditional resource use structure in response to increased population pressure, and resultant increased demand of food, fodder, grazing land, water and other natural resources in the region. This facilitated and also compelled people to utilize the critical natural resources, such as, land, water and forests beyond their ecological carrying capacity through unscientific and irrational resource development. Large-scale deforestation, mining and quarrying, and extension of cultivation, excessive grazing and of course the rapid urban growth and development of tourism contributed significantly to the depletion of natural resources in the region. Consequent upon this, the water resources have been dwindling and diminishing fast throughout the Himalayan ranges leading to rapid degradation of aquatic-ecosystems. The rapid depletion of water resources has not only damaged the fragile ecosystem but also threatened the sustainability of mountain communities directly as well as indirectly.

Kumaon Himalaya

Kumaon Himalaya encompasses a geographical area of 21035 km^2 in the eastern part of the newly carved Himalayan state of Uttaranchal. It stretches between 28^0 44' and 38^0 49' North Latitudes and 78^0 45' and 81^0 01' East Longitudes. In the north, it is separated from China by the Indo-Tibetan water divide; in the east, river Kali defines its boundary with Nepal; the plains of Ganga makes its southern boundary; and in the west the region shares its boundaries with Chamoli and Pauri districts of Garhwal Himalaya. Geographically, the region is located between the plateau of Tibet on the north and the Ganga Plains in the south. Kumaon assumes a great strategic significance as its northern and eastern boundaries makes international border respectively with China and Nepal. Physiographically, from south to north the Kumaon Himalaya is constituted by the low-lying foothill belt of *Bhaber* (the northern extension of the plains of Ganga with coarse deposits), Siwaliks hills, Lesser Himalayan ranges, Great Himalaya and the Trans Himalaya. These physiographic zones are separated by tectonic boundaries – the thrust planes. The absolute relief of the region varies from 204 m to 7436 m from the mean sea level. Owing to physiographic diversity the region enjoys a variety of climatic regimes varying from tropical to polar climatic conditions. The physio-climatic complexities obtaining in the region are reflected in a variety of natural vegetation and numerous species of wildlife. Considering its biological prosperity, the region has been identified one of the biodiversity hotspots of the world (Tiwari and Joshi, 1997). The Corbett National Park, which has the distinction of being the first National Park as well as the first Tiger Reserve of India, and the Nandadevi Biosphere Reserve are situated in the region. Administratively, the region constitute Kumaon Division that comprises six districts (Udhamsingh Nagar, Naini Tal, Almora, Bageshwer, Champawat and Pithoragarh) which put together with Garhwal Division lying to its west and comprising seven districts form the newly carved Himalayan State of Uttaranchal. The region has a total population of 29,43,199 persons of which only 20 percent is urban and remaining 80 percent lives in rural areas.

Water Resources of Kumaon Himalaya

The precipitation in the form of snow, which accumulates on the mountain slopes, is the principal source of water in Trans and Great Himalaya. Whereas, in the Lesser Himalaya and Siwalik mountains, rain water constitutes the surface and sub-surface flow systems and also forms the ground water reserves through percolation and infiltration. The Himalayan watershed can be divided into three categories on the basis of Hydrological characteristics. These are (i) the Fluvio-glacial watersheds which are marked by high surface gradient and medium drainage texture, and are confined to great Himalayan ranges; (ii) the Lesser Himalayan region is the domain of fluvio-erosional processes. Watersheds of this region are characterized by comparatively lower surface slopes, high drainage density and accelerated erosion; and (iii) the watersheds of fluvio-depositional hydrographic regime are marked with low geomorphic energy environment, and consequcntly, the process of deposition is most significant. This regime is extended over the areas adjacent to the south of the Himalayan foothills (Rawat, 1988).

Glaciers: Thc high altitude areas lying above the snow line are about 4800 m on the external and southern ranges and about 5600 m on the Indo-Tibetan water divide. There is large number of glaciers on both the slopes of these snow-clad high mountain ranges and serve as natural regulator of water and constitute the biggest reservoir of water resourccs of the region. About 380 km^2 area of Kumaon is under permanent snow cover which accounts for more than 12 percent of the total geographical area of the region. Pindari, Milam, Kaphni, Sunderdhunga, Kalaba, Baldhunga, Talkot, Poting are some of the important glaciers of Kumaon Himalaya. The Pindari glacier, which extends for about 3 km in length and 300–400 km in width, is situated between Nandadevi and Nandakot peaks and form the source of Pinder River. The Milam glacier, which lies between the Untadhura range to the northeast and Nandadevi–Nandakot massif to the southwest has the largest catchment area of 211.12 km^2 and glacier area of 39.50 km^2.

Rivers and Streams

Kumaon consists of three river systems—Alakhnanda, Ramganga, and Kali. Besides Alakhnanda, Girthi and Pindar are the principal rivers of the Alakhnanda system. All these rivers are snow-fed which have their source in the glaciers of Trans and Great Himalaya. The principal rivers of Ramganga system are Western Ramganga, Gagas, Kosi and Gaula, which have their origin in the Lesser Himalayan ranges. The Kali system, which is constituted mainly by the snow-fed rivers of Kuti, Duauli, Gori, Eastern Ramganga and Saryu, drains the largest part of Kumaon (10869 km^2) and has the highest average annual water discharge. Whereas, the average annual discharge of Kosi and Gaula rivers that originate from the rain-fed slopes of Lesser Himalayan ranges is considerably low.

Springs and Natural Lakes

Apart from the glaciers and rivers, springs and natural lakes are the important aspects of the geo-hydrology of Kumaon and constitute a significant proportion of the water resources. No detailed geo-hydrological investigation of springs has been carried out in the region. But these springs and lakes contribute to the major proportion of the discharge of the streams, particularly those originating from the Lesser Himalaya and Siwaliks Ranges. In most of the parts of the region, the springs are recharged by seasonal rainfall. Tectonic activity along the thrust – planes and diversified lithology are mainly responsible for the origin of several lake basins in the region. These are scenically beautiful and geologically very interesting. Bhim Tal with a total area of 11.20 km^2 is largest and Naukuchia Tal with maximum depth of 21. 90 m is the deepest lake of Kumaon (Table 11.1). Besides, numerous lakes in the Himalayan region have originated by damming of rivers by landslide debris, fluvio-glacial process and contemporaneous folding (Mathur, 1955; Ball, 1878).

Water Resource Potential

The watershed having independent hydrological boundaries is an ideal geo-hydrological unit for the analysis, monitoring, management and conservation of water resources. The geo-hydrological processes of a watershed are controlled and regulated by a set of geographical factors that include precipitation, transpiration, overland flow, infiltration, deep transfer, sub-surface flow etc. The amount of run-off and infiltration which play significant role in maintaining the geo-hydrological balance of a watershed is to a large extent regulated by the complexities of physio-cultural factors, such as, surface configuration, lithology, structure, land utilization pattern etc. Pathak, H. (1983) in his study of utilization and potentials of water resources of the Central Himalaya assumed that on an average the surface run-off in the region accounts for about 49 percent of the total rainfall.

Table 11.1: Important Morphometric Attributes of Principal Lakes of Kumaon Himalaya

Morphometric Attributes	Lakes				
	Naini Tal	Bhim Tal	Sat Tal	Naukuchia Tal	Khurpa Tal
Altitude (m)	1938.00	1345.00	1320.00	1320.00	1610.00
Maximum Depth (m)	25.70	24.75	18.00	41.25	38.00
Mean Depth (m)	18.55	12.13	NA	21.90	NA
Maximum Length (km)	1.46	1.75	0.87	1.05	0.35
Maximum Width (km)	0.47	0.53	NA	0.88	NA
Catchment Area (km^2)	5.50	11.20	5.00	2.60	0.59

Source: Rawat, 1987

The study of vegetation hydrology of Kumaon Himalaya revealed that the vegetal cover plays dominant role in increasing the rate of infiltration as the amount of surface run-off is as low as 0.70 percent of the total rainfall in densely forested areas (Pathak, P. C., 1983). Whereas, the experimental study of land use and hydrological parameters revealed that in similar geological, climatic and geomorphic conditions, forested, cultivated and barren land produce, 3.2 percent, 20 percent and 10.38 percent surface run-off of the total rainfall respectively (Rawat, 1988). However, the investigation carried out for measuring the water volume of the Upper Kosi watershed (480.15 km^2) of Kumaon by Thiessen Polygon method brought out the fact that the entire catchment has 210.77 million m^3 volume of water (Tiwari, 1995). Table 11.2 shows that the region has huge water potential. The North Kosi Micro-watershed with a total area of 74.90 Km^2 has the largest water volume, which accounts for more than 15 percent of the total water volume of the catchment (Table 11.2). This high water volume in the headwater region is explained by the fact that more than 65 percent of the micro-watershed has inaccessible terrain and consequently has very sparse population and dense forest cover.

Table 11.2: Average Annual Volume of Water in Different Micro-watersheds of Upper Kosi Catchment, Kumaon Himalaya

Micro-Watersheds	Area (km^2)	Percent of total Area of Catchment	Volume of Water (Million m^3)	Percent of Total Water Volume of Catchment
1. North Kosi	74.90	15.60	32.90	15.61
2. Bhutagaon Gad	34.90	7.27	15.30	7.26
3. Dhoni Gad	40.50	8.43	17.76	8.43
4. Sim Gad	53.90	11.23	23.66	11.22
5. Middle Kosi	68.90	14.33	30.26	14.36
6. Nana Kosi	62.05	12.92	27.24	12.92
7. Patia Ron Gad	44.60	9.29	19.56	9.28
8. Khul Gad	55.90	9.56	20.15	9.56
9. Shail-Jamthara Gad	24.50	5.10	10.74	5.18
10. South Kosi	30.10	6.27	13.20	6.28
11. Upper Kosi Catchment	480.15	100.00	210.77	100.00

Source: Tiwari, 1995

In order to monitor the water flow in streams and springs, experimental study was carried out in Shail Micro-watershed (1014 ha) of Upper Kosi Catchment. The density of springs is 3.06 springs per km^2, whereas, the density of perennial streams was computed to be 3.74 km of stream length per km^2 in the region (Table 11.3). The total flow of water in the streams of the region was measured to be 1,25,000 litre/day during dry months. At present, there are 31 perennial springs in the region, which put together discharge of more than 95000 litre water per day. Considering the geographical area (1014 ha) of the micro-watershed the flow of water in streams and springs is very high. On an average, the region has a total water generating capacity of more than 210 litre/day (Tiwari, 1995).

Status of Water Resource Utilization

Despite huge water potential the entire region is facing great scarcity of water for domestic as well as agricultural purposes. So far only 7 percent of the available water resources have been utilized mainly for household requirements and minor irrigation. Studies conducted in Upper Kosi Catchment of the region revealed that out of the 322 villages as many as 210 have been provided with piped water supply. But, it was observed during the field surveys that in most of such villages the water supply is irregular and partial. In 63 villages of the region, the piped water supply schemes have blocked or become inoperative mainly owing to low discharge of spring or streams from where the water flows into the distribution system or lack of active community involvement and participation. As many as 197 village of the catchment are facing acute scarcity of drinking water due to underutilization and improper management of water resources. Generally, as one moves up from the valley floors to the mid and up-slope areas and ridges, the availability of surface as well as ground water decreases owing to increased surface gradient and low water generating capacity of land.

Table 11.3: Spring and Stream Flow in Shail Gad Micro Watershed of Upper Kosi Catchment, Kumaon Himalaya

Total Geographical Area (ha)	1,014
Spring Density (per km$^{2)}$	3.06
Average Spring Discharge (Litre/Day)	95,250
Stream Density (km/km$^{2)}$	3.74
Average Stream Discharge (Litre/Day)	1,18,000
Total Water Generating Capacity of the Micro-watershed (Litre/ha/Day)	210.30

Source: Tiwari, 1995

It has not been much possible, mainly due to economic reasons, to lift the water from the rivers flowing down in the valleys for the large number of settlements situated on the higher slopes and ridges. This is one of the important reasons for the non-availability of sufficient water to rural population in Kumaon. This is substantiated by the fact that the Almora town situated along a ridge of about 1500 m height from the mean sea level receives three-time lesser water supply than the minimum requirement of water fixed for the urban centres by the government. The rural population of Shail Micro-watershed has a geographical area of 1014 ha, and water generating capacity of more than 210 litre/ha/day. This is not able to get more than 5 litre/person/day water for all purposes. This state of affairs brings out the fact clearly that in many areas of Kumaon the high water potential is being managed and utilized very poorly and inefficiently causing great hardship to local people and resulting in the underdevelopment of the entire region.

Out of the total cultivated land (22 percent of total area) of Kumaon only 11 percent is irrigated. Water resources for irrigation are managed in Kumaon, mainly through the construction of small canal, tanks, lift, hydrams etc. Canals and Tanks are the main source of irrigation as these two share 38 percent and 37 percent respectively of the total irrigated area. The irrigated cultivation is mainly confined to valley floors and other low-lying areas where the regular supply of water for irrigation is available round the year. The cultivated land lying on up-slope areas and ridges accounts for about 84 percent of the total agricultural land of Kumaon and is never irrigated due to non-availability of water.

Environmental Changes and their Impact on the Geo-hydrology

As in other parts of Himalaya, the traditional resource development process in Kumaon is interlinked with forests, farmland, and livestock (Palni, 1998). More than 75 percent population of the region is dependent on traditional biomass based cultivation. In order to preserve fertility of soil and productivity of land under sustained cropping in such a biomass-based agro-ecosystem, there must be a net transfer of energy from the support area (Forests) to arable land. This flow of energy from forest to cultivated land in the Himalayan agro-ecosystem is mediated through livestock, which is usually in the form of fodder of stall-fed cattle whose manure and labour is later applied to the cultivated land. On an average, one unit of agronomic production in the region involves nine units of energy from surrounding forest ecosystem (Singh et al, 1884). The forests and the cultivated land of Himalaya are linked in a series of dynamic relationships involving the production, transfer and consumption of energy. The optimum rate in this system at any time in terms of balance between areas (forest and arable land) and numbers (human population and cattle units), in one which permits the maximum utilization and consumption of energy produced in the system without impairing the regenerative and restorative capacity of those elements responsible for commensurate energy production (Whittaker, 1989).

In the Himalayan agro-ecosystem, 5-10 ha of well-stocked forest area is required to meet the energy requirement of 1 ha of arable land to practice agriculture on sustainable basis (Singh et al, 1984). In Upper Kosi Catchment, the forestland available to per ha of agricultural land is only 2.77 ha, and more than 60 percent of these forests are highly degraded. This clearly shows that the biotic stress on the forest of the catchment is very acute. The rapid growth of population, and the resultant increased demand of arable land, grazing areas, fodder and fuel-wood, and the inappropriate development strategies has pushed the crop farming to forests and marginal and sub-marginal areas. The expansion of cultivation in the region is now taking place at the rate of 0.79 percent/year

(Tiwari, 1995). Consequently, there is a proportional increase in the cattle population. The availability of grazing area in the region is 0.21 ha/cattle against the ecologically recommended standard of minimum 3.5 ha/cattle (Ashish, 1983). The grazing pressure is very acute, and the pastures are coming under increased grazing stress with the massive increase in cattle population. As a result, the forest and rangelands on an average up to 7 km distance from the rural settlements in the region are highly degraded and depleted (Tiwari, 2000 and 2002).

As described above, the traditional process of natural resource development has been changing fast mainly in response to high growth of population and resultant increased demand of food, fodder, fuel wood etc. Consequently, the activities of cultivation, grazing and deforestation are extended over large areas of the region. The natural ecosystem of the region has come under increased resource use pressure resulting into ecological imbalances and unsustainable resource development (Bisht and Tiwari, 1996). The proportion of degraded and wastelands have been increasing which accounts for more than 15 percent of the total geographical area of Kumaon (Tiwari, 2002). The rapidly changing land use pattern and the resultant decrease in forest area have contributed significantly in promoting the process of soil erosion in the region and decreasing the water generating capacity of land (Ives. 1989).

Retreat of Glaciers

Studies reveal that the glaciers of Kumaon have been receding and becoming smaller in size, and their regulatory effect is diminishing considerably owing to environmental changes. Most of the Himalayan glaciers have a negative mass balance (i.e. the melting rate is higher than the accumulation rate of snow) during the last 20–25 years (Cotter, 1906; Strachey, 1845; Tiwari and Jangpangi, 1962; Tiwari, 1972, Rawat, 1988). The receding trend in the Himaalyan glaciers is also indicated by several disconnected tributaries in the region, which were earlier connected with the main body of the glaciers (Bhandari and Nijampurkar, 1988). Thc Pindari glacier of Kumaon Himalaya has retreated by about three kilometres from1845 to 1966, and its size has diminished by 29 kilometre since Pleistocene glacial period (Rawat, 1988). The Milam glacier of the region is receding at an average rate of 12.5 metre/year (Bhandari and Nijampurkar, 1988). On an average, the glaciers of Kumaon Himalaya are receding at the rate of 23.46 metre/year (Rawat, 1988). In case this diminishing trend of glaciers continues, the regime of the snow fed rivers in the region will be adversely affected and the Himalayan rivers will carry far less water as there will be gradual decrease in the volume of snow-melt water released during the summers (Valdiya, 1985).

Drying of Springs

The large-scale depletion of forest resources is causing great damage to the underground water resources by reducing the water generating capacity of land to springs and streams in the region. Since, a large proportion of the rainfall is lost through surface run-off without replenishing the groundwater reserves, a large number of springs that support a variety of life sustaining activities, particularly in rural Kumaon, are drying up fast. Study carried out in the Gaula catchment of Kumaon revealed that about 45–46 percent springs have dried up or become seasonal due reduced ground water recharge (Valdiya, 1985). In Shail Micro-watershed of Upper Kosi Catchment there are 49 natural springs and 18 out of them have completely dried up and all the 9 flourmills have abandoned due to low water discharge in streams during the last 20–25 years. The heads of many of the streams in the region have moved down on an average of 37 meters during the last 25 years. In view of the reduced recharge of ground water in the watersheds of the region, it is being estimated that the Himalayan Rivers will carry 20-30 percent less water in near future (Valdiya, 1985). These geo-hydrological changes have large impact not on the geo-ecology but also on the quality of social life of rural communities in the region.

Study carried out in Upper Kosi Catchment revealed that the watershed has lost about 11 percent of its irrigation potential owing to reduced water flow in steams and springs, and consequently, the productivity of agro-ecosystem has declined by about 9 percent despite continued extension of cultivation, during the last 20–25 years (Tiwari, 1995). Owing to very low productivity of the traditional agriculture, male youths migrate out of the region in search of livelihood leaving behind large number of females, children and aged people in the region. Consequently, the responsibility of fetching water, collecting fodder and fuel wood form long distances becomes the sole responsibility of women. Survey carried out in the Upper Kosi Catchment revealed that the average travel distance for the collection of potable water has increased from 2 km to 4 km during the last 20–25 years mainly owing to drying up of natural springs within and in the surrounding of the rural settlements, in the catchment.

Diminishing Lake Ecosystems

The lake ecosystems of Kumaon are also under increased biotic stress. Most of the lakes in Kumaon are situated along tectonically alive and ecologically fragile but densely populated zones. Besides, all the lakes mentioned in Table 25.3 situated within or in the surroundings of the fast growing urban areas. More recently, comparatively less accessible areas of the lakes region of Kumaon are also coming under the process of fast urbanization mainly owing to the extension of road network, development of horticulture, gradual shift from primary resource development practices to secondary and tertiary sectors, and the growth of domestic tourism through the publicity and marketing of new tourist sites. The natural risks of this unplanned urban growth are clearly discernible in terms of increased number of landslides, accelerated soil erosion, disruption of natural drainage and silting and pollution of lakes. This is resulting into the depletion and destruction of nature as well as increased incidence and severity of urban environmental hazards in many of the urban centres, such as, the lake town of Naini Tal. Bathymetric investigations of Bhimtal and Naini Tal Lake revealed that the capacity of these important lakes has respectively decreased by 5494 m^3 and 14150 m^3 during the last 100-110 years due to rapid siltation of the lakebeds. The annual average rate of siltation in Naini Tal Lake was 65.32 m^3 (Khanka and Jalal, 1984 and 1985; Rawat, 1987). Most of the lakes of the region are heavily infested by weeds and invaded marshy conditions (Rawat, 1988).

Conclusions

It is clear from the above discussion that the water resources of Kumaon are diminishing fast owing to the rapid transformation of natural environment and resultant geo-hydrological disturbances. The huge glaciers of Great and Trans Himalaya are receding fast, and their regulatory mechanism is diminishing. The water generating capacity of land is decreasing due to reduced recharge of ground water in the region. As a result the springs are drying and the water discharge of streams is decreasing. Besides, the beautiful lakes of Kumaon are becoming smaller in size and their capacity is dwindling due to anthropogenic impact in the catchment areas. These geo-hydrological imbalances have a large impact on the fragile ecosystem of Himalaya as well as on the sustainability of mountain communities.

Forests and farmland are the most crucial components of the traditional resource utilization structure in Kumaon Himalaya. The natural forests in the region carry large human population, including forest dependent tribal groups. These rural communities are completely dependent on forests not only for the fulfilment of their basic resource needs, such as, fuel wood, fodder, timber, grazing etc. but also for their livelihood. It is therefore, not practically possible to conservc natural resources without considering the needs and problems of rural communities living interspersed them, particularly when their traditional activities are limited or prohibited in many parts of the region following the creation of National Parks, Sanctuaries and Biosphere Reserves.

Hence, the environmental conservation and resource development programs in the region should be development oriented. In view of this, the conservation of dwindling water resources of the region is very complex in nature as it is essentially associated with the management of other critical resources, particularly the land and forests. This brings out the fact that the goal of sustainable development of water resources can not attained through sectoral approach. It is therefore, imperative to analyze all crucial issues related with conservation and protection of water resources in a holistic manner by considering water conservation and management as one of the essential components of overall land use and resource development policies. This clearly underline the need of developing a Natural Resources Information System (NRIS) at micro-watershed level through comprehensive and detailed analysis, appraisal and mapping of land, water and forest resources in the socio-economic backdrops of the region. Remote sensing and Geographic Information System (GIS) techniques will be highly useful in the analysis and management of natural resources on both time and cost effective basis.

References

Ashish, M. (1983) Agricultural Economy of Kumaon Hills: A threat to Ecological Disaster, in O.P. Singh (ed.), *The Himalaya: Nature, Man and Culture*, New Delhi.

Ball, V. (1878) On the Origin of Kumaon Lakes, *Records*, Geological Survey of India, XI, Part-II, 174-182.

Bhandari, N. and Nijampurkar (1988) Himalayan Glaciers: Our Neglected Water Banks, in S.K. Chadha ed.*Himalayas: Ecology and Environment*, New Delhi, 76-92.

Bisht, B.S. and Tiwari, P.C. (1996) Land Use Planning for Sustainable Resource Development in Kumaon Lesser Himalaya-A Study of Gomti Watershed, *International Journal of Sustainable Development and World Ecology*, 3, 23-34.

Cotter, G.P. (1906) Notes on Certain Glaciers in Kumaon, *Records,* Geological Survey of India, 35 (4), 148-151.

Ives, J.D. (1989) Deforestation in the Himalaya: The Cause of Increased Flooding in Bangladesh and Northern India, *Land Use Policy*, 6, 187-193.

Joshi, S.C., Joshi, D.R. and Dani, D.D. (1983) *Kumaun Himalaya: A geographical Perspective on Resource Development*, Gyanodaya Prakashan, Naini Tal.

Khanka, L.S and Jalal, D.S. (1984) Morphological Analysis of Lake Naini Tal in Kumaon Himalaya, *Geographical Review of India*, 46 (4), 64-69.

Maithani, B.P. (1986) Towards Sustainable Hill Area Development, *Himalaya: Man, Nature and Culture*, 16(2), 4-7.

Mathur, S.M. (1955) On the Origin of Bhimtal and Neighbouring Lakes in the Naini Tal District, U.P. Quart. *Journal, Geological Min. And Met. Society, India*, XXVII, No. 4, 125-180.

Palni, L.M.S. et al (1998) Conservation of the Himalayan Agro-ecosystem: Issues and

Priorities, Technical Paper-v, *in Ecological Co-operation for Biodiversity Conservation in the Himalaya,* United Nations Development Programme, New York, 253-290.

Pathak, H. (1983) Water Resources of U.P. Himalaya: Their Uses and Potential, in O.P. Singh ed. *The Himalaya: Nature, Man and Culture*, Rajesh Publications, New Delhi, 161-169.

Pathak, P.C. (1983) *Vegetation Hydrology and Its Impact on Nutrient Cycling in Selected Forest Ecosystems of Kumaon Himalaya*, Unpublished Ph.D. Thesis, Kumaon University, Naini Tal.

Rawat, J.S. (1987) Morphometry and Morphology of Naini Tal Kumaon Lesser Himalaya, *Journal of the Geological Society of India*, 30 (6), 493-498.

Rawat, J.S. (1988) Water Resources and Burning Hydrological Problems of Kumaon, in K.S. Valdiya ed. *Kumaon Land and People*, Naini Tal, 201-212.

Singh, J.S., Pandey, U. And Tiwari, A. K. (1984) Man and Forests: A Central Himalayan Case Study, *Ambio*, 13; 80-87.

Strachey, R. (1845) A Description of the Glaciers of Pindari Kaphinee Rivers in Kumaon Himalaya, *Journal of the Asiatic Society of Bengal*, 16(2), 203,

Tiwari, A.P. (1972) Recent Changes in the Position of the Snout of the Pindari Glacier, Kumaon Himalaya, Almora District, U.P. India, *Proceedings of the Symposium of* on Role *of Snow and Ice in Hydrology*, UNESCO-WHO-IAHS, Canada, Vol.2, 1144-1149.

Tiwari, P.C. (1995) Natural Resources and Sustainable Development in Himalaya, Shree Almora Book Depot, Almora.

Tiwari, P.C. (2000) Land Use Changes in Himalaya and their Impact on the Plains Ecosystem: Need for Sustainable Land Use, *Land Use Policy*, 17, 101-111.

Tiwari, P.C. (2002) *Second Annual Progress Report of the Research Project on Natural Resources Information System for Wasteland Development in Kosi Headwater*, Department of Science and Technology, Government of India, New Delhi.

Tiwari, P.C. and Joshi, B. (1997) *Wildlife in the Himalayan Foothills: Conservation and Management*, Indus Publishing Company, New Delhi.

Tiwari, A.P. and Jangpangi, B.S. (1962) The Retreat of the Snout of the Pindari Glaciers, *Proceedings of the Symposium of Obergurage International Association of Hydrological Sciences*, 58, 245-248.

Valdiya, K.S. (1985) Accelerated Erosion and landslide Prone Areas in the Central Himalayan Region, in J. S. Singh ed. *Environmental Regeneration in Himalaya*, Central Himalayan Environment Association, Naini Tal, 12-38.

Whittaker, W. (1989) The Ecology and Economy of Himalayan Agriculture and Labour Migration; A Case Study of Garhwal District, in D. C. Pandey and P. C. Tiwari (eds.), *Dimensions of Development Planning*, Criterion Publications, New Delhi.

12

Urban Environmental Degradation: A Study of Air Pollution in Ghaziabad City of India

Ram Bilas

Introduction

Air pollution is not really a new phenomenon, as smoke from heating and cooking fires, adours from domestic waste-sewerage and garbage have been a characteristic of place where man has been living since grouping into communities began (Ambast, 1990). However, in the last century in the developed countries methods of waste disposal, sewerage treatment, domestic heating and cooking have changed the traditional forms of air pollution. The smoke and odour have been reduced and replaced by a new set of air pollutants, which result from our auto mobile, industrial and urban society (Agarwal, 1991).

The earth's atmosphere has been serving the man by providing him with life sustaining air to breath as well as a medium for disposing of his refuge throughout his existence (ESMAP, 2004). Although, the nature has equipped the atmosphere to efficiently dispose the reasonable quantities of waste associated with human activities but man's indiscriminate use of the atmosphere as a gigantic sewer has led to a number of severe air pollution episode and to a global deterioration of the quality of the ambient air (Jain, 1993). Technological advancement, industrial expansion, population explosion, urbanization and man's increasing desire for higher standard of living have together contributed to the current environmental problems (Singh, 1993).

The problem of air pollution in Ghaziabad City at the present time is due to the steadily growing demands for energy and natural resources. Activities, such as energy production, transportation and industrialization are responsible for discharge of numerous pollutants in the air affecting the environment and human health.

Air pollution is generally composed of the pollutants of gases and solid liquid particles of both organic and inorganic in nature (Gopalan, 1999). The carbon dioxide, fluorocarbons, nitrogen oxides, sulphur compounds, waste heat, water vapour, ammonia, hydrocarbons, methane, peroxyacetyln nitrates, methyl bromide, krypton-85, aerosol etc. are the main constituents of air pollution

(Chaurasia, 1992). It is significant to note that air pollution through natural sources including volcanic dusts, wind blown dusts vapour from plant leaves; rotting materials in the natural environment, pollen grains from plant flowers etc. does not warrant much concern because such pollutants can be considered to be accommodated within the global ecology. The natural pollutants are distributed all over the globe but man made pollutants are injected and concentrated in certain localities of their sources mainly in highly industrialized and urbanized pockets of the world (John, 1998). In other words, the natural environment generally absorbs the pollutants coming out of natural sources and no pollution problem arises but man-made pollutants being concentrated in certain parts of the atmosphere pollute the nearby area.

Study area

Ghaziabad city, situated in the middle of the Ganga-Yamuna plain between 28°38′24″ and 28°42′48″ N and 77°19′24″ and 77°28′36″ E occupies an area of about 88.82 km^2. Ghaziabad (a part of the Nation Capital Region, Delhi) suddenly got its prominence as the most important industrial city of Uttar Pradesh. Formation of Ghaziabad as a separate district in November 1976 was mainly because of extraordinary growth of industries at the city during post independence period.

No doubt, greatest resources of Ghaziabad city lie at the junction of three important routes coming from Calcutta, Dehradun and Moradabad. The high degree of nodality of the city in respect of its surrounding areas is further reinforced by its proximity to the national capital city, Delhi. It is well connected with all the other parts of the country. It was mainly because of its extremely nodal situation coupled with its nearness to New Delhi. Ghaziabad has been chosen by more and more entrepreneurs for extremely favourable situation for industrial enterprise

Apart from the high degree of nodality, Ghaziabad city has the sound economic base. Upper Ganga Yamuna Doab is one of the most progressive and prosperous agricultural regions of the country and contributes much to the progress of this District.

Data and Methodology

This study is based on the secondary data collected from different secondary sources. Vehicular pollution load in the Ghaziabad city was estimated by the Pollution Control Board Ghaziabad which was based on the travel in a day by a particular category of vehicle, total number of vehicles and the emission factors. The vehicles, mainly trucks and buses contribute to high level of automobile emission and causes air pollution in this city. The number of vehicles was obtained from the R.T.O. office, Ghaziabad. For the assessment of air quality and pollution load five pollutants such as SPM, NO_x, CO, HC, Aldehydes from different crossing, residential, commercial and industrial locations were taken into consideration.

Comparison of Pollution Sources

While discussing air pollution from different sources (particularly from combustion processes) it is important to compare the relative quantities of air pollutants produced (Mishra, 1992). The average quantities of the major pollutants produced for one tone of fuel consumed are shown in Table 12.1.

Table 12.1: Emission from Combustion Sources (kg/per tone fuel)

Air Pollutants	Internal Combustion		External Combustion			
	Auto Engines	Diesel Engines	Fuel		Coal	
			Fuel Generation	Commercial Domestic	Power Generation	Commercial Domestic
Carbon monoxide	395	9	0.005	0.025	0.25	25
Nitrogen oxides	20	33	14	10	10	4
Sulphur oxides	1.55	6.0	20.8[s]	20.8[s]	20.8[s]	19[s]
Hydrocarbons	34	20	0.42	0.26	0.26	5
Aldehydes and organic acids	1.4	6.1	0.08	0.25	0.25	0.0025
Particulates	2(a)	2(b)	1.3(c)	1-12(c)	1-12(c)	2-8[A](d)

s: To obtain sulphur oxides produced, multiply number by percent in fuel (S = sulphur).

A: To obtain particulate produced, multiply number by percent A in fuel (A = Ash)

(**Note:** Most coal fired units are fitted with control devices and emissions are of the order of 1 to 10 percent of these)

a) About 20 percent of this total is lead from the knock additives.

b) Largely un-burnt carbon, on which traces of aromatic compounds, such as 3, 4-benzopyrene and similar compounds, have been absorbed.

c) Largely metal oxides form impurities in the fuel oil. These include the oxides of iron and vanadium.

d) Metal chlorides and sulphates (calcium-magnesium, iron etc.) from ash inclusions in the coal.

The amount of carbon monoxide emitted from the auto engine is obviously far greater than the amount emitted from the Diesel engine in case of internal combustion system and it is quite insignificant in case of external combustion systems. Nitrogen oxide emissions are also a function of the mode of combustion, and are most easily controlled in external combustion system. Ash and sulfur dioxide emissions are primarily not a result of the type of combustion but of the type of fuel used. Motor spirit is a highly refined product containing very little sulfur and no ash. However, it has been seen that the production of refined fuel from crude petroleum inevitably results in some residual fuels, and these also need to be disposed of, usually by combustion in a manner resulting in a minimum of air-pollution (WHO, 1994).

Air Quality Standards in India

Standards specifying allowable emission can either be related to the quality of the air in the atmosphere surrounding the industry or to industrial production. In the former case they are referred to as ambient air quality standards, whilst in the later case they are called emission standards. Emission standards are useful for design and control whereas ambient air quality standards are preferable for environment quality measurement and protection (WHO, 1994). In our country, on the basis of land use pattern in particular and other factors in general, various areas of a state may be classified into 3 categories, namely A, B and C by concerned pollution control boards. Category A covers industrial and mixed-use areas whereas category B covers residential and rural areas. Category C covers sensitive areas, like hill stations, tourist resorts, national parks etc.

Table 12.2 shows ambient air quality standards in India for 4 major pollutants, namely SPM, $S0_2$, No_x and CO in $\mu g/m^3$ (Tiwari, 1992). In fact, when monitored uniformly over the 12 month of a year with a frequency of not less than once in a week with a sampling time of 8 hr. for any sample and analyses accordingly to procedure specified by the Central Pollution Control Board, the concentrations for the pollutants must be within the limits prescribed in Tables 12.2 and 12.3.

Automobile Types and Number

Automobiles include all types of vehicles using petrol or diesel oil. Table 12.4 shows the number of vehicles from year 2002 to 2004. It is evident from the table that number of vehicles is continuously increasing since 2002. At present there are more than 59121 automobiles in Ghaziabad city, which move in different parts of the city. Thousands of buses, trucks and other automobiles pass through the city. These vehicles (especially trucks and buses) contribute to high level of automobile emission causing air pollution in Ghaziabad city.

Table 12.2: Indian Ambient Air Quality Standards

Category	Area	Concentrations, $\mu g/m^3$			
		SPM	SO_2	NO_x	CO
A	Industrial and mixed use	500	120	120	500
B	Residential and rural	200	80	80	2000
C	Sensitive	100	30	30	1000

Table 12.3: Indian Emission Standards

Industrial unit	Pollutant	Capacity/Process description	Emission limits, mg/m^3		
			Protected area	Other area	Any area
Cement	SPM	Capacity: Less than or equal to 200 tpd	250	400	–
		More than 200 tpd	150	250	–
Thermal power plant	SPM	Boiler size: Less than 200 MW	150	600	–
		200 Mw and above	150	150	–
Iron and Steel	SPM	Sintering Plant	–	–	150
		Blast Furnace	–	–	–
		Steel making during normal operation	–	–	150
		During oxygen lancing	–	–	400
Fertilizer (urea)	SPM	Pilling tower	–	–	50
Thermal power plant	SO_2	Boiler size	Stack height H = 220 m		
		200 Mw or less	Stack height H = 275 m		
		500 Mw or more			
Sulphuric acid	SO_2/acid mist	Single conversion	10 kg/tone of conc.		
		Single absorption	(100 percent) acid produced/50 mg/m^3 for acid mist		
		Double conversion	4 kg/tone conc.		
		Double absorption	(100 percent) acid produced/50 mg/m^3 for acid mist		

Source: Central Pollution Control Board, Emission Regulations Part 1, July 1984

Road Pattern and Traffic Flow

Traffic flow in different parts of the city greatly affects the total emission of exhaust gases. The survey was conducted at various squares by counting number of vehicles (buses, trucks, cars, jeeps, motorcycles, scooter and other vehicles) while out-going from and incoming to the city for every road with the help of personal observation and traffic police.

Table 12.4: Number of Automobiles in Ghaziabad City

Types of automobiles	2002	2003	2004
Trucks, buses	2,911	2,527	2,540
Car, Jeep	3,200	3,304	3,417
Scooters and motor cycles	39,705	42,091	43,283
Tractor	7,342	7,570	7,754
Others	2,198	1,901	2,127
Total	55,356	57,393	59,121

Source: R.T.O. Office, Raj Nagar, Ghaziabad.

Traffic density at different squares varies from 22368 at Hindon Air Force to 66240 at Mohan Nagar crossing. The most congested square of the city was observed at Mohan Nagar crossing, where emission of exhaust gases was very high. This survey was conducted from 7 AM to 8 P.M. It has been observed that in the morning from 8 to 11 and in the evening from 4 to 8 P.M. the intensity of traffic was higher than at other hours of the day.

The analysis shows that total emission of pollutants varies from one crossing to another in quantity. Table 12.5 shows the total emission of the gases from automobiles at various crossings of the city. During the working hours from 7 AM to 11 AM, total emission of CO varies from 692.58 gm at Hindon Air Force crossing to 2604.21 gm at Mohan Nagar crossing.

The total emission of CO calculated in the city was 30213.53 gm. The emission of other exhaust gases like HC, NO_x, and aldehyde were found maximum at Mohan Nagar crossing because the intensity of traffic flow also remains there highest, while lowest quantity was observed at Hindon Air Force crossing. The second major pollutant is the hydrocarbon. It was also found maximum at Mohan Nagar crossing (i.e. 318.12 gm) and lowest at Hindon Air Force crossing 76.88 gm. Emission of NO_x was highest (33.46 gm) at Mohan Nagar crossing and lowest (9.86 gm) at Hindon Air Force crossing. Aldehydes are emanated in lesser quantity than other three selected pollutants. Its emission varies from 1.56 gm at Hindon Air Force to 5.76 gm at Mohan Nagar crossing in the city. Automobiles are the major source of air pollution in the city rather than industries.

Table 12.5: Total Emission of Exhaust Gases from Automobiles at Various Squares of the City (2003)

Name of the crossing	No. of vehicles	CO (gm)	HC (gm)	NO_x (gm)	Aldehydes (gm)
Mohan Nagar Crossing	66240	2604.21	318.12	33.46	5.76
Merut Road Crossing	51552	2176.35	234.22	24.26	3.85
Purana Bus Stand	58512	2478.18	262.23	26.50	4.10
New Bus Stand	57024	2388.27	259.62	27.68	4.18
Hapur Chungi Crossing	28368	701.26	76.46	11.01	1.75
Shashtri Nagar Crossing	23568	825.17	82.72	10.38	1.64
Hindon Air Force Crossing	22368	692.58	76.88	91.86	1.56
Lal Kuwan Crossing	38400	1640.41	166.12	17.22	2.76
Hapur Phatak	35208	1201.68	156.64	16.51	3.01
Maharajpur Crossing	33072	1156.04	127.60	14.42	2.02
Shahid Nagar Crossing	28072	685.27	74.56	10.37	1.95
Rejendra Nagar Crossing	24260	722.21	78.52	10.02	1.76
Patel Nagar Crossing	58287	2537.31	262.23	26.18	4.26
Hapur Turning	57361	2503.47	258.31	26.02	4.12
Shahibabad Crossing	32960	1072.48	118.58	12.78	2.00
By Pass Road Crossing I	41857	2358.33	242.78	23.35	3.28
By Pass Road Crossing II	31648	1031.28	124.37	12.22	2.26
By Pass Road Crossing III	56841	2230.71	240.15	26.08	4.02
By Pass Road Crossing IV	36365	1208.32	162.73	17.28	2.41

Source: Pollution Control Board, Ghaziabad.

Pattern of Air Pollution in Ghaziabad City

For the spatial pattern of pollutants and their source of emission air samples were collected from different parts of the city according to their functional characteristics and tested by pollution control board (2002). Among all the localities surveyed, Kavi Nagar shows the highest concentration of particulate matter (3619.18 mg/m^3) while Raj Nagar shows 325.78 mg/m^3. The highest concentration of particulate in Kavi Nagar locality is due to more industrial establishments whereas the least concentration in Raj Nagar is owing to purely residential area. Concentration of pollutants varies from one locality to another. The seasonal variation of particulate reveals that it was less during rainy season due to more washout of pollutant in comparison to summer season. The dispersion of pollutants is greatly influenced by wind velocity. The diffusion of particulate is also widespread if wind velocity is high. The concentration of pollutant will be high in the windward direction. Thus, the wind direction and velocity have been responsible in aggravating and diffusing the industrial pollution in the residential areas (Nath, 1990).

The concentration of particulate was found maximum during winter because of less dispersion of pollutants caused by low wind velocity. This is also because of the fact that air contamination with particulate and dense smoke does not allow dispersion and vertical diffusion of pollutants. The study also reveals that Mohan Nagar, Raj Nagar, Kavi Nagar, Lohia Nagar, Patel Nagar, Shashtri Nagar, residential areas and industrial estates near slums were worst affected owing to the high concentration of dust particles. Buland Shahar industrial area is one of the major sources of factory smoke and coal dust particles for air pollution. In this estate most of the residential areas are affected by dust and smokes. Level of air pollution in Trans Hindon river areas along G.T. Road and U.P. - Delhi border areas is high. In these areas vehicular transportation is one of the major sources of air pollution. Large number of vehicles running on various routes with diesel engines is bound to contribute a considerable amount of air pollution. The concentration of dust particle is very high along U.P.-Delhi border and in eastern part of the city. Level of air pollution is high along roads and industrial areas. Obviously, wind direction as a factor was given negligible consideration by the planning authorities while formulating the layout of city's residential, commercial and industrial areas. This is a serious mistake, which should not be repeated while planning the future urban industrial development of the city (Moore, 1994).

It has been observed that the concentration of air pollutants remains lowest during rainy season because during this season the process of wash-out of pollutants remains very effective. Winter season shows highest level of pollutants because of very scanty rainfall and end of summer season shows intermediate level of air pollution in the city. Wind velocity highly affects the concentration of pollutants in the air in residential localities. Concentration of dust particles was recorded higher inside the factory, but when wind speed is higher, concentration of air borne dust was found to be low. The analysis reveals that meteorological factors like wind speed, temperature, relative humidity and rainfall play significant role in the distribution of air pollutants in the city. The air sample analysis of different stations shows that the area around New Kavi Nagar, Mohan Nagar, industrial estate and C.B.D. of the city are under high pollution, whereas Rajendra Nagar, Shashtri Nagar, Kamla Nehru Nagar and outer part of the city are under low level of air pollution.

People's Perception about Air Pollution

Six categories of persons such as self-employed, business class, service class, pensioners, daily wagers and students were interviewed from the point of view of their perception about air pollution. The data for the general perception of people regarding air pollution shows that 32.65 percent were quite casual about it. 20.00 percent of them don't understand anything about air pollution, 32.46 percent were specific about the quality and pollutants of air and 14.89 percent had mixed opinion about air pollution. A similar type of study has been conducted by ESMAP, 2004 too. The World Bank shows interesting result of air quality trend perception in Delhi Metropolis.

As much as 58.38 percent people think that industries and motor vehicles exhaust are the main sources of air pollution and 24.26 percent considers dust as the most important factor of air pollution. About 55.0 percent people suffer from the discomforts caused by air pollution when they are out of their houses or at their working places.

The above discussion provides a general picture of the perception of people regarding air pollution prevails in the locality of their residence. Further investigations were made with the objective of studying the level of perception on the basis of occupation, education and annual income group, as these are some of the important factors influencing perception of the people regarding environment.

Among the self-employed, about 48.57 percent people think that motor vehicle exhaust and industrial smoke are the prime factor of air pollutant. 32 percent of self-employed feel the effect of air pollution on health. As may as 60 percent express their acceptance to the present condition of air and 38.4 percent preferred to control it with active participation.

In the business class, 43.65 percent persons are casual about air pollution. About 56.35 percent consider air pollution is most hazardous. Regarding the effect of air pollution, 48.6 percent persons experience it on health, clothes and house furnishing all together. However, 51.4 percent feel the effect of air pollution when they are out doors. In this class of occupation, 39 percent persons show no response or acceptance and 61 percent show awareness for controlling air pollution. Service class seems to be more aware of air pollution. Nearly 72.6 percent rank industrial smoke and motor vehicle exhaust as the most important air pollutants to be followed by dust, coal and oil consumption.

Air pollution is ranked first among the pollution factors by this class. About 78.26 percent people of this class have mentioned outdoors as most affected place by air pollution. About 22 percent belong to the no response category and 76.2 percent favour adoption of necessary measures to control air pollution.

56 percent from amongst the daily wagers were the about the quality of air. About 28.2 percent said, they don't know about air pollution, 9 percent found it effectual and another 9 percent did not have clear perception about it. Nearly 32.6 percent of the daily wagers ranked motor vehicle exhaust and industries as main source of air pollution. Only 11.8 percent of daily wagers were aware of the hazards of air pollution. 70 percent expressed an attitude of no response when they were asked about their role in controlling air pollution. Only 21.4 percent think that something must be done to control air pollution.

As far as the percentage of controlling air pollution is concerned it was found that 78.2 percent of pensioners and 74.8 percent of students expressed their response to control air pollution. Low and middle income groups have maximum number of people with casual attitudes towards air pollution, however, persons belonging to low, middle and high income groups consider air pollution most hazardous. Maximum number of people from all the three groups noticed combined effect of air pollution on health, clothes and house furnishings. They also feel air pollution while they are outdoors. Considerable difference is noticed in the perception level of persons of the three income groups. 56.4 percent persons from the lower income group show their readiness in accepting the present quality of air and 32.6 percent expressed their readiness to take active part in controlling it. It is quite reverse in case of middle-income group persons as 62.3 percent expressed active response and 37.8 percent showed their acceptance. In the higher income group 12 percent persons were ready to accept the existing situation and 84.6 percent wanted to improve the quality of air by adopting immediate or long-term air pollution control measures.

Effects of Air Pollution

The gaseous and particulate materials added to the atmosphere by the activities of humans are considered to be pollutant when their concentrations are sufficient to produce harmful effects. The majority of man-made emissions to the atmosphere also have natural sources and in many cases there are larger than the pollutant one (Chadha, 1992).

Effect on Plants: The acute toxic effects of some air pollutants particularly sulphur dioxide on plants in the vicinity of non-ferrous smelters roasting sulphide ores have been observed and recognized for a long time. The pollutants affect plants either by disturbing physiological processes such as affecting the growth productivity and quality of the vegetation without producing any visible damage or by causing visible damage. Mainly SO_2, hydrogen fluoride, ozone and peroxy acetlynitrate affect plants (Singh, 1991). Plants take up air pollutants either directly through interchange of gases with the atmosphere or through the moisture taken up from the soil. The soil may have been exposed to the air pollutants that were then dissolved in water in the soil. Acidic air pollutants can continue to affect the plants grown there, although in time they are diluted and are leached out by rain (Katyal, 1989).

The most direct effect is the entry of gaseous pollutants into the plants through open stomata. Gaseous air pollutants after entering into the plant tissue dissolve in the intercellular water. The acidic pollutants attack the cell structure within the leaf. That is why easily soluble air pollutants like sulfur dioxide, hydrochloric and hydrofluoric acids, etc. are the most toxic.

In Ghaziabad City, it has been found that near industrial areas such as Industrial Estate, Shahibabad Industrial Complex, Buland Shahar road industrial area, along Merrut road, Kavi Nagar, Mohan Nagar crossing to Delhi border and Hapur Chungie to Raj Nagar, trees and plants are affected from SO_2 pollution. In agricultural areas such near Makunpur, Sikandarpur, Pasaunda Ghukana, Garhi near Village Balharipura, wheat and vegetable crops are observed affected by air pollution. In new parts of the city such as Raj Nagar, Shashtri Nagar, Rajendra Nagar, Kavi Nagar and Vijay Nagar plants are affected by air pollution.

The plants of decorative value have sensitive leaves. Particulate deposits can seriously damage their aesthetic or commercial value as is the case with flowers, although they may not affect the ability of the plants to survive and reproduce (Table 12.6).

Table 12.6: Plant Group on the Basis of Their Sensitivity to SO_2 Exposure

Sensitive plants	Intermediate plants	Resistant plants
Mango	Jamun	Seisham
Tomato	Neem	Babul
Wheat	Eucalyptus	Tulsi
Potato	Rose	Ashoka tree
Onion	Ber	Corn

Effect on Materials: Big industrial cities like Kolkata, Mumbai, Bangalore, Kanpur and Ghaziabad etc. reflect the effect of air pollution on building and other materials. The effect of SO_2 on several materials has been observed in many studies. High concentration of SO_2 in air causes chemical action with building materials and damages them. Effects of SO_2 on building, tress along G.T. Road, Buland Shahar road, Hapur Road and Merrut road are easily noticed. Thus, air pollution affects not only human and plants but also building materials (Table 12.7).

Effect on Human Health: In Ghaziabad city, burning of coal, gas and oil are the principal source of sulfur dioxides and nitrogen oxides. Coal is burnt in many industrial processes, as well as for domestic and commercial heating purpose (Ganguly, 2001). Industrial processes produce 52 percent of particulate. Certain kinds of industry produce more particulate than others. These types of industry emit carbon, silica, aluminum, and iron dioxide; the construction industry emits various kinds of dust, cotton ginning industry is a major source of trash, dust and lint. Air pollution has direct effects and causes chronic and acute respiratory diseases.

Table 12.7: Effect of Air Pollution on Materials

Material	Typical manifestation	Measurement	Principal pollutants	Other factors
Metals	Spoiling of surface, loss of metal tarnishing	Loss of weight reduced physical strength	SO_2 and particulate	Moisture temperature
Building	Discoloration, leaching	Not usually	SO_2 and particulate	Moisture and freezing
Paints	Discoloration, softened finish	Not measured quantitatively	H_2S, SO_2 and particulate	Moisture and micro-organism
Leather	Powdering and weakening	Loss in tensile strength	SO_2 and acid fumes	Physical wear
Paper	Imbrutement	Decrease in folding resistance	SO_2 and acid fumes	Moisture, fumes and Sunlight
Dyes	Fading	–	NO_2, SO_2 oxidants	Sunlight, moisture
Rubber	Cracking	Loss in elasticity	Oxidants, O_3, SO_2	Sunlight

Source: NEERI, Nagpur Information

In Ghaziabad city, data were not available for all diseases. However, available data from the General hospitals, private medical practitioners and city board Ghaziabad may be quite useful for the study of different diseases. Table 12.8 shows the diseases related to air pollution specially Asthma, Bronchitis, Tonsillitis and TB (respiratory) in the study area. The rate of incidence of Asthma varies from 1721 in 1998 to 2310 persons in 2003. Similarly, deaths also vary from 77 persons in 1998 to 121 persons in 2003. Bronchitis is affected by air pollution. The number of persons affected by bronchitis varies from 1120 in 1998 to 1541 in 2003. Number of persons affected by tonsillitis, TB and respiratory diseases is increasing from one year to another.

Effect of Particulate on Human Health

In Ghaziabad city, there are several other matters suspended in air floating all the time. Both clean and polluted air has some particulate. Industrial dusts release large amount of particulate in the atmosphere. Industrial complex such as Shahibabad Industrial Complex, Merrut Road, Buland Shahar Road area, Kavi Nagar area, Loni Road Industrial area etc. produce large amount of metal dust like copper, iron, aluminum, zin etc. These particulates present in the air are very dangerous to human health.

The only major route through which particulate enters the human body is the respiratory tract. Relatively large particles are likely to get retained in the nasal cavity and in the pharynx. Very small particles are likely to reach the lungs and to be retained by them. Though, the respiratory system has some mechanisms for the removal of particulate matters. The particulate materials or soluble components may get transported to organs some distance from the lungs and have a detrimental effect on these organs. Particles cleared from the respiratory tract largely enter the gastrointestinal tract. Material may also enter into the blood after it is transported to the gastrointestinal tract. A strong correlation exists between the daily mortality rate and acute episodes of air pollution. In such cases, high levels of particulate matters are accompanied by high level of SO_2 and other pollutants.

Table 12.8: Number of Persons Affected by Asthma, Bronchitis and Tonsillitis

(Number of Patients)

Year	Asthma		Bronchitis	Tonsillitis	Cancer		T.B. (Respiratory)	
	Affected	Death			Affected	Death	Affected	Death
1998	1721	77	1120	1310	73	55	512	40
1999	1776	78	1221	1372	86	72	570	47
2000	1861	54	1180	1578	78	51	638	37
2001	1907	98	1275	1822	94	49	861	64
2002	2140	104	1360	2340	67	58	1022	73
2003	2310	121	1541	2631	72	69	1236	62

Source: City Board Ghaziabad, 2004.

Particles over 5.0 µm in diameter are stopped and deposited mainly in the nose and the throat Those that do penetrate to the lungs do not often go beyond the air ducts or bronchi and even these are soon removed by ciliary's action. Particles ranging in size from 0.5 to 5.0 µm in diameter can be deposited in lungs as well as in the bronchioles. Few reach the alveoli. Most particles deposited in the bronchioles are removed by the cilia within two hours. Particles less than 5.0 µm in diameter reach and may settle in the alveoli. The removal of such particles from these areas is much rapid and less complete than from the larger passages. Some of the particles retained in the alveoli are absorbed into the blood.

Conclusion

The economic development and urban expansion of the modern world is directly related to the industrial growth of the present time. Some sort of air pollution cannot be avoided if we go for development but industrial expansion can be beneficial only when air pollution control measures are also adopted. It may be pointed out that comprehensive control measures of air pollution and air quality management strategy must be based on holistic perspective of air pollution and overall improvement of the environment. The immediate concerns of human community are to reduce the emission of chlorofluorocarbons, halogen, hydrocarbons, oxides of sulphur and nitrogen, carbon monoxide, greenhouse gases and particulate matter and smokes from our various activities.

References

Ambasht, R.S. (1990) *Environment and Pollution,* Students Friends & Co., Varanasi, pp.85, 184.

Agarwal, S.K. (1991) *Automobile Pollution,* A.P. House, New Delhi, pp.147-49.

Chaurasia, B.P. (1992) *Environment Pollution Consequences and Measures*, Chugh Publication, Allahabad, pp. 241-48.

ESMAP, (2004) Toward Cleaner Urban Air in South Asia: Tackling Transport Pollution, Understanding Sources, *ESMAP* Report 281/04, March, Washington D. C.

The World Bank (2004) Urban Air Pollution in India: perceptions of stakeholders, *ESMAP*, No.15, pp.1- 4. Chadha, S.K., (1992): *Monitoring Environment in India*, Sheel Sethi Pub., New Delhi, pp.32.

Gapalan, H. N. B. and Saxena, S. (1999) Domestic Environment and Health of Women and Children, *Biofuels*, Tata Energy Research institute, New Delhi, P. 77.

Ganguly, N. K. et al. (2001) Indoor Air Pollution in India- A Major Environmental and Public Health Concern, *ICMR Bulletin,* Vol. 31, No.5, New Delhi, p.2.

John, Lenin (1977) *Environment and Man*, Blackie, Glasgow and London, pp. 64-67.

Jain, S.K. (1993) "Air Pollution Control in India", *I.J. Environmental Protection*, Vol. 13, p. 521.

Katyal, T. et al. (1989) *Environmental Pollution*, Anmol Publication, New Delhi, p. 2

Mishra, S.G. (1992) *Environmental Pollution*, Venus Pub. H., New Delhi, pp. 69-71.

Moore, C. (1994) *Urban Air Quality*, United State Information Agency, Washington, D.C.

P. Nath and S. Nath (1990) *Environmental Pollution Conservation and Planning*, C. Publication, Allahabad, pp. 80-92.

Singh, Onkar, et al. (1993) *Frontiers in Environmental Geography*, Concept Pub. Comp., New Delhi, pp. 351-360.

Singh, Savindra (2005) *Environmental Geography*, Prayag Pustak Bhawan, Allahabad.

Tiwari, R.R. and Gurdeep Raj (1992) *Man and Environment*, A.P. House, New Delhi.

W.H.O. (1994) *Health and Safety Guide*, Washington DC, pp. 15-16.

13

Physical and Cultural Landscape of Kosi Plain

Shio Muni Yadav

Introduction

Kosi plain is an integrated part of the middle Ganga plain. This is a physical region and is situated in the north eastern part of Bihar. It comprises an extensive plain formed by the detritus material brought by Kosi, Mahanda, Saura, Parwan and sursor rivers. This physical region is known as land of rivers. Kosi, the sorrow of Bihar and Hwang Ho of India has handicapped the physical and cultural landscape of this region by its shifting courses and flood. This region has rich cultural heritage. There are many sites related to Ramayan, Mahabharat and Mughal periods. Irrigation facility by Bhimnagar barrage and Green Revolution has changed the economic scenario of the Kosi plain.

Methodology, as a comprehensive term, is a system of methods, rules and techniques as well as product of scientific inquiry and research focusing on the philosophical issue of a subject searching for truth, objectivity and explicitly, and in the nature of things, also bordering on imagination and speculation. Methodology is the formulation of systematic and logically coherent methods for search for knowledge. In the present study, techniques and methods of geographical analysis have been used to portray and depict spatial distribution of physical and cultural resources in the study area. Maps and diagrams have been drawn to illustrate the site and location, shifting courses of Kosi and distribution pattern of human resources.

The heart of any research design is the collection of data. In geographical studies, it is quite possible that the necessary spatial data will be made available from different sources. Primary data for this study has been made available from field survey and secondary data from decadal Census Handbook and Data Processing Division, Government of Bihar, Patna.

Study Area

Study area, Kosi plain is located in the north eastern part of Bihar between 25^0 13' N to 26^0 35' N latitudes and 86^0 19' E to 88^0 32' E longitudes, extending over an area of 16902 square km with a total population of 13125298 person according to 2001 Census. It consists of two Divisions, seven Districts and seventy Community Development Blocks. The study area is bounded on the north by International boundary of Nepal, on the south by Khagaria, Bhagalpur districts and Sahibganj district of Jharkhannd, on the east by West Bengal and on the west by Madhubani, Darbhanga and Khagaria districts.

A. Physical Landscape:

- **Physiography:** Physical landscape of any specific area reflects its physiography, climate, vegetation and soil types. Physiography or orggraphy is a matter of surface surveying; the determination of structure demands a more intimate examination, one which probes beneath the surface. The physiography of the Kosi plain is determined by the underlying structure. Study area is a level plain. There are marked alluvial uplands in a number of localities. These alluvial uplands have examined almost untouched by the ravages of the Kosi due to its higher level. It comprises an extensive plain formed by alluvium brought by the rivers flowing in this plain. The alluvium is supposed to have been derived from the Himalayas to the north and deposited on a gradually or intermittently subsiding surface. In consequence of the flat gradient of the area the rivers that flow south-east ward trend to take pronounced meandering courses. So, the physiography of the area is in the form of flood plain by sweeping of meanders to and fro down the valley floor and later perhaps by the swinging of the meanders belt itself. As the valley floor widened in this way the slip of slopes become nearly flat and the flood plain may then have only relatively thin veneer of mud and silt generally with an underlying deposit of sand and gravel covering a planned of surface of bed rocks. Levee, meander, ox-bow Lake, marshes and Diara are common land forms in this plain. They are formed by river's deposition.
- **Drainage Pattern:** Drainage pattern refers to the particular plan or design which the individual stream courses collectively form. In the study area the drainage pattern is dendritic in general and the general characteristic features are available throughout the plains. The rivers meet at acute angles and several tributaries form parallel or sub-parallel lines to the main stream. The Kosi, the sorrow of Bihar and Hwang Ho of India is the chief river in the study area. The Kosi known as kaushiki in Sanskrit literature is formed by seven Himalayan rivers (Sapt Kosi-Arun, Sun, Bhotia, Tamba, Likhu, Dudh and Tamar.) The Arun, the chief tributary of Kosi rises from the crest of range 16km south of the bed of Tsang po and other streams rise on the slopes of the snow clad great Himalayan range. Kosi is one of the most furious rivers in India. It is notorious for its vagaries and has preferred to change its bed

very often. During the last two centuries the Kosi has shifted its course for over 125 km in west ward direction. Presently it is flowing through Supaul, Saharasa and Khagria districts and joined the Ganga at Kursela in katihar. But suddenly in the month of August 2008 it eroded its Aflux Bandh (embankment) at Kusaha in Nepal about 11.5 km before Bhimnagar barrage and shifted its course through Sursar river and damage entire infrastructure of Supaul and Madhepura districts. This is the most critical feature in the peculiar character of the Kosi. Mahananda, Parwan, Saura, Sursar, Kari Kosi, Benga, Chilauni, Gumati are other important rivers in the study area. Ganga the secret river forms the southern boundary of the study area, especially in Katihar district.

- **Flood:** Flood is a common phenomenon in the study area. Flood simply means inundation of extensive land area with water for several days in continuation. Heavy rainfall in the catchment's area of Sapt Kosi in Himalayan region of Nepal is the main cause of flood disaster in the Kosi plain. Bhimnagar barrage, its Aflux Bandh through its George at Barahkshetra in Nepal and east and west Kosi Bandh through Bhimnagar to Kursela are man made attempt to tame to furious nature of Kosi, but this attempt is not final solution of Kosi. This year on 18th August, the furious Kosi has eroded its Aflux Bandh (embankment) before 11.5 km to Bhimnagar barrage at Kusaha in Nepal and damaged physical and cultural landscape of Neapl, and five districts of north eastern Bihar. Its sever impact handicapped the central part of Supaul and Madhepura districts. This flood was declared as "National Disaster" by the Government of India. Rescue operation by Neavy, Army and volunteer organizations saved the life and property of affected people of the area and relief operation is continued for six months through Mega Siwirs. Government machineries are trying to repair the Aflux Bandh and cutting. Mahananda is another furious river in the study area. Eastern part of the study area (Kishanganj and Katihar districts) remains badly affected by its flood every year. Bakra, Parwan, Saura, Sursar, Kari Kosi, Chilauni, Gumati are also flooded in this flood prone-area.
- **Soils:** Soil refers to the loose surface of the earth as distinguished from solid rocks. According to the soil scientists, soil means that parts of the earth's crust which has been changed as a result of soil formation processes. The soils of the study area vary from sand loam to heavy clay. It is composed of alluvial soil partly old and partly new. The old alluvium is in the northern part, where it consists of course gravels and surface Kankars. The soil contains a greater proportion of sand and is in some places covered by sand deposits, which

render it absolutely, uplift for cultivation. One major type of soil is alluvial, which differs from area to area in texture and colour due to the varying amount of sand and clay particles and humus contents. Generally four sub types of soil have been differentiated on the basis of sand and clay proportion in the study area. These are loam, sandy, clayey, clay loam.

B. Cultural Landscape: Culture is like a piece of tented glass, affecting and distorting our view of the earth. Culture conditions the way people think about the land, the way they use and alter the land, and the way they interact with one another upon the land. The visible and invisible evidences of culture-buildings and farming patterns, language and political organization are elements in the spatial diversity that invites and is subject to geographical inquiry.

- **Farming Pattern:** The quality of agricultural lands varies in response to the terrain, soil productivity and physical environment of the area. The production depends upon the methods introduced, techniques adopted, irrigation provided, quality of the seeds and fertilizer used, fertility of the soil and the cropping pattern practiced. Agriculture is the main occupation of the people of the area. The principal food crop is rice followed by wheat and maize. Main commercial crops are jute, oil seeds, pulses, banana and vegetables. Tea plantation is very popular in the north eastern part of the study area in Kishanganj district. High yielding varieties of rice, wheat, maize and sunflower by Green Revolution has changed the cropping pattern and agricultural scenario of the study area. Sunflower cultivation in Purnia district and banana cultivation in the southern part of Purnia and Katihar districts is emerging as new crop. Irrigation facility by East Kosi canal is treated as boon for agricultural productivity.
- **Population:** Spatial variation in population is a function of a host of physical, economic and cultural factors, but they operate through the dynamics of population change. A significant part of a regional population study is the examination of the distribution of population in relation to the capabilities of the environment types. Study area, Kosi plain occupies 17.94 percent of the total area of the state. It contains 15.83 percent of the state population. Population density in the study area is 781 persons per square km. It is lower than state population density 880 but higher than country density 324. Decadal population growth rate of the study area was 31.71 percent. This is higher than the state's decadal growth rate 28.43 and further higher than country's growth rate 21.34 percent (Table 13.1).

C. Literacy: Literacy is the root of development. Education enhances the understanding of the behaviour of interrelationship among the tangible and intangible phenomena surrounding and imparts skill to translate the knowledge into action and make the most beneficial use of them. The educational process has to be linked with production and employment. In the words of Census of India a person who can read and write with understanding in any language is taken as literate. A person, who can merely read but cannot write, is not literate. Person should have received any formal education or should have passed any minimum education standard.

Study area has poor literacy ratio (35.71). This is lower than the state literacy of 47.53 percent and it is far behind the country's literacy of 65.30. Female literacy is treated as backbone of the development of society, but study area is unlucky in this respect as it shows minimum female literacy in the state and country. Kishanganj district of the study area shows the lowest literacy rate in the country, i.e. only 18.44 percent (Table 13.2).

Table 13.1: Population Distribution, Density and Decadal Growth Rate of the Study Area

District/State/ Country	Area (Km^2)	Population	Density	Percentage decadal growth rate
Purnia	3,229	25,40,788	787	35.23
Katihar	3,057	23,89,533	782	30.91
Araria	2,830	21,24,831	751	31.84
Kishanganj	1,884	12,94,063	687	31.50
Saharsa	1,696	15,06,418	853	33.03
Madhepura	1,788	15,24,596	855	29.45
Supaul	2,400	17,45,069	724	29.95
Total/Average	16,902	1,31,25,298	781	31.71
Bihar	91,463	8,28,78,796	880	28.43
India	32,87,782	1,02,70,15,247	324	21.34

Source - Census of India 2001, Series 11, Bihar

Religious and Historical Sites

Study area, Kosi plain has rich cultural heritage. There are many religious and historical sites related to Mahabharat and Ramayan periods. Thakurganj, Kursela, Manihari, Biratpur are related to Mahabharat period. Singheshwar and Satckhar are related to Ramayana period. Lord Shiva temple of Singheshwar (Singheshwar Mahadeo), Tara Pith at Mahishi, Sun temple of Kandaha, Puran Devi Mandir of Purnia city, Karu khirhar Asthan, Baba Bishurawat temple, Madanpur asthan are important religious sites of the study area. Study area is the land of Mandan

Bharthi and Fanishwar Nath Renu.

Table 13.2: Literacy Rate (in percent) of the Study Area

District/State/ Country	Literacy	Male Literacy	Female Literacy
Purnia	35.51	46.16	23.72
Katihar	35.29	45.51	24.03
Araria	34.94	46.50	22.14
Kishanganj	31.02	42.80	18.49
Saharsa	39.28	52.04	25.31
Madhepura	36.19	48.87	22.31
Supaul	37.80	53.23	21.02
Average	35.71	47.87	22.43
Bihar	47.53	60.32	33.57
India	65.38	75.85	54.16

Source - Census of India, 2001 Series 11, Bihar

Conclusion

The study area, Kosi plain is a flood-prone area. Flood is common phenomena in this area. The furious river Kosi has handicapped the physical and cultural landscape of the study area by its flood and shifting courses. Bhimnagar barrage is treated as man made boon to disaster of Kosi, but this man made attempt is not final solution of Kosi problem. Green Revolution has changed the cropping pattern and agricultural scenario of the study area. High birth rate and low death rate are main cause of population growth. Rapid growth of population and low rate of literacy are impediments to proper and balanced development of the study area. Labour migration is burning problem in the study area. Low wage rate and lack of proper work opportunity are push force for labour migration and high wage rate and work opportunity in the north-western and western states like-Haryana, Punjab, Delhi, Gujarat, Maharashtra are pull force for labour migration in the study area. In this respect Kosi plain reflects a peculiar physical and cultural landscape.

References

Ahmad Enayat, Bihar, A Regional Geography, Ranchi University Press, Ranchi,

Chaudhary P.C. Roy, Bihar District Gazetteers, Purnia 1963.

Chaudhary P.C. Roy, Bihar District Gazetteers, Sharsa, 1965.

Getis, Arthur, Judith and Fillmann J, Introduction to Geography,

Kumar, Arun, (2000) Recent Trends of population Mobility and Economic Development

in Katihar District. Unpublished Ph. D. thesis B.N.M.U. Madhepura.
Singh Jasbir & Dhillan S.S. Agricultural Geography, Tata McGraw-Hill Publication, New Delhi.

14

Mitigation and Management of Technological Hazards

Parbati Nandi

Introduction

Natural hazards are caused by natural events, but their impacts and society's responses to them are largely governed by the political, economic and social systems. The late 1990s and the early 2000s certainly deserve the title "Decades of Environmental Disasters". The cataclysms include Turkey earthquake, Orissa super cyclone, Gujarat earthquake, Tsunami in the Indian Ocean, Hurricane Katrina, Outbreak of Avian Flu and the perennial Flood in Bangladesh. Most of the natural disasters are either meteorological in origin or they are the results of earths organic processes. They may also be due to man-induced technogenic and anthropogenic interventions. Earthquakes are the most fatal one and more than half of all deaths attributed to natural disaster results from earthquakes. Because of extraordinary population pressure, many parts of the world are extremely vulnerable to natural disasters such as earthquake, storm, flood, fire, etc. Arsenic Contamination, toxic chemical leaches, underground mine fires and outbreak of yellow fever are disasters quite unlike earthquake, flood and tornadoes. These are technical disasters. Human intervention in the environment created the disaster and technical intervention is required to abate then. Such disasters tend to be chronic and affect individuals and communities.

Natural and Technological Hazards

Technological hazards are viewed as acts of people. Technological systems fail because of their complexities and because of human fallibility. The immediate impact of natural disaster and technical disaster represent two qualitatively different types although all natural disasters have some effects on its inhabitants and society at large. The natural disaster is an event in which a society undergoes severe danger and incurs such losses that the social structure is disrupted and fulfilment of essential functions of the society is prevented. By contrast, a technical disaster is a slowly developing, extended, humanly generated deterioration in human system-ecosystem relations, in which the entire community incurs danger to health and safety and the disruption of ongoing patterns of social and cultural relations.

The crucial differences between the two types of disasters are due to differences in time and in human/technological involvement. The technological disaster develops slowly and persists for a relatively long time. In addition, the effects of natural disaster are often influenced by human factors like population density, agricultural practices, building designs etc.

In the light of these two types of disasters, let us now discuss some of the recent and worst incidents happened during the last few years. Although not fully predictable, their cases may be dealt with chronologically following cause-events-effects and measures.

Case I: Gujarat Earthquake

An earthquake with magnitude 7.7 on Richter scale occurred on January 26, 2001 near Bhuj in Western Gujarat. It has resulted in the death toll of over 35000 people and has devastated the entire state. The numbers of affected people were several millions. The devastation has affected the area socially, economically and physically. A wide range of damage has been noted in different types of buildings in the urban areas, as well as rural areas. The rural housing had undergone severe damages and in some cases total collapse. Bridges, roads and railways were damaged with cracks; the electric substations were damaged severely. The people who had been rendered homeless were also not provided assistance. There was ample supply of tents, medicines and food items but due to lack of coordination between various departments, the relief operation suffered a lot. The rescue and relief efforts were initiated almost 24 hrs. after the earthquake. The reason for this delay was lack of credible information on the damage. All the major communication links including telephone, cellular phone, police wireless and air-traffic control systems in the affected areas had been disrupted.

The Gujarat earthquake has thrown tremendous challenge to the information systems community of India. The response mechanism following a disaster can be made more effective by taking assistance of GIS-based tools. It is therefore essential that suitable GIS-based database and tools be developed for different regions. These datasets require constant updating with decision support systems. We geographers have learnt lessons from this tragedy in Gujarat and we will put to use the GIS technologies for the benefit of our people.

Case II: Indian Ocean Tsunami and Hurricane Katrina

Institutional hazards are the outcome of national and international laws, rules and principles concerning disaster response operations. This proposition can be examined through the prism of experiences in responding to the Indian Ocean tsunami of December 2004 and more recent operations responding to the earthquake in Pakistan in October 2005 and Hurricane Katrina in the USA in August 2005.

The most visible legal issues associated with these disasters concerned the entry of international relief goods and equipments Despite the best efforts of governments, aid did not always find its way smoothly to those who needed it. For example, a year after the tsunami in Indonesia, an estimated 217 containers of tsunami relief aid were reportedly lying still with custom authorities in a port outside Jakarta. Similarly, at one point during the relief operations in Sri Lanka, over 100 relief containers were stranded at the port in Colombo awaiting inspection and approval from different government ministries. Many food items therefore perished before they could be distributed and other items, such as tents and body bags, were no longer needed. In USA nearly (4,000,00) "meals ready to eat" sent by the UK in response to Hurricane Katrina were quarantined in a warehouse because they contained British beef, banned by American health regulations.

These types of problems are by no means unique to the disasters examined here. Several other examples of similar nature may be cited. But, the inflexibility of normal customs and import regulations or the confusion arising from the hasty adoption of impromptu procedures frequently also have a role to play. On the other hand, bottlenecks can equally be caused by international actors if they deliberately fail to comply with national laws and regulations.

The civil liability of relief operations can also be an important issue. The US agencies have decided to decline any international offers of certain types of aid, including blood products, medical kits and rescue personnel arriving to assist the people affected by Hurricane Katrina. Another problem derives from the lengthy procedures required for NGO registration and it involves extensive paperwork. Consequently, it is estimated that only a small proportion of NGOs involved in Tsunami relief and reconstruction have registered with the Thai authorities. The effect of non-registration is that personnel cannot apply for work permits and must enter the country on short-term tourist visas, requiring them to leave and re-enter the country every month. Similarly, they have difficulty opening official bank accounts or employment contracts or lease agreements, as they do not have recognized legal personality.

Case III: Avian Influenza

The outbreak of avian influenza (H5N1) commonly called "Bird Flue" in Asia (Hong Kong, S. Korea, Japan, Vietnam, China, Cambodia and recently in India) has become a global crisis for animal and human health. The World Health Organization (WHO) and Food and Agricultural Organization (FAO) both had appealed for global collaboration and funding to control the outbreak. Recently in January 2008, an alert was sounded throughout India when the deadly pathogenic virus continued to spread in new areas affecting 13 districts of W. Bengal. The city of Kolkata is reeling under a bird flue scare. The International Health Regulations (IHR) seem to be irrelevant to the current avian influenza outbreak as they apply only to 3 infections diseases Cholera, plague and yellow fever and thus the IHR will not be legally applicable to the crisis. The main public health intervention is culling of poultry flocks in affected areas followed by disinfection. If public health and agricultural interests are not aligned, gaps will undermine the global containment effort. The role of trade in the unprecedented geographical spread of the H5NI virus is not presently understood. Trade restrictions on imports of birds and their products from the affected countries must be followed. The technologies to fight this virus are expensive and in limited supply. In light of the current outbreak WHO is stressing the need to develop a vaccine for the H5NI virus.

Recent experiences confirm that existing international and domestic regulatory regimes are not as effective as might be desired in facilitating international relief where it is needed. Instead of addressing potential legal issues as an integrated part of disaster preparedness, there is a tendency for governments and relief agencies to resort to ad hoc arrangements. However, awareness of the legal aspects of international disaster response is increasing. The unusually high incidence of major disaster operations over the past few years provides an opportunity to evaluate the effectiveness of existing frameworks and to find ways forward to ensure their strengthening and improvement.

When the entire world is going for pre-disaster and pre-emptive measures, India still continues to take all the mileage particularly the political groups only when the disasters occur. In our country, scientists, sociologists, economists and other decision makers seem to be still sceptical at the political decisions in this direction. We need to take up through our NGOs, through various voluntary organizations, that is, to enable them to sensitize people on the perception of the risk policy. Risks need to be analyzed. We need to take up assessment, identification and management of risks.

Agenda, Programme and Strategy

In this context the Disaster Risk Management (DRM) Programme executed by the Ministry of Home Affairs with the United Nations Development Programme (UNDP) may be mentioned. The programme aims to contribute towards the social and economic development goals enabling the governments to minimize losses from disasters and reduce vulnerability. The vital output of this project is multi-hazard risk management and sustainable recovery plans at all levels (Community, Panchayat, Block, District, State), and strengthening institutions responsible for sustainability and replication of these efforts. It would set up an institutional framework for disaster management involving four phases: mitigation, preparedness, response and recovery.

Mitigation: Mitigation efforts attempt to reduce the effects of disasters when they occur. It focuses on long term measures for eliminating risks. The measures can be structural or non-structural. Structural measures use technological solutions like construction of flood levees. Non-structural measures include legislation, land-use planning, insurance etc.

Preparedness: In the preparedness phase, emergency managers develop plans of action. Common preparedness measures include:

- Communication plans with easily understandable terminology and chain of command.
- Development and practice of multi-agency coordination.
- Proper maintenance and training of emergency services.
- Development and exercise of emergency population warning methods combined with emergency shelters and evacuation plans.
- Stockpiling, inventory and maintenance of supplies and equipment.

An efficient preparedness measure is an emergency operation centre (EOC) combined with a practiced region-wide doctrine for managing emergencies.

Response: The response phase includes the mobilization of the necessary core emergency services, such as fire-fighters, police and ambulance crews. In addition, specialist rescue teams, volunteers and non-governmental organizations (NGOS) such as the local Red Cross branch or St. John Ambulance may provide immediate practical assistance like first aid. In the response phase, medical assets will be used in accordance with the appropriate triage of the affected victims.

Recovery: The aim of recovery phase is to restore the affected area to its previous state. It differs from the response phase in its focus; recovery efforts are concerned with issues and decisions that must be made after immediate needs are addressed. Recovery efforts are concerned with actions that involve rebuilding destroyed property, reemployment and the repair of essential infrastructure.

Role of Geographers

Geographers have worked and developed applications of GIS and remote sensing in disaster management for regions around the world although these technologies are grossly under-utilized in our country till date.

It is therefore essential that suitable GIS-based database and tools along with decision support systems be developed for different regions of the country. These datasets will require information from several different sources and require constant updating. The mapping needs of the vulnerable areas for disaster preparedness must be incorporated into the Disaster management Plan. Easy availability of precise maps with spatial data and non-spatial data for each disaster focusing on the vulnerable areas would go a long way in taking preparedness measures for future disasters.

Under the guidance and leadership of IDNDR (International Decade for National Disaster Reduction), geographers around the world are working hard in developing techniques for assessing disaster risks and delineating their geographical distribution. International efforts should emphasize on scientific programmes, engineering capabilities, and in the response to humanitarian and economic needs, particularly those of the developing countries through the programmes of UNESCO, UNDRO, UNEP, IOC, UNDP etc.

As all such programmes and activities are basically concerned with human elements; human touch can hardly be overlooked. Social and cultural milieu, values and ethics can in no way be lost sight of. Community based mitigation has to holds way, reckoning science and technology. A total view is therefore a must and an integrated approach inevitably a part of daily usage. Currently increasing emphasis is being given to participatory management by the people who group together to form different types of stakeholders.

To sum up, one can say that disasters are inevitable and they are a part of our lives. Human beings must learn to live with the disasters and can pray for tranquillity and peace on earth, on our planet, in all living beings, everywhere and in everyone.

References

Biswal, T. (2006) Human Rights, Gender and Environment, Viva Books Pvt. Ltd., New Delhi

Banerjee, Antara, et all (2005 ed.) Combating Disaster, acb Publications.

Cutter, S.L. (1999) Environmental Risks & Hazards, PHI Pvt. Ltd, New Delhi

http:/en. wikipedia. org/wiki/Emergency - management

Kates, R. W. (1971) Natural Hazards in Human Ecological Perspective: Hypotheses & Models, in Economic Geography, vol. 47 (3) pp. 438-51

Mitchell, J. K, Devine, N & Jagger, K. (1989) A Contextual Model of Natural Hazard, Geographical Review, Vol. 79(4) pp 391-409.

Sinha, D.K. & Rahim, K.M.B (1999 ed.) Natural Disasters: Some Issues & Concerns, NDM Cell, Visva-Bharati, Santiniketan.

Sinha, D.K. (2002) Some Aspects of Natural Disaster Management, Institute for Rural Development, IRUDENDEM

15

Water Harvesting: An Urgent Need

Bindu M. Bhatt and Raghuvanshi Jogender Singh

Colossal Social Problem

Approaching of the summer in India, brings water crisis with it, wells, ponds and taps dry up, women begin to walk the village streets and city roads with pots and pitchers looking for water point. The municipality water tankers and government run water trains begin to traverse the length and breadth of the country, people gather on streets corners, village squares and in front of municipality offices. Protests, demonstrations, road blockades, take place. City dwellers go against farmers, villagers against towns, towns against cities and citizens against government; people against people. Increasingly, these conflicts are taking on general shape of a bitter war for water. Water is becoming a cause for social conflicts. Is there a way out? What should we do? Hang down our heads in shame? Or should we look up? Therefore, the time to do a quick rethink on water, water management and water related issues is here and now. Water is what unsettles. It may create schism or amity. It evaporates, vanishes, but transforms lives. Thus, water is what we make.

It is futile to state water is life blood of the environment; without which no living being can survive; water plays a unique role in traditional economy and culture of the native people. Availability of an adequate and usable water supply under-pins our economy. However, evidence of over exploitation and subsequent environmental stress is there.

Gross misuse of water resources causes widespread degradation of soils, disrupts the supply of potable water and generates massive economic losses. There is an urgent need for action to maintain the health of our water systems. Shortage of fresh water and its pollution threatens the quality of life of many Indians.

Water Harvesting: A Concept

Life poses us with so many contradictions. Despite being one of the wettest countries of the world, India's growing water shortage has reached alarming proportions.

Cities in India are designed in such a way that it ensures that water is wasted.

This creates an artificial scarcity to begin with. No attempt is made in city to harvest water, on the other hand, it is allowed to flow unchecked into city sewers. Sources of water recharge have been encroached upon and claimed for construction projects. Such is the fate of a pond or lake that becomes a part of urban or municipal area of a town. Rivers which were once a source of clean drinking water are dyed with effluents released by a host of industries and even ground water has not been spared by rouge units, which have directly pumped their effluents into the aquifer to avoid installing pollution control technology. With most of India hit by droughts and famines bring into sharp focus on the gross mismanagement of natural resources in country due to mal-governance, inefficiency and corruption.

Rainwater is a free source of nearly pure water. It can be used to supply potable water and non-potable water. For non-potable uses like watering landscapes it is ready to use as it falls from the sky. For potable use rainwater must be treated to remove or kill disease organisms that may be present.

For centuries the world has relied upon rainwater harvesting to supply water for households, landscapes and agricultural uses. Before city water systems were developed rainwater was collected and stored.

The natural ground water recharge has been greatly hampered by drawing of excessive water and covering/paving up all available open land. Rain water harvesting is merely "putting back rain water into soil, where it will be stored in underground reservoirs and rivers, so that it could be used whenever needed." Simply put, it is collecting whatever rain falls on the ground. It could be on rooftop, in drive way or pathway, back yard, storm water drains roads and pavements wherever. The idea is to channelize this water into some storing place, which would either be an external storage device like a tank or, as it happens these days, an underground pit. With underground recharge the logic is that the water sucked from below the surface, it is imperative that must be restored back as much into ground. Technically speaking, water harvesting means capturing the run-off in one's own village or town." Experts suggest various ways of harvesting water: Capturing run-off from rooftops; Capturing run-off from local catchments; Capturing seasonal flood water from local streams; and Conserving water through watershed management

Thus, apart from increasing the availability of water, water-harvesting systems developed by local communities and households can reduce the pressure on the state to provide financial assistance needed for water supply. Also involving people will give them a sense of ownership and reduce burden on government funds. It promotes self-sufficiency and fosters an appreciation for water as a resource It also promotes water conservation.

Water Harvesting: A Brief History

Harvesting rainwater from the rooftop and on the surface has been part of Indian social and cultural lie since antiquity. Ancient texts inscription, local traditions and archaeological evidences are suggestive of the rich tradition. Pre historic evidences are also being traced as well. The Puranas, Mahabharat, Ramayan and texts of Vedas, Jains and Buddhist contains several references of canals, tanks, embankments and wells. Kautilya, a minister of King Chandragupta Mauraya gave vivid reference of irrigation with water harvesting systems in his historic treaties called the Arthsastra. He quoted that people were not only had knowledge of the water regimes and hydrological cycle but state was supportive of such ingenious local solutions. The evidences are indicative of unique development of civilizations on the Indian subcontinents. With monsoon season being limited to three–four months only, people realized that sustaining life will require extending bounties of wet to dry months. The net result of human ingenuity was the diverse water harvesting systems to suit some fifteen different ecological regions

The Khulas of Jammu, Kuls of Himachal Pradesh, Guls of Uttarkhand, Pats of Maharashtra, Zings of Ladakh, Zabos of Nagaland, Eris of Tamil Nadu, Keres of Karnataka, Tanks, Kundis, Bawdis, Jhlaras, etc. of Rajasthan are a few of the traditional water harvesting systems, which existed but now dying a slow death in country.

In the mountains and hill regions of India, people direct water into artificial channels, which flows, into agricultural fields. In the arid and semi-arid regions where streams are seasonal, the water is led into a storage structure, which provides for the dry period. In certain villages of the Eastern Himalayan states of Nagaland and Arunachal Pradesh, the water with channel is taken through a cattle shed, which enriches the water with nutrients before it is led to the fields. Due to uneven terrain these people use bamboo for their water channels; these resemble the modern drip irrigation system. The tribals of Arunachal Pradesh combine wet rice cultivation and pisciculture. By using temporary walls, they divert the water flow of the streams from the hills towards the terraced and valley lands.

In the Haveli system of Madhya Pradesh, the nature of the soil and crops allows the storage of rainwater in agricultural fields itself, enabling complete percolation o water. This provides adequate moisture for the following dry period. Water is shared between fields through embankments.

Maldharis of the Kutch in Gujarat have developed a system called Virda, which is based on the difference in the density o sweet water and salt water. In this system, wells dug on the beds of ponds allow percolation of rainwater. The ponds remain filled up during the rains, while during dry periods; people draw water from the wells.

In the state of Tamil Nadu, a big stream collecting water from the catchment area is diverted to feed a chain of 25 to 30 tanks called the 'System Tank'.

People of dry areas of Rajasthan have traditionally used a combination of surface water and ground water for their needs. Wells and step wells have been built below tanks and other water storage structure, so that clean ground water can be harvested on drying of tanks water. In many towns of Rajas than rooftops have been used as catchments to collect rainwater. In towns of Phalodi there are cases of borrowing one's neighbour's roof to collect rainwater.

The tribals of Kikruma village of Nagaland constructs a series of speed breakers on the road at about every 10 meters to block the runoffs, which are emptied into the ponds by means of channels.

These are a few water harvesting practices and there are many more o such unique methods of which some still exist while many already out of use.

Today, this rich socio-cultural tradition is in a state of utter neglect. At several places it has just remained as archaeological evidence. The systems that sustained for centuries were sacrificed in the name of 'development during the past 200year or so. The foreign rule in country set the cycle of destruction in motion. In an effort to earn revenue from the society, the water management system was brought under the control of the state. Within a few decades the British rulers faced with recurrent famines. The top irrigation engineer, Sir William Willcocks advised them to learn from the natives. It is now widely acknowledged that our forests began disappearing and water resources polluted or destroyed as the management and control forcibly snatched away from the local communities. However, when the ecological crisis becomes unmanageable, the government has to acknowledge traditional system of water harvesting.

The Present Status

In India the monsoon is brief. It rains about 100 hours a year, where in from water must be caught, stored and used over the other 8,760 hours that make up a year. In 2050, when the population of India will be 164 crore, per capita water availability from rain and snow will be 1,600 cubic meters (cum). As per the norms set by World health Organization, small natural hazards will shift India from the stressed to scarce status, which in turn will affect our economic, social and political stability.

The drought, which hits many states of the country for few consecutive years points at the gross mismanagement of the country's natural resources. There was a new sensation a wave with people declaring "no crippling dependency on the government", they began to take charge of their own environment with the expectation from the state either leave them alone or play supportive role. Thus, the community initiative first in the rural areas because our villages have been neglected than urban centres, it became very necessary to regain control over their own lives. The cities and metropolitans also followed the footsteps.

Water Harvesting: A Solution

Urban Scenario: The total amount of water that is received in the form of rainfall over an area is called rainwater endowment of the area. The amount that can be effectively harvested of it is called the water harvesting potential. Thus, Water harvesting potential = Rainfall (mm) x Collection efficiency.

This is because all the rainwater falling in an area cannot be effectively harvested as evaporation, spillage etc. also needs to be considered. Factors like runoff coefficient and the first-flush wastage are taken into account while estimating the collection coefficient. An illustration will further emphasis such a potential and it could be applied to get potential for any plot or rooftop area, using rainfall data for that area as follows:

Consider a building with a flat terrace area of 100 sq.m. Assume that the average rainfall is approximately 600 mm (24 inches). Now this means that assumed that the terrace floor being impermeable and all the rain water retained without evaporation, then, in one year there will be rainwater on the terrace floor to a height of 600 mm. Now, putting all these as following step wise data:

- Area of the plot =100 sq. m (120 sq. yards)
- Height of rainfall =0.6 m (600mm or 24 inches)
- Calculating volume of rainfall over the plot=Area of plot x height of rainfall.
- Assuming that only 60 percent of the total rainfall is effectively harvested then
- Volume of water harvested = 36,000 litres (60,000 x 0.6)

Considering the average daily drinking water requirement of 10 litres per person, this volume of water is about twice the requirement of a five member family.

Rural Scenario: Community based rainwater harvesting in rural areas –a model of the past has in it much strength today as it was earlier also. It is with this technology that people were able to survive in water scarce area.

Now, the simple statistic India's total land area is over 300 million hectares. Assuming 587,000 villages in our country can harvest the runoff from 200 million hectares of land, excluding inaccessible forest areas, high mountains and other inhabited area that still gives every village on an average access to 340 hectares or a rainfall endowment of 3.75 billion litres of water. These calculations show the potential of rainwater harvesting is enormous and undeniable. Needless to mention, can drought be called as natural disaster in our country? Not at all. They are government made disasters. There are many advantages thus of water harvesting as to

High agricultural returns so it can potentially solve the problem of rural unemployment and poverty. This will improve over all national economy.

Rainwater harvesting involves the participation of local community, this promotes self-sufficiency and fosters an appreciation for water as a resource. It also promotes water conservation.

Self Rule: In countries like India, as the ecological crisis becomes unmanageable, it is acknowledged that traditional systems of water harvesting organized by self governing communities work far better than any modern systems of water management and supply devised. This is being repeatedly demonstrated by numerous initiatives being undertaken by village communities in different parts of the country to assert their rights to manage their natural resources. Its revival will actually make modern democracy more meaningful, deep rooted and more functional. Non-partisan efforts made for common good spontaneously sets a unifying processes promoting collaboration and cooperation.

Conclusion

On the threshold of a new century which means development, growth, population pressure on natural resources and urbanization on one hand and environmental crisis on the other. There is flooding during rains and depleting of ground water in all parts of the country. It is wise to rejuvenate our dying wisdom and adopt traditional water harvesting systems so as to suit our present demand for urban and agricultural sectors. A great amount of water which goes waste every year on our terraces, storm water drains which could be hardly distinguish from sewer pipes, needs to be "catched" and "captured". The Real Green Revolution is about water harvesting. Let us catch water where it falls. Let it transform human lives. Let it change social existence. If this happens, the world will merely be an agglomeration of ecological-rain water harvesting–democracies (Anil Agrawal, Founder Director, CSE)

References

Agrawal Anil (et al) (2000) Making Water Everybody's Business: Practices &Policy of Water Harvesting, CSE, New Delhi.

Bank loans to harvest water: Jalvanni, a news letter on rural water and sanitation in India, Vol.1 No.3

Catchwater, (2001) a CSE newsletter, June 2001.

Gosh G. K. (2002) Water of India (Quality and Quantity), APH Publisher Corporation, 57 Ansari Road, Daryaganj, New Delhi

Kothari Ashish (1999) Bhaonta: A village Wild Life Sanctuary, The Hindu Survey of the Environment.

Mahapatra Richard (2001): A story of hope and of major change, Down To Earth, August 15,2001, CSE New Delhi.

McCully Patrick (2002) Water Harvesting in India Transforms Lives, World Rivers Review, December 2002.

Narain Sunita (2001) Harvesting Rain Drop, Down To Earth.

Parthasarthy G.S (et al) (2002) A manual of Water harvesting, GSFC Foundation, Vadodara.

Raju K.C.B. (et al) (1996) Water Harvesting In Coastal Areas, 22nd WEDC Conference, New Delhi, 1996.

Sudhirendra Sharma (2000) Food Security through Rain Water Catchment (UNDP, World sanitation programme)

Water Harvesting: Urgent Need to Reap Rich Rewards (September 2002) www. teriin.org/energy/waterhar.htm.

Part III: Developmental Profile

16

Urban Development Policy in South Korea

Nak-hun Song

The pace of urbanization varies throughout the world. Developed countries experienced rapid urban growth during and after the Industrial Revolution, while developing countries are currently in the throes of a great urban transformation (Dugler, 1988:1). During the last Four decades, urbanization in Korea as an outcome of economic modernization, significantly affected Korean society. Successful macro-economic performance accelerated urbanization and gave the country a highly urbanized population.

Three interdependent processes-economic development, migration and urbanization have interacted in many countries. Macro-economic success brings about a huge migration from rural to urban areas resulting in the increased pace of urbanization. In the rapid urbanization process, urban areas operate as an engine of growth by producing a higher return of investment, an increased productivity, and increased employment opportunities, together with a several negative effects such as shortage of housing and urban services, overburdened infrastructure, increased crime, unplanned and rapid migration and accentuation of the rural/urban income gap. Urbanization affected South Korea quite differently than other developing countries. Urbanization influenced significantly the demographic process, cultural level, per capita income and income distribution. Changing growth pattern of cities from an early emphasis upon the two largest metropolitan areas, Seoul and Pusan, to a later emphasis upon eight regional centres, was a significant directional change resulting in more balanced national urban development. This directional change was partly the result of national government policy. It is, however, impossible to make such a change without a concomitant change in economic setting. Nonetheless, macro-economic success in Korea made this directional change possible. The outcome has been a rapid urban growth in regional centres since the 1980s.

The purpose of this paper is to analyze the characteristics of urbanization in Korea by examining the evolving pattern of the policy instruments developed to deal with the phenomenon. The first section deals with the urbanization process as affected by economic development, migration, and urbanization. The second section analyzes urbanization characteristics which have significant impact on Korean society. The third section describes, briefly, the problems associated with the dominance of metropolitan growth. The fourth section evaluates urban development policies used for decentralization and in the last section; the paper suggests theoretical perspectives for future urban development and management in Korea.

Urbanization Process

As of 2000, 87 percent of Korea's population was urbanized (KNSO 1, 2001: 48-52). This compares with only 28 percent in 1961, the beginning point of the economic modernization. Thus, in 40 years the urban population has more than threefold. During the last four decades, urban population grew by an average annual rate of 2.5 percent, while the total population grew by about 0.6 percent (MGAHA, 2000: 124). The former has increased much faster than the latter. It may be a common characteristic of today's developing countries in relation to urbanization.

Before 1961, the urban population in Korea was much lower than that of the world figure. However, since 1970, it has exceeded the world standard and has continuously increased its proportion. The United Nations has projected that Korea will have an urban population of 87.9 percent by the year 2025 (United Nations, 1989: 43). Currently, nine out of ten people in Korea live in urban areas. This is quite similar to that of Israel where a high rate of urbanization with high income is maintained (Renaud, 1981: 49).

The main factor behind rapid urbanization was the success of macro-economic performance. Traditionally, Korea has been an agricultural country with limited natural resources. This has resulted in small capital formation as a consequence of a small domestic market. To break this vicious circle, Korea prescribed a strong policy to increase investment for industrialization with foreign aid and focused on an export-led strategy (Sohng, 1989: 514). To maximize goals, growth poles were restricted to a few metropolitan areas, mainly to the capital city, Seoul. This strategy made sense owing to a high rate of expansion of foreign trade which allowed the country to enter the world economy.

The success of macro-economic performance brought about a rapid structural change from agriculture to industry and with the acceleration of industrialization, metropolitan areas required many young workers. As a result, the massive shifts of human and other resources to metropolitan areas followed, especially to Seoul. At the initial stage of economic development focusing development strategy on a few metropolitan areas was inevitable to achieve high economic efficiency under limited financial circumstances (Renaud, 1981: 37). From this time, Korea began to experience serious rural to urban migration and the relatively well-developed road system allowed migrants to move easily to metropolitan areas.

Young migrants were eager to move to metropolitan areas for better economic opportunities. Urban areas were very attractive to rural dwellers because urban areas possessed, in their minds, everything needed for a better life. Moreover, migrants preferred urban areas rather than living in isolation in the countryside, because cities were considered the best places for socialization. Thus, several combined factors-economic, psychological, and social-prompted young workers to migrate to metropolitan areas (EPB, 1977: 16-17). An urban pull factor generated an intense attraction.

Table 16.1 shows the high migration rate resulting from economic development in Korea for the period between 1962 and 2000. The total migration rate nearly doubled from 11.7 percent of total population in 1962-70 to 18.9 percent in 1996-2000. A large increase in the rate began to occur in the mid 1980s. During the 1980s the rate plateaued, but remained high. Intra-provincial migration exceeded inter-provincial migration for all of the periods since it was easier to move within a province. However, as a small country, migration in Korea either within or between provinces could occur easily because the distance barrier was not excessive. The direction of inter-provincial migration in the 1960s was mostly toward the two largest metropolitan areas, Seoul and Pusan, since industries were primarily located in these areas. Thus, migration was the main factor of urban growth in this period of a two centre-based rapid economic development.

Table 16.1: Migration Total and Rate
(Unit: total in thousands and rate in person)

Year	Total	Intra-Provincial	Inter-Provincial
1967-1970	3,504 (11.7)	2,490 (8.5)	1,014 (3.2)
1871-1975	5,414 (14.6)	3,757 (11.5)	1,657 (3.1)
1976-1980	7,633 (21.1)	5,276 (14.6)	2,363 (6.5)
1981-1985	8,866 (22.4)	5,916 (15.0)	2,950 (7.4)
1986-1990	9,343 (22.4)	6,350 (14.7)	3,208 (7.7)
1991-1995	9,073 (21.4)	6,109 (14.4)	2,864 (7.0)
1996-2000	9,009 (18.9)	6,164 (12.9)	2,864 (6.0)

Source: Economic Planning Board (EPB), Republic of Korea, Recalculation from Annual Report on the Inter-Net Migration Statistics, National Bureau of Statistics, 1977: 7, 1992: 12, 2000: 9-16.

The Seoul metro area has continued to be the major recipient of migrants.

During 1965-75, it alone absorbed half a million migrants annually which was about equal to the country's natural growth. In the early 1980s, 55 percent of Seoul's population consisted of lifetime migrants, 67 percent of whom were in the working age-group (14-44). Among the migrants, 90 percent of the males and 83 percent of the females from 14-59 year age group were employed (U.N., Seoul, 1986: 6-7).

Growth patterns of urban areas have evolved through four decades. First, before the pre-industrialization period of the 1960s urban growth took place primarily due to natural increase caused by high fertility rate of 4.8 per woman in the 1960s for the nation as a whole (World Bank, 1989: 170). The ratio of national increase of migration during this period in Seoul was almost 7 to 3. Second, with industrialization in the 1960s, the ratio between the two reversed to almost 3 to 7 (EPB, 1990: 67). This was a period during which urban growth was primarily due to migration and secondarily due to natural increase. With decentralization policy in the 1970s the migration rate much declined (EPB, 1992: 69).

Third, since 1980, with the end of rapid migration the ratio between national increase (7.4) and migration (2.6) in Seoul reversed back to the situation of the 1960s, but with a much lower fertility rate. Population increase due to migration in Seoul during 1980-1990 was 0.6 million, while due to natural increase it was 1.7 million (EPB, 1992: 69). The magnitude of reduction in migration can be gauged from the fact that by the end of the 1980s, the fertility rate for the nation had further declined to 2.14 per woman (World Bank, 1989: 170). By the way, this trend changed steeply by entering the 1990s. In-migration to Seoul was not over 0.1 million and the fertility rate also decreased sharply to below 1.7 (KNSO 2, 2001: 107). Any way, urban growth generated by a large scale rural migration was coming to an end with the depletion of younger working age group persons in the rural areas. Consequently, migration among urban areas and natural increase in the urban areas become more important.

There have been many administrative reclassification and boundary changes since 1960. Settlements are reclassified after they reach population of 50,000. Between 1960 and 1990, 40 settlements gained city status as a result of boundary changes. On the other hand, annexation and boundary changes for urban growth have been relatively minor. Less than 10 percent of all population growth in cities was because of a boundary change (KHC, 1992: 25-39). Since 1971, the areal expansion of urban areas was severely restricted by the establishment of urban greenbelts and urban land use (Kim and Mills, 1988: 159).

Density in most urban areas increased sharply creating traffic congestion and environmental degradation, while the quality of urban amenities declined. Korea has tried to address these negative effects of urbanization through a decentralized policy by attempting parallel development in rural areas and by building high rise apartments and related amenities in cities through urban renewal.

Urbanization Characteristics

Relatively well developed transportation, communication, and information systems helped the acceleration of the urbanization process in Korea. The speed apart from quality, therefore, was very fast. The urbanization process did not seem complete because it lacked enduring interdependent socio-economic change. However, in the process of rapid urbanization, macro-economic success helped policy makers to implement a broad spatial distribution policy quite different from the earlier and narrowly focused metropolitan area's development. Thus, urbanization was supported by economic growth. This was the main factor that allowed Korea to induce a relatively faster urbanization process unlike other developing countries in which urbanization preceded industrialization (Alam, 1989: 234). In other developing countries population pressure induced rural push and forced the rural population to migrate to cities in search of employment, while urban pull produced only a limited inducement for such migration.

Five main urbanization characteristics are apparent in Korea. First, urbanization affected significantly the demographic process. Both crude birth rate and crude death rate decreased, while life expectancy increased due to an increase in the proportion of elderly people. Between 1961 and 1980, the rate of fertility declined sharply from 4.9 per 1000 women to 1.7 and this trend continued (World Bank, 1992: 271; KNSO 2, 2001: 107). As a result, the annual growth rate of population decreased from 2.0 percent during 1965-80 to 1.1 percent during 1980-1990 (World Bank, 1992: 269). By 2020-25 the projected annual rate should reach - 0.39 percent (United Nation, 1991: 156).

Normally, it is believed that urbanization and fertility rates have a negative relationship. For example, in a country where the rate of urbanization is high, the rate of fertility is low (Berry, 1981: 78). Urbanization experiences in Korea support this theory. The main factor favouring a lower fertility rate seems to come from the advantages offered by urban areas. In urban areas the percentage of people having higher education is more. Medical facilities are easily accessed. The urban dwellers are exposed to mass media and various other sources of information. Young woman migrants have greater chances to become better educated through their companies, formal education and the mass media.

Second, the need to reverse urbanization trends resulted in the development of many regional centres as counterbalances to Seoul and, thus, initiated a process of region-based development. Table 16.2 shows the growth patterns of cities and proportion of urban population by rank groups in Korea. The overall number of cities with population over 50,000 increased to threefold from 26 in 1960 to 78 in 2000. The general urban hierarchy before 1960 in Korea tended to weigh toward two metropolitan areas and 17 small cities with populations of 50,000-100,000.

Table 16.2: Growth Patterns of Cities and Proportion of Urban Population by Rank Groups in Korea

(Figures in parenthesis are in person)

Population Size (thousands)	1960	1970	1980	1990	2000
over-1000	2 (52)	3 (64)	4 (65)	6 (66)	7 (55)
500-1000	1 (9)	1 (5)	2 (6)	5 (10)	9 (15)
200-500	3 (14)	3 (9)	11 (15)	15 (14)	24 (18)
100-200	3 (7)	11 (12)	17 (10)	14 (6)	31 (11)
50-100	17 (18)	14 (8)	6 (2)	30 (7)	7 (1)
Total	26	32	40	70	78

Source: KHC (The Korea Housing Corporation), Recalculation from Housing Statistics Yearbook, the Korea Housing Corporation, Republic of Korea 1992: 22-45. Korea National Statistical Office (KNSO 1), Regional Statistics Yearbook, National Statistical Office, 2001: 48-52.

During 1960s, the growth pattern of cities changed as an emphasis was placed on metropolitan areas and cities with populations of 100,000-200,000. This period was an era of growth for the largest metropolitan areas. This period was also the initial stage of economic development which required high efficiency as reflected in the bi-polar growth, based on Seoul and Pusan. During 1970s, emphasis was placed on growth of small and medium sized cities; cities with populations of 100,000-200,000 and 50,000-100,000, respectively. During 1980s, the growth pattern of cities shifted to larger cities with populations of 200,000-500,000, together with small cities with populations of 100,000-200,000. During 1990, maintaining the growth pattern of 1980s, the growth of small cities with populations of 50,000-100,000 was remarkable. On the other hand, in Table 16.2: Number of Cities and Proportion of Urban Population by Five Size Groups, 1960-2000 the 2000s, cities with populations between 1000,000 and 100,000 were grown rapidly, especially the population size of 100,000 -200,000. These evolving urban growth patterns resulted in the transformation of an uneven hierarchy into an even one. For example, compared with the urban hierarchical pattern of 1960, the hierarchy of the 2000s seems relatively balanced, but it is still weighted more toward the largest metropolitan areas.

One remarkable phenomenon noted through the analysis of Table 16.2 is growth of regional centres. Especially, between 1980 and 1990 many regional centres grew rapidly and some were raised to the rank of metropolitan area or came to possess a population of over 0.5 million. These growth patterns of cities were significant because they were made possible under an elaborate plan based upon economic capacity. Owing to its economic success, Korea could induce region-based development cantering on regional centres with its strong decentralization policy.

Even though Korea tried to create small cities to stimulate rural well being, 55 percent of urban dwellers lived in seven metropolitan areas in 2000. Though there are many different sized cities, people strongly favour metropolitan areas as the most desirable living places. More decentralization seems to be possible only by suburban movement like America and West Europe.

However, urban primacy in Korea remains high as seen in Table 16.3. For example, if using the four-city rule, the ratio of population between the larger city and the sum of the next three largest cities, as of 2000, the primacy ratio is 1.1, a somewhat high rate. Using the two city rule, the ratio of population between the largest city and the second largest, the primary ratio is 2.7 as can be seen in Table 23.3. Either way, the primacy rate in Korea is a little high. The highest rate occurred in the 1970s. Since then, the rate has been slightly reduced. The Capital Regional Plan, adopted in 1981 allowed the Seoul region to decentralize, but intra-regional decentralization had precedence over inter-urban dispersal (Yeung, 1989). Such a policy in actuality did not slow the process of Seoul's growth, but continued to favour it's primacy within the national context.

Table 16.3: Urban Primacy and Population of Regional Centres

Rank	Cities	1960	1970	1980	1990	2000
1	Seoul	2,445	5,423	8,351	10,628	9,895
2	Pusan	1,164	1,839	3,157	3,798	3,663
	Two-city Ratio	2.10	2.95	2.65	2.80	2.70
3	Taegue	677	1,061	1,604	2,227	2,481
4	Incheon	401	631	1,081	1,798	2,475
	Four-city Ratio	1.0	1.5	1.4	1.3	1.1
5	Kwangju	314	493	727	1,145	1,353
6	Taejon	229	406	651	1,062	1,368

Hansen argues that most developing countries imitate the Western industrialization model as a vehicle for their economic development without modification. This, in turn, results in a pattern of urban primacy. As a consequence, the rank size rule which is applicable in Western countries cannot be applied to developing countries (Hansen, 1979: 217). Western countries have different city sizes such as metropolitan, medium, and small towns. Korea also used the same Western logic though it has tried to create many small and medium size cities.

Third, urbanization brought about a high increase of per capita income, US$150 in 1961 to US$6,330 in 1991 (World Bank, 1993: XIV), and has helped to maintain a relatively equal distribution of income between rural and urban areas. Unequal income distribution between rural and urban areas is considered as the main force behind rural-urban migration in developing countries. There are no consistent opinions about Korean income distribution. Haggard points out that before the industrialization of the 1960s, Korea had maintained a relatively even income distribution. However, with industrialization, rural/urban income distribution became unequal (Haggard, 1990: 225). It is true that at the beginning of economic development, income levels in urban areas were higher than that of rural areas. This is reflected in the rapid migration to urban areas. However, the Korean Statistical Office does not show a significant income gap between rural and urban areas. It reports almost even distribution from 1970 to 1990 (EPB, 1991: 81). Mills and Song support EPB's report by pointing to a relatively equal income distribution in Korea (Mills and Song, 1979: 26). Since the 1970s, Korea has focused on the development of rural areas for balanced national development under the slogan of 'rural reconstruction for rural people' in order to persuade villagers to remain in rural areas. Policy makers realized that urban development without a parallel development in rural areas was almost impossible.

Korea first concentrated its effort to reduce the income gap between rural and urban areas by modifying rural policy from simply developing infrastructure and light industries to developing heavy industries and improving living condition through the national land development plan adopted in 1972. This emphasis resulted from the lesson learned in the 1960s that without employment opportunities in rural areas, migration could not subside (Kim and Donaldson, 1979: 670). In other developing countries, the rural-urban income gap is greater. Gilbert and Gugler pointed out that in Indonesia the per capita income gap between the richest and the poorest regions in 1972 was twelve fold. However, Korea is different from other developing countries because urbanization grew with per capita income (Gilbert and Gugler, 1878: 29).

Fourth, urbanization depleted valuable rural human resources because of the strong pull factors of the urban areas. Migrants were the main instrument of industrialization, which absorbed labour surplus in the period of rapid economic growth. They also planted an urban subculture which was mixed with wider, varied life styles of different regions. This subculture strengthened ties among urban areas (Berry, 1981: 82). As a result, they played a crucial role in urban development. Illegal settlements, rising crime and growth of slum areas in the initial stage of national development were the negative effects of rapid migration.

In contrast, rural areas sent young and educated workers to urban areas resulting in a big loss of a valuable rural asset. The depletion of young workers in rural areas affected the future of rural areas as it was related to productivity. Rural poverty in many ways is caused by routine work, limited land, lack of innovative ideas, and lack of improvement in the quality and quantity of agricultural products. Regardless of how good the government policy for rural dwellers, distribution of effective resources did not take place. As a result, urbanization made urban areas more productive through absorption of young, educated migrants from rural areas, while rural areas lost creative young workers.

Lastly, urbanization contributed in reducing the cultural gap [1] between rural and urban areas, which before 1961 was wide. During that period, modern civilization had no significant impact on rural areas. With the movement towards modernization, rural areas rapidly absorbed urban culture and mass media accelerated this process. This was particularly possible because Korea is small country. The increase in per capita income made the availability of radio, television, telephone and newspapers to the general masses possible. Electrical appliances became indispensable for daily life and private automobile ownership increased. Urbanization influenced the thinking process of the rural dwellers significantly.

Consequently, urbanization in Korea followed a relatively uniform process unlike other developing countries. Here, the impact of urbanization was quite different. It affected significantly the demographic process, per capita income, and cultural standard, and accelerated the growth of regional centres while depleting rural human resources. The main reason why Korea could induce a relatively strong urbanization is the economic success emanating from the urban areas' productive role. The general economic uplift of the country made policy makers focus on regional centre's development by dividing national functions among regional centres.

Problems of Metropolitan Growth

A higher concentration of population and facilities in a few metropolitan areas can be effective in bringing about higher economic efficiency. Metropolitan areas can register higher investment returns, productivity, and employment opportunities. However, in the longer term, it is not desirable because the lopsided growth of metropolitan areas is not cost effective and constructive investment is not directed to new areas (Sussman, 1976: 174).

Overexpansion was the most important spatial problem of the country and in Seoul it was related to the issue of national security. Korea has been divided since the end of the Second World War. South Korea has made a conspicuous upward movement economically with developing democratic institutions, while North Korea remained economically backward with an emphasis on military might within a framework of a Marxist Socialist system. These two countries have confronted each other with different ideologies. Seoul, which also possesses the most important administrative facilities, is located within the range of North Korean artillery fire. Despite Seoul's location in strategically disadvantageous position, it continued to play a premier role, which was vitally linked to Korea's security and sustainable development (Song, 1990: 23).

The second problem was the inefficient and unbalanced land use of the country, Growth in a few metropolitan areas means that other regions sacrifice much of their chance for development. Especially, migration of young educated workers to metropolitan areas brought about great damage to rural areas which in turn dampened the vitality of urban areas as a result of declining productivity potential of the former. Thus, in a country like Korea which lacks the required natural resources, the efficient use of land was as important as national security.

The third problem was related to environment. The effects of environmental problems are subtle and do not appear vital for current life, as they are initially intangible. Because of this, the development goal was based on a one-sided decision without consideration of environmental problems. Ultimately, development decisions that do not take into consideration of the environment are counter productive to a sustainable development (Lau, 1990: 206).

Consequently, concentration of development in a few metropolitan areas requires additional social costs to meet increased demand for housing, public services and infrastructure for the migrants (Sussman, 1976: 174). It reduces efficient urban development by increasing ongoing costs in the metropolitan areas and deferring new social development programs. The motivating force in determining the approach to the national land development policy was guided by Seoul's vital role in national security. This was the narrowly focused development strategy of the 1960s.

Urban Development Strategy

The ultimate goals of urban development in Korea are to restrain Seoul's growth and to induce balanced national urban development. To control Seoul's growth, the urban development plan has been revised four times to achieve a rational approach. The policy change required selection of a reasonable counterbalance to Seoul based on economic capacity (Renaud, 1981: 37). This policy, therefore, could not be confined to a few small urban areas because it was impractical. A few small towns were too little as a counter balance to a mega city like Seoul. Regional centres, the second level of urban hierarchy located evenly throughout the country, were the most reasonable counterbalance to Seoul. Thus, a policy of region-based urban development was adopted in 1971.

Strategies of the 1960s: Four different urban development strategies were used in each of the last four decades. The main strategy in the 1960s was the effort to apply the growth pole concept used in both the developed and the developing countries as a decentralization policy (Bergman, 1991: 242). The central concept of this policy was to generate and spread effects from the designated growth poles to surrounding areas by establishing and promoting industrial activities in the designated areas. Functional relationships between designated areas and surrounding urban areas were emphasized.

Korea chose two metropolitan areas, Seoul and Pusan (about 500km apart from each other) as growth poles to achieve higher economic efficiency in this period (Kim, 1979: 55). Korean planners and policy makers thought if these two metropolitan areas develop, other urban areas would also develop as a result of their functional economic relationships. Thus, a trickle down effect would take place. The expectations were not fulfilled as the two metropolitan areas grew rapidly while the growth rate of other urban areas decreased. The national urban hierarchy changed vertically rather than horizontally and the imbalance between regions deepened.

If balanced development was the principal goal, the main mistake in this period was the wrong selection of growth poles. Growth poles should be selected from backward areas to accelerate industrialization and to keep pace with other developed areas (Gore, 1984: 82).

Korea, on the other hand, chose relatively well-developed cities because they were easily developable under conditions of limited financial resources. As a result, these two metropolitan areas grew rapidly, while other cities lagged behind in industrialization releasing part of their working age population to the metropolitan areas. Also the growth poles ignited huge rural to urban migration and Korea began to suffer seriously from migration problems due to unplanned development. The result was an example of a failure of the functional approach.

Strategies of the 1970s: Beginning with the 1970s and on the basis of 1960s' experience, Korea established the first national land development plan (1971-1982) to induce balanced national urban development throughout the country and approached development problems from the perspective of areal development.

The principle of the plan was based on area-wide development by focusing on regional centres together with other regional cities away from the two metropolitan areas (LPB, 1992: 25). At the same time, rural development programme was implemented. Policy makers already knew that without parallel development in rural areas successful urban development was virtually impossible.

For decentralization of Seoul, three policy measures were established. The first measure was to establish new towns around Seoul for resettlement of population, housing squatters and for the relocation of industries. The second measure was the establishment of a greenbelt to apply a brake to Seoul's physical growth. Later the greenbelt concept was expanded to other urban areas of the country. The third measure was administrative decentralization. National administrative functions, concentrated in Seoul, were to be decentralized into other designated areas (Yeung, 1989: 313-319).

However, in many ways, Seoul's decentralization policy was not successful because of the strong containment policy in Seoul which produced a huge conurbation beyond the greenbelt and spilling into the outer part of the metropolitan area. Overspill of population and industries moved to existing small and new towns surrounding Seoul taking all advantages of easy accessibility to the city. Compared to the metropolitan area's periphery, the city of Seoul did not register a very rapid population increase. The designation of the greenbelt in 1970 led to leapfrogging development across the belt and into the satellite cities (U.N., 1986, Seoul: 19). Construction of cheaper housing in the peripheral areas attracted lower income groups while the better environmental possibilities attracted higher-income families (KHC. 1983). Neither business nor government was really interested in reducing the growth of Seoul and the built-up area in the metropolitan area continued to increase. The greenbelt policy was looked upon both positively and negatively as some thought it to be a major contributor to metropolitan decongestion" and others thought that it was a source of land scarcity and the high cost of housing in the city of Seoul (U.N., 1986, Seoul: 49). Seoul also suffered from traffic and environmental problems resulting in additional social costs.

However, at the end of the 1970s, regional centres were beginning to recover from their stagnation because of the location of large scale public sector industrial complexes within them. Also some entrepreneurs settled as permanent residents in the regional centres and participated actively in regional reconstruction. New urban growth patterns began to reduce the dominance of the two major metropolitan areas and to foster development in regional centres. Regional centres grew rapidly, while the two major metropolitan areas grew at a much reduced rate.

Strategies of the 1980s: With the advent of the 1980s, Korea adopted its second national land development plan (1982-1991). The adopted approach was for fostering a more balanced national urban development. If the first land development plan provided an opportunity for balanced urban development, the second plan sought to achieve it with a much more elaborate spatial distribution plan than before (LPB, 1992: 5).

The main focus of the plan was to consolidate a changing pattern of growth which began to shift from Seoul to regional centres at the end of the 1970s. Also, the plan focused on the development of rural areas as well as smaller urban centres in order to induce real balanced development throughout the country. This plan divided Korea into 28 Integrated Regional Settlement Areas (IRSAs) according to the criteria of homogeneity and size of central city which was designed to act as a centripetal point for each region (Rondinelli, 1983: 202). The IRSAs include five large metropolitan cities, seventeen local cities and six rural cities.

The five large metropolitan areas are Seoul, Pusan, Taegu, Kwangju, and Taejon. The last three were designated as growth poles in order to counterbalance Seoul and Pusan by absorbing a portion of their functions. The area-wide policy was applied to regional centres and other larger cities. The purpose of designating regional centres as growth poles was to increase significantly the functions of regional centres while reducing those of the largest metropolitan areas. The rationale for this policy was that unless the same functions were allocated to the regional centres, their growth goals could not be achieved (LPB, 1992: 25).

The seventeen local IRSAs were designated as second level growth poles and were planned to develop to the level of Taejon, a city with about 500,000 populations. The intent was to develop these cities as centres for labour intensive manufacturing, trading, and administrative services which provide crucial support for rural dwellers (Rondinelli, 1983: 203). Six rural cities were designated to help stabilize rural areas by providing modern rural facilities and establishing agricultural and fishery processing activities to absorb rural migrants closer to their homes.

Compared with the 1960s and the 1970s, planning in the 1980s emphasized a much more balanced spatial distribution. The plan shifted completely from the narrowly focused development strategy to a broader areally spread out growth poles and by designating many growth poles throughout the country. This plan, coupled with the need for more spread out economic development reduced greatly the population and industrial concentration in the two largest metropolitan areas compared to the 1960s and 1970s (EPB, 1992: 69). The most significant result in the 1980s was the consolidation of the growth of regional centres and other larger cities which could then counteract the growth of the two largest metropolitan areas. During this period, the growth of small sized cities with populations of 50,000-100,000 was also stimulated. Such stimulation was necessary for balanced urban growth as shown in Table 23.2. The outcome was the beginning of emergence of a much more balanced urban hierarchy throughout the country.

Strategies of the 1990s: Until the end of the 1980s, Seoul's growth had continued but with much reduced rate. Entering the 1990s, the Korean government introduced the capital region maintenance law as a more effective policy measure for restraining the concentration of Seoul. As a result, at the end of the 1990s, the growth of Seoul, at last began to maintain stagnant situation with the population of around 10 millions. The main strategies of the 1990s were as follows:

In 1991, the Korean government established the third 10-year national land use plan (1992-2001). This plan was basically meant for developing both the capital region's area and the local area keeping in mind the trend of globalization and localization.

In 1993, the Korean government confirmed the reform plan of the capital region's maintenance policy for simplification of the capital region's development zone, conversion of regulation methods and reorganization of the capital region's spatial structure. In 1994, to support this institutionally the capital region's maintenance law was completely revised and announced and as the follow-up measure the enforcement ordinance of the capital region's maintenance plan was revised. The major contents of it are as follows (Bae etal, 2000: 7-9).

First, it simplified the development zones from 5 to 3 and adopted differential regulation method for each zone. Second, it relaxed the regulation contents much and at the same time converted regulation method of facilities from each to overall one. An overall regulation method is a method in which an overall quantities of new and enlargement construction of universities and factories in the capital region each year was included. Third, relaxing the sturdiness of physical regulation method and permitting location for essential facilities to reconsider the efficiency of regulation on the capital region, it introduced economic regulation method charging overpopulation costs.

In 1994, the Korean government enacted the regional balanced development law. Under the recognition that the capital region policy could not be succeeded with only the containment policy of the capital region, it enacted the regional balanced development law as a means for both the restraint of the capital region and the upbringing of the regional areas. In 1997, on the basis of the complete revision of the capital region maintenance law, the second capital region's plan was established. It grounded on reconsidering the function and role of the capital region under the basic recognition that until now the firm capital region policy had weekend the capital region's competition.

Consequences of Four Decade Strategies

The urban development policy, thus, was directed towards containment of the growth of the two largest metropolitan areas and decentralization of their function to regional centres and other regional cities. Though, this containment policy for the two metropolitan areas was strongly advocated during the 1960s and 1970s. Korean decision makers could not restrict their growth at that time. As a result, the two largest metropolitan areas grew continuously during this period. However, since the adoption of the second national land use plan a more balanced national urban development pattern has been evident since the 1980s. In the early 1990s, the development pattern displayed a rapid growth of regional centres while Seoul's growth slowed. Imbalances between regions continued and national policy continued to pursue both growth and balance at the same time (LPB, 1992: 5). However, at the end of 1990s, the population of Seoul began to maintain the stagnant status around 10 millions. We might think that the urban policy in Korea is just a series of containment policy of the metropolitan area's growth rather than the policy of considering quality of life or wellbeing in all urban areas. In other wards, it shows that a developing country like Korea, how much efforts and time should be given and spent to restrain the metropolitan areas' dominant growth since designated them as the growth poles. This may be common characteristic suffering most of the developing countries by introducing the growth pole strategy.

Urban Development and Management in the Future

The direction of policy for urban development in Korea has changed since 1960 from bi-polar growth poles to multi-and -areal growth poles. The outcomes of the 1980s growth pole policy are impressive in terms of broader spatial distribution and a much more balanced urban development throughout the country. These changing patterns of urban growth resulted from the national urban development plan and the nature of spatial development occurred in the free market economy when evolving from a pre-industrial to mature industrial level. The remaining issue is how Korea can induce further balanced urban development in a situation of declining urban growth.

When viewed as a series of urban development stages, the planning policy in each decade emphasized a specific level of urban hierarchy, metropolitan areas in the 1960s, metropolitan and regional centres in the 1970s, regional centres and large cities in regions in the 1980s, and balanced development in the 1990s. If this trend changes further from the current regional centres and other large cities to local centres which are closely related to the economic and social activities of rural dwellers, Korea can achieve a completely balanced urban development (Renaud, 1981: 48).

When considering future urban development in Korea, two policy issues emerge. The first is related to the development of local cities. Current rural areas in Korea are in crisis due to the lack of educated young people who continue to migrate to urban areas. This trend tends to reduce the efficiency of production in rural areas and lowers the potential for supply of high quality agricultural products to urban areas.

To revitalize rural areas, they will have to be changed into multi-functional space by converting the current conventional production system to a manufacturing based system. Small towns in rural areas can then combine functions of residence, leisure amenities, garden-like environment, and industrial production. To accomplish this conventional agricultural system will have to be changed into a mechanized system so that urbanization can occur in local areas (Todaro, 1985: 287).

The second suggestion is related to management of urban areas. Current trends through out the world are tending towards a declining population growth rate because fertility and birth rates are falling in most countries. Future world population projections for 2025 by the United Nations also reflect a gradually decreasing rate of growth as it was 93 percent during 1950-1985 and 61 percent during 1990-2025 (United Nations, 1991). The projected Korean population growth of 21 percent during 1990-2025 is much lower than the projected world rate. In addition, a second important trend is the suburban movement in the high income economies. These trends occur to a significant degree in America and Europe where the standard of living is relatively high (Hall, 1991: 293). Based on a per capita GNP of US$6,330 in 1991, the World Bank placed Korea at the higher level of upper-middle-income group country (World Bank, 1993) and considering its development record since the 1960s, it is expected to be ranked as a high-income-economy soon. Korea, thus, is at a transitional level. Its level of suburbanization is rising and will continue to rise. Lower population growth and the desire for improved quality of life, emanating from the higher GNP per capita, favour living in suburban areas over the inner cities. U-term migration, a migration from large urban centres to small or rural areas, could occur (Mera, 1979: 193).

In the 1970s and 1980s, the industrial sector remained the most dynamic sector of the Korean economy as it improved its share of GDP from 29 percent in 1970 to 45 percent in 1991, while agriculture's share withered from 26 percent to 8 percent and the service sector remained almost constant, going from 45 percent to 47 percent during this 21-year period (World Bank, 1993:243). Seoul, which is a pace setter of modernization, reflects the changes that have taken place in the country: the city "has modernized rapidly, building up a diversified export-oriented manufacturing base and then moving into tertiary and, more recently, quaternary activities"(U.N., 1986:1). Korean cities in early 1990s reflect the characteristics of the late industrial cities, while they are evolving into a post-industrial level like that of cities in high-income economies. When this happens, the share of service employment will greatly increase and the proportionate share of industrial employment will decline. Korean cities, particularly Seoul, are more likely to feel the problems of derelict industrial land uses, abandonment of sub-standard central city housing and deterioration of the urban core. The government and urban planners must be ready to meet such challenges in the near future.

Korea also has experienced a decreasing rate of population growth and fertility. The decrease in the fertility rate from 4.8 in the 1960s to 1.8 after 1980 was a remarkable change and this trend is projected to continue into the future (World Bank, 1992: 271). By the year 2020 the Korean population will reach 51 million and will stabilize at that level (United Nation, 1991: 147). Also the era of the rapid urban growth by migration has become a thing of the past. Considering these trends, current concern with quantitative expansion of urban space has to be replaced by a concern for qualitative expansion and management in the future. To do this, the current expansion of heavy infrastructure such as roads, schools, and sewers, needs to be changed to new forms of infrastructure such as telecommunication networks and high quality environmental equipment to improve the quality of urban life (Homme, 1989: 46). This shift will require not only greater economic resources, but more innovative ideas.

Conclusion

The nature of urbanization reflects the interaction of interdependent processes such as economic development, migration, and growth of urban population. Urbanization in Korea was a result of migration caused by macro-economic success. Korea created a relatively stable and successful urbanization process as a result of economic success. With the increased pace of urbanization beginning in the 1960s, demographic variables and cultural change were significantly affected. Also, the income gap between rural and urban areas was not excessive and continues to remain so. An initial development strategy based on regional centres to check Seoul's growth seemed to be a reasonable policy, but a change in development strategy were required because there were many other sized cities, which needed government and private enterprise-sponsored investments to achieve a balanced national economic setting. In the 1980s such steps were taken by the government and private investors have responded favourably. The fast pace of Seoul's growth has been checked and the growth rate became faster in other cities. Such decentralization occurred both as a result of government policy-inducement and spontaneous processes taken by private enterprises.

Urban policy in Korea has been guided by a combination of spatial, political, and economic factors. Among them, the economic factor was the most essential because without the growth of the economy, spatial redistribution of activities was virtually impossible. The reason for failure of growth pole policy in several developing countries was mainly the result of an erroneous assumption that many growth poles could be chosen. Such an assumption lacks pragmatic considerations and undermines a rational assessment of prevailing economic conditions. Urban policy in Korea had benefited by a realistic assessment of the development level of the economy. Such an effective policy direction in the 1990s induced much more balanced urban development than in the 1960s and 1970s.

Remaining issues to be resolved are how Korea can maintain more balanced urban development between regions and redevelop existing urban areas to accommodate additional population.

As Korea is passing through an industrialization process, its cities reflect the characteristics of industrial cities, but as the country's industrialization matures and it moves into more capital intensive, "high-tech", automated and information-system-oriented manufacturing, the country will advance into a post-industrial stage. As in high income economies, Korean cities, particularly Seoul, will then have to meet the challenge of transition from industrial to post-industrial conditions.

Note

1. A cultural gap resulted from a shortage of facilities, such as, modem appliances, communication and electronics and a low level of education in rural areas. Increased levels of urbanization and acceleration of development reduced this gap by spreading modem conveniences to rural areas along with the increased use of transportation and information systems, Differences in life-styles of rural and urban areas were wide during the pre-1960 period. Rural areas lacked modem facilities, whereas, the urban areas enjoyed them. Rural areas did not regard education to be important because the laborious traditional agriculture did not require it. Modernization brought about a revolution in the communication and information systems narrowing

the rural-urban gap and promoting mechanization of agriculture.

References

Alam, M. Shahid (1989) the South Korean Miracle: Examining the Mix of Government and Markets, The Journal of Developing Areas, Vol. 23, Jan., p.234.

Bae Sunsek, Kim, Hyunsic, Park, Sangwoo, (2000) Growth Management of the Capital Region and New Town Development, National Land Development Institute.

Bergman, E.M., Maier, G. and Todtling F. (1991) Regions Reconsidered, New York; London, Mansell Publishing Limited.

Berry, Brian J.L. 1981. Comparative Urbanization, St. Martin's Press, (1981), pp. 78-82.

Economic Planning Board (1977) Annual Report on the Internal Migration

Statistics, National Bureau of Statistics, Republic of Korea, pp. 7-17.

—— 1990, p. 67.

—— 1991, p. 81.

—— 1992, pp. 12-69.

Gilbert, Alan and Gugler, Josef (1989) Cities, Poverty, and Development, New York, Oxford University Press.

Gore, Charles (1984) Regions in Question, New York: London, Methuen and Co. Ltd., p.82.

Gugler, Josdf (1988) The Urbanization of the Third World, New York, Oxford University Press.

Haggard, Stephan (1990) Pathways from the Periphery, Ithaca, N.Y., Cornell University Press.

Hall, Peter (1991) Cities of Tomorrow, Oxford, England, Basil Blackwell Ltd.

Hansen, Niles M. (1979) Growth Strategies and Human Settlement Systems in Developing Countries, in Lo, Fuchen and Salih, Kamal(eds.), Growth Pole

Strategy and Regional Development Policy, London, Pergamon Press, p.217.

Homme, Remy Prud (1989) New Trends in the Cities of the World, in Knight, Richard V. and Gappert, Gary(eds.), Cities in Global Society, Beverly Hills Ca., Sage Publications.

Kim, An-jae (1979) Industrialization and Growth Pole Development in Korea: A Case study of The ULSAN Industrial Complex, in Lo, Fuchen and Salih, Kamal (eds.),

Growth Pole Strategy and Regional Development Policy, London, pergmon Press. Kim, Song-Ung and Donaldson, Peter J. (1979) Dealing with Seoul's Population Growth, Asian Survey, Vol. xix, No. 7, July, p. 670.

Kim, Kyung-Hwan and Mills, Edins. (1988) Korean Development and Urbanization: Prospects and Problems, World Development, Vol.16, No1, p.159.

The Korea Housing Corporation (1983) Housing Policy Development Research, Seoul: Korea National Housing Corporation.

——1992. pp.25-45.

KNSO 1 'Korea National Statistical Office', (2001), Regional Statistics Yearbook, National Statistical Office.

KNSO 2 'Korea National Statistical Office', (2001), Social Indicators in Korea, National Statistical Office, p. 107.

Lau, Lawrence J. (1990) Models of Development, An International Centre for Economic Growth Publication.

LPB 'Land Planning Board' (1992) Republic of Korea, The Third National Land Development Plan, Ministry of Construction, pp.5-25.

Mera, Koich (1981) The Changing Pattern of Population Distribution in Japan and Its Implications for Developing Countries, in Lo, Fuchen and Salih, Kamal(eds.),

Growth Pole Strategy and Regional Development Policy, London, pergmon Press.

Mills, Edin S. and Song, Byung-Nak (1979) Urbanization Urban Problem: Seoul Korea, Cambridge, Mass., Harvard University Press.

MGAHA(Ministry of Government Administration and Home Affairs), Municipal Yearbook of Korea, 2000, MGAHA, p. 124.

Renaud, Bertrand (1981) National Urbanization Policy in Developing Countries, Beverly Hills, Ca.., Sage Publications.

Rondinelli, Dennis (1981) Secondary Cities in Developing Countries, Beverly Hill, Ca., Sage Publications.

Seoul Metropolitan Administration (1983) Seoul Metropolitan Government.

Song, Byung-Nak (1990) the Rise of the Korean Economy, New York, Oxford University Press.

Sohng, Soong N. 919890 "The South Korean Model for Industrialization: Theory and Practice", Asian Profile, Vol.17, No.6, Dec.,p.514.

Sussman, Carl. 1976. Planning the Fourth Migration, Cambridge Mass., MIT Press.

Todaro. Michael, P. 1985. Economic Development in the Third World, Longman Ind.

United Nations (1986) Population Growth and Policies in Major City Seoul, Population Policy Paper No.4, New York.

United Nations (1989) Prospects of World Urbanization 1988, Population Studies, No.122, New York: United Nations Publications.

United Nations (1991) World Urbanization Prospects 1990, Series a 1121, New York: United Nations, pp.147-156.

World Bank (1989) Social Indicators of Development 1989. Baltimore and London: The Johns Hopkins University Press.

World Bank (1992) World Development Report, New York: Oxford University Press, pp. 269-279.

World Bank (1993) Social Indicators of Development 1993. Baltimore and London: The Johns Hopkins University Press.

Yeung, Yue-Nam (1989) "Bursting at The Seam: Strategies for Controlling Metropolitan Growth in Asia", in Costa, Frank J., Dutt, Ashok K., Ma, Laurence J.C. and Noble, Allen, G.(eds.), Urbanization in Asia. Honolulu: University of Hawaii Press, pp.313-319.

17

Spatio-temporal Analysis of Urban Human Resources Development in India

B.R.K. Sinha

Introduction

Human Resource Development is one of the challenging global issues of the twenty first century. The concept of Human Resource Development (HRD) is universally and equally applicable to both the urban and rural areas, yet there is wide gap between rural and urban human resource development. This is a result of wide range of factors of social, cultural, economic, political and environmental aspects. Urban areas are the pockets of concentration of population, population density, educational and health infrastructure, secondary and tertiary services, employment opportunities, in-migrants, industries, etc. The socio-economic condition of the urban people is better than that of the rural. However, urban areas suffer from many problems such as health problems, environmental pollution, population explosion, lack of proper and adequate social facilities, core and periphery differential, slum areas, poverty and urban misery, housing problem, unemployment, inadequate transport, waste and sewage disposal, lack of community connectedness, cultural heterogeneity, etc. Over population is most pressing HRD problem because influx of rural population to urban areas places great burden on developmental efforts. No doubt, India possesses abundance of human resources (in quantitative sense) but in reality the majority of them are poor in terms of their ability, ingenuity, knowledge, talents, energies and other mental and physical capabilities. This is a result of cumulative effects of several factors. Therefore, HRD is considered as a key issue in the field of developmental studies.

Human resource development is an important and more reliable indicator of development than any other single measure. It is one of the necessary conditions and helps the people in maintaining the social mobility or social order in achieving the growth of wealth, prosperity, exaltation, beatitude and also in enjoying the life of peace and comfort by liberating them from poverty, illiteracy, illness and other socio-economic bindings. That is why, human resource development is considered as the core concept in the field of geography of human welfare. HRD is a life long process of promoting qualitative values in all people of an area. HRD, according to Gupta, S.P. Das (1998, p. 397), is the complete form of physical and mental growth of individuals. Rao, T.V. (1999, p. 41) has emphasized the importance of HRD and stated that it has the role of getting the right kind of people, creating a culture that nurtures and retains talent, providing avenues for competence development at all levels, ensuring utilization of talent and aiding in renewal of various productive human processes. Nadler, L. (1994, pp. 16-22) defined HRD as planned continuous effort by management to improve employee capacity levels and organisational performance through training, education and development programmes. Similarly, Kumar, B. and Hansra, B.S. (2000, pp. 17-18) defined HRD as an approach to facilitate the development of individual's competence, environment and organisation. HRD lays stress on development of individual, the family and the village community.

HRD has two major dimensions. The first is 'on formation' and the latter is 'off formation' of human resources. When population of an area continues to acquire knowledge, skill, ability through formal and non-formal educational systems, job training or learning by some other sources with an integration of health, food and nutrition is called as population 'on human resource formation'. But that population which has already achieved the above ability or functional values (by the first process of HRD as feed-back) is called as population 'off human resource formation'. Such usable achievement (knowledge, skill, ability, talents, energies and other mental as well as physical capabilities) in such population is termed as 'a stock of human resource'. According to Harbison, F.H. and Myers, Charles A. (1964, pp. 24-27) the stock of human capital indicates the levels of HRD already achieved, which is measured by the levels of educational attainment and net addition (through the process of human resource formation) to the stock of human resources indicates the rate of accumulation of human capital over a certain period of time. This rate of accumulation is measured by the enrolment of students at various educational levels. In this way, HRD creates the resources in human beings and adds to the stock of human resources of an area. Thus, HRD deals with the on going human capital formation as well as the existing situation of human resources already achieved as a stock.

HRD takes place in space and time. Here, space is related to the extent of an area in which elements of HRD are distributed and time is related to the fixed period during which changes in human resource elements take place and inequalities emerge. Therefore, space and time are collectively called as spatio-temporal dimension and the interpretation of this gives us an idea about human resource situation and its future scope of development for well-being of the people. With this end in view, attempts have been made to map out the spatial pattern of the stock of human resources of 1981 and 1991 census year and to note and interpret the distribution and changes.

Objectives of this paper are to:

- map out the stock of urban human resources and interpret the spatio-temporal pattern of this,
- find out the urban male-female human resources development differential at two points of time along with their vertical temporal movement,
- extend appropriate suggestion for reducing the male-female HRD gap in space and time.

Methodological Approach

Human resource development encompasses a variety of elements of both the mental and physical aspects of an individual. The complete measurement of HRD is not easy. Harbison, F.H. (1973, pp. 17-13) also admitted that to fix an yardstick to measure HRD is a difficult task. According to him, no one has yet devised comprehensive indicators of human resource development. If one were constructed, it should probably include as a minimum: measure of educational achievements, school participation ratio, persons with strategic skills, measure of health by data on life - expectancy, infant mortality, diseases or critical measure of food and nutrition, etc. In another study, Harbison, F.H. and Myer, Charles A. (1964, pp. 24-22) adopted various quantitative indicators and computed composite index in measuring human resource development. Educational achievement according to them was most ideal indicator of HRD. Schultz, T.W. (1961, p. 17) also suggested education at elementary, secondary and higher levels for developing and measuring human resources development. Similarly, Singh (1982, pp. 12-13), Prodi, R. (1996, pp. 126-127) and Kaur Parmider (1996, pp. 37-45) too considered educational achievements as an indicator of HRD.

Other scholars such as Das, P.K. and Karak, N. (1988, p. 65), De, N.K. (1988, p. 97) considered and adopted decennial growth rate of population, density of population, literate and educated persons, proportion of urban population, working and non-working persons, etc. as indicators for measuring and mapping human resources development. Harbison, F.H. and Myers, Charles A. (1964, p. 26) further considered the rate of literacy as an important indicator of human resource development in some studies. However, according to them it is relatively a poor indicator. Sinha, B.R.K. (1999, pp. 88-89) used composite index technique in measuring human resource development. For this human resource development index was calculated using composite scores of individuals obtained by putting certain weightage to several quantitative and qualitative parameters directly or indirectly related to physical and mental capability.

Since, there is dearth of data on relevant quantitative and qualitative indicators relating to physical and mental aspects of individuals either at local, regional or state level, the author has taken into consideration only educational achievements, right from illiteracy level to graduation, post-graduation as well as professional/technical levels of education as ideal indicators of HRD. Therefore, this paper is exclusively based on the HRD index calculated on the basis of total composite scores of all educational levels of both urban male and female population of respective states. For this the secondary data relating to all educational levels were collected from the 1981 and 1991 (the 2001 census figures were not available when this paper was prepared) Census Series-India, Part-IVA-C, Social and Cultural tables.

While calculating the composite scores each educational level was given certain weightage on the basis of its respective rank order. The weightage assigned are as follows: Illiteracy-1, literacy-2, below primary-3, primary-4, middle-5, secondary/matriculation-6, higher secondary/intermediate-7, non-technical certificate or diploma not equal to degree-8, technical certificate or diploma not equal to degree-9 and graduation and above (including post-graduation, teaching, veterinary, agriculture/dairying, medicine, engineering and technology and others-10. After putting the assigned weightage to respective educational levels the composite scores of both urban male and female human resources of 1981 and 1991 were calculated separately for each state and employing the equation: HRD = Actual value - Minimum value/Maximum value - Minimum value, human resource development indexes for both urban male and female human resources of 1981 and 1991 of respective states were calculated. Actual value here is meant for total composite score of male or female human resource of each state; minimum value considered was 100 (that is slightly less than the lowest composite score); and maximum value selected was 500 (that is slightly more than the highest composite score). Finally, five levels of HRD such as very high, comprising >0.80 HRD index; High falling between the HRD index of 0.60 and 0.80; Medium, joining the HRD index from 0.40 to 0.60; Low, relating the HRD index between 0.20 and 0.40; and Very Low, showing <0.20 HRD index, were made depending upon variation of the HRD indexes.

Spatio-Temporal Pattern of Urban Male Human Resource Development

Table 17.1 portrays variation in the levels of urban male human resource development of 1981 and 1991. When we look into the detailed picture and distribution pattern of males across states we find that only five (16.13 percent) states such Pondicherry, Tripura, Chandigarh, Delhi and Himachal Pradesh belonged to very high (>0.80) level HRD range in 1981 and all (except Delhi being fallen in high level) maintained their position in 1991 also. 22(70.97 percent) states forming the majority belonged to high level (0.60-0.80) HRD category in 1981 and from them only Tamil Nadu, West Bengal, Goa, Daman & Diu, Kerala and Maharashtra moved to higher rung of the ladder of development in 1991 and the remaining states such as Andhra Pradesh, Karnataka, Orissa, Madhya Pradesh, Bihar, Gujarat, Rajasthan, Haryana, Punjab, Meghalaya, Arunachal Pradesh, Nagaland, Manipur and Sikkim remained in the same position after ten years in 1991. Only Andaman & Nicobar Islands came down to medium rage of HRD in 1991. Similarly, only Uttar Pradesh, Dadar and Nagar Haveli, Jammu & Kashmir and Lakshadweep forming 12.90 percent of the total states of 1981 were in medium range (0.40 - 0.60) of HRD and from among them Dadar & Nagar Haveli made a very good progress jumping to very high level HRD range in 1991, Lakshadweep and Uttar Pradesh moved upward to high level HRD range in 1991. Since census was not held in Jammu and Kashmir in 1991 and as a result this state did not show any change.

Table 17.1: Temporal Pattern of Urban Male and Female Human Resources Development in India, 1981 – 1991

Level and index of HRD	Number and %age of States			
	Male		Female	
	1981	1991	1981	1991
Very high >0.80	5 (16.13)	12 (38.71)	...	1 (3.23)
High 0.60 – 0.80	22 (70.97)	18 (58.06)	4 (12.90)	12 (38.71)
Medium 0.40 – 0.60	0.40 – 0.60	4 (12.90)	1 (3.23)	14 (45.16)
Low 0.20 – 0.40	...	...	13 (41.94)	2 (6.46)
Very low <0.20	...	...	...	...
Total	31 (100.00)	31 (100.00)	31 (1000.00)	31 (100.00)

Source: Census of India, 1981 and 1991.

In short, it can be said that the development of urban male human resource in Himachal Pradesh, Tripura, Chandigarh and Pondicherry was very good as these states maintained very high (>0.80) HRD index in both the years and Tamil Nadu, Kerala, Maharashtra, Goa, Assam, Daman & Diu, Dadar & Nagar Haveli and West Bengal moved to >0.80 from 0.60-0.80 HRD index in 1991. Majority of the bigger states from central, western, south central, north eastern India maintained status quo (high level) in both the years, however, still there is need for an effort to uplift them to very high level HRD range. Important states like Uttar Pradesh, Jammu & Kashmir, Lakshadweep also need much care for their development. Situation of Delhi and Andaman & Nicobar Islands is not satisfactory because of their falling trend from very high to high and from high to medium level respectively in 1991 and therefore need special emphasis on upgrading them in future.

Spatio-Temporal Pattern of Urban Female Human Resource Development

Table 17.1 depicts variation in the level of urban female human resource development of 1981 and 1991. When we look into the detailed picture we find that no state had its position in very high HRD range of >0.80 in 1981, however, Tripura occupied this position in 1991 after moving from high level of 1981. Even Kerala like Chandigarh and Himachal Pradesh remained in high level HRD range (0.60-0.80) in both the census years. Majority of the 1981 states (14/45.16 percent) were in medium range (0.40-0.60). From among them Mizoram, Meghalaya, Punjab, Sikkim and Delhi progressed to high level HRD range after ten years in 1991 and Andaman & Nicobar Islands slumped down to low level in 1991 and the remaining states such as Gujarat, Karnataka, Maharashtra, Tamil Nadu, West Bengal, Pondicherry, Arunachal Pradesh and Haryana maintained their grade in 1991. Thirteen (41.94 percent) states of 1981 were in low level (0.20-0.40) and only Rajasthan from among them did not change its position even after ten years. However, Nagaland, Goa and Madhya Pradesh progressed to high level in 1991 and Andhra Pradesh, Orissa, Bihar, Uttar Pradesh, Manipur, Lakshadweep, Dadar and Nagar Haveli and Daman & Diu moved to medium level of HRD in 1991.

After having a close view we find that Tripura, Himachal Pradesh and Kerala women had overall better picture in term of their development. Some other states such as Mizoram, Meghalaya, Punjab, Sikkim, Delhi, Nagaland, Goa, Madhya Pradesh, Damam & Diu, Dadar Nagar Haveli, Lakshadweep also made progress moving to upper levels in 1991 from lower levels of 1981. Situation of Rajasthan and Andaman & Nicober Islands even in 1991 was not good. Majority of the states in medium and low levels of HRD in 1981 showed poor quality of India's urban women resource. But a good progress in the quality of urban women in 1991 became satisfactory as indicated by the majority of 1991 states in medium and high level of HRD. But when we compare the development of urban male human resource with the development of urban female human resource we find that the situation of urban male human resource development was fairly better in both the census years.

Vertical Structure of Urban Human Resource Development

This section deals with the vertical structure of human resource development of urban male and female population and highlights the male-female difference at two points of time (1981 and 1991).

Male-Female Difference (1981): After having a close view of India's urban male-female human resource development differential, it was found that the highest HRD index (0.97) of urban males was in Pondicherry and the lowest value of HRD index (0.53) was in Lakshadweep. Rest of the states were found varying between 0.53 and 0.97 HRD index. The position of Pondicherry, Delhi, Chandigarh, Tripura and Himachal Pradesh in 1981 was fairly good in comparison to other major states and union territories as these states recorded its HRD index well above 0.80. The states having its position between 0.60 and 0.80 HRD index were Andhra Pradesh, Arunachal Pradesh, Assam, Bihar, Daman & Diu and Goa, Gujarat, Haryana, Karnataka, Kerala, Madhya Pradesh, Maharashtra, Manipur, Meghalya, Mizoram, Nagaland, Orissa, Punjab, Tamil Nadu, West Bengal, Andaman & Nicobar Island. The states having less than 0.60 and above 0.52 HRD index were Rajasthan, Sikkim, Uttar Pradesh, Jammu & Kashmir and Dadar & Nagar Haveli (union territory). These states showed quite unsatisfactory human resource situation.

Similarly, in context of human resource development of urban females it was found that the lowest index was 0.20 as shown against Lakshadweep and highest index (0.72) was against Chandigarh. In fact, only Chandigarh and Kerala had better position as its HRD index was above 0.60. The condition of Daman & Diu and Goa, Rajasthan and Lakshadweep was vulnerable. Rest of the major states and union territories had their position between 0.33 and 0.60 HRD index and shows unsatisfactory condition.

The male-female gap of urban human resource development was wider in Pondicherry, Daman & Diu and Goa, Lakshadweep, Delhi, Rajasthan, Uttar Pradesh, Tripura, Orissa, Nagaland, Manipur, Maharashtra, Madhya Pradesh, Karnataka, Haryana, Himachal Pradesh, Gujarat, Bihar, Assam, Andhra Pradesh, Dadar and Nagar Haveli; and it was less wider in Arunachal Pradesh, Kerala, Meghalaya, Mizoram, Punjab, Sikkim, Andaman & Nicobar Islands, Chandigarh. But overall situation of HRD in context of both urban male and female population in 1981 (except few states) was not good.

Male-Female Difference (1991): It is clear that all the states were above 0.44 and below 0.94 HRD index, whereas in context of urban female human resource development all the states were between 0.33 and 0.82 HRD index. The detailed picture of male human resource development shows that only Andaman & Nicobar Islands recorded 0.33 HRD index. Uttar Pradesh, Lakshadweep, Madhya Pradesh, Rajasthan, Mizoram, Assam, Gujarat, Bihar, Haryana, Andhra Pradesh, Delhi, Sikkim, Punjab, Nagaland, Orissa, Meghalya, Manipur, West Bengal,

Karnataka, Arunachal Pradesh were between 0.65 and 0.80 HRD index. These are socio-economically poor states in India. Only Chandigarh, Himachal Pradesh, Goa, Kerala, Maharashtra, Tamil Nadu, Tripura, Dadar & Nagar Haveli, Daman & Diu and Pondicherry were between 0.80 and 0.94 HRD index. These states have relatively better socio-economic condition and have high score of total education.

In comparison to that of males the HRD of females is poorer. Andaman & Nicobar Island, Rajasthan, Uttar Pradesh, Bihar, Dadar & Nagar Haveli, Lakshadweep, Gujarat, Andhra Pradesh and Arunachal Pradesh were between 0.33 and 0.50 HRD index. This is a result of cumulative effect of social, cultural, economic and political factors.

Particularly, Bihar, Uttar Pradesh and Rajasthan are the partners of Bimaru (ill) states. Rest states of India (except Chandigarh with 0.81 and Tripura with 0.82 HRD index) were between 0.50 and 0.78 HRD index. Such states in majority do not have satisfactory progress in female education.

The above male-female difference forms a clear cut gap between urban male and female human resources development. The male-female gap in Bihar, Gujarat, Andhra Pradesh, Arunachal Pradesh, Haryana, Orissa, Rajasthan, Dadar & Nagar Haveli, Daman & Diu, Uttar Pradesh, Pondicherry, Karnataka, Maharashtra was more and in Assam, Goa, Haryana, Himachal Pradesh, Madhya Pradesh, Nagaland, Sikkim, Tamil Nadu, West Bengal, Delhi, Lakshadweep was comparatively less. In Kerala, Mizoram, Tripura, Meghalaya, Punjab, Andaman & Nicobar Islands and Chandigarh was least as most of these are matriarchal and forward looking (towards female education) states.

Vertical Temporal Change in HRD of Urban Male and Female Population

All the states and union territories, except Andaman & Nicobar Islands, Delhi and Pondicherry (male category), had upward movement on the scale of HRD of urban males and females. The downward sliding of Andaman & Nicobar Islands, Delhi and Pondicherry (male category) may be either due to less educational attainment through less enrolment of students particularly at higher level or out-migration of educated persons for jobs and other reasons towards other states.

The length of upward movement (on HRD scale) of urban males between 1981 and 1991 was greater in Assam, Goa, Kerala, Sikkim, Dadar & Nagar Haveli. This shows better progress of these states in terms of development of urban male human resource. The remaining states (mainly bigger states) showed less progress as indicated by shorter length (gap) between 1981 and 1991 on HRD scale which may be due to overall poor development performance of the states.

Similarly, the gap between 1981 and 1991 HRD index points caused by upward movement in urban female human resource development over a period of ten years was much wider in Goa, Nagaland, Tripura and Madhya Pradesh and indicates good progress in urban female human resource development. This may be due to more enrolment of girl students particularly at higher level education and also due to in-migration of educated females through jobs and marriage. The wider gap between 1981 and 1991 HRD was in Himachal Pradesh, Bihar, Assam, Kerala, Manipur, Mizoram, Orissa, Rajasthan, Sikkim, Tamil Nadu and Lakshadweep. The gap was less in Andhra Pradesh, Haryana, Kerala, Maharashtra, Megahalaya, Punjab, Uttar Pradesh, West Bengal, Chandigarh and Dadar and Nagar Haveli. Almost no change in Arunachal Pradesh and a negligible positive change in Gujarat and Delhi were noted. This may be due to almost status quo in overall development of these states.

Conclusions and Suggestions

After having gone through the spatio-temporal analysis of urban male and female human resource development between 1981 and 1991 one finds that the overall development of urban male human resource was comparatively better than that of urban females. This is indicated by the majority of states from both the years in high and very high levels in case of urban males and in medium and low levels (1981) and medium and high levels (1991) in case of urban females. This indicates that the qualitative development of urban male human resource was fairly better than that of the urban female human resource.

In case of urban males Kerala, Tamil Nadu., Maharashtra, West Bengal, Tripura, Himachal Pradesh, Dadar & Nagar Haveli, Daman & Diu, Chandigarh and Goa showed good progress in 1991 from 1981 but most of the major states from central, western, south central and north eastern India did not change their levels. They maintained status quo (high level) in both the years. Therefore, there is need for an effort to uplift them also to very high level HRD range.

Similarly, in case of urban females the performance of HRD in most of the northern, eastern, central, western and north eastern states is not so good. The major reasons of such condition are higher illiteracy, relatively less enrolment of female students at school, college and at university levels; low participation rate in economic activities, poverty, and general backwardness. Western and Southern costal states including Himachal Pradesh, Punjab, Haryana, West Bengal, Arunachal Pradesh, Tripura, Mizoram and Meghalaya had relatively better performance in case of female human resource development. This may be due to some better socio-economic conditions. Therefore, there is need for some special human resource development programmes in almost all the states and union territories for the betterment of the urban female human resource.

It can also be said that generally most of the smaller states and Union Territories showed better HRD performance (in case of both males and females) leaving aside few cases in exception.

The male-female gap on vertical scale of urban HRD (1981) was wider in Pondicherry, Daman & Diu and Goa, Lakshadweep, Delhi, Rajasthan, Uttar Pradesh, Tripura, Orissa, Nagaland, Manipur, Maharashtra, Madhya Pradesh, Karnataka, Haryana, Himachal Pradesh, Gujarat, Bihar, Assam, Andhra Pradesh, Dadar and Nagar Haveli; and it was less wide in Arunachal Pradesh, Kerala, Meghalaya, Mizoram, Punjab, Sikkim, Andaman & Nicobar Islands and Chandigarh. This indicates that the overall situation of HRD in context of both urban male and female population (except few states) was not good.

The gender difference on vertical scale of urban HRD (1991) forms a clear cut gap between urban male and female human resources development. The male-female gap in Bihar, Gujarat, Andhra Pradesh, Arunachal Pradesh, Haryana, Orissa, Rajasthan, Dadar & Nagar Haveli, Daman & Diu, Uttar Pradesh, Pondicherry, Karnataka, Maharashtra was more. This was a reflection of gross educational achievement influenced by several socio-economic factors of respective states. The gender difference in Assam, Goa, Haryana, Himachal Pradesh, Madhya Pradesh, Nagaland, Sikkim, Tamil Nadu, West Bengal, Delhi, Lakshadweep was comparatively less. Kerala, Mizoram, Tripura, Meghalaya, Punjab, Andaman & Nicobar Islands and Chandigarh showed least gender gap as most of these are matriarchal and forward looking (towards female education) states.

The upward movement (as shown on HRD scale) of urban males between 1981 and 1991 was more in Assam, Goa, Kerala, Sikkim, Dadar & Nagar Haveli. This shows better progress of these states in terms of development of urban male human resource. The remaining states (mainly bigger states) showed less progress as indicated by shorter length (gap) between 1981 and 1991 on HRD scale. This may be due to overall poor developmental performance of the states. A downward sliding of Andaman & Nicobar Islands, Delhi and Pondicherry (in male category) was also noted.

The upward movement of urban female human resource development (as measured on vertical scale of HRD) over a period of ten years (1981-1991) was greater in Goa, Nagaland, Tripura and Madhya Pradesh and indicates good progress. This may be due to more enrolment of girl students especially at higher level education and also due to in-migration of educated females through jobs and marriage. The gap between 1981 and 1991 HRD was observed wider in Himachal Pradesh, Bihar, Assam, Kerala, Manipur, Mizoram, Orissa, Rajasthan,

Sikkim, Tamil Nadu and Lakshadweep. The gap was less in Andhra Pradesh, Haryana, Kerala, Maharashtra, Megahalaya, Punjab, Uttar Pradesh, West Bengal, Chandigarh and Dadar and Nagar Haveli. Arunachal Pradesh, Gujarat and Delhi showed a negligible positive change over a decade. This may be due to almost status quo in overall development of these states. Only Andaman & Nicobar Islands showed a downward movement over a decade, which may be due to some certain reasons.

After looking into the above findings and keeping in mind the objective of achieving optimum level of HRD, which would go a long way to make the entire development effort a real success, it would be absolutely necessary to set up an adequate machinery for human resource development at both formal and non-formal educational levels from the very grass root level of the society. Not only this, but also there should be fair allocation and equitable distribution of adequate social, cultural, economic and political infrastructure or resources at all spatial levels in all the states. While doing so special focus should be on the development of human resource of S.C, S.T and of the socio-economically poor people from other section of the society too. Women of all age groups and at all spatial units should be given more priority in utilising the HRD infrastructure. Similar facilities should be made available to those who are not well sheltered, well-fed, well clothed and having no access to education, health, training, food and nutrition etc. Thus, there should be development and proper use of required infrastructure at all spatial units of various types and levels particularly relating to education, health, food, nutrition, shelter etc. for narrowing down substantially the gender gap of HRD and in bringing the urban areas to the road of rapid progress.

References

Das, P.K. and Krak (1988) Identification of Human Resources Development Zones and its Mapping, In Resource Mapping at District Level, Monograph 8, NATMO, Calcutta.

De, N.K. (1988) Mapping of Human Resources in Bankura District, West Bengal, In Resource Mapping at District Level, Monograph 8, NATMO, Calcutta.

Gupta, S.P. Das (1998), Geographical Review of India, Vol. 60, No. 4, December 1998, the Geographical Society of India, Calcutta.

Harbison, F.H. (1973) Human Resource as the Wealth of Nation, Oxford Univ. Press, London.

Harbison, F.H. and Myers, Charles. A. (1964) Education, Manpower and Economic Growth: Strategies of Human Resources Development, McGraw-Hill Book Company, New York.

Kaur, Parminder (1996) Human Resource Development for Rural Development, Anmol

Publications Pvt. Ltd., New Delhi.

Kumar, B. and Hansra, B.S. (2000) Extension Education for Human Resource Development, Concept Publishing Company, New Delhi.

Nalder, L. (1994) The Handbook of Human Resources Development, John Wiley and Sons, New York.

Prodi, R (1996) The Evolution of Economic Organisation in Contemporary Societies, In Barnado, C.; Paul, D and Max, F.P. (1996) Resource and Population, Clarendon Press, Oxford University Press, New York.

Rao, T.V. (1999) HRD Audit: Evaluating the Human Resource Function for Business Improvement, Response Books, A. Division of Sage Publications, New Delhi.

Schultz, T.W. (1961) Investment as Human Capital, American Economic Review, March 1961, Quoted in Ghosh B.N. (1985) Fundamentals of Population Geography, Sterling Publishers, N. Delhi.

Singh, J.P. (1982) Human Resources of North Eastern India, Inter India Publications, New Delhi.

Sinha, B.R.K. (1999) Mapping of Human Resources Development in Rampurhat Block-1 of Birbhum District, West Bengal, In the Indian Journal of Landscape Systems and Ecological Studies, Vol. 22, No. 2, Institute of Landscape, Ecology and Ekistics, Calcutta.

18

Patterns of Urban Living and Quality of Life in Bucharest during the Post-communist Period

Mariana Mirela Nae

Introduction

Bucharest is organised on the basis of the classical model: the old central area (transformed and revitalised over the past decade), a mixed intermediate area with (semi) detached and collective apartment blocks—overwhelmingly those of the communist era that dominate the urban landscape—and a peripheral area heavily influenced by its rural origins (despite recent housing growth) with only limited amenities apart from communist era factories and warehouses and recent housing development.

Through unemployment and suppressed demand for new housing, transition has proved problematic producing widening disparities in status among social groups (generating considerable urban poverty and deprivation—even in comparison with other former communist states) with a lack of political will to contemplate radical action. Although there has been a major shift to private ownership, which has given more respect to the former tenants. There are major contrasts between different areas on the basis of such 'quality of life' indicators as the per capita living space and green space; relations between neighbours and involvement in community/local matters.

Bucharest: from Integrated Residential Urban Space to Relocation Dynamics and Housing Renewal

The urban physiognomy of the capital city is the direct effect of the historical-geographical evolution and is the direct result of the great construction campaigns from the 20th century (1920-1940-1948). Starting with this incredible campaign takes place the process of parcelling with small housing of 1 or 2 floors, which were either isolated or grouped in lots, especially in its intermediary – residential area.

All these mutations will bring about the differentiation of the socio-cultural inequalities and discrepancies between districts. Thus, the central area, that is today a strong economical target and used almost exclusively for the service sector, still keeps reminiscences of the 20th century atmosphere, with blocks of 3 or 4 floors or semi detached houses. The intermediate residential area will be affected in turn by these changes by the emerging parcelled semi detached houses of 2 or 3 floors.

The configuration of the geographical space preserves the traces of the market-town from the second half of the 19th century and is marked by the functional areas of the city from that time. These are *the central part* with narrow streets, inns, different shops along with the big bourgeois houses, gardens and parks; *the residential districts* with small residences with gardens and yards bourgeois houses, situated in the central area or near the Mogoşoaia Bridge (Victoria Avenue of today); *the suburbs*, used agriculturally, situated outside the city's boundaries. This spatial configuration was shaped, changed and transformed by complex urban projects, which were highly necessary to a capital-city that underwent a series of physical-geographical restrictions, and had a lower degree of modernization and with a low quality of life.

The 2000s represented a certain ground mark in the social- economic changes of the city (socio-political changes, investments and entrepreneurial interest in the economic development, urban legislation, new real estate actors, etc). Thus, all these interventions have influenced in time the entire social organization of the city and at the same time the population's quality of life, distinguished and outlined by complex phenomena of social and spatial polarization, (the northern part of the city is more developed compared to the southern one), gentrification, the residential mobility has "rearranged" the social and geographical distances.

Uncontrolled Urban Sprawl and Rise of New Residential Neighbourhoods

The Bucharest spatial physiognomy has acquired the attributes of a transitional space, slower from 1990 and more pronounced after 2000, thus risking an urban chaotic and uncontrolled sprawl, by setting up residential parks and commercial spaces (for example, the neighbourhood Pipera, outside the city, without access to public utilities and the flood problems from 2005-2006). The risks of the uncontrolled urban sprawl can be the source of many shortcomings in the field of urban legislation, directly correlated with the absence of a series or plans and coherent strategies of urban and real estate planning. As a result of these facts, in some areas of the city especially towards the suburbs there have emerged neighbourhoods of semi detached houses, some isolated or not integrated in the urban landscape, without any access roads or public utilities networks (the construction of which implies high costs). As a matter of fact, the big private companies have (re)oriented themselves towards investing *within the city,* exploiting to the maximum the terrains, by sacrificing some green spaces and building tower like vertical block of flats.

The multiple causes and unwanted effects exist the residential and real estate domain (we build a lot and we do it badly), artificially prolonging the agony of (post)transition:

- the lack of clear instruments of measurement of the value of the real estate property, real estate agency that inexactly evaluating it by directly negotiating with the owners;
- launching the mortgage credits on the medium and long term;
- the high level of the prices of the real estate market, as a result of the pressures made by certain interest groups, especially regarding terrains, and real estate brokers (representatives of agencies of speculators);
- the debatable quality of some NRP (new residential parks);
- the spectacular rise of prices in 2003/2004 due to mortgage credits, the fluctuations of the conditions for grating them has given birth to serious dysfunctions on the market;
- the mental factors induced by the media assault two or three years ago regarding the expected growth of the apartments prices as a result of the EU accession or that on the market there is a stock of monetary resources (most of the mortgage credits have been oriented towards the new residential projects)
- the illusion created by the EU accession process by introducing the idea of the growth of the prices per dwelling, usually, the real estate companies will not purchase old dwellings, and will prefer to build new ones, thus the pressure that exists for the already existent blocks will not raise.

Geographical Patterns of Urban living

The urban space represents both the product between the will of the public forces and urban planning, of firms, individual owners of real estate properties, each of them using more or less rational strategies. This complex and chaotic logical of decision and production of the urban space is full of contradictions and oppositions between the actors: pollution, uncontrolled urban sprawl, traffic jams, inflation, high land prices, real estate speculation and behaviour of clandestine passengers are often the bases of the spatial regulations (Humain- Lamoure, Le Goix R., 2006).

As a matter of fact, in Bucharest, the forces that are involved in this game can produce initial phenomena of spatial fragmentation and voluntary aggregation of the population that have a certain cultural and social capital. The causes of the urban fragmentation can be many and complex (Edwards Michael, 1991). Among those we note: the law infringement associated both with the separate decision of the investors, promoters and local power factors and with the visual and functional fragmentation phenomena; the speculative market, the accelerate rhythm of changes that occur in the field of industrial fields; functional locations; costs of the apartments and the transformations of the production organization (Vidal Rojas 2002: 34).

The geographical patterns of urban living are mirrored by a complex mix of factors which could be especially related to the communist heritage within the city: obsolete apartments, high residential densities and reduced medium surfaces of living, including the residential attachment.

The number of persons/dwelling and also the residential density represent undoubtedly one of the most determinants of the quality of living which could give us some suggestive images of spatial differences between the central, semi central or peripheral zones of the city. Areas with high levels of the residential density implies undesirable social temporal effects such as more intergenerational conflicts, a difficult cohabitation between two or more families or social disorganization.

A norm *i.e.* a room/person represents a *sine qua non* condition to a better quality of life in the city. The sensitive issues seem to be more delicate in the communist blockhouses where a reduced median surface of living are predominantly associated to a high multi functionality of the rooms. Thus, the perception of the precarious habitat of living seems to be more recurrent in the collective apartment blocks and also in the peripheral zone with semi detached houses.

According to the late census data (2002), the values of the residential density are situated between 1.56 persons /dwelling (the low value) in central part of the city and 3.81 persons/dwelling (the high value) in the peripheral zone.

The reduced values (1.5–2.00) of this indicator characterizes the central part of the most neighbourhoods considered *chic,* with an urban patrimonial value (Universităţii, Unirii, Calea Victoriei-Bd. Lascăr Catargiu) or the northern part of the city (Calea Dorobanţilor-Bd. Aviatorilor, Herăstrău, Floreasca, Primăverii, Aviaţiei). All this north-central part of the city could be designed in terms of specific urban territoriality.

This urban territoriality could be more visible into a particular appropriation of the urban space, in fact realised by an influential and selected social population groups within specific forms of voluntary aggregation or voluntary regrouping of persons with high income. This is all particularly about a regrouping created especially by the real estate's restrictions, urban areas with a social prestige, mostly revealed by the presence of important addresses, playing the role of a huge symbol (so called the "effect addresses").

The values 2.5–3.00 persons/dwelling are more specific to the peripheral zone, particularly in the southern, western and eastern parts of the city, including the residential communist flats build up beginning to 1950-1960, typically communist neighbourhoods: Berceni, Progresul, Ferentari, Rahova, Pantelimon, Colentina, Dudesti, Giulesti.

The residential model of the most identical communist flats had tried obediently to follow the soviet model based upon "cvartale", *i.e.* an urban unit with reduced surfaces about 5-10 ha and also a density about 3,000 inhabitants/ha.

The high values (up to 3.5) characterized the whole obsolete residential area, in the proximity of the industrial zone, where more industrial units are nowadays in decline or relocated (Industriilor in the 3rd district, Aparatorii Patriei, in the 4th district or S. Alexandriei-Odai, Calea Rahovei in the 5th district).

Changes in the Urban Design of the City During the Post-communist Period

The nowadays restructuring of the post-modern urban spaces bring to our attention more and more to the notions of *urban territoriality* and *neighbourhood* and a central notion of that territoriality. The lack of a series of tangible activities and initiatives of participative planning (advocacy planning), with the citizen, the inexistence of *bottom-up* development strategies and involvement, the absence of an education and mentality of empowerment and civic involvement of the Romanian society have led to significant spatial differences at a city level.

The northern area and central-northern of the city was and will undoubtedly remain the most attractive one especially the perimeter Băneasa - Ion Nicolae, Primăverii, Herăstrău, is always wanted by investors and having the benefits of a series of natural factors, green areas, amenities and numerous recreation or leisure facilities.

The central and semi central areas are rendered profitable by big real estate projects that are either in their beginning phase or approach their finalization. Some of them were placed in closed down areas or on the location of former factories and industrial units (for example the residential complex Central Park, built on the location of the Dâmbovița bread factory, in Ștefan cel Mare neighbourhood). The real estate investors considered not only the residential market but also the office one – type A and B office– or commercial spaces.

The suburb area was less attractive for such projects. The western area presents investing potential (residential, commercial, logistical parks), thanks to the existence of highway. Meanwhile the southern area (Rahova, Ferentari) is continuously avoided except a series of future residential projects.

On the other hand, part of district 4, 3 or 2, some areas from Berceni, Titan or Colentina neighbourhoods will represent the signs of an incipient revitalization, by constructing new neighbourhoods, with different standards and recreation facilities. Unfortunately, many of the city's neighbourhoods have mixed authentic urban morphological standards, proven both by the coexistence of numerous social categories and of the industrial activities, closed down industrial areas and vacant lands. These still bear the marks of their industrial past, with mix parcels, either houses that often don't have basic infrastructures, derelict area or vacant lands, garages and workshops mostly closed down (Mirela Nae, 2008).

The socio-geographical differences of the entire city, especially in the second and fifth districts seem to adjoin to heterogeneous elements of the urban design, transcribing into pavilions and communist blockhouses, the last one almost described as being the workers neighbourhoods.

The central part of the 2nd district is more eclectic with patrimonial villas and pavilions of ancient commercial functions (Barbu Văcărescu-Floreasca-Beethoven, M.I. Glinka-Ceaikovski–Verdi, Str. Polonă), while the semi central part is dominated by the communist neighbourhoods with 8-12 floors like Colentina, Pantelimon, Obor or the functionalist neighbourhoods *Vatra Luminoasă*.

The peripheral zone is characterized by rural antecedence with modest pavilions affected by the suburbanization. The whole residential image is dissected by the obsolete industrial zone along the boulevards such *Gara Obor* boulevard (*Aversa S.A., Mecanică Fină, Sintofarm*) or in its marginal zone (*Pipera, Electronica, IEMA, Helitube, RECO*).

In the first decade of the post transition period (1990-2000), the local authority doesn't tackle the serious problems of the precarious infrastructure, urban development, public services or recreational facilities, due to lack of the financial resources or the absence of an integrated vision of the urban development. This is one of the reasons that some areas are still in decline with waste terrains of rubbish, obsolete industrial zone or neglected neighbourhoods in "ghettoization" process (Obor, Baicului, Pantelimon, Colentina, Fundeni).

Starting with 2004, the local authorities have made an attempt to reconfigure a little bit the "face" of the district by redundant initiatives or superficial ones with a speculative and punctual direction of the life quality domains such as social assistance for the elderly or for the persons with disabilities, ecological actions of the green spaces.

The information provided by the internet communicates lacunas about ecological actions of the greengrocers market, such as Obor and Delfinului, identification of homeless persons and social assistance for Roma population lived in Ostrov, Colentina, Plumbuita, Morarilor neighbourhoods, the consciousness of the civically implication or voluntary actions.

The rising of the EU integration stimulates the urban renovation process, rehabilitation of the neighbourhood's perimeters and modernization of the infrastructure.

The poor dwellings initially designated to members without families and rented by the local authorities for the low income persons have become the key-point for social delinquency phenomena, squatting, drogue consumption or depositing for stolen goods (Baicului neighbourhood).

In these conditions, according to the local major data, the dwellings were taken over by the local major, renovated and modernized with a total investments for 44,5 million lei, afterwards rented or sold out at the local market price or according to the Law 260/2006 (average price 32,000 € for each apartment). Other major investments could transform the urban design of the district by creating underground passages, local market modernization or new modern residential housing parks. New powerful foreign developers have invested in mix functional spaces like *NeoCity Group* or *Hercesa Imobiliaria.*

Obsolete Industrial Zone of the City and its Urban Renovation

The derelict urban area from within the cities or at their suburbs can benefit from a process of hypothetical revitalization, especially in speculative purposes (land estate reserve). Many industrial areas are abandoned especially due to the deindustrialization process and delocalization of some industrial units towards the periphery (including Bucharest and all the major Romanian urban centres).

After 1989, once the markets were opened the communist productive system, based on a centralized and planned structure became obsolete to the new social and economical requirements. Under the pressure of globalization the city had to overcome a series of constraints regarding the distribution of a products and different services related to them. As a result, the "atomization of the factories" has become a current problem, through delocalization or by establishing its core unit within the city and its fabrication units outside its boundaries.

There have been already announced 15 industrial locations that will be relocated and 49 non functional railways courses that used to serve the communist factories.

Strategic investors from the real estate environment have speculated the real estate value of the state patrimony. Apart from its esthetical and functional characteristics, the industrial patrimony has an important identity or role for the city or neighbourhood, transmitting its memory. Although of great identity value, this heritage is affected and threatened, seldom neglected, and usually associated, in the collective memory, with a "very sad memory".

Pierre Nora (1984:25) sustains that a memory represents a "significant material or ideal unit, which, by the will of the people and the passing of time, has become a symbolic element of any community". Unfortunately, this symbolic element is not sufficiently explored and emphasized upon large scale projects.

The central and semi central areas are benefited from urban projects, using either communist factories, or old abandoned buildings, called *circuri ale foamei* [1], turned into modern and complex commercial centres like *malls* (*Plaza Romania, Vitan Mall, City Mall, Liberty Centre)* or even private universities headquarters like the *Dimitrie Cantemir* University.

Important Disparities in the Urban Design within the City

Even if for the other administrative units, there are some positive and symbolic elements for an improved life quality or for the presence of the natural advantages, amenities, with a specific urbanity and patrimonial values (except *Cotroceni* area). In southern part of the city (5th district), these elements are not recognizable for their citizens anymore.

This is a zone that seems to be organically more segmented and "fractured" of the city, with an urban desolated and dissonant landscape, especially in the peripheral area, with a profile to a rural antecedence, where the urban fragmentation is more visible in the proximity of the obsolete industrial zone (e.g. the neighbourhood *Zăbrăuţi* with the ghetto status inhabited predominantly by the Roma population). The entire administrative unit is "dissected" by the industrial zone (*RECOM, Uzinele Chimice Române, Vulcan - Electromagnetica, Excelent, Muntenia, Rocar*, etc). Some of these communist plants should be relocated, becoming nowadays a preferred target for the new developers, especially for the urban regeneration activities (e.g. *Vulcan*).

The residential duality is conferred by the two opposite areas: the north, north- western by the *Cotroceni* area, with a good image, dominated by *chic* villas owned by middle income families vs. the south, south-western (a typically rural area) with pavilions without basic amenities (lack of the infrastructure) and communist flats. Such geographical contrast is doubled by a social one, by a negative image which had been perpetuated due to the presence of the predominant Roma population located here (especially Rahova and Ferentari neighbourhoods, well known in the collective memory to the *Ferentexas* or *Ghettoland*).

This stereotype construction was made throughout composite images and social representations about an area or a neighbourhood based on information collected from different sources. It's all about the pejoratives connotations to what that mean, the symbolic geographies which could reconfigure entirely the geographical space by creating new territories.

The constitutive attributes created through time a negative image, based especially on different stereotypes, related to Roma population, have been also real social elements such as the presence of the ghettos, social disorganization, vulnerable social persons, smuggling and gangs, prostitution or drogue dealers.

In Zabrăuți ghetto, the majority of the Roma population is immigrant originated from small towns around the city, like Giurgiu and Oltenita. They are very poor; their typical survival techniques are very different. Their behavioural characteristics are different as they are day labourers or the informal commercial persons. After they earn some little money, they spend it or they prefer to find out the people who lend out money at usurious rates of interest.

The social image is formed by the predominance of the low income families, unemployment (3-5 percent), especially in the Ferentari and Salaj neighbourhoods, with a mixed urban design (collective apartments and individual dwellings) which could enhance the patterns of a poor and obsolete zone area of the city.

During the post transition period, main activities/initiatives related to new urban development and configuration have, unfortunately, not been taken into consideration or applied here, except some activities in order to rehabilitate scholar units (for subliminal electoral reasons), greengrocer markets modernization (*Piata Rahova*), the transformation of the communist boutiques type *Alimentara* into popular cheap units designated for the poor people with low income or for the retired persons, called *magazine tip economat* or actions to so called rehabilitation of the blockhouses, in fact some cosmetic or aesthetical operations of the *façade* of the communist flats realised by the local authorities in the past few years.

This zone hasn't represented the interest of major developers, except for the local commercial activities in *Cotroceni* or 13 *Septembrie* neighbourhoods. The big projects which have to become a key point into valorisation of this area, is the *Liberty Centre*, a mall which will be constructed on the ancient place of a communist ruin construction (known and remain in collective memory to "*circul foamei*").

The peripheral zone is still confronted with a big infrastructure issue, especially water canalization. The financial resources of the local authorities have been dissipated into useless and furtive auctions, misappropriations or disagreements and conflicts between the residents and the local major, plaints and petitions unsolved.

Homogeneity of the Social Urban Morphology

The social component defines an urban territory by giving it its significant characteristics with (in) direct effects upon the quality of life. The income creates and determines a different accessibility related to the basic needs of the population. The differences are induced by the level of education or age mark important social-territorial repartitions, but such differences are perceived at a lower level or at a micro-geographical scale. Thus, the overall character of a social homogeneity or the level of the urban territory, with some exceptions of course, depending on activity sectors or types of professional groups is indeed relevant.

The social homogeneity overlaps with the homogeneity of the urban habitat, either individual or collective, with influences that have repercussion upon the life style, upon a more or less degraded urban habitat. Such social-professional concentrations, more or less homogeneous, result also through the existence of certain logic imposed the market mechanisms for the access to a better dwelling, determined particularly by financial constrains.

The lack of efficient and coherent housing policies can influence the perpetuation of the apartment's crisis, the degradation of the collective habitat, pretty obsolete, their transformation into popular neighbourhoods (having the status of modest social residence), and decline of the standard of living of the certain group of population. Therefore, many families will be constrained to choose these kind of dwellings, bought at very high prices on the market, but labelled as being social (term used regarding the physical residential parameters, said to be under the required standards). This degradation of the urban habitat is found in all the dimensions of life leading to restrictions towards other everyday life requirements or basic services (health, recreation and leisure).

One can say that the level of income corroborated with the social-professional morphology configuration marks and determines life styles shaped exclusively after them (with the risk of giving the income level a deterministic significance). In order to attenuate the discrepancies between the rich and the poor persons, different solutions were sought, like projects of urban renovation or adequate housing policies. The purpose of these was to limit the concentration of low income families in sensible neighbourhoods, with social dwellings, by certain modalities of attracting the high income population to those areas.

The professed objective of this policy was to diminish the differences between rich and the poor people, sustaining a idea that a more heterogenic mixture of people with different social and cultural heritage will have a positive effect upon the families and persons less favoured (after the French example from 1996, of the program (*Pacte de relance de la ville)*.

In the manner, there could be opportunities of improvement of the image of sensible districts, the social cohesion would be consolidated, the chance of equality could be guaranteed, and the quality of life would be better. Unfortunately, this mixed social policy is on the limit of an urban utopia, the objective of social diversity not being mostly realized.

The territorial distribution of the social and professional categories, on activity sectors, shows an overall *relative homogeneity of the socio-professional urban morphology,* with slight exceptions, like the concentration of a series of categories that are more advantaged, with a structure employment in services and high-order services in certain areas or neighbourhoods (even a socio-spatial segregation is obvious in some areas of districts 1 - Herăstrău - Aviației - Primăverii, Banu Manta - I. Mihalache - Turda - Domenii, 3 - Unirii - Centru Civic - Piața Alba Iulia - Bd. Decebal - Calea Călărași - Matei Basarab or 5 in Cotroceni neighbourhood).

The inequalities of the territorial distribution of the socio-professional categories are determined mostly by the income level and the financial power of population, depending on which they have access to a better dwelling enjoying qualitative services, thus having a higher quality of life, some of them being more advantaged then others.

The distribution of population in the service sector also determines spatial discrepancies within the census units. The lesser percentages under 50 percent are found at the periphery of the city, in the 3rd district, in the proximity of the Republica industrial platform, in Industriilor neighbourhood in the eastern part of the city.

The areas surrounding the 2nd district (parts of Baicului - Obor, Pantelimon neighbourhoods), 3rd (Titan - Bd. 1 Decembrie1918, Vitan - Dudești), 4th (Apărătorii and Patriei neighbourhoods, and partially Berceni and Progresu), most of the southern part of the 5th district namely Rahova and Ferentari neighbourhoods, part of Roșu-Militari and the proximity of the Laromet industrial platform (Chitilei Av. - Marginei Av. – Mimozei Av.) from the 1st district is characterized by a population involved in the service sector in proportion of 50–60 percent. Percentage of population engaged in service sector in the rest of the central and semi central districts was between 60 and 70, while more than 70 percent population was found in some parts of the central and north-central area of the city Aviației, Primăverii, Dorobanți, Universitate, Dacia Av., Unirii - Calea Călărași) or Cotroceni area.

Perception of the Income Level from the Perspective of the Quality of Life

Inquires made regarding the degree of satisfaction/dissatisfaction of the urban population have the advantage of reviewing both the strong and weak points of the activities made by the local or central authorities. These have a direct effect on the elements that lead to the improvement of quality of life of the inhabitants, but, knowing the opinion of the population allows for a series of actions to be made indirectly by the local authorities. In order to answer the complex issue of the quality of life in Bucharest and in order to verify the hypothesis, author's inquiry consisted of a double process of observation, build on a geographical base of general-urban perspective and on the other hand of a local perspective of the area and districts. The general analysis is supplemented by a local one by presenting the specific representation of the dimensions of the quality of life at a territorial level.

The investigation of the inequalities and the social-spatial representations implied the adjustment of the research methods to the geographical and statistical reality. In general, hypothesis is tested by the data collected from the 2002 population census and from the personal interviews conducted especially on 36 marked perimeters, made at equal time intervals for a term of four years: 1998, 2004, 2005 and 2006.

The elements that make up the personal quality of life are extremely complex and are related or associated differently depending on numerous variables (gender, education, social-professional background, age, social-cultural environment, etc.). Thus, all the elements pertaining to each aspect of life have a more or less powerful effect in the local relation: quality of life – individual.

In order to have a synthetic overview of the importance of everyday issues that influence in a more or less negative degree the quality of life, the inquired people were asked to name two of these elements: concern for their personal health status, the state of the environment (pollution), precarious housing conditions, negative social relations, low perspectives for finding a job in the city (unemployment), bad working relations, low incomes and stressed family relations.

The personal quality of life varies a lot depending on the level of education and gender distribution. If we are to mark their importance, one can see that for the more disadvantaged social-professional sections of the population (pensioners, unemployed people, housewives and workers) level of education starts with low income and bad living condition and health issues. These are the first three variables in order of their importance that have a negative influence of their life environment.

A very interesting fact is that a negative social relations (social disorganisation, anomy, incivility, delinquency) and bad working relationships exist on the last position with "0" importance. Also, the investigation of the main (negative) fears about the personal quality of life is very important, because it can reveal characteristics of the citizen profile.

Thus, the data gathered through the inquires show the following differentiations of *the negative elements* upon the quality of life: low income (52.6 percent), pollution (35 percent), concern regarding the personal health status (34.9 percent), unemployment (21.6 percent), negative social relations (16.8 percent), precarious housing conditions (16.7 percent), tensioned family relationships (13.5 percent) and conflicts at the working place (9.1 percent).

In addition to this, the profile of the social professional class characterizing the poor neighbourhoods related to the quotidian anxiety or the fear for the future substantially touching the life quality is constructed through some hierarchical elements such as income family, precarious housing conditions, personal health status or unemployment (Table 18.1).

Table 18.1: Negative Elements Affecting the Life Quality Considering the Secondary Education Form (personal survey data)

Rank	Variable	Importance	Education form	Profession/Statute
1.	Low income	+	Secondary education form	Unemployment Retired person Housekeeper Worker
2.	Precarious housing conditions	+		
3.	Personal health status	+		
4.	Unemployment	+		
5.	Pollution in the city, conflict families relationship	+		
6.	Negative social relationship	-		
7.	Work tensional relationship	-		

+ with importance
- without importance

The hierarchical importance of the elements affecting the life quality seems more different in the case of the residents with high college education form. The low income and the health status are more important than precarious housing conditions variable or the negative social relationship (Table 18.2).

Table 18.2: Negative Elements Affecting the Life Quality Considering the High College Education Form (personal survey data)

Rank	Variable	Importance	Education form	Profession/Statute
1	Low income	+	High College education form	Student
2	Personal health status	+		Retired person
3	Pollution in the city	+		Employee
4	Unemployment	+		Worker
5	Conflict families relationship	+		
6	Precarious housing conditions	+		
7	Negative social relationship	+		
8	Work tensional relationship	-		

\+ with importance

\- without importance

Significant changes appear at the social-professional categories that have a higher education level. This can have different explanations: higher living standards, social-cultural differences, value systems, mentalities and a specific *modus vivendi*. Therefore, the pollution or the precarious state of the environment is their first concern that influences their health status; also social and domestic conflicts are more important for them than for other social-professional categories. The precarious living conditions and unemployment are not less important. The social homogeneity overlaps with the homogeneity of the urban habitat, either individually or collectively, with influences that have repercussion upon the life style, upon a more or less degraded urban habitat. These social-professional concentrations, more or less homogeneous, results also through the existence of certain logic imposed on the market mechanisms for the access to a better dwelling, determined particularly by financial constrains. The geographical analysis of the life quality can be realized on several research levels, out of which the most important ones are the spatial and social perspectives.

The urban territory bears the indubitable mark of these dimensions, both at individual and collective levels. The spatial analysis of the urban life quality can be detached from the urban social representation of the inhabitant; so knowing the way the people perceive quality of life but also reveal the reference criteria (resulted from the intensity of frequency or their main dimensions) that will remain the main dimensions and levers for obtaining a diagnostic.

Conclusions

The Bucharest urban space has without a doubt the signs of an almost uncontrolled urban sprawl, mostly due to the real dysfunctions of the nowadays urban planning legislation. The role of the local public administration, in particular, needs to be consolidated in order to apply serious project of urban revitalization. The immediate results refer to the legislative process and the local authorities and encouraging the public-private partnerships (PPP).

Unfortunately, the attractive offers of the new residential parks and new neighbourhoods in different construction stages (approximately 80) are considered to be palliative, especially for the lower middle classes, for which there does not exists some advantages offers yet.

We can discus about a *financial dynamic*, as a result of the financial capitalism, for promoters and investors that aim the areas with spatial natural amenities (parks and lakes). We are confronted with *growing phenomena of readjustment of the integrated residential neighbourhoods*, circumstantial phenomena without any continuity of vision or projects.

Urban and social groups working with competent institutions should realize *diagnostic and intervention analysis* by involving all the urban actors in order to increase the urban life quality. Also, there should be stimulated all the subventions possibilities even up to 90 percent in certain areas that have privileged initiatives, like areas of readjustment of the habitat centres and districts by applying integrated policies of revitalization.

The territorial distribution of the social-professional categories, from activity sectors, reveals a *relative homogeneity of the social-professional urban morphology,* with some exceptions like the concentration of a series of advantaged groups belonging mostly to the service and high-order service sector in some preserved neighbourhoods.

Meanwhile, the suburbs of the city that overlap with the communist residential parks or the peripheral habitat, are underrepresented in terms of a percentage of an elite formed by businessmen or employers.

The differences brought about by the level of education or age mark important social-professional repartitions are visible mostly at a small scale or at a micro-geographical level. An investigation of the public perception of the current income from the perspective of the life quality, depending on the basic needs of the population, can reveal a series of characteristics of the urban profile.

If we have to form a hierarchy of the elements that have a negative effect upon the quality of life, one can see that in fact the low incomes are the most important ones, before pollution of the environment of the personal state of health.

Note

1. Circul Foamei: It is an expression related to an architectural form and urban design referring to a cupola or huge 'cirque' and ironically reflecting Ceausescu's megalomania for huge state shops ('complexe alimentare') generally unfinished in 1989 since these great works of urban reconfiguration were delayed by the priority for exports to pay off foreign debts.

References

Anne -Lise Humain- Lamoure, Le Goix R.,(2006), *Points chauds sur la ville, La Géographie urbaine, au defi de la métropolisation*, „Géopoint," p.4, Angers.

Edwards Michael (1991), *Fragmentation dans le contexte urbain*, "Architecture et comportement", vol.7, No. 4, p.339-348

Élisabeth-Dorrier Apprill (dir.) (2001), *Vocabulaire de la ville, Notions et références*, Éditions du Temps, Paris.

http://halshs.archives-ouvertes.fr/docs/00/25/82/16/PDF/GP06C_rlg_alh.pdf (accesat pe 10 mai 2008)

Nae Mariana Mirela (2008), *La taille des logements, densité et attachement résidentiels – facteurs limitatifs de l'habitat urbain bucarestois à l'impact visible sur la qualité de vie*, « Analele Universităţii Bucureşti », Editura Universităţii din Bucureşti.

Nora P., (1984) (dir.), *Les lieux de mémoire; vol . I : La République*, Gallimard, Paris.

Vidal Rojas Rodrigo (2002), *Fragmentation de la ville et nouveaux modes de recomposition urbaine*, L'Harmattan, Paris.

19

Women Participation in Dairying: A Case Study of Rajasthan, India

M.K. Khandelwal

Dairy development plays a vital role in the subsistence economy of Rajasthan particularly in rural and semi urban areas. In view of the frequent occurrence of droughts and famines adversely effecting agriculture, a large section of the population is bound to dependent on the livestock. Infect, as an important component of mixed farming system, bovine rearing has always been an integral part of the Indian rural life for several centuries. By virtue of its environment, animal husbandry is the only major occupation especially in western Rajasthan, where scarcity of water, vegetation coupled with adverse climate has made the life of population miserable.

It is very much pertinent to emphasis upon the dairy industry, not only to fulfil the demand of milk add milk products to urban areas and for the physical development of child, pregnant and lactating women, but also from the employment point of view for unemployed and housewives in recent years in Rajasthan. Even today it is a symbol of material prosperity among the rurals. Dairying has been a part and parcel of Indian culture and civilization from ancient period and remains so even today. The importance of cattle in the economic recognized by our ancestors, they elevated the cow of the level of 'Mother' and incorporated the protection of cow as an integral part of their religion and culture. This sentiment continues with the Indian masses and it is a big tool in development of Indian dairy industry on scientific lines.

Selection of the Problem and Study Area

Participation of women in India in dairy farming is dominating since the beginning of Hindu culture and civilization from ancient time and even today. Hence, women are the real milk producers who spent lot of time in dairy activities at home.

Dairy farming has significant importance at present time. Dairying is not considered as an occupation, but it is a supplementary activity of crop farming in India. Both agriculture and livestock are the interdependent. However, in other countries it is an occupation. Hence, it is desirable that the integrated development strategy of the needs and requirements of the crop farming for supply feed and fodder for livestock population be kept in mind. It is fact that bovine keeping is a supplementary economic activity in the country; it also provides additional employment and income to the farmers. Crop farming does not provide income regularly to seasonal fluctuation and drought conditions. But, during farming gives steady and regular income, reduces the oscillations in the farmers income. Milching animals are the assets in the form of liquid, which can be converted into cash whenever needed. The significance of dairy development is increased with the income elasticity. Whole state of Rajasthan has been taken into consideration for study purpose. In arid, semi-arid region of the state ladies participation is increasing fast and dominating.

Milk cooperative is an organizational institution where processing and manufacturing of milk has been undertaken. Hence, dairy development through milk cooperatives can be evaluated. In rural areas adoption of dairying by women in arid and semi-arid region is a supplementary occupation in Rajasthan.

Objectives of this paper are:

- to examine the participation of women in dairy in rural areas.
- to examine the employment generation for women by dairy.
- to analyse the organizational and functional pattern of milk cooperatives.
- to examine the various policies and programmes of milk cooperatives with respect to enhancement of milk production and adoption of dairy farming by women to strengthen them.

Animal husbandry and dairy farming is the most dominating supplementary occupation in arid and semi-arid areas of the State, in which women participation is very significance. All the related activities of dairy are done by women. Therefore, number of the ladies milk societies increased at large scale in the state of Rajasthan. The ladies participation is the good sign of progress in the state from which rural poor masses economically benefited from dairy. It has a most significance in job orientation for rural masses.

Methodology

Data have been collected from both primary and secondary sources. In order to have concrete idea of economy of dairy farming and livestock management practices sample societies of milk cooperatives of Jodhpur, Bikaner and Jaipur district were selected. Livestock owners, farmers, ladies were interviewed about the management of livestock including grazing of animals, collection of grass from field, providing of milk to societies etc.

While examining the contribution of animal husbandry and dairy development programmes in Kerala, K.N. Nair (1979) concluded that there was a considerable increase in productivity of milch animals and total milk production in Kerala during the period 1964-65 to 1975-76. It was largely due to the increase in level of feeds inputs of milch animals. In recent studies the emphasis has shifted on analysing the problems and possibilities of developing dairying as an instrument of social and economic upliftment of weaker sections in rural areas. B.L. Jain and Avadh Prasad (1982) observed that organised marketing has positive impact on the milk yield in Bikaner region. I.J. Singh, A.C. Gangawar and I.R. Chakravarty (1979) have found in Haryana that the cost of milk production from cow was lowest in summer and the highest in winter. In the case of buffalo, it was highest in summer and lowest in rainy season. National Commission on Agriculture (1971), reveals that 70 to 75 percent of the households possessing cattle, according to the size of land holding in different areas of country, belong to the category of small and marginal farmers and agricultural labourers. They are already keeping milk animals to supplement their income. Thus, dairying by and large is a small man's business.

D.S. Thakur (1974) stated that dairying is especially suited to the weaker section with small land base and abundant labour force. A.H. Somjee and Geeta Somjee (1978) observed in village of Kaira district (Gujarat) that mostly people from the lower status of the community have benefited as a result of milk cooperatives. They increased their land holding as well as number of buffaloes possessed by them and they have used their daily income to pay off their loans, for repairing of dwelling houses and meeting wedding expenses etc. S.M. Patel, D.S. Thakur and M.K. Pandey (1977) have observed that the milk cooperatives are of considerable benefit to the weaker sections in the villages, provided these people own milch animals and their milk is accepted by the milk societies. B.K. Narayan (1971) studied the milk unions of Gujarat state and found that it has brought out a change in attitude, enterprise and way of life. It embraces a large percentage of the rural population and provides opportunities for earning substantial additional income. Women folks find in it a way to utilize their spare time productivity, P.K. Das (1978), Surendra Singh (1979), Haria, V.K. (1980), S.S. Grewal and D.S. Rangi (1980) and number of other educationist, scientists worked on dairy development. They advised that the women participation in dairying is more beneficial and time utilizing when they are having not any kind of employment.

The study of the participation of women in dairy development become as essential and important exercise as there are abundance of potentialities and possibilities to participation of women in dairy development.

Dairying is the major industry after agriculture farming to provide employment opportunities in rural masses in the state. It was studied of Bikaner Milk Union and found that in the rural areas where there are more than one milch animal in mostly households, it is a major source of family labour input. It was replied that by the cattle households that the dairying is their family occupation which avails them substitute of food, income and employment round the year. It was noticed that about 90 percent of cattle house hold employed 100 percent of their women labour for livestock serving with agricultural activities. All the tasks included grazing of animals collection of grass, bathing of animals, cleaning of cattle shed and feed, milking and feeding the various feed stuffs done by the women. India has major proportion of world's livestock wealth, buffaloes, sheeps, goats and camels are the significant livestock breeds contributing considerably to the national income of the country. The dairy farming has two distinct features in India, which distinguish it from the dairy industry in other countries. In India the farmers generally domesticate bovines for the supply of milk and drought power, rather then for getting milk and meat in western countries. It has not only been considered as an occupation, but also regarded as an activity which supplements the agriculture.

Origin of Organized Dairying

Organization of cooperatives is the most successful sector for production, procurement, processing and marketing of milk in the world. This kind of agencies has been working efficiently in the countries where there is a large production of milk, such as Denmark, Sweden, Australia, New Zealand and the U.S.A. The first dairy cooperative society in India was established at Allahabad (U.P.) in 1913. For supply of clean pasteurized milk to consumers a dairy cooperative organization was established as Kolkata Milk Supply Society Union in 1919. During the pre-independence period some dairy farms were established by private entrepreneurs, military cantonments, princely estates, charity institutions and the Indian Agricultural Research Institute. Such milk colonies were set up at Aarey (Mumbai), Haringhata (Kolkata), Madhuvaran (Chennai). There after at large scale and systematic dairy cooperatives in India was established in 1948 by Kaira District Cooperatives Milk Producers Union Ltd. at Anand. This unit produced milk products for market located all over the country and provided technical inputs for milk production enhancement. The Kaira Union emerged as a pioneer in milk cooperative movement in India.

Operation Flood Programme

In 1965 National Dairy Development Board (NDDB) was set up at Anand in pursuance of a government directive. The NDDB draw up a programme known as "Operation Flood", it was largest in the world dairy development programme which under took the gigantic task of upgrading and modernizing milk production, procurement and marketing. Rajasthan Dairy Development Project was launched in July, 1970 and it is one of the three dairy development projects implemented in India with the assistance from International Development Association (IDA) of World Bank. Then the Rajasthan Cooperative Dairy Federation was set up in 1978 to give an extended boost to the dairy programmes.

The Operation Flood-I, II, III and IV were extended to the year 2000-2001. It covers 32 districts of the state. The major activities envisaged under Operation Flood are formulation of village level milk producers cooperative societies by the milk unions enrollment of membership in the cooperatives, implementation of technical input programmes for bread improvement, animal health care, distribution of fodder, seed for fodder development, sale and supply of balanced cattle feed.

Organizational Pattern

The organizational pattern of milk cooperatives in the State is a three-tier structure. It envisaged the organization of milk producers into a primary dairy cooperative society (DCS) at the village level. At the district/division level milk producer cooperative union have been established. At present all the district dairy unions are the constituent members of the Rajasthan Cooperative Dairy Federation (RCDF). There are 16 district dairy unions in the State. Thus, some of the unions have members from more than one district, for instance the Jodhpur union affiliates the societies (units) in Jodhpur, Jaisalmer, Barmer and Nagaur districts. Similarly, Tonk union affiliates Tonk and Sawai Madhopur district. Dungarpur/Banswara union registered societies from both districts. At the same pattern, Sikar and Jhunjhunu have jointly registered union. RCDF is engaged in supplying good quality milk and milk products to the customers. It provides animal health facilities for cattle feed and make all efforts to get fair price to milk producers. 14 dairy plants and 24 chilling centres are engaged in collection of milk at present. Their capacity of milk collection is 13.5 lakh litres and 3.5 lakh litres per day respectively. There are 4 cattle feed mills which capacity is 400 tons.

In Rajasthan 4 milk unions were registered in 1972-73 year which increased to 12 in 1981-82 year and in 2001-2002 year 16 milk unions perfectly and efficiently working. During the year 1972-73 year 32 DCS were registered and in which 27 DCS were working. In the year 1995-96 4931 DCS were registered and 2967 were functioning with incentives provided by the NDDB, in 2001-2002 year 6306 DCS have registered in which 4174 DCS were effectively working.

The trend of milk procurement have been recorded, it was 0.05 lakh litres in 1972-73 year, 5.48 lakh litres in 1985-86, 7.81 lakh litres in 1999-2000 year and 10.52 lakh litres during 2001-2002 year per day average were obtained (Table 19.1). It was very interesting that in January, 2002 milk procurement has been recorded 15.19 lakh litres per day which was highest milk procurement in north India. This production of milk was more than Punjab, Uttar Pradesh and Haryana states (Table 19.1).

Table 19.1: Trend in Procurement of Milk by Cooperatives in Rajasthan from 1972-73 to 2000-2001

Year	No. of Milk Unions	No. of Societies		Membership (in 000)	Milk procurement per day (average) (lakh litre)	Amount paid (Rs. lakh)	Average price paid per litre (Rs.)
		R	F				
72-73	4	32	27	1	0.05	5	0.88
73-74	5	124	83	5	0.12	50	1.02
74-75	7	346	274	10	0.36	150	1.24
75-76	7	691	615	24	0.88	460	1.42
76-77	7	1196	905	52	1.82	910	1.36
77-78	9	145	1064	72	2.10	1080	1.41
78-79	10	1721	1215	87	2.36	1270	1.47
79-80	10	1989	1365	105	2.22	1280	1.58
80-81	10	2202	1474	121	1.75	1070	1.71
81-82	12	2352	1654	135	2.06	1487	1.99
82-83	12	2551	1624	150	2.88	2267	2.16
83-84	14	2782	165	167	3.09	2502	2.22
84-85	14	3095	2002	197	4.95	4629	2.56
85-86	16	3477	2474	226	5.48	5364	2.68
94-95	16	4764	2757	363	3.06	6259	5.68
95-96	16	4931	2967	370	4.20	10885	7.09
96-97	16	5049	3269	376	5.43	14451	7.29
97-98	16	5205	3352	385	6.61	19210	7.96
98-99	16	5380	3386	400	7.17	22451	8.58
99-00	16	5595	3571	415	7.8	26238	9.18
01-02	16	6306	4174	436	8.86	30961	9.57

R = Registered; F = Functional

Source: Rajasthan Cooperative Dairy Federation, Jaipur, 2003.

Payment was made to the milk producers Rs. 5.00 lakh in 1972-73 year; Rs. 1070 lakh in 1985-86 year; Rs. 4551 lakh in 1991-91 year; Rs. 30317 lakh in the year 2001-2002. It is a good sign of increasing of income of the rural milk producers, RCDF providing all kinds of infrastructure, technical inputs to the milk producers, hence, they are gaining faith, good income and are being prosperous (Table 19.1).

Manufacturing of Milk Products

The major technological and refrigeration innovations enhanced the growth of dairy industry. It was the major problem of conservation of milk before operation flood programme was launched in the country. At that time India was importing large quantity of milk powder and other products. During the flush period quantity of milk increased and rates decreased in market. Hence, a significant amount of surplus milk has been converted into various products. The dairy industry has made efforts to convert milk into ghee paneer (cheese), butter, SMP, WMP, Chhachh, Lassi, Shri Khand, and various other products. During the year 1985-86 ghee production was 3420 ton, SMP 2500 ton, WMP 1397 ton, butter 1742 ton and paneer 16 ton, which increased with the demand of urban consumers, tendency of consuming of various milk products. Hence, the products of ghee was 6030 ton, SMP 1480 ton, WMP 584 ton and butter 141 ton during the year 2001-2002.

Women Participation in Dairying

Participation of women in India in dairy farming is dominating since the beginning of Hindu culture and civilization from ancient time and remains so even today. Women have been the kingpins in the home and farm economy in rural areas. Hence, rural women are called "Treasure of her Husband". Which describing about Jat community of Haryana state, Darting (1925) said "Jatani is an economic treasure". "A Jat wife for me, all the rest is a more waste of money", says a Multani proverb. In rural areas women power is engaged in some work or labour. They do plough or drive a cart. All types of agricultural and dairy farming activities done by them. Majority of them form invisible category of works from the years of planners. Maximum women avoided in distribution the fruits of growth and development. But during the past decades it was observed and explicitly recognised that the development process and discrimination against women as it is against weaker section of society, while the role of them was not recognised in rural development and upliftment.

Women Dairy Cooperative Societies (WDCS)

Women are the real milk producers, who spent lot of time in dairy activities at home. With this reason and awakening towards the education, it had been decided to be given participation in milk societies. Therefore, number of lady members has been registered as a member of WDCS in all the milk unions of the State. Jaipur Milk Union having highest 292 DCS of women and in decreasing orders were recorded 218; 108; 58; 57; 57 WDCS in Bhilwara, Pali, Ganganagar, Bikaner and Ajmer respective milk unions during the year 2000-2001. Therefore, number of ladies milk WDCS increased at large number up to 1040 ladies dairy milk societies (Table 19.2) on the basis of large scale participation of women only women milk societies have been registered, where all activities of the society are being performed by women themselves. The ladies participation is really a good sign of progress in the State. Increasing coverage of number of villages under cooperative movement has been started. Therefore, the women participation during Tenth Five Year Plan was proposed to organize about 2770 WDCS of women milk producers.

Table 19.2: Women Dairy Cooperative Societies (WDCS) And Their Membership in Different Milk Unions of Rajasthan during the Year 2000-2001

S. N	Milk Unions	Women DCS of Total	Women Members of Total
1.	Ajmer	57	5666
2.	Alwar	11	9470
3.	Banswara	39	968
4.	Bharatpur	4	1510
5.	Bhilwara	218	137715
6.	Bikaner	57	3774
7.	Churu	26	1281
8.	Sri Ganganagar	58	-
9.	Jalore	5	1451
10.	Jaipur	292	20480
11.	Jodhpur	73	5730
12.	Kota	3	1293
13.	Pali	108	5727
14.	Sikar	30	756
15.	Tonk	25	1238
16.	Udaipur	34	1711
	Total	1040	74830

Source: Rajasthan Cooperative Dairy Federation, Jaipur and Field Survey 2003, year.

Registered Women Member in DCS

With increase of education, awakening and incentives given by government the membership in dairy cooperative societies is being increasing rapidly during past decade. Strengthen the ladies. WDCS by creating transparency in the democratic system has been taken up in good progress. It boost up the confidence of milk producers in cooperative and more ladies milk producers associated with the movement of dairy. Hence, the ladies membership during the year 2000-2001 was recorded highest 20,480 DCS in Jaipur dairy cooperative milk union. It was observed the membership in decreasing order 13775 in Bhilwara, 9470 in Alwar, 5727 in Pali, 5666 in Ajmer milk union and so on. Involvement of members as a whole in the State in different unions was 74,830 during the same period. In ladies WDCS, milk collection, testing of milk, maintenance of record, making of payment, milk marketing, and providing balance cattle feed, technical and infrastructure inputs works are doing by the women only.

Women Development Programme

In the year 1991 a long step was taken by the Ministry of Human Resources, Government of India for women development and independent participation in dairy co-operative milk societies. The programme of development of ladies, it was started in Western Rajasthan Milk Union Ltd. (WRMUL) Jodhpur. At that time in 50 villages women dairy cooperative societies registered only for ladies, in which all kind of activities were performed by the women only. During the year 1999 in WRMUL, Jodhpur 72 Women Milk Cooperative Societies (WDCS) were registered where as in (Uttari Rajasthan Milk Union Ltd.), Bikaner 57 women milk cooperative societies enrolled for registration. The activities performed by ladies in WDCS were to collect the milk, to test the milk, to check up the fats, registered the new lady members, prepare the pass books, maintenance of accounts, to organise fortnight/monthly meetings to make the payments, to provide the technical inputs, selling of cattle feed, marketing of milk and milk products. The women milk societies involve in other activities which are gainful to them, such as stitching, spinning, weaving, ladies adult education and number of self employed activities supplements their income. These dairy societies started the works of sanitation, child care, female training, literacy, community welfare, vaccination, distribution of piles to birth control etc. programmes of women development.

During 1999 year 5,699 women members were registered of WDCS in WRMUL, Jodhpur. Two dairy societies as Malavas and Roopnagar at the first time in India at the dairy cooperative society level the women prepared 1128 National Cooperative Flags during the year 1995 and send them to Uttar Pradesh,

Madhya Pradesh, Andhra Pradesh, Karnataka and Orissa states. It provided the employment to unemployed women in the areas.

In the year 2000-2001 the URMUL, Bikaner have recorded milk procurement by their women participants. During past few years drought and famine conditions prevailing, but the government and RCDF boost up the milk producers. Each and every types of assistance as balanced cattle feed, artificial insemination provided to them, therefore, the record milk were collected in URMUL, Bikaner.

Women Insurance Scheme

The Life Insurance Corporation of India started new insurance policy for ladies of dairy societies. In this scheme the registered lady member or husband of the dairy society of died or handicapped due to accident the LIC would pay the premium to them. The lady members have to pay Rs. 15 per annum, the remaining amount of LIC premium would be paid by dairy cooperative. In WRMUL (Jodhpur) about 25,000 lady members of dairy milk societies were benefited from this scheme. Such schemes have been started in URMUL, Bikaner also.

Land Holding and Dairying

Most of the agricultural practices and dairy farming are done by the women in rural areas and dairy farming is a supplementary of agriculture. The big and medium milk producing farmers have big land holdings. The involvement of women from such farmer's family in dairy activities is not much. Their works are done by landless people. It was observed in WRMUL that they consumed about 35 percent of milk production and remaining they sale in dairies. Quantity of milk supply was at maximum. Small and marginal farmers as well as landless labourers supply less milk. They consumed about 27 percent of their milk production and surplus milk they supply to DCS. Women of these groups performed all dairy activities themselves and their involvement is increasing.

Training and Extension Education to Rural Youth

For the improvement and development in milk yield at grass-root level, the rural youth, male and female were being sent for extension education and training to Anand. It is essential ingredient of the Anand Model. Under this model the unions carry out the various responsibilities of their own such as the maintenance of record of the societies, collection of milk, its testing, payment to the milk producers, primary knowledge of veterinary first-aid, technique of artificial insemination (A.I.) distribution of cattle feed, fodder growing in the farmers field.

The training is preferable to residents of the village where the society is to be organized. In the state there are seven training centres one each at Jaipur, Ajmer, Alwar, Bhilwara, Udaipur, Jodhpur and Bikaner. The centres give the training to rural youth (male-female), to secretaries, their helpers, members of management committee of the societies, livestock supervisors and village extension workers. The duration of the course is of ten weeks.

During the year 1986 the training centres imparted training in basic courses to 4,458 secretaries and helpers and refresher courses to 2,664 male, female for the same. During the same year about 3,606 batches of members of DCS managing committee were imparted orientation training course.

Extension activities are organised by the Kaira Union (Gujarat) with which milk producers and union maintained communication link. In the programme the farmers are induced to join cooperatives, to adopt new technical inputs and scientific animal husbandry practices which are the main activities of the programmes. The milk producers also learn how to get rid of the middle men. RCDF deputes the male/female milk producers to AMUL project area.

Dairying and Employment

Dairy is the most important and major sector of agriculture and provide employment opportunities in rural areas of the State. Where there are more than two-third milch animals in the household, dairying is the only source of income of the family. During the field it was observed that households having cattle were mostly involved in dairy activities. Dairy activities provide them substitutes of food, income and employment round the year. It was noticed that about 90 percent of households having cattle in desert region employed all family lady members in livestock rearing. In management of livestock, a number of activities have to be carried out for the maintenance of animals. Such activities are grazing of animals, collection of grass from the field, providing of water for drinking and bathing to animals, cleaning of cattle feed and shades making and feeding of various feed stuffs, providing milk to milk society. The women participation as family labour in such activities is highest. The female children have to confine to grazing, collection of grass and fodder from field and grazing lands, providing water for bathing and even marketing of milk to DCS. In this operation female participation is very high.

Women Strengthening Year, 2001

To strengthen the women, the year 2001-2002 was celebrated as a "Women's Strengthening Year". About 1102 WDCS of ladies were registered in which 50,430 woman members were involved and benefited. With the milk marketing about Rs. 17 crore was earned by the women milk societies. There has been a substantial increase in average income of women. It shows a great job opportunity in rural areas in future. In women DCS the tasks of balanced cattle feed, mineral mixed urea, molasses breeks, calf starter, providing seeds for green fodder, artificial insemination facilities, animal first aid, emergency veterinary services are done by the women. During the off season of agriculture, they spend lot of time in dairy activities which provided employment and regular income.

During the death of husband of lady member the dairy society have provided Rs. 2,500 to 7,500 as a premium. The women DCS have collected maximum milk and sold balanced cattle feed to the milk producers. Women milk societies share about 20 percent of the total milk produced by RCDF. In selling of cattle feed ladies supersede males. 659 animals of high yield milk producing have been provided to only women members of dairy society.

There are more possibilities in generation of jobs and increasing income with better dairy planning and better availability of credit to members of society. During the drought and famine period number of people sits idle without any employment or migrate to nearby cities and other distant places for jobs. To prevent them dairy farming seems to be a logical source of service in such conditions; which can provide self employment to the people inhabiting the region and it can protect them from the vagaries of drought and famine.

Livestock and dairy farming are more labour intensive. It has been observed that on an average five members per day per household during the rainy season were utilized in dairying. Hence, at present a level of production with animals, dairy alone provides employment to ten million man hours per day in the desert areas of the State.

Dairying as a Source of Income

Dairying is a major source of income for rural mass in desert and semi-desert regions, where uncenainty of precipitation, scarcity of fodder and grazing lands, low production of cereals, and lack of infrastructure technical education exist. Basically, dairy cooperatives have provision of development of livestock and enhancement of milk. Women milk societies have emerged at a large scale and they have been provided loan facilities from banks to purchase high yielding milch cattle. During the field survey it was observed that the share of dairy income increases with an increase in household income. Medium household income group earns about Rs. 1500-2000 per month, lower income group earns below Rs. 1500 per month, where as higher income group earns more than Rs. 2500 per month. This increasing income of milk producers is due to balanced cattle feed and good management of milch animals.

Socio-Economic Upliftment

It was observed that the big and medium household farmers commands the dairy societies, lower landless and marginal household farmers were not much benefited. Livestock rearing occupation is done by women in rural areas; they spend maximum hours in livestock management, feeding, milking, collection of fodder etc. Hence, they are the real milk producers. Green fodder development programmes were started at many places in the State such as in Bilada, Bhopalgarh tehsils of Jodhpur district, Merta and Nagaur tehsils of Nagaur district, Rojadi farm of Bikaner and Bassi farm of Jaipur district. To strengthen the women in dairying a ladies fair programme was started in March, 2002 in Bikaner. More than 5000 women participated in that fair, where they discussed various plans, problems and suggested solutions, so that the maximum participants of women could be started.

Change in Life Style

It was observed that ladies openly discussed at length and look optimist in dairy development. It was also observed that the changes took place in their life style, food habits, clothing and health habits and taking care of children and family. All these are related with social, economic and cultural conditions of rural area. The dairy industry is the assessment of status of the households in rural areas as cattle and buffaloes are the important measures of their earning. In rural areas milk, curd, Chhachh and Ghee are the major items of their food. It was noticed that those farmers who sell milk to dairy society or in market earn money every day. Hence, they used to take pulses, vegetables. The use of tea has also become usual in almost every family.

With increasing income from dairy development, most of the young and adult males and females use good quality of cloths in place of old fashioned khadi cloths. It can be seen that in the rural areas school, college going children wear good quality shorts, shirts, trousers and shoes. It was observed that on the occasion of marriages, fairs and festivals they put good quality multi-coloured cloths and ornaments. They are awarc of their family health care and services. At the time of illness, they go to the dispensaries and hospitals to take medicines and avoid traditional treatments.

In rural areas every households prefer to domesticating bovines in place of other animals. It is the major source of their life because of traditional use of milk as a food. This tendency has made their minds for having bovines for their social prestige in the society and with this little bit earning, they could educate their children and feed them properly. The present tendency will enhance the dairying a lot. The participation of women is a very good sign of their positive response.

The dairy has changed social and economic conditions of the rural masses. Their life style is changing. Poor, marginal and land less milk producers are provided medical, educational services, food and fodder, infrastructure and technical input services from RCDF at reasonable rates and financial assistance from banks. They are only expected to supply a certain quality of milk to cooperative dairy societies. The people have understood the benefits obtained from dairy industry.

References

Annual Physical Progress Report of RCDF.

Annual Physical Progress Reports of WRMUL, Jodhpur and URMUL, Bikaner.

Dass, P.K. (1978): Crossbreed Cattle in Orissa- Prospects and Constraints NDDB-Anand.

Grewal, S.S. and Rangi, D.S. (1980): Economic and Employment of Dairying in Punjab - Indian Journal of Agricultural Economic Vol. 35.

Haria, V.K. (1980): Indian Grass Land, FRI, Jhansi.

Jain, J.L. and Avadha Prasad (1982): Organized Milk Marketing in India, Socio Economic Impact- A Study of the Delhi Milk Scheme in N.W. Rajasthan, Jaipur.

Khandelwal, M.K. (1989): Dairy Industry in Rajasthan-A Case Study of Urban Resource Development, unpublished Ph.D. Thesis, University of Rajasthan, Jaipur.

Nair, K.N. (1979): Milk Production in Kerala, Trends and Progress, Eco and Pole Weekly Vol. 14.

National Commission on Agriculture (1971).

Patel, S.M.; Thakur, D.S. and Pandey, M.K. (1977) Spread Effects of Dairy Enterprises- A Case Study of Anand-Hyderabad.

Singh, J.: Gangwar, A.C.; Chakravarty, I.R. (1979): Economics of Milk Production in Haryana State, HAU, Hisar.

Singh, Surendra (1978): Operation Flood-II Some Constraints Implications, Eco and Pole Weekly. Vol. 14.

Somjee, A.H. and Somjee, Geeta (1978): Cooperative Dairying and Profile of Social Change in India, Eco Development and Culture Change Vol. 26.

Thakur, D.S. (1974): New Approach to Dairy Development, Dairy as an Instrument of Change, New Delhi.

Part IV: Population-Environment-Development: Inter-linkages

20

Status of Population, Development and Quality of Life in Japan

Shii Okuno

This paper aims to study the status of quality of life in Japan through three perspectives, namely the population and development, the environment, and the vital and health perspectives, with an objective to compare whether there is any difference between Japan and other Asian nations, and also, between Japan and other industrially advanced nations in the west.

Population and Development

It is assumed that societal development or growth can be traced by looking at its population growth and change, income per capita, growth of per capita gross domestic product and change in the metropolitan/urbanization rate.

Statistics of population show a steady rise of total population of Japan from approximately 20 million in 1920 to 120 million in 2000-2010, which coincides with her rapid industrialization and modernization. After 2010 her population decreases, actually assumed to drop from the year 2007, to approximately 100 million in 2050 and perhaps to approximately 70 million in 2100. Her population over the age of 65 rises steadily till 1990, and rapidly upwards in 1990s and in the early quarter of the 21st century, giving a rate of 20 percent in the first decade of 2000s and 25 percent in the following decade. The aging process is pushed forward by the presence of baby boomers born just after the Second World War in late 1940s. This rate of aged population is predicted to rise to 30 percent in 2040 and then go even around 28 percent at the second half of the century.

Taking the world's growth rate as an focal point of quarters, Pakistan, Nepal, Bangladesh, India and Vietnam are the first group of countries with growth rate more than 1.5 percent and density over 100 people per sq. km. China, Thailand, and Sri Lanka are in the second group with low annual population growth (0.7-1.5 percent) and around 100 people per sq. km. The third group of countries is those with similar density or higher, but low annual growth at 0.2-0.4 percent, namely Japan, Germany, Italy and France. USA and Brazil form the fourth group, and have an annual growth rate at 1.2-1.5 percent and population density at 30-50 people per sq. km. Australia is the only country in the fifth group, with an annual population growth rate at 1.2 percent and very low density, less than 5 persons per sq. km..

In terms of Parity Purchase Price Gross National Income (PPP GNI) against their Gross National Product per capita growth rate for selected countries, Japan has a PPP GNI at over US$ 27,000. However her per capita GDP growth is negative. India has a PPP GNI well below US$ 2000 but her per capita GDP growth rate is approximately 2.6 percent. In the same period, China, with a PPP GNI at around US$ 2500, enjoy an exceptionally high growth rate (6.5 percent).

Japan's population stands sixth in Asia after China, India, Indonesia, Pakistan and Bangladesh with 127 million people in 2001. Her average annual growth of population in the decade of 1990s is 0.3 percent, much lower than the average world growth at 1.4 percent, and lower than the South Asian nations (1.3-2.4 percent), and USA (1.2 percent), and appears at similar level with European nations like Germany, Italy, or France. Her population density at 350 people per sq. km. in 2001 is much higher than the world average at 47 people per sq. km., rather similar with India (348 people/sq. km.) or Sri Lanka (304 people/sq. km.), or Vietnam (244 people/sq. km.), or Germany (230 people/sq. km.) but much different from Bangladesh at the top (1025 people/ sq. km.), or USA(31 people/ sq. km.) and Australia (3 people/sq. km.) at the bottom.

Her gross national income in 2001 ranks second only after USA, and per capita income makes her rank first at US$ 35,990. However, the adjustment by Parity Purchase Price (PPP) reveals that Japan only makes US$ 27,430 per capita, after USA, Australia, Germany, or France, but much higher than the world average at US$ 7,570 or other Southern Asian nations.

The adjustment of gross national income by PPP gives USA the first, China the second, and Japan the third among the given list. However, in 2000-2001 her GDP per capita is minus, marking herself out from slow growth nations (Germany, USA) or fast growth nations (China or Vietnam).

Life expectancy at birth in 2000 shows that Japan ranks highest in the longevity of life among other nations, averaging at 81 years of age, and followed by Australia (79), France (79), Italy (79), Germany (77), USA (77), Sri Lanka (73), and then China (70). The world average is at 66 years of age. India gives the life expectancy at 63, lower than Sri Lanka, on the same level with Pakistan, but higher than other South Asian countries such as Bangladesh (61) and Nepal (59).

The mortality rate for children under 5 years of age per 1000 people at 2000 shows Japan has a rate of only 5 percent, performing well among other developed and developing countries. Most developed countries give a rate ranging from 6 to 9 percent, and developing nations in Asia at a rate ranging from 2 to 3 digits, take for example, Sri Lanka (18 percent) is outstanding among the rest, then followed by China (39 percent), Thailand (33 percent), Bangladesh (83 percent), India (88 percent), Nepal (105 percent), and Pakistan (110 percent). The world average marks at 78 people per 1000.

The adult illiteracy rate for people at 15 years of age or above shows that most developed nations have only negligible problem, and developing nations show one-digit rate for Thailand, Vietnam and Sri Lanka, and the followed by Indonesia (13 percent), Brazil (15 percent), China(16 percent), Iran (24 percent), and India (43 percent).

Figures on the emissions of carbon dioxide shows nations with large population size or intensive industrial activities such as USA, China, Japan (1134 million tons), and India (1061 million tons) produce more than a thousand million tons in 1998. When per capita emission data of carbon dioxide for surveyed nations in 1998 are calculated, the result shows that developed nations rank much higher, exemplified by USA (19.2 tons), Australia (17.1 tons), Germany (10 tons), Japan (8.9 tons), Italy (7.2 tons), and France (6.2 tons), when developing nations rank much lower, exemplified by Thailand (3.1 tons), China (2.4 tons), Egypt (1.6 tons), Indonesia (1.1 tons), India (1.0 tons), Pakistan (0.7 ton) and Nepal (0.1 ton). It is assumed that the level of modernized style of living, mode of industrial production, and also culture come together to explain for the differences among developed and developing nations

Lastly, another characteristic of the population of Japan is urbanization, and exemplified by concentration of her population at the three metropolitan regions (MR), namely, Tokyo (or Keihin), Osaka (or Keihanshin), and Nagoya (or Chukyo). The actual conurbation of built-up areas spread over an area of 60-70 kilometre radius for Tokyo Metropolitan Region, an area of 40-50 kilometre radius for Osaka Metropolitan Region, and 20-30 kilometre radius for Nagoya Metropolitan Region. In 2001, these three regions, when calculated at an average radius of 50-kilometers, contain a population of over 30 million people in Tokyo MR (24.2 percent of the nation's population), over 16 million people in Osaka MR (12.9 percent), and close to 9 million people in Nagoya (6.9 percent), making a total of over 55 million(44 percent).

This so-called metropolitanization percentage has increased from 33.4 percent in 1960, to 40.5 percent in 1970, and then with much slower growth since 1970s. All these three Japan metropolitan regions are well served with subways and suburban mass transit, allowing for concentration and efficient distribution in these regions. The actual area of these three metropolitan regions only takes over 22,000 square kilometres, or only 5.9 percent of the national land. The densely inhabited areas give an average of 2481 persons per square kilometre for the three

MRs, with the highest at Tokyo MR, over 4000 persons per square kilometre. Disadvantages of dense inhabitation are many, to name some of them, high land price or rental, and relatively small size of apartment or little amenity in residential areas, long-distance work-trips, and congested trains and traffic at rush hours. Now the trend for residential mobility is live within the metropolitan core areas rather than at suburbs or outskirt, and more public projects come in for renovation of and environment improvement for urban space.

Environment

Linking to the above-mentioned population, we see that development is more than the increase of gross domestic product, but includes aspects such as quality of life, development in human resource, and also environmental aspect. In this session, we select forest area, energy resources, and waste treatment to further the discussion on environment.

Forest area of Japan has decreased a little from 25,212,000 hectares in 1990 to 25,146,000 hectares in 1995. In terms of percentage of coverage, nearly 67 percent of her land is covered with forest of some kind or another, giving a variety of natural beauties over a latitudinal difference over 20 degrees stretching from north to south. It is worthwhile to mention the nations which have put efforts on greening and conserving the forest, and as a result have achieved increase in forest cover at the end of the period of 1990-95; examples are USA, Canada, France, India and Italy.

Coal was the largest primary resource (38 percent) in 1960 whereas petroleum (52 percent) in 1999. A breakdown of the different primary energy supply reveals that the percentages for hydro and coal decline in the survey period, and steady increase for LNG & others, and atomic and rapid increase and then decrease for petroleum due to diversification of energy sources. In terms of local energy resource supply, Japan did well in 1960, but has turned rapidly to depend on imported resources since 1970, over 80 percent in the last three decades. So Japan is vulnerable to any energy crisis or abrupt change in oil prices, she has stored an amount of petroleum for a period of 30 days as a precautionary measure.

Japan has been making efforts in waste treatment and reuse of refuse in order to attain an environmental or a resource recycling society. Her waste treatment was over 50 million tons in 1997, and the same figure per capita reveals Japan treats 400 kilograms per person, lower than those of most developed nations. The recycling percentage of Japan in paper and glass ranks her after the environmentally advanced nations of the Netherlands and Germany at 54 percent for paper, and 56 percent for glass in 1997.

Vital and Health Features

What are characteristics of Japan's vital and health features, and how have they changed in the last century? As data is available for a time series over the past hundred years, we shall look into the trends of birth rates, death rates, infant and neonatal mortality rates, death causes, HIV infection, and daily calorie intake as an aspect of Japanese way of life, as a whole to present the quality of life in terms of vital and health development.

Vital Statistics: The trends of birth rates, death rates, and natural increase rates of Japan in the period of 1899-2001 show the population transformation of Japan towards a general decline of growth in four visible stages. What is usually mentioned as the first stage of population transformation, namely high birth rate (over 40 percent) and high death rate (over 20 percent) as common to many developing countries in the early period of development, was not found within this period. The birth rate of Japan in late 19th century and early 20th century (1890-1940), that is, right after modernization period started at the Meiji Restoration (1868), moved downwards gently with the "medium high" level at 29-35 percent, and "medium high" death rate at 20-23 percent, as a result the natural increase rate dropped steadily at a medium rate of 10-15 percent. This is the first period.

The second period (1940-1949) is an abrupt rise of population growth before and after the end of Second World War (1945), as represented by relatively high birth rate at 17-20 percent and relatively low death rate at 11-16 percent, and an average of natural increase at 16-20 percent. This abrupt rise of population growth has caused the baby boom which maintains its swelling effects along each life-stage of these boomers like schooling age, university age, first employment, marriage and first children, and retirement. They then produce cycles of baby booms approximately every two decades onwards along with social effects and market segment expansion.

The third period (1950-1973) is characterized by general fall and then slight rise in birth rate, fluctuating between 14 percent and 19 percent, whereas the death rate a steady fall from 9.9 percent to 6.5 percent, resulting a fall of natural increase rate from 17 percent to 10 percent, and then slight rise to 13 percent. The rise in birth and natural increase rates is caused by the first boomers, who have produced the second generation.

The fourth period (1974-2001) is a general decline of birth rate from 19 percent to 10 percent at 1990, and then to single-digit rate in the 1990s to the present. The death rate is a slight upward trend. It has risen from 6.5 percent to

6.7 percent in 1990, and then further rise to 7.7 percent, perhaps partly due to the increase in the proportion and size of aged population. As a result the natural birth rate has dropped down from 12 percent to 3 percent in the 1970s and 1980s, and then from 3 percent further down to 1.6 percent in the 1990s.

During the last century there were four abrupt falls in natural increase rate in single years in Japan and the reasons are respectively given as follows: (1) at a rate of 9-10 percent in the years of 1906 and 1907 due to belief that girls born on that calendar year of 'hinoeuma (a cycle reappears every 60 years)' would bring forth misfortune to the family; (2) at 6 percent in 1918 due to Spain influenza and possibly also due to the rise in rice price and its shortage; (3) at 9 percent in 1938 and 1939 due to national mobilization to enter into War with China; and (4) at 7 percent in 1966 due to what people perceived as the unlucky calendar year.

Infant and neonatal mortality rates, that is to say, death rates per thousand live births below 5 years of age, and that below one-month old respectively. The general trend goes downwards for both of them. However, the infant mortality rate has increased between the years of 1909-23. According to the record of vital statistics, infant mortality rate declined from 154 deaths per thousand live births in 1889, and 78 deaths for neonatal the same year. The infant mortality rate was reduced from 3-digit to two- digit figure (90 deaths per thousand live births) in 1940, whereas the neonatal declined to 39 percent. And then the next milestone is in 1976 with infant mortality rate came below one-digit figure at 9.3 percent and neonatal at 6.4 percent. The last few years stabilized at 3.1 percent for infant mortality rate and 1.6 percent for neonatal. These two rates reflect the advance and practice of medical technology and the health system itself in Japan.

Death Rates and Their Causes

Japan found herself somewhat in the middle with 706 deaths per 100,000 persons, between Russia at 1500 at the upper end, and 502 deaths at the lower end. Her major causes of death rates are ranked as follows: malignant neoplasms, heart diseases, cerrebrovascular diseases (C.V.D.) and then pneumonia. Countries/regions like Hong Kong, Canada, Italy, and France followed similar pattern, except the fourth cause varied somehow. Another pattern was with heart diseases as the first, malignant neoplasms the second, and C.V.D. the third, this was seen in U.S.A., U.K., Germany, and Norway.

In the year 1950, the causes of death, according to descending order, was tuberculosis at the top, followed by C.V.D., and then pneumonia and bronchitis at the third. In the next period, as represented by 1960, 70, and 80, the C.V.D. came into the first place, followed by malignant neoplasms and then heart diseases. In the third period, which is consistent with the present at 2001, shows that malignant neoplasms have claimed the first place since around 1985, and for the second and third, the general pattern are heart diseases and C.V.D., with some minor variations. The first cause of death has shown stronger presence, representing 146 deaths per 100,000 people (approximately 122,000 actual deaths) caused by tuberculosis in 1950, and 176 deaths per 100,000 people (approximately 181,000 actual deaths) caused by C.V.D. in 1970, and 235 deaths per 100,000 people (approximately 295,000 actual deaths) caused by malignant neoplasms in 2000.

HIV/AIDS

The situation of HIV/AIDS infection in 1999 is taken as an index to understand the social and prostitution problems in various regions in the world. The total number of HIV/AIDS infected persons in 1999 was 34,300,000 people, of which 73 percent distributed in Africa and 27 percent in non-Africa regions. Among the 2,800,000 persons died of AIDS, 80 percent in African and 20 percent non-African countries.

Regions such as South and Southeast Asia, North and South America have a larger number of infected persons, averaged over 900,000. When we come to the nations involved, India (3,700,000 infected persons), USA (850,000), Thailand (755,000), P. R. China (505,000), Ukraine (240,000), Russia (130,000), and Vietnam (100,000) show they are more seriously affected. It is worthwhile to note that India has the largest number of infected persons shown in the table, and at the same time the death rate caused by AIDS is higher than those of other regions, and moreover, a little bit higher in the number of infected children, that is persons under 15 years of age. In general the female (young persons at 15-49 years of age) is less that of the male. The causes of HIV/AIDS are rather complicated: some are affected since birth, some are affected through blood transfusion, and the rest because of social interactions like free sexual intercourse, or prostitution. The social background for the infected may be insufficient knowledge of the diseases, and insufficient or inappropriate medical treatment of the diseases. A macro point of view is that countries with rapid economic change or in the transition stage seem to have higher figures of infected persons. Last comment is that Japan is one of the countries with the least number of people infected or died of AIDS. Inappropriate and sufficient medical treatments are mentioned to be the major causes of HIV/AIDS infection in Japan.

Life Expectancy

The life expectancy at birth shows that Japan ranks the highest among other nations with an average of 77.6 years of age for male and 84.6 female of her population. The causes for this high rate of life expectancy are suggested to be her diet of food, medical system, average person's health knowledge and practice, etc. In the next paragraph we shall look into the average daily calorie intake in further detail which might give some hints to the health and life expectancy.

Daily Calorie Intake

Daily calorie intake is a complex indicator indicating the way of eating and drinking habits of the people and how they are possibly related with the local farm produce, cultural practices and endowment of natural environment. Of course it also reveals the sufficiency or insufficiency of calorie intake to carry out the daily human activities.

When we look into the composition of the diet, cereals consist of a higher percentage in East/Southeast and South Asian countries, usually over 40 percent. Japan's cereals composition is 39 percent. When compared to other Asian countries, Japan maintains a medium amount of calorie intake (2,782 kcal per person), less cereals, similar level of meat and vegetables, more eggs, and much more fish, and more milk products than other East/Southeast Asian but not South Asian countries. When compared to other developed nations like European or USA, Japan maintains a lower profile in calorie intake, more cereals, less beans and potatoes, much less met, much more fish, and much less milk products. It is worthwhile to note that India has a rather low profile in total calorie intake (2417 kcal per person), and characterizes herself with higher percentage in cereals, more beans, less vegetables, much less meat, much less eggs, much less fish, and medium level in milk products.

Towards a Resource-Recylable Society

To summarize, the major findings are the following:

1. Japan has experienced expansion of population growth and metropolitanization during the economic growth in the 1950s to 1970s.
2. Though Japan has one of the worst kinds of environment pollution in some industrial cities during the 1950s and 1960s, but in 1970s environmental control law and measures have been drawn. Her forest resource, covering 67 percent of national land area, is well conserved. And her citizens, after the first Oil Crisis in 1973, have been paying great attention to work towards efficient energy consumption, and recycling of wastes, and reuse of resources. Japan is also vulnerable to rapid price change in energy, lumber, and foodstuff sources as she depends on import of all these resources.
3. Vital statistics, and indices on health and calorie intake show that Japan has similarities with other East Asian Countries in terms of low calorie intake, but

lower content in cereals and higher in fish, eggs, and milk products. Compared to European nations, Japan's average diet consists of more cereals, less meat, more eggs, less milk products and much more fish. And her leading causes of death now are malignant neoplasms, heart diseases, and C.V.D. in descending order. Her high life expectancy and very low birth and natural increase rates give further evidences on her quality of life, and also indicate problems ahead for her rapidly aging society.

To conclude, we have compared ways of lifestyles and varieties concerning people, urbanization/metropolitan development, births and deaths, calorie intake, and etc. of different nations or regions. We agree that empowering the potential of each human being to help attain their goals in life is very important. Industrially developed countries in Europe, North America, Oceania, or Asia have shown interesting examples of their diversified paths in development. Social systems, cultural values, lifestyles and urban forms and transport patterns assist each citizen/resident to work collaboratively for a secured and satisfying life. Simple grading or ranking different nations or ethnic groups may be insufficient in understanding the true nature of leading such a life in other nations or ethnic groups.

First of all, adopting a collateral point of view on comparative cultural contexts or socio-economic systems is necessary to help us understand, and more important, to respect the beliefs and moral virtue of our neighbours.

Second, in the 21st century, human studies or social science try to follow the new goal of sustainable development, that is, satisfying the needs of the present generation but without minimizing the possibilities of coming generations in achieving their potentials in development. Japan shows an example in working closely with more efficient usage of energy in her industry or daily living, efficient urban mass transportation, less but sufficient calorie intake, and recent efforts to treat and recycle wastes and to work towards a resource-recyclable society. She is more than willing to discuss and exchange her development practices and experiences with other countries. However, Japan has been suffering from deflation and weak domestic demand in recent years, and present policies are aimed to vitalize her industries and regions, and create new areas in technology and businesses.

Third, interdependency and exchanges should be enhanced among and within north-south, north-north, and south-south nation relationships. Nations or regions are not and cannot be isolated. We have evidenced the rapid growth of Newly Industrializing Asian Economies and others in the last quarter of 20th century. That has also urged China and Vietnam to open her doors and minds for more foreign direct investment, modern business management, and trade. Trade flows, development aids, technology transfer, and cultural and academic exchange activities are needed for a global society. Japan always puts emphasis on environment technology transfer, preservation of important cultural and historical assets, and industrial development program consultation in high priority in her overseas development aids. She has learned from her mistakes against the environment during the age of rapid economic growth. As a member of the world community, Japan should have a lot to learn from the varieties of cultures, histories, regions or nations, and their harmony practices and thoughts with natural environment, all of which integrate to represent and celebrate the complexities and charm of mankind.

Acknowledgement

Gratitude is due to Professor Masakazu Nagayama and Mrs. Chisho Okuno for their advices and information on historical population development of Japan.

References

Kito, Hiroshi (2000) *Jinkou kara Yomu Nippon no Rekishi (Interpreting Japanese History through Population)*, Kodansha-Gakujutsu Bunkou.

Hayami, Yuzuru (2001) *Rekishi-Jinkougaku de mita Nippon (Japan from the Viewpoint of Historical Demography)*, Bunshun-Shinsho.

Maruo, Naomi, et al (1997) *Ekosaikuru Shakai (Eco-cycle Society)*, Yuhikaku.

Ministry of Environment (2001) *Junkangata-shakai Hakusho (White Paper on Resouce-Recyclable Society)*, Gyousei.

National Land Agency (1998) *21-seiki no Kokudo no Gurandodezain (Grand Design of National Land in the 21st Century)*.

Nomura Sougo Kenkyusho (2000) Nomura Research Institute, Shoshi-Kourei-ka to Gen'eki setai no Kasseika (Less Children, Aging, and Vitalization of Present Generation).

Okurasho-Zaiseikinyu Kenkyusho (1998) Azia no Jizokutekiseichou wa kanouka (Is the sustainable Development of Asia possible?), Okurashou.

Ohbuchi, Hiroshi (1997) *Shoushika-jidai no Nippon Keizai (Japanese Economy in the Age of Less Children)*, Nippon Hosou Kyoukai.

World Bank, *World Development Report (*2003) *Sustainable Development in a Dynamic World: Transforming Institutions, Growth and Quality of Life,* Oxford University Press.

21

Environment, Population and Land Use Conflicts in the Coastal Savannah of Ghana

Michael O'Neal Campbell

Introduction

Coastal Savannah of Ghana is an important part of Ghana. In West Africa, vegetation change, especially changes in forest/savannah boundaries, has been strongly associated with population and development issues, largely because of the dominant discourses that ascribe such change to population growth and increased land use intensity. Established discourses generally describe savannah vegetation as the result of a linear sequence of deforestation from an 'original' pristine forest vegetation to grass and farm dominated mosaics, with the main contributory factors for this metamorphosis being population growth, and the increased intensification of land uses of various competencies (Fairhead and Leach, 1995, 1998) incorporating a narrative of declining resources and unequal power relations which leads to the marginalisation of poor land users and further environmental degradation is a powerful theme in the global environmental literature (Bell and Roberts, 1991; Blaikie and Brookfield, 1987; Redclift, 1987).

Reardon and Vosti (1995, 1495) write of a common tendency in the literature to envisage a 'vicious circle' in socio-environmental relations, a co-evolutionary sequence that contributes to impoverishment, within the context of population growth, poverty has also been described as 'one of the greatest threats to the environment' (United Nations Human Development Report 1990).

However, the perspective of a positive relationship between increased population and poverty and environmental degradation is 'highly disputed' and some narratives of environmental degradation under population growth, poverty, disempowered populations and modernisation are held to be 'exaggerated' (Batterbury et al. 1997: 126).

Some studies challenge this general hypothesis by citing examples of indeterminate, variable or multi-directional environmental change, or even landscape enrichment in areas of poverty and intensive land use (Fairhead and Leach 1995; Tiffen, Mortimore and Gichuki 1994; Campbell 1998; Elliott and Campbell 2002). Commenting on this narrative, Broad (1994: 812) also describes research that deconstructs 'oppositional thinking in the poor-environment dyad by bringing forth evidence that some poor people act not as environmental degraders, but as environmental sustainers'.

An important issue in the consideration of these contested positions concerns the reliability of the research tools and analytical methods that enable the construction of the narratives (Batterbury et al. 1997; Leach and Mearns 1996). In this regard, four relevant themes may be noted in the literature. Firstly, there has been increased recognition of the importance of studying social dynamics of environmental change within savanna contexts. Savanna contexts plainly merit attention, as there are a vast number of contexts that are described as savanna (Hopkins 1992), and they cover one fifth of the earth's land surface, and half of the area of the African continent (Scholes and Walker 1993). Despite this, some authors have noted that tropical savannas are less studied than are tropical forests (Stott 1991).

Secondly, in the examination of nature/society relations in such problematic contexts, there has also been acknowledgement that the reliable measurement of physical environmental change is vital for informed assessments of some of the contextual factors for land use issues. This has involved the increased use of single date or time series field and aerial photographs, and satellite images, especially for the documentation of vegetation change at landscape and patch levels (Campbell 1998; Fairhead and Leach 1994, 1995, 1996; Herwitz et al.1998; Innes 1998; Ite 1997; Lieberman 1979; Millington et al.1992; Nsiah Gyabaah 1992; Spaeth 1996; Tiffen et al. 1994).

Third, there has also been an increase in studies that examine nature/society relations from several perspectives. Particularly relevant in the construction of micro perceptions of environmental change are actor oriented and actor/structure dualities (Craib 1992; Giddens 1979, 1984; Long and Long 1992), gender perspectives (Agarawal 1994, Budget-Meakin 1995; Jackson 1993, 1994; Mellor 1997; Rao 1991; Rocheleau et al. 1996) and participation studies (Baidu Forson 1997; Baur and Hoffman 1997; Bebbington 1996; Peet and Watts 1996; Pretty 1995; Pretty and Shah 1997; Riley and Alexander 1997; Thomas Slayter 1994; Teme et al. 1996; Witcombe and Joshi 1996; Witcombe et al.1996; Zimmerer 1994;).

Fourth, despite these developments, there has been a paucity of studies that integrate these multiple research methods and paradigms in the documentation of the dynamic and sometimes multi-directional environmental change that is a fundamental factor underlying many land-use issues (Redclift 1987; Campbell and Palmer-Jones 1999). Dominant discourses argue for narrowly defined methodologies and narratives of linear environmental change under destructive actions. Therefore, this article integrates the research methods described above in the case study of the Tuba-Aplaku Plains of Coastal Ghana. It goes beyond the dominant deforestation narrative by documenting the variable actions taken by local actors, which enable multidirectional environmental change.

A comprehensive methodology was evolved, involving social and ecological methods. The social survey, conducted from June 1995 to July 1996, involved three forms of social contacts: (1) Semi structured interviewees and individual discussions; (2) Group discussions; (3) and social observations. Four hundred and sixty eight people were interviewed, selected to allow broad representation of the stakeholder groups, from Bortianor, Kokrobite, Oshiyie and Aplaku. Investigated variables comprised education, gender, age, livelihood activity and religion. The theoretical framework for the social survey was based on Giddens' (1979; 1984) structuration theory, which holds that actor volition and cultural structures should be viewed as a duality or two sides of the same coin: people construct, maintain and reinforce structures, which also influence people's behaviour. Therefore, people were interviewed concerning actions, motives and belief in the fetish and other social structures (gender specificity, respect for elders, education, religion, environment perception). Different reactions to cultural structures were also charted.

The ecological field survey was conducted in four stages: Firstly, vegetation was classified into closed canopy forest, mixed forest and shrubs, shrub dominated, grass–shrub mosaics and grass dominated areas. Further examination of the structure and species composition allowed the selection of two groups: forest (closed and open canopy forest, thick shrub sized tree species) and non-forest (grass, light shrubs, farms, and beach). Secondly, there was the random application of quadrats in each of the classified areas, involving 21 10x10 quadrats within which there were 525 2x2 metre quadrats, based intensive field exploration, involving local people, field photography and specimen collection for species identification. Thirdly, the land use and related vegetation was classified into protected and un-protected areas. This required intensive interviewees and group discussions, and allowed the differentiation between unprotected forest and fetish. Fourth, several field features, such as large trees, farm borders, road corners and buildings, were identified and compared with those in the aerial photographs. In several cases comparison between the two sets of aerial photographs and the field measurements showed changes. The resolution of the aerial photographs was sufficiently detailed for the identification of individual trees, canopy sizes, road width and differentiation of trees and shrubs.

GIS methods and times series images were also used. Black and white aerial photographs, scaled at 1:10,000, were dated 1960 and 1986. Because this study dealt with trees that took several years to reach maturity, the widely spaced dates of the time series images were acceptable. The photographs, scanned and saved in TIFF format, were then registered to common grid, and digitised feature maps, were created using geomatics software (IDRISI). Through the overlaying and cross tabulation, of the images, matrices were also created. Forest loss and expansion between 1960 and 1986 were documented. The changes in the protected and un-protected areas were compared, to determine the effectiveness of the fetish edict.

The rest of this chapter is divided into four sections. The first section examines literature on the historic problem of land use conflicts in Ghana, and the background issues for socio-environmental relations in the coastal savannah of Ghana. The second section examines the socio-environmental relations of the case study of the Tuba/Aplaku plains of Coastal Ghana. The third section documents the evidence for land use conflicts that were revealed by the field survey. This is followed by the conclusions that summarize the socio-environmental dynamics revealed in the study.

Land Use Conflicts in Ghana: A Significant Historic Problem

In Ghanaian history, the documentation of land use conflicts, environmental change and social group responsibility for real or exaggerated environmental degradation is fraught with disputed assessments. During the first third of the twentieth century, colonial authorities, miners and local farmers blamed each other for deforestation in the forested eastern and central regions (Howard 1978). For example, Kay (1972: 126) quotes a letter dated August 17, 1922, from the colonial Governor to the Secretary of State for the Colonies which stated that the colony of the Gold Coast (the colonial name for Ghana) was 'threatened with ruin through the promiscuous denuding of its forests'. Land use intensification, mainly local shifting cultivation, forestry and cocoa farming was blamed for this problem. Another contemporary writer, Ormsby Gore (1926, in Kay 1972: 25) blamed the savannisation of the forest regions on the local people, arguing that it was 'almost impossible to persuade the native' of the need for forest conservation in the face of agricultural intensification, brought on by losses of areas of shifting cultivation to colonial agriculture and mining. Frequent inter-tribal conflicts and the declining status of traditional land authorities were also identified as contributory factors in deforestation. Environmental legislation was argued to be necessary to restrict the expansion of land use and consequent deforestation (Tudhope 1918, in Kay 1972: 243).

The coastal savannah of southern Ghana has also been described as an area where intensified and sometimes conflicting land uses have created particular vegetation patterns. It is an area relatively neglected in the literature on land use issues in Ghana, due to the economically peripheral position of its resources (flat land, vegetables, cereals, firewood and bushmeat) compared with the exportable resources of inland Ghana (minerals, cocoa and timber). The vegetation is a mixed tree/shrub/grass savannah, generally termed coastal thicket where shrubs predominate and coastal grassland where grasses predominate (Campbell 1998; Carson 1985; Dickson and Benneh 1988). This is the driest region of Ghana (Ahn 1969; Carson, 1985) and is believed by some to be a degraded landscape, an example of the final result of the intensification of land use patterns which are taking place nation-wide. It is assessed by others to be under more complex, contextual patch dynamic change, based on both degradation and enrichment (Campbell 1998; Hall 1985; Jenik and Hall 1976; Keay 1959; Talbot 1981).

Several historical studies describe human activities as the main factors for the conversion of a formerly forested area into a savannah ecosystem (Booth 1956; Dupuis 1824; Macdonald 1898 Irvine 1947; Taylor 1952; La Anyane 1956; Lane 1962; Dickson 1966; Dickson and Benneh 1988). Here, it is believed that, largely due to population increase and resultant land use intensification, there is evidence of 'man's use or misuse of the land' (Amoah 1976: 3) and 'centuries of farming resulting in the impoverishment of the soil' (Lane 1962: 167). In particular, natural and anthropogenically created fire (Hawthorne 1994), intensive farming (Gyasi et al. 1995), firewood cutting (Campbell 1998; Jampoh 1989; Ocansey 1985; UNICEF 1990) and cattle herding (Sarris and Shams 1991) are activities that are believed to have created long term environmental degradation. There is also belief in continual deforestation and desertification in the last quarter of the twentieth century (Benneh and Agyepong 1990; Folly 1995; Iddrisu and Tropp 1995; Lieberman 1979; Oduro-Afriyie 1996). In this region, as in the rest of Ghana, the narrative that emerges from these studies is highly generalised, neglecting patch level changes and the multidirectional changes that may result from the human activities contributing to both degradation and enrichment. Rather than employing integrated research methods, many studies focus on single themes and hence are unable to answer the complex questions concerning nature-society dynamics.

The Tuba/Aplaku Plains of the Coastal Savannah of Ghana

The Tuba-Aplaku plains cover approximately fifty square kilometres of hilly, undulating and flat land approximately twenty kilometres south-west of Accra, the capital city of Ghana. The main vegetation type is a mixed tree/shrub/grass mosaic. The population of the six settlements of the area -Bortianor, Oshiyie, Kokrobite, Tuba, Aplaku and Langma- increased from 1,972 in 1948 to 7,065 in

1984 and over 8,000 in 2000 (Census Reports 1948, 1984, 2000). The main livelihoods were based on primary activities, which were usually practised simultaneously, seasonally, temporarily or semi-permanently. In the field survey farming, cattle ownership, tractor operation and firewood cutting were found to be practised by both males and females. Fishing, hunting and herding were male dominated activities, while fish smoking, fresh fish and meat trading, were almost exclusively female activities.

The main crops planted and traded were tomato *Lycopersicon esculentum* Mill, maize *Zea mays* L., pepper *Capsicum annuum* L., garden eggs *Solanum melongera* L and *Solanum aethiopicum* L., and cassava *Manihot utilissima* Mill and *Manihot esculenta* Crantz. Livestock reared were cattle *Bos taurus* L, *Bos indicus* L., sheep *Ovis aries* L., goats *Capra hircus* L. and a few pigs *Sus scrofa* L. Birds kept were domestic chickens *Gallus gallus* L., ducks *Anas platyrhynchos* L. and the wild guinea fowls *Numida melagris galeata* L. Hunters hunted primarily the Crowned Duiker *Sylvicapra grimmia* L., Black Duiker *Cephalophus niger* Gray., Red Flanked Duiker *Cephalophus rufilatus* Gray., Maxwell's Duiker *Cephalophus maxwellii* H.Smith. and Bushbuck *Tragelaphus scriptus* Pallas. Some hunters used dogs *Canis familiaris* L. Favoured tree/shrub species for firewood include *Cassia siamea* Lam., *Mangifera indica* L., *Fagara zanthoxyloides Zanthoxylum zanthoxyloides* L. and *Azadirachta indica* A.Juss. Fishermen hunted primarily round sardine *Sardinella aurita* Valenciennes., flat sardine *Sardinella eba* Valenciennes., club mackerel *Scomber japonicus* Houttuyn., common treadfish *Galeodis decadachylus* Bloch and sika sika *Pagus ehronbergi* Valenciennes.

Vegetation Distributions

The above activities, especially farming and firewood cutting, affected the mixed tree/shrub/grass mosaic. The field survey and the image-based assessment supported the classification of the landscape based on processes of change into three main types. There were deforested areas, where farming and firewood cutting had virtually destroyed all the large trees, and the short fallow prevented forest regrowth. There were also areas where change in vegetation was barely noticeable, with slight variations in canopy diameter, shrub canopy density and grass patches within shrub dominated areas, and grass densities. In some areas, there was also reforestation, or increased tree/shrub density due to farm abandonment or traditional land protection schemes. Some areas under cultivation in the 1960 images were covered with tree/shrub mosaics in the 1986 images, and in some cases this change could also be judged in the 1998 satellite image. The land use activities that contributed to these vegetation variations created characteristic contexts.

The contexts of intensive farming and firewood cutting were mainly grass-dominated areas. The commonest species were *Andropogon guyanus* L., *Sporobulus pyramidalis* L. and *Panicum maximum* L. In these areas there were very few shrubs, usually *Azadirachta indica* A.Juss and *Fagara xanthoxyloides,* and these are mostly shrub sized. The open nature of these contexts was due to the farmers' preference for light thickets of grass, due to the difficulty of tree/shrub clearance. Root removal was a precondition for mechanised ploughing, a recent development. In past and current hoe clearance, the total removal of roots was not as important. Some trees, especially the mango *Mangifera indica* L. were sometimes tolerated for shade or fruits, but such occurrences were under thirty percent of the farms surveyed.

In the contexts of firewood cutting and some isolated patches of farming, shrub/grass mosaics dominated. Shrub and shrub sized tree species occurred either as individual specimens in grass stands or in scattered clumps. The main tree and shrub species were *Azadirachta indica, Fagara xanthoxyloides, Baphia nitida* Lodd and *Securinega virosa* (Roxb.ex Willd) Baillon. The commonest grass species were those mentioned above. This vegetation type existed mainly in the short fallow areas, where farming ceased either seasonally or for up to two years. Most firewood cutters were also farmers and much of the wood was obtained during farm clearance, but all the participants in such multiple-activity livelihoods acknowledged that intensive farming was the key factor behind tree stand losses

The contexts of hunting and/or firewood cutting were largely wooded. The hunters preferred thick wooded stands, because these were the preferred habitats of their main prey, the duikers. Here the dominant vegetation comprised thick shrub and shrub sized tree growths. These occurred mostly in areas left fallow for more than two years. The main species were the tree and shrub species mentioned above. Due to firewood cutting and coppicing, tree species such as the neem (*Azadirachta indica*) were sometimes kept at shrub size, about two to three metres high. Isolated patches of grass and occasional full sized trees (usually *Mangifera indica*) also occurred.

The contexts under fetish or conservation control (the woodlots) and in the proximity of graveyards, were also wooded. Some tree species, which were common in the inland forests, occurred in these limited areas, even though they were extinct or extremely rare elsewhere in the study area. These included *Samarea saman* (Jacq.) Merr, *Entandrophragma angolense* C.E.C. Fish. *Casia siamea* Lam., *Triplochiton sceleroxylon* K.Shum., *Antiaris africana* Lesch., *Sterculia tragacartha* L., *Albizia zygia* Durraz., *Ceiba pentandra* Mill., *Antiaris toxcana* Lesch., *Ficus thonningii* L. *and Diospyros mesopiliformis* L. Other species, common in the areas outside the forest clumps (usually stunted to shrub size by firewood cutting) occurred in full size (e.g. *Azadirahta indica, Mangifera indica, Milletia thonningi*, and *Fagara zanthoxloides*).

Land Use Conflicts in the Tuba-Aplaku Plains

The literature on the livelihood dynamics described above is scanty. Also relatively neglected is the issue of land use conflicts in the area. Occasional sources may be derived from the national media. For example, Mensah (1996) and Mezikpih (1996) described the acrimonious social upheavals that resulted from the arbitrary sale of farmlands to developers in the Bortianor area. The situation in April 1996 was so serious that the Greater Accra Regional Security Council attempted to ban further sales of land. Graphic Reporter (1995: 3) also described a meeting of traditional rural landowners of the coastal savanna west of Accra. At this gathering it was argued that land disputes 'have claimed many lives, left others permanently impaired and destroyed property worth millions of cedis (the exchange rate at the time 2000 cedis to the pound sterling). Medzikpih (1996: 16) also describes the decline of the Densu Ramsar Conservation Area 'as a result of the wanton destruction of the environment', the main factors being 'excessive' farming, 'unsuitable' fishing methods, the work of developers and sand extraction for building. There was no attempt however, to link these activities and assess how the conflicts over land may have contributed to the multi-directional environmental change.

In the current research, four main conflict scenarios were noted to be especially problematic. Firstly, there was a general perception among land users that the available land for livelihood activities was being progressively reduced, leading to livelihood change, rural to urban migration and intensification of rural activities. Secondly, there was the contested usage of flat land by farmers and developers, which contributed to the increased cultivation of lowlands. Thirdly, there was some marginalisation of farmers, from lowlands to hilltops and slopes, under pressure from developers. Fourth, there were the conflicting land use needs of certain livelihoods (farmers who prefer open grassland for its easy clearance and firewood cutters and hunters who prefer wooded areas) and the problems that affect people engaged in multiple-activity livelihoods. These increased local awareness of patch level vegetation change.

Tables 21.1 to 21.5 provide a broad matrixed summary of the livelihood dynamics in this area and of the intra-activity relations and environmental impacts. The main factors for land use conflicts are then described. This information builds on the description of the vegetation contexts described above.

The conflicts in the needs of activities were strongly related to the patch level changes. There were several social issues that contributed to the exacerbation of land use conflicts. These principal factors were population increase, preferences for flatland among stakeholders and farmer marginalisation.

Table 21.1: Analysis of Aerial Photographs, Field Photographs and Satellite Images

Area	Primary Form of Vegetation Change (1960-1998)		
	Aerial Photographs (1960- 1986)	Field Photographs, Quadrat Survey,1996	Satellite Image, 1998
Aplaku/ Densu/ Eastern Bortianor	• Deforestation. • Increase in grassed areas • Little change in shrubs	• More deforestation. • Increased farms and developers • Most areas grass covered	• More deforestation • Increased developers.
Bortianor/ Kokrobite/ Oshiyie	• Losses and gains of trees and shrubs. • Intensive farming	• Deforestation. • Farming unchanged • Increased developers. • Some reforestation	• More deforestation, • Increased developers
Tuba/ Langma	• Grass dominated fields dotted with small tree/shrub clumps.	• Loss of tree/shrub/grass mosaics to the irrigation project.	• Little change visible.
Hinterland of Bortianor, Oshiyie and Kokrobite.	• Deforestation. • Increased farm/grass/ shrub mosaic	• Patch dynamic variation. • Expansion of developers	• Patch dynamic variation. • developer expansion

Source: Campbell 1998; Campbell and Palmer-Jones 1999

Population Increase

All the older respondents contacted in the field survey believed in a tenfold increase in population between the 1960s and 1996. They based their estimate on their knowledge of absentee farm owners and occasional farmers with multiple residences. Field interviews, local documents and media sources point to an increase in the number of rural actors engaged in primary activities. Issues discussed included the increased food demand in the area and increased need for farmland. The result of these changes was the reduction of the land available for farming, firewood cutting and hunting between the 1960s and the 1990s. This also resulted in the general transition of the dominant farming patterns from shifting cultivation to permanent plots and in some cases to scattered semi-permanent plots and farm abandonment.

Table 21.2: Effects of Combined Livelihood Activities on Farming

Effects of activities	Farming	Hunting	Firewood cutting	Developers
Farming	Conflicts occur between farmers over good land, (flat or fertile), marketing and authority for sales. Richer and more powerful farmers tend to marginalize poorer farmers to the edges of profitability and land use capability, creating inroads into tree/shrub areas on less preferred slopes.	Hunters burn the bush and in rare cases this may spread to farms. The awareness of the needs of hunting does not however lead some actors to restrict farm expansion, nor do hunters restrict their activities to non farmed areas.	Firewood cutting, where the roots of the trees and shrubs are removed assists the clearance of farmland. However, where there is coppicing, the thick roots cause a problem, as they must be dug up before ploughing.	Factor behind collapse of shifting cultivation (reduction of land available for farming) and also of the resultant intensification of farming in limited areas. Both farmers and developers prefer low-lying land. The influence of developers is patchy, dependent on the preferences of the buyers of land.

Source: Campbell 1998; Campbell and Palmer-Jones 1999

Preference for Flatland

All the stakeholders in the area- farmers, hunters, firewood cutters and developers preferred the lowlands to the steeper slopes of hilly areas. The farmer preference for lowlands was largely due to the higher incidence of erosion and desiccation on steep slopes. More than sixty percent of the farms surveyed on the hill slopes had severe problems with desiccation and erosion. In some cases there was a total loss of the crop (mostly tomatoes but also some maize and cassava). These problems also occurred on the lowlands but were far less severe: less than twenty percent of the farms in such areas suffered severe losses. Also, tractor ploughing was difficult on the steeper slopes. The tractor drivers were reluctant to plough farms located on steep slopes for fear of damaging their vehicles or ploughs. This was a very important limitation for all the farmers, as most of them had been dependent on tractor tillage since the introduction of mechanisation in the 1970s. Hand tillage, the previously dominant form of land preparation, was time consuming.

Table 21.3: Effects of Combined Livelihood Activities on Hunting

Effects of activities	Farming	Hunting	Firewood cutting	Developers
Hunting	Farming degrades the natural habitat of the larger animals. This is despite the fact that all the hunters are also farmers, and hence are aware of the issue. Landscape effect is the diversification and areal reduction of the animal habitats.	Conflicts occur between some hunters because they believe that their increased numbers and the intensification of activities are among the main factors behind wildlife depletion.	Firewood cutting depletes hunting areas when whole trees or shrubs are removed. However, where coppicing is employed the habitats are not destroyed. Constant proximity of cutters is also believed to scare off animals	Developers work destroys the habitats of the hunted animals However, when land purchased for development is not usually farmed, and if building is delayed thick shrubs may grow, providing a new habitat, depending also on the proximity of settlements.

Source: Campbell 1998; Campbell and Palmer-Jones 1999

Even in lowland areas the hiring of tractors resulted in substantial problems: women took an average of twelve days to obtain the tractor service, as opposed to about nine days for the male farmers, whom the tractor operators described as being more forceful in bargaining. These problems were exacerbated for female farmers on slopes. Hunters and firewood cutters preferred lowlands because of the difficulty of walking up slopes. Developers also preferred flat land, because many future house-owners believed the pumping of water to their homes up a steep gradient would be difficult, especially in this area where the water supply was generally unreliable. The transport of heavy materials and the operation of heavy machinery were also difficult on steep slopes. As the most powerful stakeholders, these developers were able to take over lowlands previously covered by rain fed farms.

Table 21.4: Effects of Combined Livelihood Activities on Firewood Cutting

Effects of activities	Farming	Hunting	Firewood cutting	Developers
Firewood Cutting	Farming destroys firewood stands. This problem has become especially pronounced as fallow periods have been reduced and farm sizes have increased. This is despite the fact that many farmers are also fire woodcutters.	In some cases the use of fire by hunters has destroyed wood stands.	Competition between firewood cutters results in further expansion of their work, and the further depletion or coppicing of wood stands.	Developers work destroys the firewood stands. However, as noted above, delays in building sometimes for several years, due to financial problems may allow new stands to grow as farmers rarely touch such areas. Firewood cutting continues however.

Source: Campbell 1998; Campbell and Palmer-Jones 1999

Farmer Marginalisation

The pressure from developers and plantation agriculture 'pushed' many farmers up the slopes. Some farmers also farmed hilly areas, because they were prepared to risk losses to desiccation and erosion. Some upland areas were perceived by some to be less prone to such problems. However, the majority of farmers preferred lowlands and argued that upland farming was largely due to pressure from more powerful stakeholders with a preference for lowland.

Table 21.5: Effects of Combined Livelihood Activities on Developers

Effects of activities	Farming	Hunting	Firewood cutting	Developers
Developers	Farmers may protest at land sales to developers, and these protests may hamper the spread of developer work.	Hunting has no direct effect on the work of developers.	Firewood cutting has no direct effect on the work of developers. However, the clearance of previously cut stands for development is easier than older trees. Coppicing does not affect the thick roots which are difficult to remove	There is competition among developers for low-lying land, and this may increase the efforts to acquire such land.

Source: Campbell 1998; Campbell and Palmer-Jones 1999

An important issue concerned land sales to developers. The areas purchased by developers, on which farming was prohibited, had greatly expanded over the period 1995 to 1999 and these areas were largely on the lowlands. These sales contributed to the Bortianor land dispute, which had been occurring sporadically during the 1980s and early 1990s, but reached extreme violence in 1996. The rising profitability of land sales for landowners (a plot 20 by 30 metres could sell for the equivalent of C1.2 million or £600 pounds, while farming a similar area would bring an average profit of C30000 or £ 15) influenced two of the twelve family heads in Bortianor to sell cultivated land to developers and to the Ghana Tourist Board during March and April 1996, appointing a Burkinabe (a native of Burkina Faso) land guard to supervise in this process. The clearing machines destroyed about thirty farms, totalling about sixty hectares. This angered the non-participating family heads, and the affected farmers reacted violently. Due to their superior wealth, the land sellers were able to bribe the police to arrest some of their opponents, the retaliation being the 'smashing' of four houses, two roofs, a corn mill and a water pipe. The intervention of the government led to a land sales ban and the temporary separation of the combatants: the land sellers were forced to reside temporarily in the suburbs of Accra. When the violence diminished they returned to Bortianor. Some farmers argued that 'we showed them that they can't take our land'.

There was also the Government supported seizure of productive rainfed farmland for the irrigation project. This project was envisaged because of the dry weather, and the close proximity of the Weija dam, which could ensure a good supply of water. Work started in 1983, with 200 hectares under rainfed cultivation being cleared to make way for what was believed to be a more technologically advanced and efficient system of farming. The enabling grant of 3,125,000 ECU from the EEC for the project's development funded only 200 of the proposed 1500 hectares (the 200 hectare Block C and a Central Farm) a preliminary development to ascertain the problems—environmental, economic and political—which might occur with a larger scale development (TAWEICO Final Report 1986). Several conflicts affected the work of the project.

Firstly, there was the forcible acquisition of the land. The land on which the project is located was acquired by the government from the Chiefs of Bortianor, Kokrobite, Tuba, Weija and Nyanyano. This was followed by the forcible displacement of peasant farmers, largely from Tuba, causing violent encounters between farmers and government workers operating land-clearing machines. Equipment belonging to the Irrigation Development Authority (I.D.A.) was damaged, and many farmers were arrested, but these 'weapons of the weak' as described by Scott (1985: 1) were, however, insufficient to prevent the opening of the project in 1983. Secondly, there were enforced cropping schemes. During the early stages of the project, cropping schemes were developed to enforce the planting of particular crops at particular times, for up to five and ten years (TAWEICO Final Report 1986). Farmers disputed these attempts at agricultural regimentation, as they based their planting choices on their knowledge of crop market demand, and their choices invariably differed from official directives. Thirdly, there was financial tension. The withdrawal of funded support from international sources and the Ghanaian government (1987 to 1990) increased the financial and social burden for farmers: there were numerous dropouts, increased problems with mechanisation and non-participation by female farmers. Coping strategies also created more land use tension: farmers were forced to intensify their participation in other activities (rainfed farming, firewood cutting, hunting, fishing and fish smoking) to support the cost of their participation in irrigation farming.

Traditional land protection was also important. Similar landscape pressures from traditional authorities denied farmers access to potentially productive lowlands. Traditional religious beliefs emphasised the existence of environmentally based deities, and every settlement in the Tuba/Aplaku plains, with the exception of largely Muslim Tuba, had at least one such deity. The enforcing agents of these beliefs (the fetish priests) had power to forbid cultivation and wood harvesting within a respectable distance of the believed habitation of the god (usually between ten and fifty metres). This resulted in the thickening of the vegetation within the protected areas and the loss of some good farming land and wood sources. Despite a currently declining belief in the power of the fetish (in 1996, eighty one percent of the people surveyed did not believe in this religion compared a near total belief in the 1960s) the fetish groves still existed in 1998 (visible from the SPOT satellite image). There was also a fetish ban on the keeping of goats in Bortianor and Aplaku. As goat keeping is an extremely viable supporting activity for farmers (most people prefer goats to sheep because they are perceived to be stronger) this action frustrated some farmers and contributed to the farm abandonment by some individuals to whom goat trading was a strong supporting source for financing farm expenses.

Responses to Marginalisation

The respondents described several responses to the pressures described above. These were individual and varied according to season and location. The two main responses were farm dispersal and livelihood diversification.

Farm dispersal: This was carried out to exploit local variations in soil moisture and fertility, and the increasing likelihood of farmland loss to soil desiccation and degradation and/or developers. The majority of interviewees argued that this strategy had merits. Wide spacing of farms allowed the growth of patches of shrubs and later trees. This benefited hunters, because the mixed patches of farmland and fallow provided habitats for hunted animals to a greater extent than the intensively farmed areas with clear forest boundaries. Firewood cutters also preferred such vegetation, because their preferred wood sources of young shrubs were commoner than in a landscape dominated by trees and farms.

This strategy was however, difficult because of the limitations of land access, as more influential and/or richer farmers obtained most of the 'good' land. Also, arranging for the mechanised ploughing of scattered farms could be more difficult, due to the tractor operators' fear of mechanical damage during long journeys. Weeks frequently passed between the ploughing of two widely spaced farms belonging to one farmer. These burdens hit the female farmers particularly hard, they emphasised the stress of daily walks over long distances (sometimes up steep slopes) between farms, the difficulty of hiring help for farm work in remote locations, weeding of plots after long walks, carrying of fertilisers to farms and the additional burden of child rearing household duties. Were farmland was permanently abandoned; reforestation would take place, this being dominated by faster growing trees such as neem *Azadirachta* indica and *Mangifera indica*.

Livelihood Diversification: For male farmers, the alternative activities were fishing trading and transport driving. Hunting was seen as complementary to farming rather than a replacement, because the income derived from sales of bush meat was insufficient to provide full support for individuals. For the female farmers the alternatives were farm produce and non-food trading, and fish smoking. With a few exceptions, firewood cutting was generally considered a supporting activity rather than an alternative. This was because, like hunting the income derived from this activity was usually insufficient to comprise a full livelihood. The presence of these alternative or supporting activities often motivated farmers to drop out of farming during hard times (drought, crop losses to disease, high cost of inputs, loss of lowlands to developers and reluctance to farm hill sides). Farmland thus abandoned might either remain under the ownership of the farmer or his/her family, or revert to the traditional authorities from whom the land may have been obtained in the first place. In any case, a long fallow situation would be created, and this resulted in the regrowth of shrub-dominated vegetation, or tree stands if the duration of the fallow period was more than a few years. This networking had similar environmental effects to shifting cultivation and bush fallowing, as variable fallow periods in farming practice created patches of shrub dominated vegetation which either reverted to grassland after farming or intensive wood cutting, or changed to young forest under light or selective coppicing.

Conclusions

The above discussion of landscape and patch level vegetation change, land use conflicts and a consequent process of socio-environmental dynamics has introduced several important issues. The sources of environmental degradation and change could not necessarily be blamed on single activities, but were the result of 'give and take' among individuals, social groups and the environment.

The scenario of linear environmental degradation positively correlated with increased inequality and poverty could not be fully accepted in this case study. What emerges is a more complex narrative of multidirectional environmental change, variably perceived by different stakeholders. The term environmental degradation became subjective during the study, as it was plain that land perceived as degraded by, for example, wood cutters (e.g. grassland) might be favoured by farmers, and due to the multiple-activity livelihoods practised by many actors this perspective might vary daily, seasonally or be permanently based on multiple re-appraisals according to the simultaneous practice of different activities in patch sized contexts.

People's activities contributed to environmental dynamics that shaped long-term change and these environmental changes also shaped social dynamics that obtained relationship with them. In some areas there was steady deforestation under intensified farming and firewood cutting that contributed to the decline of hunting and wood harvesting as economic supports to farming. In other areas farm intensification and abandonment existed side by side, leading to both deforestation and reforestation, the contributory factors being both social and natural (for example contextual variables such as land sales, alternative activity options, soil desiccation and topography). The effects would be both social and natural: for example the expansion or retraction of wood harvesting in response to vegetation change and tree growth.

Strong social conflicts were revealed to be occurring. These problems existed at the actor level: for example, individual choices between activities requiring similar or mutually exclusive environmental contexts. They also existed at the group or class level: for example the conflicts between farmers and developers/land owners. These disputes were clearly enabled by individual volition, as individuals reacted differently (for example some people abandoned their farms temporarily or permanently, other practised farm dispersal or multiple- activity livelihoods). Yet there was clearly an element of cultural and economic structuralism: many life spaces were regimented according to gender, traditional religion and power

These findings have implications for socio-environmental planning and management in such contexts. Awareness of the social constructions of life spaces at the individual level, and structural manifestations of these at the group level, as well as the environmental factors that coevolve with these social phenomena is necessary for effective understanding. Integrated research methods provide the tools through which useful materials may be gathered, the better to construct more critical narratives. This basis, upon which a deeper understanding of the dynamics of livelihood management, environmental change and nature/society relations is built, represents a first step to the solution of the serious land use problems in the case study area. Applications to other contexts are also possible.

References

Agarwal, B. (1994) 'Gender, Resistance and Land: Interlinked Struggles over Resources and Meanings in South Asia', in *Journal of Peasant Studies* 22 (1): 81-125.

Ahn, P. (1969) 'The Ecological Zones of Ghana in Relation to Agricultural Planning and to Fertiliser' *The Ghana Farmer* 13 (3): 96-101.

Amoah, F.E.K. (1976) 'Evolution of Urban Settlements on the Accra Plains: Early Times to 1700 AD', *Bulletin of the Ghana Geographical Association* 18: 1-14.

Baidu Forson, J. (1997) 'On-Station Farmer Participatory Varietal Evaluation: A Strategy for Client-Oriented Breeding', *Experimental Agriculture* 33 (1): 43-50.

Batterbury, S. T.Forsyth, and K.Thomson (1997) 'Environmental Transformations in Developing Countries: Hybrid Research and Democratic Policy', *The Geographical Journal* 163 (2):126-132.

Bauer, E. and V. Hoffman (1997) 'Participatory Rural Appraisal: Challenges and Recommendations', *Quarterly Journal of International Agriculture* 36 (1): 81-99.

Bell, M. and N. Roberts (1991) 'The Political Ecology of Dambo Soil and Water Resources in Zimbabwe' Transactions of the Institute of British Geographers 16 (3): 301-317.

Benneh, G. and G.A. Agyepong (1990) *Land Degradation in Ghana* London, Commonwealth Secretariat.

Blaikie, P. and H. Brookfield (1987) *Land Degradation and Society* London: Methuen.

Booth, A.H. (1956) 'On the Mammalian Fauna of the Accra Plain', *Journal of the West African Science Association* 5 (1): 26-35.

Broad, R. (1994) The Poor and the Environment: Friends or Foes? *World Development* 22 (6): 811-822.

Budget-Meakin, C. (1995) 'Technology, Women and the Environment', *Science, Technology and Development* 13 (1): 72-78.

Campbell, M. (1998) *Interactions Between Biogeography and Rural Livelihoods in the Coastal Savanna of Ghana* Unpublished Ph.D. Thesis University of London (Wye College).

Campbell, M. and R. Palmer-Jones (1999) *The Utility and Problems of GIS Methods in the Analysis of Social Imprints on the Landscape of the Coastal Savanna of Ghana: A Report to ESCOR*, Norwich, UEA.

Carson, W.P. (1985) 'State of Knowledge Report: The Ecology of the Accra-Winneba Plains with Some Aspects of Related Savanna Ecosystems' in *Man and the Biosphere Project 3: Impact of Human Activities on the Structure and Productivity of the Savanna Ecosystem in Ghana Phase 1: Following and Rotation in the Accra-Winnable Plains, Report on Preliminary Activities* pp.4-74, Accra, Environmental Protection Council.

Craib, I. (1992) *Anthony Giddens* London, Routledge.

Dickson, K.B. (1966) 'Historical Geography: Some Problems of Presentation and Interpretation', *Bulletin of the Ghana Geographical Association,* 2: 5-14.

Dickson, K.B. and G. Benneh (1988) *A New Geography of Ghana* London, Longman.

Dupuis, J. (1824) *Journal of a Residence in Ashantee* London. Cited in Dickson, K.B. (1964) 'The Agricultural Landscape of Southern Ghana and Ashanti-Brong Ahafo: 1800 to 1850', *Bulletin of the Ghana Geographical Association* 9(1): 25.

Elliott, J.A. and Campbell, M. (2002) The Environmental Imprints and Complexes of Social Dynamics in Rural Africa: Cases from Zimbabwe and Ghana. *Geoforum* 33: 221-237.

Fairhead, J. and M. Leach (1994) 'Contested Forests: Modern Conservation and Historical Land Use in Guinea's Ziama Reserve', *African Affairs* 93 (373): 481-513.

Fairhead, J. and M. Leach (1995) 'False Forest History, Complicit Social Analysis: Rethinking Some West African Environmental Narratives', *World Development* 23, (6): 1023-1035.

Fairhead, J. and M. Leach (1996) Misreading *the African Landscape: Society and Ecology in a Forest Savanna Mosaic* Cambridge: Cambridge University Press.

Fairhead, J. and M. Leach (1998*) Reforming Deforestation: Global Analysis and Local Realities - Studies in West Africa* London: Routledge.

Folly, A. (1995) 'Estimation of Erodibility in the Savanna Ecosystem, Northern Ghana' in *Communications in Soil Science and Plant Analysis* 26 (5): 799- 812.

Giddens, A. (1979) *Central Problems in Social Theory* London: Macmillan.

Giddens, A. (1984) *The Constitution of Society* Cambridge, Polity Press.

Government of Ghana (1948-2000) Accra: Census Reports.

Graphic Reporter (1995) 'Help End Land Disputes', in *Daily Graphic* November 23 1995.

Gyasi, E., G.T. Agyepong, E. Ardayfio-Schandorf, L. Enu-Kwesi, J.S. Nabila and E. Owusu-Bennoah (1995) 'Production Pressure and Environmental Change in the Forest-Savanna Zone of Southern Ghana', *Global Environmental Change* 5(4): 355-366.

Hall, J.B. (1985) *Personal Communication* in Carson (1985) *op cit* p.45.

Hawthorne, W.D. and M.Abu-Juam (1995) *Forest Project in Ghana: With Particular Reference to Vegetation and Plant Species* Gland: International Union of Nature and Natural Resources (IUCN).

Herwitz, S.R., R.E. Slye and S.M. Turton (1998) 'Corcgistered Aerial Stereopairs from Low Flying Air from Lowflying Aircraft for the Analysis of Long-Term Tropical Rainforest Canopy Dynamics', *Photogramm. Engng Sens.* 64: 397-405.

Hopkins, B. (1992) 'Ecological Processes at the Forest Savanna Boundary' in Furley, P.A., J. Proctor and J.A. Ratter (1992) *Nature and Dynamics of Forest-Savanna Boundaries* pp. 21-33, London, Chapman and Hall.

Howard, R.(1978) *Colonialism and Underdevelopment in Ghana* London, Croon Helm.

Iddrisu, A. and S. Tropp (1995) 'Land Degradation and Desertification in Ghana' in Atchia, M. (ed.) (1995) *Environmental Management: Issues and Solutions* pp.125-127 Chichester, John Wiley and Sons.

Innes, J.L. (1998) 'Measuring Environmental Change' In Peterson, D.L. and V.T. Parker (1998) *Ecological Scale: Theory and Applications* pp. 429-457 New York: Columbia

University Press.

Irvine, F.R. (1947) *The Fish and Fisheries of the Gold Coast* London, Longman.

Ite, U.E. (1997) 'Small Farmers and Forest Loss in Cross River National Park, Nigeria', *The Geographical Journal* 163(1): 47-56.

Jackson, C. (1993) Doing What Comes Naturally? Women and Environment in Development', *World Development* 21(12): 1947-1963.

Jackson, C. (1994) 'Gender Analysis and Environmentalisms' in Redclift, M. and Benton, T. (1994) *Social Theory and the Global Environment* pp.113-149, Routledge: London.

Jampoh, E.L. (1989) *The Organisation of Fuelwood and Charcoal Trade in Ghanaian Urban Centres: Case Studies in Accra and Kumasi* Unpublished B.Sc. Dissertation, Institute of Renewable Natural Resources, Kumasi: University of Science and Technology.

Jenik, J. and J.B. Hall (1976) 'Plant Communities of the Accra Plains', *Folia Geobot Phytotax Praha,* 162-212.

Kay, G.R. (1972) *The Political Economy of Colonialism in Ghana: a Collection of Documents and Statistics 1900-1960* London: Cambridge University Press.

Keay, R.W.J. (1959) *Vegetation Map of Africa: Explanatory Roles* London: Oxford University Press.

La Anyane, S. (1956) 'An Historical Account of Agricultural Development in the Gold Coast Before 1900,' *New Gold Coast Farmer* 1 (1, 2): 28-65.

Lane, D.A.(1962) 'The Forest Vegetation' in Wills, J.B. (1962) '*Agriculture and Land Use in Ghana*', London, Oxford University Press.

Leach, M. and R. Mearns (1996*) The Lie of the Land: Challenging Received Wisdom on the African Environment*, London, James Curry.

Lieberman, D.D. (1979) *Dynamics of Forest and Thicket Vegetation on the Accra Plains, Ghana.* Unpublished Ph.D. Thesis, Accra: University of Ghana.

Long, N. and A. Long (1992) (eds) *Battlefields of Knowledge: The Interlocking of Theory and Practice in Social Research and Development* London, Routledge.

Macdonald, G. (1898) *The Gold Coast Past and Present: A Short Description of the Country and its People* London: Longman, Green and Company.

Mellor, M. (1997) 'Gender and the Environment' in Redclift, M. and Woodgate, G. (1997) *The International Handbook of Environmental Sociology* pp.367-385, , Cheltenham: Edward Elgar.

Mensah, G.E. (1996) 'Minister Freezes Sale of Bortianor Lands' *Ghanaian Times* Friday May 24: 3.

Mezikpih, E. (1996) 'Ban on Sale of Bortianor Lands' in *Daily Graphic* May 24: 8.

Mezikpih, E. (1996) 'Wetlands Must be Protected' in *Daily Graphic* July 24: 16.

Millington, A.C., P.J. Styles and R.W. Critchley (1992) Mapping Forests and Savannas in Sub-Saharan Africa From Advanced Very High Resolution (AVHRR) Imagery' in Furley, P.A., Proctor, J. and Ratter, J.A., (1992*) Nature and Dynamics of Forest-Savanna Boundaries* pp.37-62, London, Chapman and Hall.

Nsiah Gyabaah, K. (1992) *Environmental Degradation and the Threat of Drought and Desertification in the Upper West Region of Ghana: a Search for Sustainable Development Solutions* Unpublished Ph.D. Thesis University of London.

Ocansey, J.M. (1985) *A Survey of Wood Energy Utilisation within a Rural Community* Unpublished Diploma Dissertation, Kumasi: University of Science and Technology.

Oduro-Afriyie, K. (1996) 'Rainfall Erosivity Map for Ghana' *Geoderma* 74, (1-2): 161-166.

Peet, R. and M. Watts (1996) *Liberation Ecologies: Environment, Development, Social Movements* London, Routledge.

Pretty, J.N. and P. Shah (1997) 'Making Soil and Water Conservation Sustainable: From Coercion and Control to Partnerships and Participation' *Land Degradation and Development* 8(1): 39-58.

Pretty, J.N. (1995) 'Participatory Learning for Sustainable Agriculture', *World Development* 23(8):1247-1263.

Rao, B. (1991) 'Dominant Constructions of Women and Nature in Social Science Literature', *Capitalism, Nature, Socialism Pamphlet 2*, New York, Guilford Publications.

Reardon, T. and S.A. Vosti (1995) 'Links Between Rural Poverty and the Environment in Developing Countries: Asset Categories and Investment Poverty' *World Development* 23(9): 1495-1506.

Redclift, M. (1987) *Sustainable Development: Exploring the Contradictions*, London, Methuen.

Riley, J. and C.J. Alexander (1997) 'Statistical Literature for Participatory on-Farm Research' in *Experimental Agriculture* 33 (1): 73-82.

Rocheleau, D., B.Thomas-Slayter and E.Wangari (1996) *Feminist Political Ecology* London, Routledge.

Rowe, J. S. (1997) 'From Reductionism to Holism in Ecology and Deep Ecology' *The Ecologist* 27 (4): 147-151.

Sarris, A.H. and H. Shams (1991) *Ghana under Structural Adjustment: the Impact on Agriculture and the Rural Poor* New York, New York University.

Scholes, R.J. and B.H. Walker (1993) *An African Savanna: Synthesis of the Nylsvley Study* Cambridge, Cambridge University Press.

Spaeth, H.J. (1996) 'Land Degradation in West Niger', *Desertification Control Bulletin* (UNEP) (28) 34-41.

Stott, P.A. (1991) 'Recent Trends in the Ecology and Management of the World's Savanna Formations', *Progress in Physical Geography* 15: 18-28.

Taylor, C.J. (1952) *The Vegetation Zones of the Gold Coast* Accra: Government Printing Department,

Technical Assistance to the Weija Irrigation Company (TAWEICO) Final Report (1986) Technosynesis SpA, Roma.

Thomas-Slayter, B.P. (1994) 'Structural Change, Power Politics and Community Organisation in Africa: Challenging the Patterns, Puzzles and Paradoxes' *World*

Development 22(10): 1479-1490.

Teme, B., H. Breman, and K. Sissoko (1996) *Agricultural Intensification in the Sahel: Myth or Reality*? Bamako: Institut d'Economie Rurale.

Tiffen, M., M.Mortimore and F.Gichuki (1994*) More People, Less Erosion: Environmental Recovery in Kenya* Chichester, John Wiley and Sons.

United Nations Human Development Report (1990) New York: Oxford University Press.

UNICEF (1990) *Children and Women of Ghana: A Situational Analysis* Accra: UNICEF,

Witcombe, J.R. and A. Joshi (1996) 'Farmer Participatory Crop Improvement: 2. Participatory Varietal Selection, a Case Study in India', *Experimental Agriculture* 32 (4): 461-477.

Witcombe, J.R., B.R. Sthapit and K.D. Joshi (1996) 'Farmer Participatory Crop Improvement: Participatory Plant Breeding, a Case Study for Rice in Nepal', *Experimental Agriculture* 32 (4): 481-496.

Zimmerer, K.S. (1994) 'Human Geography and the 'New Ecology': The Prospect of Integration', *Annals of the Association of American Geographers* 84(1): 108-125.

22

People, Environment and Development of Upper Ganga Basin Area, Uttarakhand, India

S.C. Mukhopadhyay

Prolouge

The author has considered primarily the complex geomorphological setting, structure and tectonics, rivers and river basins, climate and the related aspects for the physical and population/demographic with particular emphasis on the most significant tribal population (both S.C. and S.T.) and their occupational patterns, land use, the prevailing socio-economic status, and the recent environmental changes in cultural landscape. These include the role of women in the society in the context of development and the regional socio-economic disparities particularly among the Gads, Jaunsaries and Rajis mainly district wise in brief (Upper Ganga Basin area, Mukhopadhyay, 1998, 2002, 2007).

Due weightage has been given on the study of some aspects of people, environment and development of the Upper Ganga basin with particular emphasis on Uttarkashi and adjacent areas, Uttarakhand. The tribal communities represent the vast diversity in their socio-economic life, cultural heritage, land and other resource uses. Despite their habitations in different zones, there prevails a common feature in the economic and social life of almost all tribal communities, with variations necessitated to maintain a harmonious coordination between resource availability and population structure. The socio-cultural life of the tribal communities is interwoven with the economic life and their resource management strategies that are expressions of their inherent cultural traits. The qualitative symbiotic relationship of the tribal people with their close environs like forests is the strenuous outcome of the centuries old experience of their difficult survival. The undulating terrain of the Western Himalaya includes major mountain districts of North Uttaranchal State. These districts are Uttarkashi, Chamoli, Rudra Prayag, Tehri, Dehradun, Pauri, Pithoragarh, Champawat, Almora, Bageswar, Nainital and Udham Singh. The total population of these districts is about seven million. Out of this scheduled castes and scheduled tribes constitute nearly 16 percent and 4 percent respectively. The five tribes numbering to 3 lakh (approximately) within the upper Ganga Basin spreads over the ridges-mountain side and valley side slopes. These are (a) the Tharus, (b) the Jaunsaries, (c) the Buxas, (d) the Bhotias and (e) the Rajis and others are Gujjars etc. Some development projects/schemes have been adopted to ameliorate the existing problems especially concerning poverty and healthy intra-zonal disparities as well as over all socio-politico-economic development of the entire tribal communities.

The objectives of the investigations are:

- to elucidate the relationships of mountain people, environment and development of Uttarakhand.
- to minimize the difference of regional imbalances, the existing gap between the levels of development of especially the tribal communities themselves and tribal areas and the adjacent areas, within the upper Ganga Basin.

It may be mentioned here that these tribal communities represent the vast diversity in their socio-economic life, cultural heritage and land use/resource use. Although their habittories are scattered in different zones, there prevail common features in the economic and social life of all tribal communities, with variations necessitated to maintain a harmonious coordination between resource availability, population structure as well as occupational patterns. The socio-cultural life of the tribal communities is closely tied with the economic activities virtually involving their resource management strategies which are expressions of their inherent cultural traits. The development strategies are primarily concerned with the following:

- to safeguard against exploitation of tribal people in terms of land, indebtedness, labour, trade and marketing of minor forest product, surplus agricultural products,
- to raise the productivity level in the field of agriculture, animal husbandry, forestry, cottage and small industries,
- to foster human resource development for the upgradation of the tribal skills and the staff engaged in tribal development work,
- to raise the level of education both formal and non-formal including technical especially for girls.

In order to achieve the aforesaid objectives, the tribal sub-plan of this part of the upper Ganga basin has four major points of the programme:

(1) Infrastructure development relating to minimum needs programme, (2) development of agriculture and allied sectors, (3) programme of family-oriented economic development, and (4) development of human resources. Under Integrated Tribal Development project, about 86 percent of the population of the five tribes has been benefited. Most of the objectives of these programmes were

fulfilled by the end of the last decade (1991-2000) in terms of the targets of crossing the poverty level to a considerable extent.

Area and Location

The author has studied an area of about five thousand sq. km. of the Upper Ganga Basin, Uttarakhand. It includes mainly the (a) Bhotias (especially the Jad Bhotiya), (b) Jaunsaries and (c) Rajis. It seems reasonable to discuss about the recent changes in the communities of Jad Bhotiya after the Jaunsar, Bhotias and Rajis. Author intends to focus on the contemporary problems of the Jaunsaries, the Bhotias and the Rajis inhabiting mountain terrains of the Indian Central Himalaya. The Jaunsaries inhabit in Chakrata Tehsil, which is also known as Jaunsar-Bawar region of district Dehradun. The Jaunsaries are agriculturists and a conservative tribal community with unique cultural practices like polyandry and black magic, which are continuously wanting. In the hierarchical classification of the Jaunsari community the high caste Brahmins and the Rajputs (Khasas) occupy the top, the shilpakara (artisan castes) the middle and the Koltas or Doms at the bottom. A traditional institution called 'Sayanachari' maintains the law and order and social justice and settles disputes and conflicts within the village.

On the other hand the Bhotias, a trans-human community of mongoloid origin, are spread over three districts (Pithoragarh, Chamoli and Uttarkashi) or Uttarakhand in Uttar Pradesh at Indo-Tibetan and Indo-Nepal Borders, a zone of ethnic intermixing and cultural assimilation. They show close racial and cultural affinity to the Tibetans and probably for this similarity, the Bhotia region is called Bod or Bhot which is synonym for Tibet. The major Bhotia groups are the Johari or Saukas, Rang, Marchha, Tolcha and Jad, and are scattered over eight main river valleys known as Johar, Darma, Byans, Chaudans (Pithoragarh district), Mana, Niti (Chamoli district), Nilang and Judung (Uttarkashi district). The Bhotias covered in the present study, inhabit the high altitude regions of two tehsils Munisary and Dharchula.

Actually, the Rajis, socially and economically, are the most under-developed tribal community of Central Himalayan region of India. The community is numerically small and is reported from 11 villages in total, from Pithoragarh, Champawat and Udham Singh Nagar district of State of Uttaranchal. The tribe is primitive and nomadic. The Rajis were recognized as a primitive tribe in 1975, and they represent themselves as descendants of one of the aboriginal princes of Kumaon. The Rajis were complete nomads about three to four decades back, and at present settling down as agriculturists under interventions (Mukhopadhyay, 2002) Distinct differences in social and economic development were found although all the three tribes inhabit in, more or less, a set of similar geo-physical and ecological conditions and are subjected to similar policy/development interventions. An effort is made in this paper to characterize these differences and discuss the role of economy and culture in the development of the tribal people. The integration of the advantages and limitations of these variables in policy of the tribal people will make the development more meaningful and sustainable.

Recent Changes among the Jaunsaries, Bhotias and Rajis

Major socio-politico-economic aspects including the various occupation, education, health hazard etc. have been considered for the purpose of ascertaining the occurrence of changes among these tribes.

The differential trends in economic development of the tribes are distinctly displayed by the occupational structure and spatial contribution of source to total economy of particular tribe. Heavy dependence on agriculture was observed for the Jaunsaries as 70.6 percent of the main workers were engaged in agriculture, against 39.3 percent in Bhotias and 44.60 percent in Rajis. Nearly 13.5 percent of Bhotia main workers were engaged in cottage industry against almost nil in case of the Jaunsaries and the Rajis. The extent of differences in economic development can be perceived more by deliberately looking at the present scenario of their spatial pattern of economy in terms of percentage contribution of different sources to total income. The per capita income was Rs. 1,427.00, Rs. 1,957.00 and Rs. 1,351.00 for the Jaunsaries, the Bhotias, and the Rajis, respectively. Economy of the Jaunsaries is based on agriculture. They have been agrarian by tradition and the villages of Jaunsar-Bawar were self sustaining until late fifties, they grew their own food, making agricultural and domestic implements themselves and weaving woollen clothes for themselves. Traditionally, the Bhotias are traders and their trade with Tibet was the mainstay of their economy. The act of trade with Tibet resulted in evolving distinct socio-economic structure like seasonal nomadism. In 1962, after the Indo-China war, their trade with Tibet was banned by the Government of India. The sudden disruption of the Indo-Tibetan trade, which was the mainstay of Bhotias economy and adjunct to their socio-cultural life, resulted in their niche-deterioration, forcing them to seek alternative courses of livelihood.

At present the economic organization of the Bhotias is an agglomeration of trade and business, terraced cultivation, pastoralism, woollen industry and service. They have two settlements, the upper or summer settlement where they stay from May-June to October-November and lower or winter settlement where they stay rest of the year. Before three to four decades the Rajis were totally nomads, pursuing a life of hunter-gatherers taking shelter in caves or temporary huts. The traditional economy of the Rajis was primarily built around the forests.

Tarur *(Dioscoroil deltodia)* and Geenthi *(Dioscoraja bulbifera)* have been their staple food. Rajis are reputed for their craftsmanship in wooden utensil. Initially, interactions of the Rajis with other communities were limited in the darkness of night. During nights, they used to disguise themselves and keep the products like wooden utensils at the door of non-tribal Kumaon households and go back to their forest dwelling without being seen by them.

On the next morning, these articles were collected by the households and replaced by some food grains, clothes, sugar etc. which would be collected by the Rajis during night. Due to such exchange at night, Rajis are also known as the Traders of Night. Similar to the African Pygmies, such kind of trade was completely based on mutual belief between the Rajis and the other local communities in the upper Ganga Basin area. The economic condition has influenced the demographic behaviour in case of the tribes. The agrarian Jaunsaries have more joint family structures (78.2 percent, the Bhotias having a multiple occupations have almost equal percentage of joint and nuclear families and the Rajis have more nuclear families (78.4 percent). Size of family was also determined by the production system or the economy of the tribal community. Average size of family for the Jaunsaries was 11 against 6 in case of the Bhotias and 4 in case of the Rajis. The prevalence of large sized joint family system among the Jaunsaries is also one of the unique socio-cultural advantages of the polyandry system, prevalent among them, whereas, among the Rajis, prevalence of nuclear family and its tradition among the Rajis was some sort of adaptation to their nomadic economy based on hunting and food gathering.

At present, predominance of nuclear family among them is largely due to the nature of their livelihood i.e. the hand to mouth condition, the strong traditional resource base of Bhotias in term of trade and pastoralism supported them financially to provide formal education for new generation which decade more and more intended towards organized service sector leading to out-migration. Such conditions have also played an important role in emergence and prevalence of more nuclear families. The Bhotias have frequently been in contact with Tibetans and their surrounding Kumaoni society since time immemorial in connection with trade which demanded certain level of formal education. That is why; the literacy is highest among them in contrast to the Jaunsaries and the Rajis. The Bhotias had a higher literacy rate (63.17) against 40.40 percent and 35.06 percent for the Jaunsaries and the Rajis respectively. The economically better of Bhotias showed comparatively better demographic behaviours reflect adequately about the quality of life. Particularly from the perspectives of gender, one gender issue that distinctly asserted the better quality of life of women in the Bhotias was the sex ratio. The Bhotias had also much less average number of pregnancies, low fertility rate and low infant mortality rate, etc. compared to others. The linkages between culture and social and economic development were apparently visible.

Table 22.1: District-wise Annual Rainfall (mm) (2005)

Name of the Districts	January to March	April to June	July to September	October to December
Dehradun	118	211	731	28
Uttarkashi	173	193	524	34
Haridwar	46	164	671	54

Table 22.2: Salient Demographic Features (2005)

Name of District	Area (sq.km.)	Rural	Male	Female
Dehradun	3,088	5,10,199	27,412	2,36,087
		S.C.77,287	41,862	35,426
		S.T.81,005	42,686	38,319
Uttarkashi	8,016	2,22,448	1,14,723	1,07,725
		52,355	26,842	25,513
		2,240	1,174	1,066
Haridwar	2,360	7,76,346	4,19,974	3,56,372
		2,05,386	1,19,460	93,926
		2,004	1,117	887

Contd...

Name of District	Urban	Male	Female	Density of population per sq. km.
Dehradun	5,15,480	2,82,320	2,33,160	343
	60,177	32,390	27,787	
	3,071	1,824	1,247	
Uttarkashi	17,261	10,255	7,006	42
	2,239	1,240	999	
	60	31	29	
Haridwar	3,48,142	1,89,089	1,59,062	497
	37,272	20,192	17,080	
	22	11	11	

The Conservative Jaunsaries preferred to remain agriculturist and have not taken the risk of diversifying their economy. The nomadic Rajis are continuing to remain economically backward and are largely dependent on forest produce. Nomadic way of life coupled with superstitions in Rahis influenced the demographic behaviour like literacy, sex ratio, fertility, mortality rates, etc. Till now, the Rajis after the death of a family member, even a child, pull down the house, quit the village and settle in another village. They may come back after a couple of years. The practice had affected their quality of life in many ways, like children's education, agriculture and allied activities, health and medicare. The upward looking Bhotias have taken advantage of their inherent cultural traits, i.e. enterprising nature, and have aptly diversified their economy after economy. However, their way of life did not fail them and they have today a highly diversified occupational pattern and probably one of the economically, socially and educationally richest tribal communities in India. Their tradition and culture are still significantly finding their way in their livelihood patterns like pastoralism, trade, use of medicinal plants, etc. They did not break down under pressure.

Table 22.3: District-wise Population by Religion (2005)

District	Total Population	Hindus	Muslims	Christians	Sikhs
Dehradun	10,25,679	8,74,160	98,748	89,490	30,417
Uttarkashi	2,39,709	2,35,509	2,464	89	214
Haridwar	11,24,488	7,68,688	3,38,146	1,990	18,822

Contd...

District	Buddhists	Jains	Other Religions	Religion not stated
Dehradun	8,345	4,159	225	76
Uttarkashi	1,177	284	2	2
Haridwar	359	2,397	17	69

It may be mentioned that the Bhotia's most remarkable cultural character is their identity of religion, despite being in contact with the Tibetans for centuries. They have never absorbed into their own simple religion the extravagances and the demonology of Lamaism. The Bhotias do neither practice Buddhism nor idolatry of the Hindus. A significant aspect of behaviour of the intelligent and mercantile community, the Bhotias, is that when they visited Tibet for trading, they worshipped the deities of that country and when they came to lower plains in India, they reversed the deities of that country and they revered the deities of Hindus, They back in their own land 'Bhot', in their social and own religion with no hand over of Buddhism or Hinduism. The simplicity in their social and cultural functions is another cultural adaptation that helped them save their income unlike the Jaunsaries who are famous for extravaganzas during festivals. Further, Jaunsari married women keep the double standard of morality as observed by Majumdar (1962).

Table 22.4: Important Economic Indicators of Development among the Three Tribes, Upper Ganga Basin (1995-2005)

Indicators	Gads	Jaunsaries	Rajis
Total main workers	52.6	55.7	63.2
Agricultural workers in main workers (percent)	41.4	67.8	48.3
Labourers in main workers(percent)	9.4	7.2	41.5
Forest produce gatherers in main workers (percent)	16.9	19.6	21.8
Service holders in main workers(percent)	24.8	15.4	3.2
Businessmen/traders in main workers (percent)	32.2	9.7	8.6
Income from agriculture(percent)	18.3	43.8	17.2
Income from wage labourers (percent)	9.3	14.6	57.5
Income from forest produce(percent)	6.2	4.4	33.8
Income from service (percent)	42.4	35.2	9.4
Income from trade/business(percent)	39.7	12.3	6.4
Household income per annum (Rs.)	13873	19718	8754
Per capita income per annum (Rs)	2447	2468	1522

(Based on Census 2001and Field study 2006)

Jad Bhotiya: Sheep Herding/Trading Tribe

Broadly speaking, the Jad occupy at present two major villages, one, Bhagori, situated near the small town of Harsil, at a height of 2,591 meters above the sea level. This was locally known as the village Haniya but has developed into a tiny town with a post office and a bank and a few eating places and shops due to the presence of the army headquarters. Also present are the Indo-Tibet border police. The area is surrounded by dense forests and has numerous streams running through it and deep gorges. In fact, the approach to the village is only on foot and one has to cross several bridges across fast flowing mountain streams to get there. It has a secondary, school and a government owned rest house as well as an inspection bungalow. The physical inaccessibility of the place may be one why one does not see many visitors here in spite of its breath taking scenic beauty. The second village occupied by the Jad is the village Dunda, at a much lower altitude near the religious town of Uttarkashi at a height of 1.167 meters above sea level. This is the winter village of the Jad who are transhumant, coming down to the lower altitude village in winter and going up in summer. In winter, Harsil remains under several feet of snow, and the approach road is often cut off. The mountain side is prone to landslides and for many months in the year this area is completely isolated from the mainland.

The Jad travelling by the mountain route rather than the roads can travel up and down on their mules and on their sure feet adapted to the mountains but vehicular traffic comes to a stop. Actually, the winter village and Duda bring the Jad closer to the culture of the people on the plains. The relatively busy and populated town of Uttarkashi is a window to the urban world where they have television, moves and the telephone. There are also urban markets and most importantly, a predominantly Hindu culture.

Major Economic Activities-Sheep Herding, Trade etc.

In earlier times the Jad used to go hawking their wares in the nearby villages. Some persons in the villages in the vicinity of Hrishikesh told me that even a couple of decades back they came hawking heeng Jabhu, Chora in these villages but now they have become prosperous. The changing political relations of the two countries, on whose borders they lived, critically affected the economic and social life of the villagers. The Jad are a pastoral community herding sheep and goats and had trading as an important adjunct of their pastoral way of life. The Jad are not unique in carrying on these activities and in the past, such was the mode of life of most of the small pastoral communities living on the borders of the countries lying across the Himalayan range, referred to as buffer for example he Na and Mara tribes of the North eastern border. With the closure of the Tibetan border, the trade links with Tibet stopped altogether and their shift to a lower altitudc also meant that they now had closer links with the population of the Hindu mainland. A number of other factors have also affected their way of life and also their world view. Now, the primary factors of change have been the opening of this rcgion to the travellers from the lower altitudes by thc building of motorable roads and communication links. The establishment of an army basc in their vicinity has been a major source of change. Since they are primarily identified as a janjati (tribe) in the government records, there has been a considerable development input. They have a secondary school and also a government PHC that is the only one in the block of eight villages that forms the Gram Sabha.

At present, the Jad have thus been brought in closer interactions with the Indian mainland and from where they get all their requirements. With the severance of earlier trade links with Tibet they have picked up new trade avenues with the Indian side of the border. Another traditional avenue of income that has almost become redundant is that of provider of transport on the hills. Since they are the only pastoral community in this region, they provided animal transport on this part of the country to neighbouring villagers as well to the pilgrims who came to visit the holy shrine of Gangotri. For this, the Jad reared mules, horses and castrated male sheep called Khadu. They also served as guides and porters to the pilgrims. With the introduction of vehicles and the construction of proper roads and bridges, this income generating activity of the Jad came to a virtual standstill. They still rear a few animals but it is mostly for their own use and for a limited hiring out. The pilgrims are now entirely dependent on buses, jeeps and taxis for transport. Most of them simply pass by Harsil because of its small size and lack of tourist facilities. The main income generating activity of the Jad is now knitting of woollen garments by the women, making of carpets and the sale of wool, sheep, goats and dogs. They have of late taken to planting apple orchards and some of them are making a good profit from them. A significant aspect of change has been education. For the last two decades or so formal education has gained in popularity. At the time of my field work from 1998-2000, all the children in the village were going to school. A large number of boys and girls had received college education.

Further, the Jads have been most frequently referred to as Buddhists in census and other reports. But during the course of my field work I found that they were neither Buddhists nor Hindus. They are a little of both. They believe in their own world of the supernatural that is composed of deities and a spirit and have primordial character closer to a tribal folk religion rather than either of the two universal religions from both of which they have borrowed elements. Their primary deity is the village Meparang, who stands guard over their high altitude village at Harsil. They are uniquely different from the Hindus in that they have no anthropomorphic deities and have no idols in their village. Tall bamboo poles decorated with pieces of red clot represent Meparan. Other deities are likewise represented by sticks and stones.

It is beyond the scope of this paper to describe their religion in details but it is suffice to say that they have their own integrated belief system that is uniquely Jad although it borrows from both Hinduism and Buddhism. In their rituals they follow a unique pattern made up of Buddhist, Hindu and primordial tribal elements. Traditionally, the men sell animals and raw wool from where they take it off the animals. They also carry on trade in Chor Pani with traders from the plains. But whatever is handed over to women becomes their property. It is they who both sell and keep the proceeds of the sale. The Jad are uniquely individualistic in that whatsoever makes an item sells it and also keeps the money. Thus young teenaged girls, who knit, sell the items they have made in the market places and keep the money to spend as they please. I have often seen girls as young as 13 or 14 driving hard bargains in the market place, and negotiating on their own with local shopkeepers. The girls and the women have a great deal of independence of movement within and near their villages but they do not go so far out that they have to spend the night out of their homes alone. In this context, it seems reasonable to mention some relevant points on the social life of the Jad especially the recent attitude of the women in their families. But the women carry on horticulture activities in the nearby field to their residence. Actually, the Jad villages have central cluster of houses surrounded by fields, and they grow mainly potatoes, chhimi (red blans), black gram, sundry vegetables and spices i.e. chillies, ginger etc. using a hoe.

Recent Development in the Activities of Women

Actually, the Jads have reorganized some of their economic activities, they primarily remain pastorals and still about several thousands of sheeps and goats are reared by them in addition to some larger animals like cows, mules and horses. The sheep are taken on their grazing routes that extend from high reaches of the Himalayas in summer to the foothills in winter. Thus a Jad herdsman and his animals cover a long route that takes them practically the entire year to complete. The route is along mountain streams and keeps the herdsman in the forested and isolated areas away from the human habitations. Thus the men in Jad community belong to the rega, the forests. Unlike some other pastoralists the Jad women and children do not accompany the men on their herding routes. The women and the family members stay in the villages, which move seasonally. But while the grazing routes of the men takes them through the wildernesses where they live in temporary shelters of tents. Thus, for the Jad, the appropriate place for the women is the village and for the men, it is rega, the forests. Since the social activities take place in the village, the women are seen as centres of the social world. All activities within the village including economic activities are in the hands of the women. The men rear the animals in the forests near thc village and pass on the raw wool to the women who take over the entire process of wool processing and spinning. They then knit beautiful items from the wool and make carpets. Some of these items are sold and others are used within the domestic group. It has been observed that the girls in the area enjoy latitude in thcir movement and sexual preferences while the Jaunsari married women maintain double standard of morality with prevalence of polygunandrous marriage (Majumdar, 1962).

Current Trends

The analysis advocates that the trends of development in all the three tribal communities were guided by economic and cultural forces. The mode of economy and cultural conservatism of the Jaunsaries did not allow them much to diversify their economy. The Jaunsaries remained traditionally agriculturists and economically poor. Their demographic behaviour, to a larger extent, is guided by conservative cultural principles which had affected the quality of life, particularly of females. The Rajis with nomadic way of life coupled with superstitions and beliefs are in the lowest level of economic and social development. The enterprising Bhotia tribe with an upward looking way of life had successfully taken advantage of their improved economic and cultural elements to promote growth with prosperity. They used their culture as framework for trying out new ideas and changes. It makes imperative that policies and programmes to be undertaken for development of tribal people must understand the nature of economy and culture of the community. It is suggestive that any development policy must be formulated, implemented and evaluated in the light of both economic and cultural specificities of the concerned community. The introduction of wheeled vehicles, the importance of keeping mules and horses is also decreasing. As less people are keeping horses, the need to come down to the camp at Chor Pani is gradually declining. On my visit to the camp in the winter of 1999, I was told that many families had not come down and in coming years the number of families may even decrease further.

They were also adapted as an Ambedkar village and received grants that lead to the building of several steel bridges to their village. Earlier the people had to partly wade through water and partly make use of temporary log bridges to reach the village. Also a road within the village was metalled although no vehicle can cross the narrow bridges to enter the village, yet some limited use can be made of it. It mostly serves the villagers as a place to sit and work.

Decision making activity among the Tribe is uniquely confined to the women in so far as these concern domestic matters. Even very young girls can take decisions provided they are of an age to start earning money by selling their produce. While doing field work I was often invited to dinner or a meal by a girl as young as 12 or 13 who would even cook the meal and serve it to us, without having to take consent from any one. But even a grown up man would say come to my house for a meal. I will ask my wife or my mother etc. The women do the cultivation, storage and the preparation of meals. It is they who serve to guest and to family members. The preparation and distribution of change is the exclusive domain of women. Thus, at a wedding feast where change is pooled to be served to guests one sees a procession of women arriving with vessels of all descriptions containing change.

Concluding Remarks

The living habits of the people including the tribes of the Upper Ganga Basin, and interference in the complex mountainous environment should be treated with a holistic approach. These include social and economic interactions with the network of dependences, of course an effect relationship which require inter-zonal and inter-sectional considerations. It becomes difficult to adopt regional development planning for spatial utilization as a standard practice for the rapid development programme especially in trade and commerce other than agriculture in the seismic-tectonically unstable terrain of the upper Ganga basin. Recently, the local people and the tourists have started to exploit the environment intensively, without having any systematic and standard land use as well as management of the resources in the area. However, the River Ganga with several glaciers as well as vast natural resources has been regarded as the gift of the Himalaya. It should be mentioned that recently (since 1980) there have been notable changes in a number of physical and social parameters involving the undulating mountainous terrain of the Upper Ganga Basin (Mukhopadhyay, 1998).

Greater rate of urbanisation and rapid population pressure cause scarcity of some commodities especially water compared to past decades especially whenever there are fluctuations in incidences of rainfall. The nomad people especially the male members of the region (Bhotias, Rajis, Jaunsaries, Gujjars etc.) have depended much on the forest and arable lands-cultivated terrains and preferred also the forest belts. They have come in conflict with the system of resource management and conservation of the region. Now, the importing of basic technical and commercial skills to the mountain populations is a vital necessity. Here, author would like to stress much on the urgent need for local people's participation further for integrated management of mountainous environment with a thoughtful planning in consideration with the introduction of the task of deagrarianisation (Mukhopadhyay 2002) and application of the nine-tier unit model at different elevations and river valleys of the study area . It will be helpful thus in minimizing the regional socio-economic disparities through establishing a social harmony towards the improvement of balanced regional economy of the Ganga Basin.

It seems reasonable to present the relevant observation of Tolstoy who begins Anna Karenina with the famous sentence: All happy families are alike but an unhappy family is unhappy after its own fashion. Perhaps that is also the case in the world of economic misery and well being. The diversity of experience of the poor countries in the world is much wider and sharper than them that of the rich countries. This is partly because the number of people and countries that are poor is much larger (and, socially, geographically, and institutionally, far more heterogeneous) than that of rich countries.

Such socio-economic situations appear to be justified in the study of People, Environment and Development of the Upper Ganga Basin Area, Uttarakhand, as presented in the text.

References

Agarwal, N.C. and Kumar Gopendra (1973) Geology of Upper Bhagirathi and Yamuna Valleys, Uttarkashi District, Kumaun Himalaya, Jr. Himalayan Geology. Vol.3, Kolkata, pp 1-23.

Bardhan and Udry(1999) Micro economies , Oxford University Press, Oxford, pp-1-9.

Channa, S.M. (2002) Changing altitudes and Gender relations among the pastoral Bhotiyas of Garhwal Himalaya, Jr. Indian Anthropological Soc., Kolkata, Vol.37, pp.41-50.

Mukhopadhyay, S.C. (1998) Environmental Changes of the Dehradoon Terrain : A Study in Human Interference, Indian Journal of Landscape Systems and Ecological Studies, ILEE, Vol. 21(2), Calcutta, pp.130-165.

Mukhopadhyay, S.C. (2002): Man and Environment of the Upper Ganga Basin, Uttaranchal, Indian Journal of Landscape Systems and Ecological Studies, ILEE, Vol. 25(2), Calcutta, pp.109-129.

Mukhopadhyay, S.C. (2007) Some hints on scale and models in applied geography (Earth System), Indian Journal of Landscape Systems and Ecological Studies, ILEE, Vol. 30 (1), Kolkata, pp.205-230.

Nag, P. (2001) The Atlas of Uttaranchal, (ed) Dr. P. Nag, Director, National Atlas and Thematic Mapping Organisation (NATMO), Government of India, Kolkata.

23

Environment and Demography: A Hostile Relation in Dholpur District of Rajasthan State of India

Rama Prasad and Rani Singh

Introduction

The Homo sapiens (Human beings) is known new in the Earth's history. Homo sapiens appeared first in Africa continent, but they quickly spread throughout the world. Because of their mental abilities and activities they have been able to modify or change the Earth's environment according to their needs.

Early human beings totally depended upon the environment like other animals. The ability to control and use fire allowed them to modify environment and the domestication animals eventually resulted in over-grazing and soil erosion. The domestication of plants also led to the destruction of natural vegetation to make their shelter and the demand of wood for fuel.

While human populations remained small and human technology modest, their impact on the environment was localized. As populations increased and technology improved and expanded, however, more significant and widespread problem arose. Rapid technological advances after the middle ages culminated in the Industrial Revolution, which involved the discovery, use and exploitation of fossil fuels, as well as the extensive exploitation of the Earth's mineral resources. With the Industrial Revolution, humans began in earnest to change the face of the Earth, the nature of its atmosphere, and the quality of its water. Today, unprecedented demands on the environment from a rapidly expanding human population and from advancing technology are causing a continuing and accelerating decline in the quality of the environment and its ability to sustain life.

Now-a-days Man and Environment both directly or indirectly affect each other. While environment richness is the base of Economic development of any country provided that the country has enough technique to utilize the present resource. For the development of mankind and satisfactory development of every man, deforestation or the disturbance of the environment is not only the way. Actually, Natural Resources are the type of capacity that must be utilized for the welfare of mankind for that it may be compulsory to the best use of natural resources for maintaining the ecological balance. It is possible then only, when the growth of population will be in control.

The present study is an attempt to explain the relation between Environment and Demography in the Dholpur district.

The aim of present study is to evaluate the effect of population on environment so that suitable step can be taken to reduce the hostile relationship between Environment and Demography in Dholpur district. Keeping in mind the above-mentioned facts the main aim of the present study is to gain the awareness of Demography features and Environment aspect, also the generated reason, which makes them hostile.

Several scholars such as Chorley, R.J. (1959); Burton, I. and Kates, R.W. (1965), Walton, W.C. (1970), Flawn, P.T. (1970), Birch, J.W. (1973), Coleman, D.J. (1975) Mathur, H.S. (1987), Bhatanagar, N.K. (1987) have worked a lot on man-environment, but no one has done some specific work on the hostile relation between demography and environment. Therefore, the present study concentrates on geology, agriculture, geomorphology, industries, irrigation, and development programmes.

The hypotheses of the study are:

- to change the view of people toward Environment,
- to create the new ideas for better use of Environment gain,
- to know the harm of increasing population.

The Study Area

The study area is situated in the east of Rajasthan, which is located between 26°22'N and 26°57'N Latitude and 77°14'E and 78°16'E Longitude. This district is bounded by District Bharatpur in the east, district Karoli in the west, Uttar Pradesh is in the west and east and River Chamble is in the south, which separates this district from state of Madhya Pradesh. The study area is just 109 km. away from Bharatpur city, 84 km. away from Agra city and situated on Agra-Mumbai National Highway number-3. The district occupies 3008.98 sq. km. area, which include 3 city, 4 Tehsil, 4 Panchayat samiti and 551 villages.

According to geological structure, landform and drainage system, the study area is mainly divided into three major groups, which are further divided into five sub-groups for the detail and micro study.

Table 23.1 shows that most of the area of Dholpur district is covered with the mountain ravines, which is not in the favours of population and environment.

Table 23.2 clearly shows a population decline from the census year 1911 to 1921. In comparison to India and Rajasthan, the population of the Dholpur district decreased more which was a result of the outburst of Plague, Malaria, and Drought etc. It also shows that during 1961-1991 the population grew faster than that of Rajasthan Population.

Table 23.1: Physical Division and Feature of District Dholpur

S.N	Main Division	Sub-Division
1.	Khader Region	Khader region of river Parbati
		Khader region of river Ghambeeri
		Khader region of river Chamble
2.	Bhanger region	Bhanger region of river Parbati
		Bhanger region of river Ghambeeri
3.	Uplands of Vinyachal	

Table 23.2: Decadal Population Growth Rate in District Dholpur

Year	Total Population	Decadal difference		
		District	Rajasthan	India
1901	2,98,547	-	-	-
1911	2,73,322	-08.45	+06.70	+05.73
1921	2,41,508	-11.64	-06.29	-00.30
1931	2,46,660	+02.13	+14.14	+11.00
1941	2,86,788	+16.27	+18.01	+14.23
1951	3,02,123	+05.35	+15.20	+13.31
1961	3,63,727	+20.39	+26.20	+21.64
1971	4,59,655	+26.37	+27.83	+24.66
1981	5,85,059	+27.28	+32.38	+24.08
1991	7,49,479	+28.10	+28.44	+23.16
2001	9,83,000	+31.13	+28.33	+21.34

Source: Census of India 2001

Sex-Ratio is one of the major factors and influence economic aspect of any country by changing working population ratio. In district Dhopur economy is based mainly upon agriculture therefore the sex-ratio effect is much more than the other affecting factors. In the study area the sex-ratio is 795 persons per 1000 males. This is the lowest among all the districts of Rajasthan. The sex- ratio of different census years is shown in Table 23.3.

Table 23.3: Distribution of Sex Ratio

S.N	Year	Sex Ratio	
		District	Rajasthan
1.	1901	838	905
2.	1911	820	908
3.	1921	800	896
4.	1931	816	907
5.	1941	819	906
6.	1951	814	921
7.	1961	807	908
8.	1971	806	911
9.	1981	796	919
10.	1991	795	910
11.	2001	828	922

Source: Census of India 2001

Population Distribution

Population is not equally distributed in the district. More than 50 percent of the populations lived in the fertile plains of tehsil Dholpur and Rajakhera and the less densely populated area are Besadi and Bandi tehsil where stone bedded plain and the ravines of Chambal river are found.

Density: Population density is the ratio of total population lived in an area and the total area of that land. The density in district Dholpur varies from place to place due to its landform features, which create the pressure on the environment of that area. From the point of environmental aspects the density of population of Dholpur district has been calculated. These are as follows:

A. Arithmetic Density: This type of density is calculated by the following formulae:

Arithmetic Density = Total population/Total geographical area

Arithmetic density varies in the study area. High density is found near city, town and river banks. Maximum density found in tehsil Dholpur, then in tehsil Rajakhera, near river Parbati. Medium density found is found in tehsil Basari and Bandi and less density is found in Ravines area of river Chambal.

B. Agricultural Density: This density is useful in examining the pressure of population on agriculture. It is calculated by the following formulae:

Agricultural density = Population engaged in agriculture/Total agricultural area

Agricultural density of the study area as calculated was 349 person/sq.km. This density also varies across tehsils. The Maximum agricultural density (401 persons/sq.km.) was found in tehsil Basari. Tehsil Dholpur shows 373 person/sq.km. Rajakhera stands with the lowest agricultural density (Table 23.4).

Table 23.4: Tehsil-wise Distribution of Agricultural Density

S.N	District/Tehsil	Population engaged in agriculture	Total agriculture area (in Km.)	Agricultural density/Sq.Km.
1.	Dholpur district	6,20,654	1776.66	349
2.	Basari	1,51,187	376.74	401
3.	Badi	1,17,351	377.41	311
4.	Dholpur	2,66,899	715.08	373
5.	Rajakhera	85,217	307.43	277

Source: Census of India 2001

C. Physiological Density: Physiological density is the ratio of population and agricultural area. It shows the pressure of population on per unit agricultural land and is calculated by the following formulae:

Physiological Density = Total population/Net agriculture area

Physiological density as found in the district Dholpur was 521 person/sq.km. This is found higher in urban areas, where the size of population is more. Maximum density is found in the tehsil Dholpur, which is 589 person/sq.km. The lowest physiological density was found in tehsil Rajakhera (Table 23.5).

Table 23.5: Tehsil-wise Distribution of Physiological Density

S.N	District/Tehsil	Total Population	Net agriculture area (in Km.)	Physiological density/Sq.Km.
1.	Dholpur district	7,49,479	1437.29	521
2.	Basari	1,51,187	311.59	485
3.	Badi	1,54,888	311.60	497
4.	Dholpur	3,35,432	569.50	589
5.	Rajakhera	1,07,972	244.60	441

Source: Census of India 2001

D. Nutritional Density: This density calculates the load of population on agricultural land. It is calculated by the following formulae:

Nutritional Density = Total population/Total area under food crop

The nutritional density of the district as calculated was 770 persons /sq.km. Tehsil Dholpur recorded the highest (935 persons /sq.km.) nutritional density. Tehsil Badi stands with 704 persons /sq.km. Nutritional density is found higher in city region only or in densely populated area (Table 23.6).

Table 23.6: Tehsil-wise Distribution of Nutritional Density

S.N	District/Tehsil	Total Population	Total area under food crop (in km.)	Nutritional density/Sq.Km
1.	Dholpur District	7,49,479	972.15	770
2.	Basari	1,51,187	236.50	639
3.	Badi	1,54,888	219.78	704
4.	Dholpur	3,35,432	358.87	935
5.	Rajakhera	1,07,972	157.00	688

Source: Census of India 2001

Rural-Urban Population

Dholpur is village and agriculture based district, therefore the development of the district is directly affected by the villagers. The ratio of urban-rural population also affects the agriculture and economic growth of Dholpur district (Table 23.7).

Table 23.7: Growth of Rural and Urban Population

S.N	Census year	Total Rural Population	percent to District Population	Total Urban Population	percent to District Population
1.	1971	3,95,565	86.05	64,090	13.95
2.	1981	4,95,924	84.76	89,135	15.24
3.	1991	6,20,654	82.81	1,28,825	17.19
4.	2001	8,06,551	82.05	1,76,448	17.95

Source: Census of India 2001

Table 23.7 shows that the rural population is continuously decreasing, since 1971 census. This was 86.05 percent in 1971 and it became 92.05 in 2001. There are only three city regions namely; Badi, Dholpur and Rajakhera. On the other hand maximum rural population was found in tehsil Dholpur. Bandi tehsil has the lowest percentage of rural population.

Effect of Population Growth on Agriculture

Production, consumption and management are the main aspects and are related with agriculture. On the other hand continuous rise in population creates pressure on agriculture. This in turn causes change in the agricultural pattern, use of machine and fertilizer etc. Effect of population on agriculture creates many developments in agriculture. During the recent period many kinds of wild plants are today used as food crops. Technology in agriculture has also changed the pattern of agricultural land use. Modern fertilizers and machines are introduced in agriculture. This helps increases agricultural output and also fulfils the requirement of employment. So, the change in agriculture is mainly due to increase in population.

Due to the increasing population Dholpur district has experienced the following changes:

- Net agricultural land has increased.
- Multi cropping pattern is largely adopted.
- Fallow land and Wasteland are continuously decreasing.
- Use of machines in agriculture has increased.
- Chemical fertilizer, irrigation and Hybrid seeds are commonly used.
- Food crop area has increased.

Effect of Population on Environment

Man's demands are unlimited and ever-increasing which result in thoughtless degradation of the natural environment. Development of science and technology, growth of population and industrialization made the tremendous changes in the natural environment. Man and Environment both are directly or indirectly affected by each other. Richness of environment is the base of economic development of any country provided that the country must possess enough technique to utilize the present resources. Increasing population is one of the major reasons of environmental degradation. Some of the effects are given below:

A. Chlorofluorocarbons: Population plays a considerable role in damaging the natural environment. The rapid increase in the use of chlorofluorocarbons (CFCs), for example, had much to do with changes in technology than an increase in population. The subsequent damage to the ozone layer from the use of CFCs cannot therefore be blamed to any significant extent on population growth.

After 1990, many industries are established in the Dholpur district to fulfil the requirement of population, which are also responsible for spreading chlorofluorocarbons in the environment.

B. Global Warming: On the other hand, population does appear to be a significant factor in the increase in carbon dioxide (Co_2) emissions. According to an estimate, over a third of fossil fuel emission in the developed countries between 1970-2000 was due to increased population, and nearly a half of Co_2

emissions in developing countries was due to the same cause. The threat of climatic change and global warming has therefore been heavily influenced by population growth.

Dholpur district experiences rapid increase in population and industries and follows the path of development. This is likely to add greatly to the problem.

C. Deforestation: Deforestation is one of the important factors in damaging environment. Deforestation leads to the loss of wetlands and species, soil erosion, forest loss, and increases emissions of methane gas.

Most of the experts are agreed that population pressure in the Dholpur district contributes directly to the continuing loss of forest cover. Most of the forestland is cleared in developing countries for human settlements, roads, and other non-agricultural developments. About 20 percent of forest cover have been lost because of clearance for farmland driven by population pressure.

D. Species Extinction: One consequence of the loss of forests, in the Dholpur district, is the destruction of wildlife and the threat to the biodiversity of life on Earth. The current extinction rate has been variously estimated at between 2 and 5 species a day, with millions of species facing extinction in the present decade. Much of this must be attributed to population growth in the Dholpur district. Other consequences of forest loss include the shortage of fuel wood, and erosion, as slash-and-burn cultivators are forced to return too frequently to the same plot, or are forced too high on to sloping land.

E. Water Use: Another environmental element that is very sensitive to population growth is water. It was estimated in 2000 that more than half of the population in the Dholpur district could be living in water-stressed or water-scarce. Population projection for further year shows that, water scarcity is likely to affect all of the population living in the Dholpur district. Success in slowing population growth could thus have a major impact on the scale of water shortages in the coming century.

Suggestion for Future

The above effects show that the future of this district is not so good. It may disturb the environment and ecological balance. So, the following steps may protect the environment.

- The use of chlorofluorocarbons may be controlled or there should be a substitute of chlorofluorocarbons.
- Population is a significant factor in the increase in carbon dioxide (Co_2). So, to get safe from global warming it is necessary to arrest the faster increase in population. This may decrease the carbon dioxide.

- Deforestation is totally prohibited and plantation programme may be launched at a large scale.
- Pollution control is necessary, either it is of soil, water or air.

References

Bhatanagar, N.K. (1987) *Population Projection of Rajasthan* (1981-2001), Directorate of Economics and Statistics, Government of Rajasthan, Jaipur.

Birch, J.W. (1973) "Geography and resources Management", *Journal of Environmental Management*.1.3-12.

Burton, I. And Kates, R.W., eds. (1965). *Readings in resources Management Conservation*, University of Chicago Press, Chicago.

Chorley, R.J. ed (1959) *Water, Earth and Man, Methuen, London.*

Coleman, D.J. (1975) *An Ecological Input to Regional Planning*, School of Urban and Regional Planning, University Ow Waterloo, Waterloo, Ont.

Flawn, P.T.(1970) *Environmental Geology : Conservation, Land-use Planning and Resources Management*, Harper and Row. New York.

Mathur, H.S. (1987) *"Wastelands in Rajasthan: Spatial Perspectives Reclamation and Development"* Occasional Paper: Department of Geography, University of Rajasthan, Jaipur. P.17.

Walton, W.C. (1970) *"Groundwater Resources Evaluation*" McGraw-Hill Inc. London.

Maps

Reference Chapter 3: Counties with High Rates of Elderly Populations

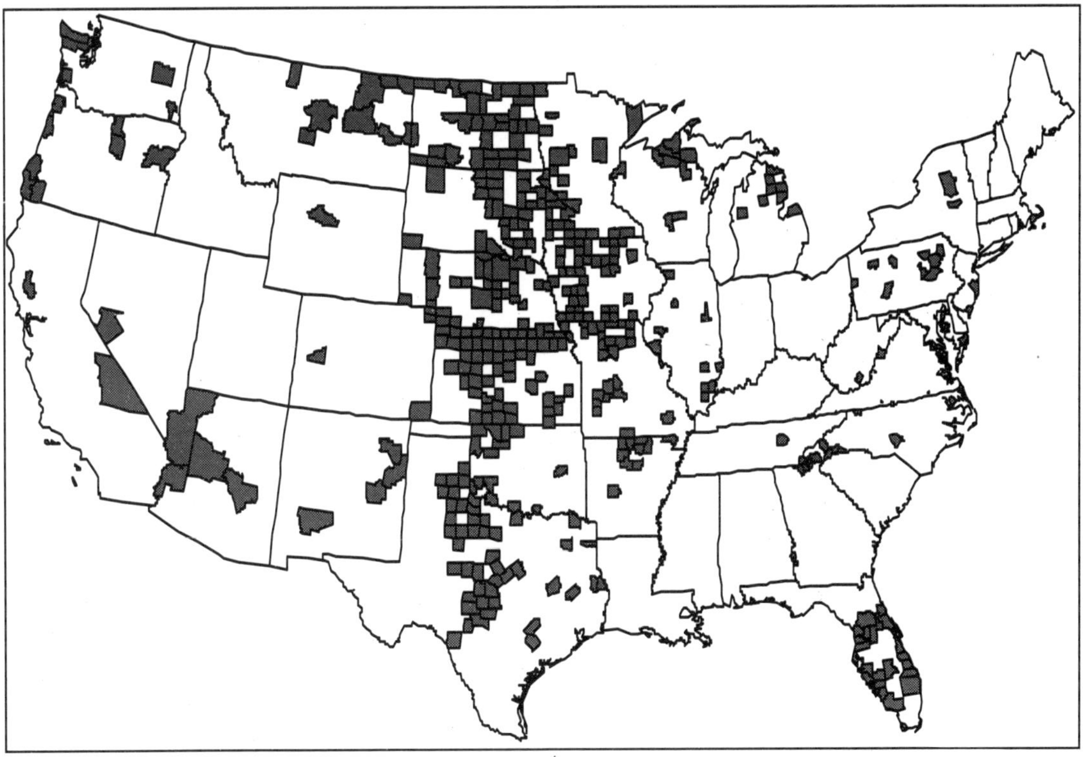

Reference Chapter 4: Location of Organ Pipe National Monument

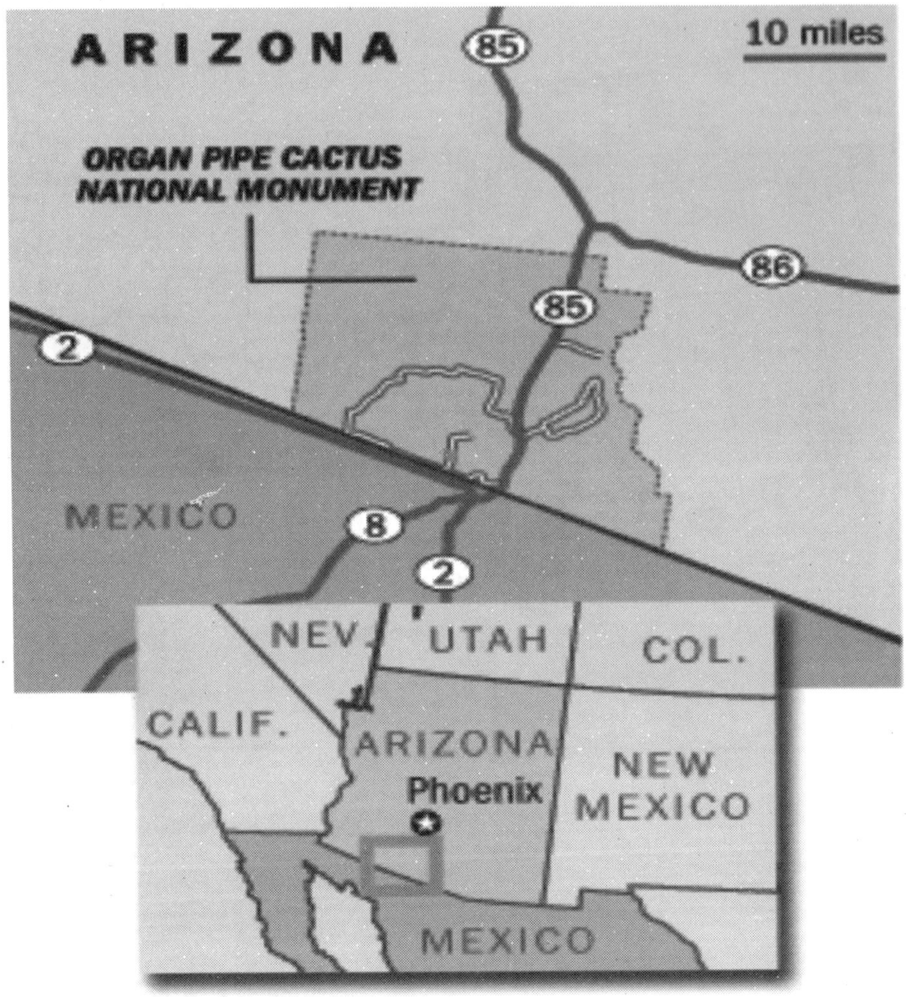

Reference Chapter 5: Health State of the Romanian Population (1990-2001)

Reference Chapter 8: Location of Raul Targului River Catchment's Area in Romania

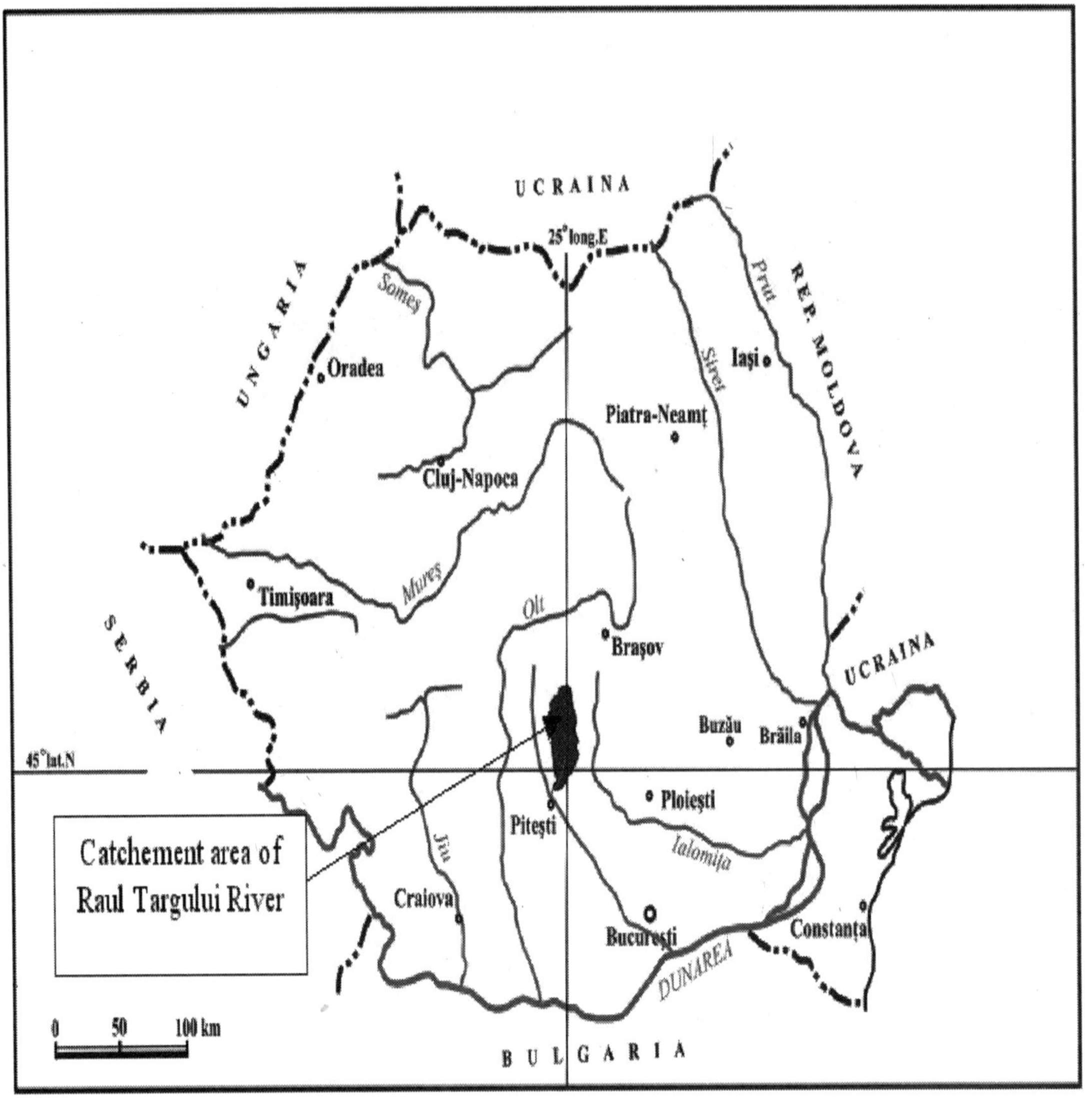

Reference Chapter 17: Spatio-Temporal Pattern of Urban Male Human Resource Development

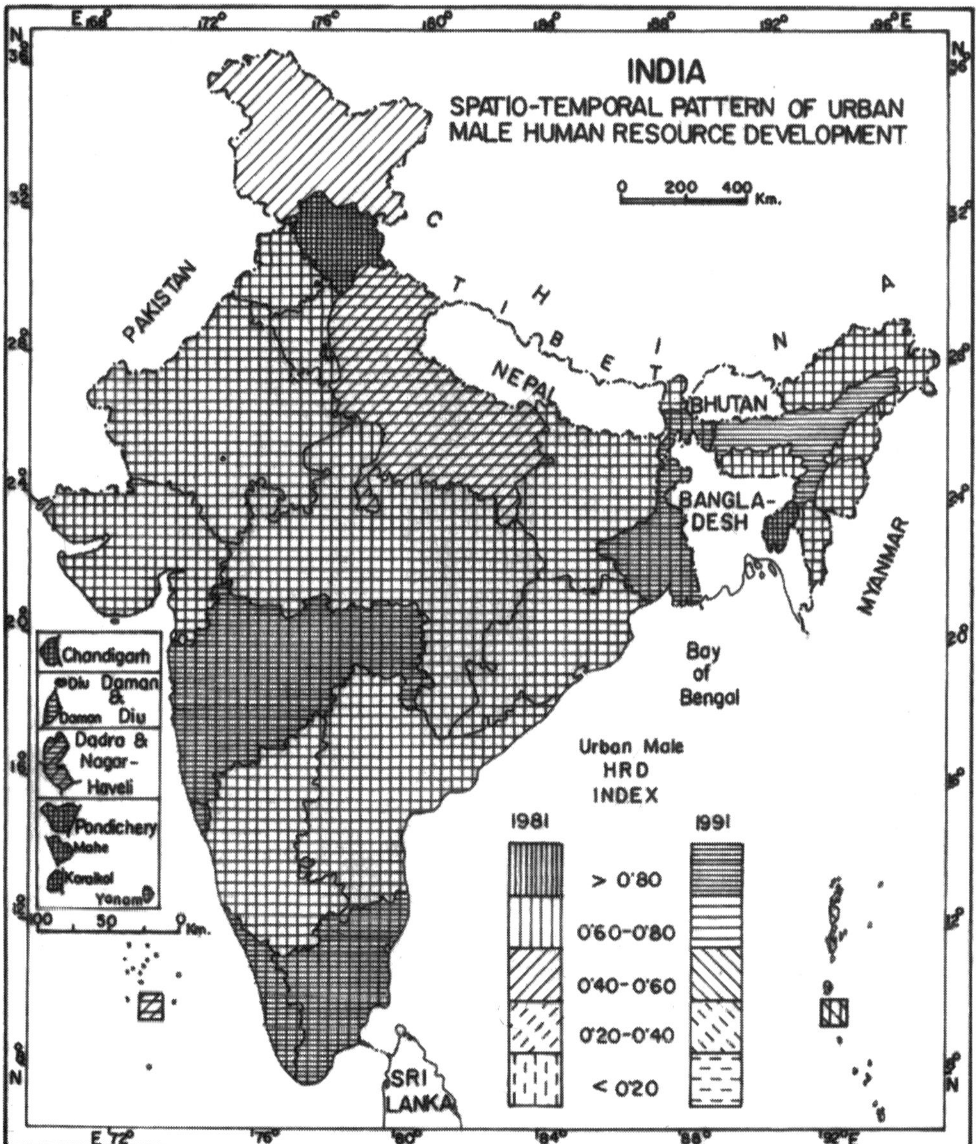

Reference Chapter 17: Spatio-Temporal Pattern of Urban Female Human Resource Development

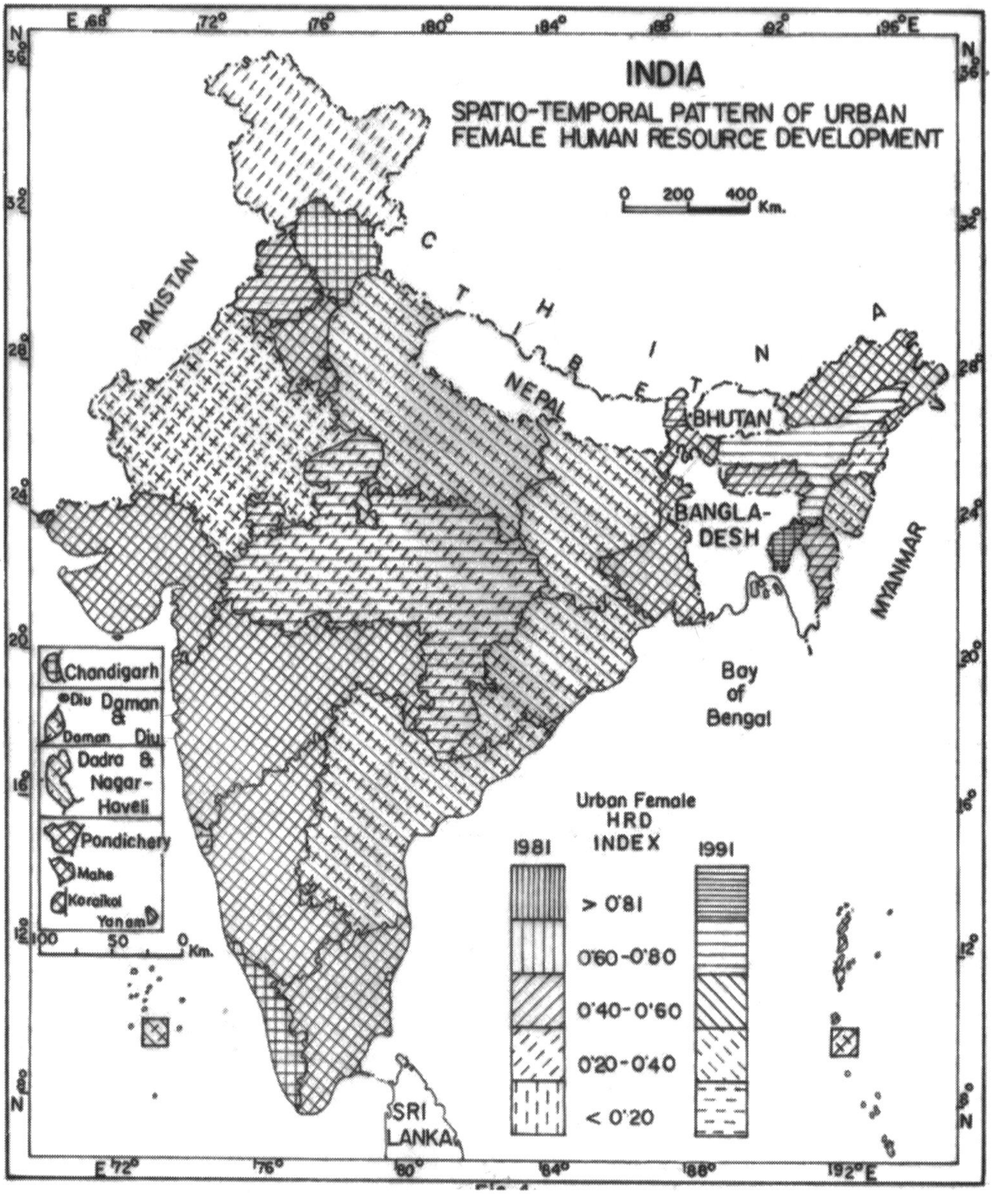

Reference Chapter 18: Residential Density in Bucharest City (Number of Persons/Dwelling)

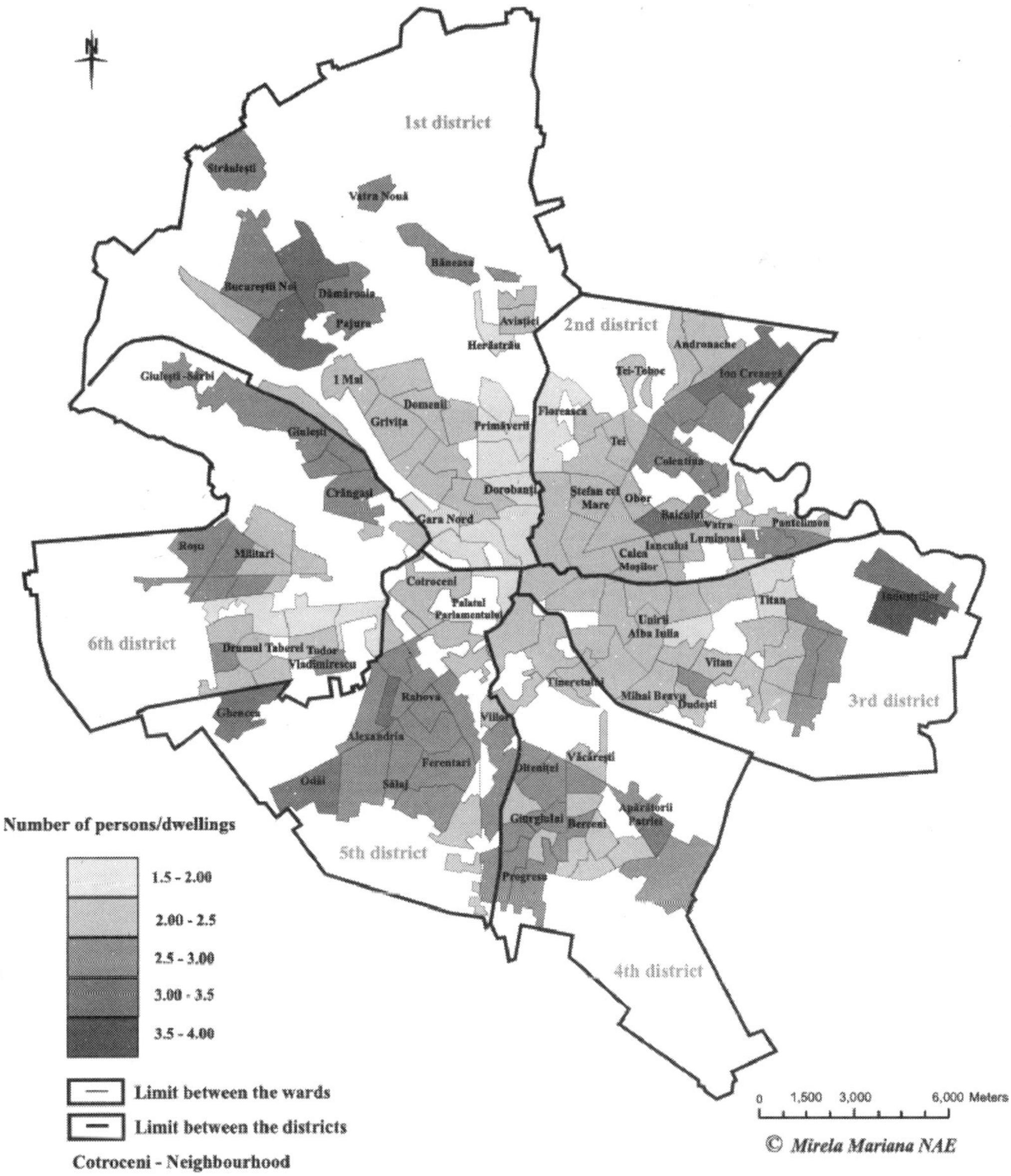

Reference Chapter 21: Map of Ghana

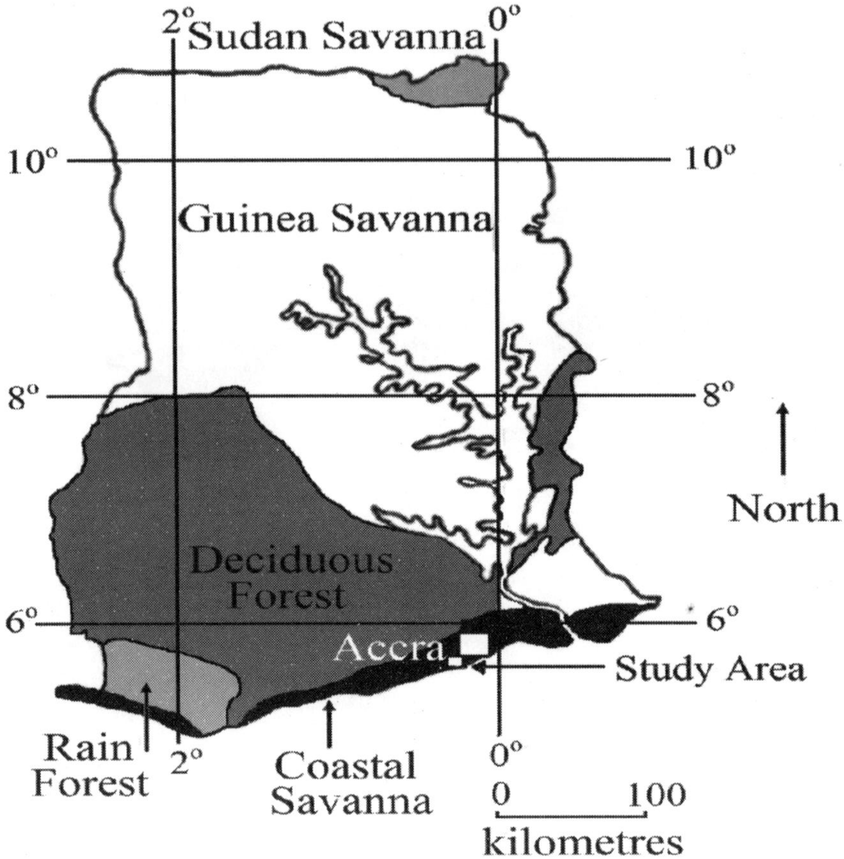

Figures and Photographs
(Reference Chapter 9)

Figure 1: An Environment and Cancer Framework as proposed by Ann Novogradec

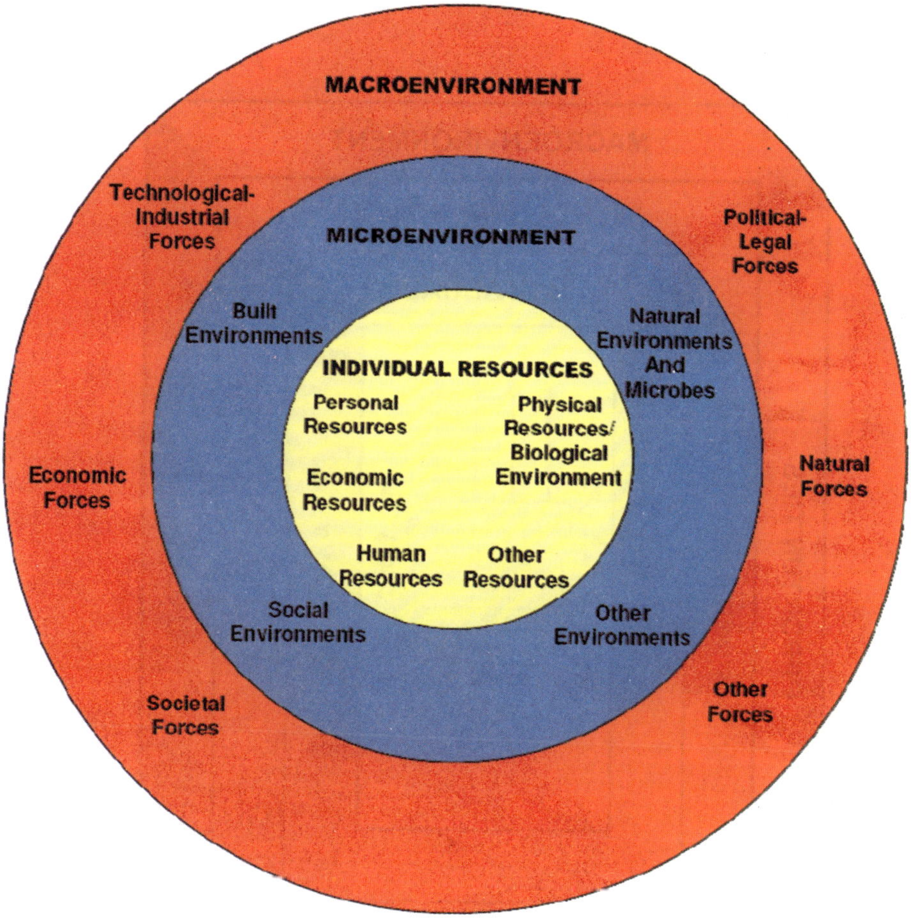

Some components of this model have been used in a different context and have been adapted with permission from: Wright, P. et al., (1998) Strategic Management Concepts, 4th Edition, New Jersey, Prentice-Hall Inc.

FIGURE 2: Levels of Analysis relating to the S.W.O.T.

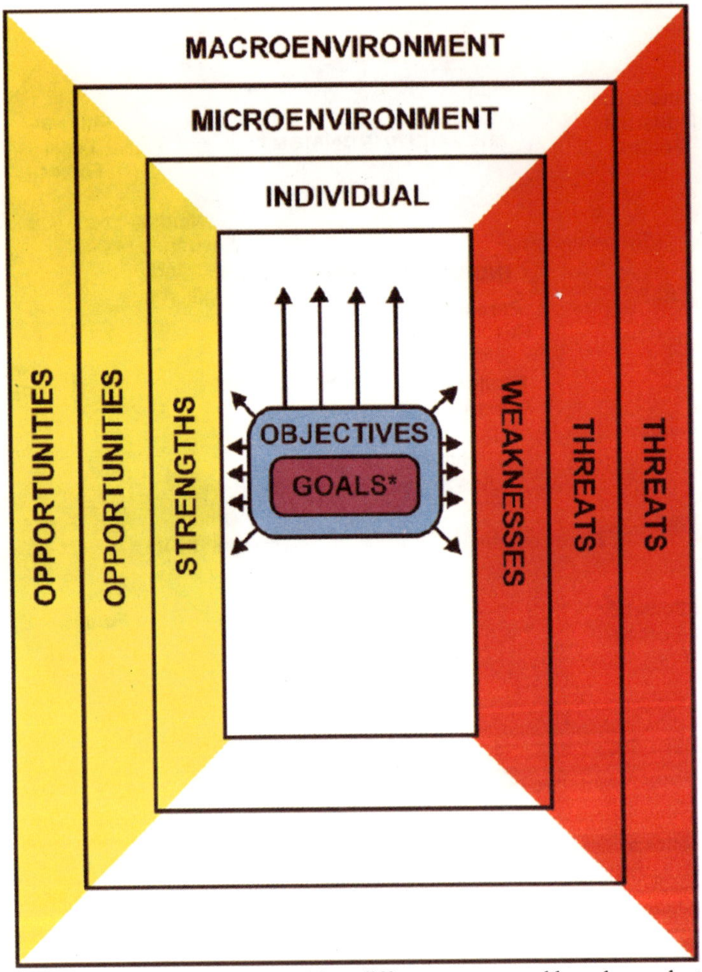

Some components of this model have been used in a different context and have been adapted with permission from: Wright, P. et al., (1998) Strategic Management Concepts, 4th Edition, New Jersey, Prentice-Hall Inc.

PHOTOGRAPH 1

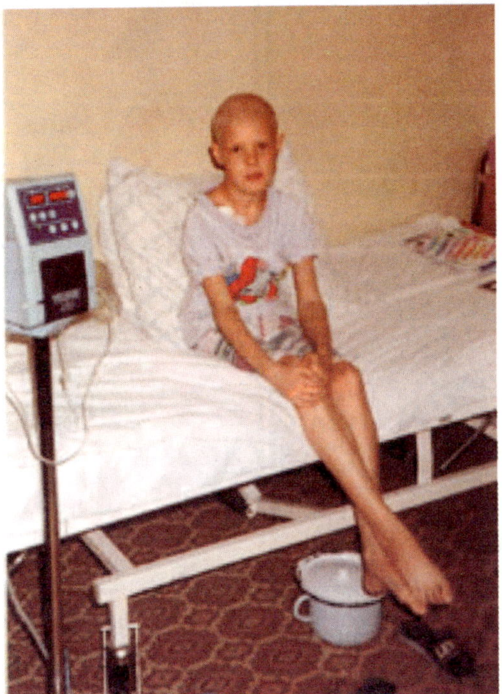

Photograph has been provided with permission, courtesy of Chernobyl Children's Project International.

PHOTOGRAPH 2

PHOTOGRAPH 3

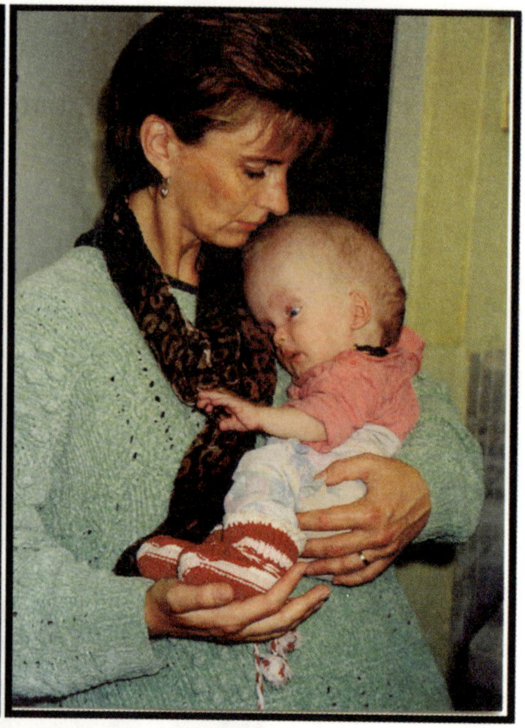

Photographs has been provided with permission, courtesy of Chernobyl Children's Project, Ireland.
Fore more information regarding the Chernobyl Children's Project, please refer to http://www.chernobyl-ireland.com/home/default.asp

PHOTOGRAPH 4

Photograph By: © Bill Biggart

The Late Bill Biggart's photograph has been provided with the permission, courtesy of Wendy Doremus.
Fore more works of Bill Biggart, please refer to http://www.billbiggart.com/index.html

PHOTOGRAPH 5

Photograph By: © Bill Biggart

The Late Bill Biggart's photograph has been provided with the permission, courtesy of Wendy Doremus.
Fore more works of Bill Biggart, please refer to http://www.billbiggart.com/index.html

Index